Wallace Lloyd

Houses of Glass

A philosophical Remance

Wallace Lloyd

Houses of Glass
A philosophical Remance

ISBN/EAN: 9783337072513

Printed in Europe, USA, Canada, Australia, Japan

Cover: Foto ©ninafisch / pixelio.de

More available books at **www.hansebooks.com**

A PHILOSOPHICAL ROMANCE.

BY

WALLACE LLOYD, M.D.

"But the greatest of all is charity."

NEW YORK:
COPYRIGHT, 1898, BY
G. W. Dillingham Co., Publishers,
MDCCCXCVIII.
[*All rights reserved.*]

PREFACE.

In endeavouring to frame in fiction a little of the philosophy of every day life, I would crave the reader's indulgence upon the methods I have employed.

In a task of this kind, I felt that I could best serve the cause, not by startling events and striking characters, but by a closer analysis of those conditions and occurrences, which form the warp and woof of life.

Believing, that truth after all, is stranger than fiction, I have not gone afield for highly coloured heroes and villains, but have taken characters from real life— men and women, with all their faults and imperfections. In venturing thus on the uncertain sea of public opinion, I have no guiding star but my own conscience, no compass but my own experience, and no excuse but the importance of my theme.

From the cradle to the grave there is no step fraught with such momentous consequences to ourselves and our posterity, as the joining of our hands in holy wedlock. In these days of divorce, when incompatibility of temperament and dissimilarity of religious faith are legitimate pleas for the severing of sacred ties, it behooves us to cultivate more fully the spirit of benevolence and charity. The frequency with which "lack of unity" is brought forward, points clearly to the duty of investigating the magnetic relations of the sexes. We cannot surely show greater respect for the laws of society than by endeavouring to harmonize them with the laws of nature.

A union based on the moral, physical and spiritual affinity of man and woman, is the only one which nature stamps as genuine, and any violation of this principle brings with it its own punishment.

During twenty years of active professional life, I have had the grand privilege of occasionally bringing together separated husbands and wives, and restoring harmony to unhappy homes.

The hope of stimulating philosophers, scientists and thinkers, and furthering discussion and investigation, has cheered me on. If a word, a hint or a thought, which I have dropped, will bring hope to any hearth, or sunshine to the heart of some poor suffering creature, then I shall feel that my effort has not been in vain.

To honest, earnest men and women, who have at heart the welfare of our race, to husbands and wives, to fathers and mothers, do I dedicate this work, in the hope that through all its obscurity, they will grasp the spirit in which it was written, and view with charity its many mistakes and imperfections.

WALLACE LLOYD, M.D.

CONTENTS.

CHAPTER		PAGE
I.	New Arrivals	9
II.	Disenchantment	15
III.	Getting Acquainted	20
IV.	Gore Farm	25
V.	Two and Twenty Years After	30
VI.	Broadview and its Proprietor	42
VII.	Adaptation	48
VIII.	A Child of Nature	53
IX.	An Unwelcome Guest	60
X.	An Interview	66
XI.	Retrospection on Wheels	72
XII.	Mother and Son	77
XIII.	Gowanstone	82
XIV.	"When the Cat's away the Mice will Play."	88
XV.	A Lucky Hit	96
XVI.	Aftermath	103
XVII.	A Disagreeable Surprise	111
XVIII.	"When Greek Meets Greek"	116

CONTENTS.

Chapter		Page
XIX.	The Honeymoon	121
XX.	The Home Coming	127
XXI.	A Vacant Chair	132
XXII.	Motley and Monarch	137
XXIII.	An Evening at the Doctor's	142
XXIV.	A Broken Pane	150
XXV.	Marion's Debut	156
XXVI.	Purer Light	163
XXVII.	A Touch of Nature	169
XXVIII.	"Uneasy Lies the Head that Wears a Crown"	174
XXIX.	An Old Acquaintance	180
XXX.	"Multum in Parvo"	185
XXXI.	A Friendly Call	190
XXXII.	Crossed Wires	196
XXXIII.	"The Land o' the Leal"	201
XXXIV.	Dr. Bennet's Spectacles	205
XXXV.	A Difficult Problem	214
XXXVI.	The Deep, Dark Valley	219
XXXVII.	A Stranger in a Strange Land	225
XXXVIII.	A Needle in a Haystack	232
XXXIX.	Jake Fetterly's Conversion	237
XL.	The Spider and the Fly	245
XLI.	Cupid's Capers	252
XLII.	A Legacy and a Lover	259
XLIII.	A Tempest of the Soul	264
XLIV.	Ways and Means	269
XLV.	Where Paths Divide	273
XLVI.	Gotham's Griefs	277
XLVII.	Propriety's Holiday	283
XLVIII.	The Skeleton of the Feast	290
XLIX.	Vicarious Atonement	296
L.	A Crown of Thorns	302
LI.	A Documentary Diagnosis	306

CONTENTS.

CHAPTER		PAGE
LII.	The Wages of Sin	311
LIII.	Gilding a Grief	319
LIV.	The Rose and Its Thorn	323
LV.	A Thunder-Bolt from a Blue Sky	328
LVI.	The Evils of Procrastination	333
LVII.	Oil on Troubled Waters	339
LVIII.	Adversity's Jewel	344
LIX.	Bill Niger's "Ketch"	348
LX.	A Welcome Visitor	354
LXI.	Sapping and Mining	360
LXII.	A Lay Sermon	368
LXIII.	Turning Towards the Sun	377
LXIV.	Reconciliation	381
LXV.	Christmas Chimes	391

HOUSES OF GLASS.

CHAPTER I.

NEW ARRIVALS.

ONE sultry summer afternoon, a group of people were gathered at the door of the post office at Grazely's Mills. In fact, this little assembly represented two-thirds of the entire population of the village, if, indeed, a few scattered buildings in the heart of a wilderness really deserved that name.

One solitary store, an inn, a blacksmith shop and a school-house, made up the list of public buildings, and these, with a few dwellings of the most primitive kind, constituted the entire settlement.

All the buildings were constructed of logs, with the exception of the hotel, which had the proud distinction of being composed of lumber, rough and unplaned though it was.

But the inn had other marks of distinction, which made it a *triton* among the *minnows*. It was fully twice as large as the other buildings. It had an upstairs, a full complement of windows, brick chimneys and pannelled doors. In view of all this grandeur, the inhabitants considered that it was fully entitled to the imposing signboard, which swung from a huge post in front, and announced, " The Bay Horse Hotel, by E. Blake." This very signboard, with its gilded letters was admired by all and sundry, and what purported to be a rampant steed, immediately over the name, was considered by the juveniles of the village to be a triumph of the painter's art. Indeed, the hotel had a modern appearance, which contrasted oddly with the store adjoining it.

The latter building was low and long. It had several front doors, and had evidently been extended from time to time, either in proportion to the growth of the family or the increasing revenues of its owner.

At the end adjoining the inn, was a window of many panes, on whose sill there sat several yellow cans of mustard; a box labelled starch, and a venerable glass dish covered with dust. These were flanked right and left with bottles of castor-oil and pain-killer, while from a nail at the door hung a pair of cowhide boots and a wash board. Out of compliment, no doubt, to the prosperity of the place, the whole front, signboard and all, had been whitewashed so extravagantly that one could scarcely trace over the door, the words " Post Office."

The two buildings were connected by a rough platform running along the front, forming a sort of sidewalk, and halfway between them was a solitary tie post for the convenience of travellers and customers.

About half a mile down the river, which followed a circuitous course through the broad valley, was a recently-erected saw and grist mill, the importance of which industry had lately changed the name of the place from, " Langtry's Hollow " to " Grazely's Mills."

Despite its primitiveness, the little hamlet was a very important feature of the district, being widely known amongst the settlers for miles around. In many cases they were forced to make a journey of several days on foot or with an ox team to get a grist from the mill. Mr. Grazely, the proprietor, was considered a great man, for with the exception of a small mill, built by a man named Gowan, about thirty miles up the river, there was not another industry of the kind in the county.

There was one other resident of the village who was almost as widely known as Grazely. A citizen, who not only rivalled the mill-owner in his greatness, but detested him with all his heart.

NEW ARRIVALS.

This was Mr. Langtry, postmaster, and first settler in the place. Diversification of talent was *his* strong point. He was merchant, bailiff, magistrate, apothecary, local preacher, and veterinary surgeon.

Not satisfied with alleviating the ailments of the equine and bovine races, he occasionally tried his hand on the nobler animal, man.

He could cure fits, worms, and colic. Indeed, some enthusiasts went so far as to say that he could relieve pain of any kind. Whether he had ever relieved any of his patients of the burden of life, it is impossible to say, but if such was the case, it neither shook his confidence nor disturbed his conscience. But Mr. Langtry's talents were not confined to professional lines, for he could put a rung in a chair, a pendulum in a clock, or a patch on a shoe.

His neighbours had truly great cause to wonder how any single head could contain so much. If he did occasionally mix molasses with his mail matter, or politics with his preaching, the settlers were not too fastidious, and any one of them would have told you that Mr. Langtry was the smartest man in the district.

The strong feeling of jealousy between him and the mill-owner ripened into bitter hatred when the place changed its name. Every letter and paper the postmaster took from his mail bags, reminded him of his hated rival.

Yet he had some advantages over the mill-owner, and he made the most of them. He could preach a fairly good sermon, play on his melodeon all the necessary hymns, and lead the singing with a fine baritone voice. Every Sunday after church, his popularity ran high, and held good till about the middle of the week. Then it took a sudden drop till by Saturday night his rival was generally a full length ahead in the race for public favour.

Mr. Grazley was young and unmarried, he gave employment to several men and was not "stuck up."

Langtry had knowledge, which was useful to the community, but Grazely had horses. The mill-owner not only had a multiplicity of horses and waggons, but he actually owned the stage, and drove a buggy with a top to it like those they had in the city. These features, and the hum of his saws, gave him the privilege and prestige of naming the place.

On this particular afternoon, the stage was away late, causing many conjectures to be offered as to the cause of delay.

The narrow, white road (called the State Line), in its gradual slope into the valley, was almost hidden from view by the trees, which in some places formed a canopy overhead, so that from the post-office the eye could only trace its course by a long, straight gap in the giants of the forest.

This had been watched for an hour past, till everybody was tired waiting. The maidens in their pinafores giggled aside by themselves, the boys cut whistles and traded knives, and the old timers seated on sundry barrels and boxes, discussed the " p'ints " of Grazely's new team, or aimed tobacco juice at flies.

A yoke of oxen, hitched to a " jumper " containing some sacks of flour, were drowsily nodding their heads and switching their tails, and a pair of fat hogs were wallowing contentedly in the shadow of the water trough.

The screeching of the saws over at the mill was softened by distance into a cooing song, and acted like a lullaby on the little gathering. The maidens subsided, the boys quit blowing their whistles, and Phil Snider, the most talkative man in the settlement, was snoring against the tie post.

At last, after several hours of waiting, the peaceful elysium was broken by a shout of—" here he comes."

The slumberers were astir in a moment, like a hive of bees.

The men gave an extra hitch to their trowsers, readjusted their broad brimmed hats and exchanged exhausted quids for fresh ones.

The postmaster rushed to the door, glaring with an air of stern authority through his spectacles, and everybody was on the *qui vive*.

So slowly did the cloud of dust come down the slope, that some one suggested the approaching vehicle to be an ox team.

"No siree," exclaimed Snider, annihilating a fly with his deadly aim, "that's Bill's dust all right and I'll go you ten to one he's got a load on."

The vehicle's unusual tardiness served only to heighten the general curiosity, and when at last the stage burst from its canopy of leaves, it was greeted with a perfect storm of exclamations.

There, in the front seat of the big yellow "democrat," sat a lady and a gentleman, the former holding in her arms an infant, which she was endeavouring to protect from the rays of the sun with a shining black parasol.

Away up in the rear, upon a throne of trunks and boxes, sat Bill Innes, the driver, proud as an emperor. With a calm dignity peculiar to himself, he held the reins high above the heads of his passengers, and, as the team with a spurt (specially prepared for the occasion) came dashing up to the tie post, he jauntily shied the mail bag at the head of the postmaster.

Strangers at any time caused great excitement, but here were species of the *genus homo* hitherto unknown.

The gentleman had flowing mutton-chop whiskers, a white waistcoat, kid gloves and eyeglasses. Not honest spectacles with wires at the sides to fasten to your ears; but glasses that sat on his nose, and were attached to the button-hole of his vest by a black cord.

The lady was tall, plump and dark, while he was fair and slender. Then her attire was out of all reason. Her cape was a mass of beads neither good for wind or weather, and in some places where the dust had failed to settle, her dress glistened in the sun. But it was her bonnet, fearfully and wonderfully constructed, which marked her as a bird of plumage hitherto unknown in an American forest.

All the open doorways in the village were temporarily transformed into frames for living pictures, where buxom dames and grey-haired grandmas, gazed with wondering eyes at the new comers. They casually noticed that the baby was in long clothes and that the mother was a trifle awkward in handling it.

Mrs. Dorris (the village midwife), gave a professional nod to her neighbour across the way, and shouted, "her first I guess."

The group at the post office stood rather on the defensive, against what appeared to them a common enemy. They huddled together at one end of the platform, and defiantly awaited developments.

Two or three of the more inquisitive ones crowded up to Bill to inquire who the swells were, but the driver, with an authority which no one thought of resenting said, "hold yer jaw will ye. Here Jim, Hank, give me a hand to rub the mares down! I'm afraid they're overheated!"

Left to themselves, the strangers dismounted from the vehicle as best they could, and stood on the platform a few moments, evidently awaiting some one to greet them. Finally the gentleman spoke.

"Is this Grazely's Mills?"

"Tain't nuthin else," replied Snider with a wink that exploded the juveniles, and relieved to some extent the uneasiness of the villagers.

The lady's large black eyes flashed through her veil, and the gentleman glared through his glasses. Turning to a bright-looking lad, the stranger handed him a piece of silver and asked where the inn, or public house was.

The boy looked astonished. "Why right there," he said nodding his head towards the open door. "Don't you see that sign," and he pointed proudly to the cinnamon-coloured steed with its forefeet in the air.

"Thank you, my boy. You are a gentleman. Gentlemen are always civil to strangers." This last remark was made with a meaning glance at Snider, causing the village Nestor to slink back into the crowd.

Turning again to the lad the stranger asked where the landlord was.

"Gone fishing."

"Well, where is the landlady?"

"Gone over to Charley Walker's, cause the baby's got the measles."

The gentleman smiled at the boy's precocity, but the

lady hugged her baby tighter, and raised her veil to kiss it.

Fortunately for them, Bill at this moment came round from the stables, and took the situation in at a glance. " Sorry to keep you waitin', mam," he said deferentially to the lady, " but my team had to be seen to at once." " Come right in and make yourself to home. The folks don't appear to be in, but they'll show up presently. I seed Julia and Sally lookin' out the top windows a minnit ago."

"*Are* this the only public house in the place," inquired the lady.

" Yes, mam," responded Bill with a polite bow, " and for twenty miles around. But don't you git scared. If you never get worse bed and grub than Ted Blake 'll give ye, you'll get through the world slicker'n most of us. Leastways that's how I've got it figgered up."

CHAPTER II.

DISENCHANTMENT.

THE excitement caused by the advent of the strangers kept steadily increasing all afternoon, and before sunset it was at white heat.

The villagers might have overlooked the fact that these new arrivals did not look like any other persons who had ever come to town, but the quantity and formidable appearance of their baggage was something beyond their comprehension. The trunks, which were piled high on the stage, bore no resemblance to emigrant boxes. They were rivetted and shod with iron, and consequently must contain something of unusual value.

Nobody could guess who the strangers were or what their business was, but everyone agreed that the trunks meant business, and were made " a purpose."

They were fairly covered with red and blue tickets. Phil Snider climbed up on the wagon to read them. "Boscastle to London. Gee whiz, they're Britishers!"

"You might a knowed that by the eyeglasses," said another. "London to Liverpool," "Liverpool to New York," and so on till the strangers were traced from starting point to destination.

That evening an informal meeting was held in front of the post-office, to discuss the situation, and the town fathers were all on hand to lend their assistance. Neither the landlord nor the stage-driver had given the faintest clue, but Mr. Langtry was expected to offer some solution of the mystery.

"It is quite certain," said the postmaster, "that the gentleman is not a United States Government official, as some of you have suggested, and it is equally certain they are not ordinary emigrants. Boscastle is in Cornwall. I know the place well. In fact, I was born within a few miles of it. But what can be their object in coming here, I am at a loss to say. I shall probably be able to tell you all about it to-morrow before mail time," and with a bow, Mr. Langtry returned to his sanctum.

This, however, did not satisfy the meeting, and the investigation went on. "Perhaps he is some timber speculator."

"Not he," said one of Grazely's sawyers, "he don't look sharp enough."

"He's sharp enough for Phil Snider, I hear," exclaimed the landlord with a laugh which went through the whole assembly.

"That's all right, Ted, but mebbie I ain't *throo* with the *dood* yet," growled Phil. "He's a sort o' 'smart Aleck,' just a leetle shade too fresh."

"There's two of a kind then, Phil," laughed Blake. "Julia," he shouted to his wife standing in the doorway, "where's Bill Innes gone?"

"He took the girls over to the party at Binkley's," replied his spouse.

"'Tain't any use if Bill was here," said Sweeney,

"He don't know a bit more'n the rest of us. He told me so, hisself."

The inquiry came to a dead stand still. It looked as if further investigation would have to be postponed, when a small boy who had been listening attentively to the discussion, came to the rescue.

"I seed him open a black box an' take out a long shinin' thing what had a glass end onto it. Me'n Harry Bowles wuz lookin' throo the winda. Wuzn't we, Harry?"

"Sure thing," replied Harry with a complimentary nod.

"What did it look like, Harry?" queried the landlord. "Tell us as near as you can."

Bowles, junior, thus appealed too, was fully alive to the gravity of the situation. He jauntily stuck his hands into his trowsers' pockets and squirted a jet of saliva through an opening in his front teeth. "Well, gentlemen, it 'peered to me like a spy glass or sumthin' to look through."

"Dollars to doughnuts he's a surveyor for the new railroad," exclaimed the landlord, slapping his thigh, "and them big trunks has got his kit in them. Come, boys, I'll take chances on it and 'set them up,' all round. Then you can help me unload the boxes. We'll go in and 'wet our tubes' on the head of it."

The foam on Blake's beer, was a sort of argument that usually carried conviction. Everybody seemed satisfied with the landlord's solution of the mystery.

As they were about to drink to the success of the new railroad, Lem Dorris, with his squeaky soprano voice tainted with Irish brogue, made a new suggestion. "Mebbie it's the ne-ew ma-an what's cumed to tak the Gore Farm on the hill."

This was greeted with roars of laughter. The idea of the "dood" being a farmer was too ridiculous for anything.

"Well, yez may laff, but Grazely telt me he had a letter frae the company, an' it is selt to an Inglishman frae Lundun. Isn't that so, Grazely," Lem continued, turning to a young man who had just entered.

"Quite so, quite so, Mr. Dorris, but I'm afraid by the looks of the trunks that he ain't your man, no, indeed."

* * * * * *

A different scene was being enacted upstairs in the "spare" room. "My God, Jane," said the husband, pacing the floor, "we can never stay here. The prospectus said, 'a town.' A town, indeed. Why, it is a wilderness peopled with savages. God knows what the farm is like if they call this a town. I have not the courage to ask about the farm. They can't give me a civil answer. They would only jeer at me." The baby was sound asleep on the bed, and the mother sat with her face buried in her hands.

"Just fancy," he continued, "living in a place like this. It would be worse than death. It would be a living death. Just imagine, this is the best room in the house," he went on, waving his hand at the rough unplaned boards while the floor creaked and rattled under his feet. "Why it is more like a box stall, and the bed there—why it is simply a litter on stilts."

"The bed are clean, William," said his wife, speaking for the first time, and looking towards where the infant lay under a flaming-colored, loud-patterned quilt. "Marian have gone asleep, dear, please not to wake her. If you like you can lie down beside her. It are needful I should think it over."

She sat with folded arms deeply absorbed in thought, looking the very picture of sullen despair. The husband was evidently of a less fretful disposition, for after carefully and suspiciously inspecting the cleanliness of the bed, he threw himself down, and in a few moments was sound asleep.

She took out her purse, and counted their store of wealth. Ten five pound notes, four and sixpence English, besides some American silver she could not count.

"Will us let the forty pounds go and get shut of all this? Will there be any farm at all or are it all a hoax," she said.

She opened a small hand satchel, and took out a document, which she read to herself in a subdued whisper. "Tract of land known as Gore Farm near the town of Grazely's Mills."

She paused and heaved a sigh at the deception of calling this wilderness a town. "Two hundred acres more or less. Ten acres clearing. House and barn in fair state of repair." "Dear me," she said to herself, "we are tricked and rogued. How his father would laugh at the 'low-bred hussy' and his foolish son. But they shall never know. I shall fight and work. I are not afraid of work. I have all when I have him."

She replaced the document in her satchel and sat looking at her large but shapely hands, as an important part of her capital. Ha! there was his ring on her finger. She turned it round and round, with a gratified look in her face.

It was a plain gold hoop with nothing particular to admire about it, but she looked at it fondly for a long time.

Diving into her satchel again, she drew forth her marriage certificate. After reading it over, she carefully placed it in her purse beside her other valuables.

"There are not many would be so good and true as William. Poor fellow, he have no idea what are before him, but if he be only contented us will get along. No matter, us will go and see the farm. I shan't flinch or give in."

Her attitude was now full of a determination which almost amounted to defiance. The responsibility of her position seemed to make her grave beyond her years. She was young and strong, and her self-reliance had been fully developed by her past life. She was already recovering from the shock of disappointment. Hope was again asserting itself.

Then she opened the window to get a breath of fresh air, and looked out into the night.

It was a clear, beautiful, balmy night, but everything looked so strange and terrible, that her courage seemed to leave her. Even the moon appeared to have risen in the wrong direction, and there, in its pale light were the relentless dark-green wooded slopes stretching away to the southwards.

Forest, forest everywhere as far as the eye could

reach, and in her morbid fancy, the dark shadows seemed hungry to engulf her. The noises downstairs had ceased, and all the lights had disappeared. Something about the solemn stillness seemed to crush her with a sense of her own helplessness—a stillness, broken only by the far off song of the whippoorwill, and the quiet swish of the river down at the sluice-way.

The same treacherous moon that shone so softly through her own little window in far distant Cornwall, was smiling and mocking at her grief in this terrible wilderness.

She laid her forehead on the rough sill of the window, and gave vent to the first tears she had shed since the shores of old England faded into sea and sky.

CHAPTER III.

GETTING ACQUAINTED.

ON the following morning, Mr. Langtry was somewhat surprized and very much gratified, when the strange lady with stately step came along the platform, and, first stopping to decipher the sign over the door, entered his establishment.

He was astonished at the massiveness of her figure, which he mentally noted was about five feet nine, with a probable weight of thirteen stone or more. A young giantess with coal black eyes, and rosy cheeks, holding an infant in her arms. Yet there did not seem to be any masculinity in her shape or form, for her outlines were rounded and graceful, and her carriage was peculiarly dignified and lady-like. But when she spoke, the postmaster modified his first estimate of her.

"Be you the postmaster here?"

"Yes, mam," replied that functionary, bowing politely. "Can I do anything for you?"

"I have a letter here to read if you'm oblige me by

GETTING ACQUAINTED.

hearkening to it," and taking a paper from her pocket she read,

"To Postmaster, Grazely's Mills.
"Please deliver to Mrs. Jane Halford the keys of Gore farm, and render her peaceable possession of the said estate."
Signed,
"J. L. Fish & Co.,
"*Agents Eureka Land Company.*"

"Let me look at it," said the postmaster, reaching out his hand for the document. She drew back, and hesitated. "I don't wish to offend, sir, but you'm better give me the key first. You see my husband thinks they have rogued us out of forty pounds, and us don't know who to trust."

"Ah! I see," laughed Mr. Langtry. "Yankee tricks eh! Well, to tell you the truth there is no key at all. We fastened the door by a bolt inside and crawled out of the window."

The lady turned a trifle paler and leaned against the little counter for support. "It *are* even worse than we thought," she exclaimed in a despairing tone.

Mr. Langtry now came out of his sanctum to comfort his visitor. "Don't let a little matter like that annoy you, Mrs. Halford. The place is a good one. The timber alone is worth ten times the money you paid for it. The forest may not look very inviting to you, but every tree is as good as money. And now let me welcome you to our little village and offer you the hand of a Cornishman."

A look of pleasure and surprise passed over her face. "What! You a Cornishman? You can have the letter—and welcome."

"Well, I am an American citizen, now, and I love the land of the free, but I was *born* at Tregoodwell, and though I was only young when I came out I can faintly remember the name of Halford. Pshaw! never mind the letter or the key. We will see that you get possession. Well, well! So your husband is a Halford of Boscastle!"

The young mother bent her head over her babe to hide the wave of colour which swept over her face. "I don't think he are any relative. Halford *are* a common name in Cornwall." How did he know where she had come from, she wondered.

"No matter, we shall be great friends, Mrs. Halford, I feel that instinctively. Milly," he shouted, "come here immediately. Here's a lady all the way from Boscastle, within a few miles of where I was born."

As Mrs. Langtry came waddling in she reminded the stranger of the fat woman at a Punch and Judy show.

"Our new neighbour, Milly," said the postmaster, introducing them. "Her husband has bought the Gore Farm. Mrs. Halford, my wife."

"You might come in and sit down," said Mrs. Langtry, smiling and leading the way into the parlour. "Sit down and rest yourself. *You* don't need to stand in order to grow big. Let the baby come to me," she continued, reaching out her arms to receive it. "No fear, it won't cry. Babies and dogs like good people," at which remark her fat body shook with laughter.

"Don't mind my wife, Mrs. Halford," pleaded the postmaster, apologetically. "She is always laughing, even when there's nothing to laugh at."

"Well, it are better than crying," responded their visitor, "or growling, either," and they all laughed in chorus.

Even the baby, as it was dandled up and down, seemed to catch the merriment from the fat lady's face. It gave a little crow of laughter and was rewarded by a shower of kisses.

"What is the little darling's name?"

"Her are called Marian."

"She's got your nose and eyes," said Mrs. Langtry, looking critically at the little face, "but I can't say whether she is like her Pa, for I have never seen him. When Charley was born," she continued, with suppressed laughter, "Mr. Langtry kept remarking how good looking the child was and wondering who he looked like. So I told him one day he needn't trouble himself as long as the boy didn't look like any of the neighbours."

Though the stranger was somewhat shocked she could not help joining in the hearty laugh, more especially as her hostess was fairly vibrating in her chair.

"Now, Milly, really you ought to be ashamed, talking so before a stranger."

"Oh, never mind," responded the visitor. "Jokes go free. I think when I get down-hearted I'll call on your wife, Mr. Langtry."

"And you shall always be welcome," returned the postmaster with a polite bow. "Come, Christina, and shake hands with the lady," he said, turning to a lanky, awkward girl of twelve. "Go and get Charlie, too."

"This is our little family," said the hostess, "and this is *my* baby," she added, pointing to a little fellow with fair, curly hair and nut-brown legs. "Look at the size of him. He isn't quite two years old yet."

"You have only two, then?" queried the visitor.

"Yes, but we have as many kinds as anybody," responded Mrs. Langtry. "and we may have more yet." This was followed by another outburst of laughter and more expostulations from the scandalized postmaster.

"Come, Charlie, won't you come and give me a kiss?" said Mrs. Halford, catching the little fellow up in her arms. In a moment his little brown fist came smack on her face, and with a squirm he jumped to the floor and ran behind his mother.

"You little rascal, how dare you!" shouted his father, giving him a shake. "Go off about your business, you young ruffian. Christina, you go and lock him up in the room for awhile. Really," continued Mr. Langtry, in apologetic tones, "he is a spoiled boy. He gets his own way in everything. Why, he has actually cut your lip and made it bleed."

"Oh, it are nothing but a scratch against my tooth; but now I must be going. I have everything to do."

"Can I do anything for you in the way of groceries or kitchen hardware?" inquired the merchant, rubbing his hands and bowing suavely.

"Dear me, yes! I shall want everything. I have plenty of bedding, dishes, ornaments and clothing, but where shall us get some furniture?"

Mr. Langtry smiled and shook his head. "We don't

keep furniture here. You see settlers, as a rule, don't want much. I can lend you a table, a bench and a couple of chairs, and I will get anything you wish on a week's notice. You will have to put up with a shake-down till then, for we lent our spare bed to Mrs. Sweeny, who is ill. Just make out a list of what you want, and I will attend to it."

"I am most ashamed to take all this kindness," said Mrs. Halford when everything was arranged. "I shall leave a five-pound note on account."

"Here is a customer worth having," said Langley to himself: as he tenderly fingered the note, and placed it away in his pocket book. It was the first he had seen for many a day and was all the more welcome on that account.

"Now you want to get moved out. Let me see! The only way will be to get one of Grazely's teams. This Grazely, madam, is a perfect young upstart, but his teams are the only ones within reach. Christina, show the lady down to the mill, but, remember, don't go in yourself. The only enemy I have in the world, Mrs. Halford, but you can pay him and no thanks to him."

Mrs. Halford found the young mill-owner more civil and courteous than she expected. She was surprized to see so young a man the proprietor of such an extensive business.

His large nose was slightly hooked at the point, and his keen gray eyes had a slight squint, but otherwise the expression of his face was rather pleasant and kindly.

"Certainly, certainly, you can have a team," he said in a sharp thin voice. "You needn't mind the pay just now," he added as she opened her pocket-book.

"My motto is, pay and be paid, Mr. Grazely, thank you. I shall want a barrel of flour as well."

"Very well, very well. Hiram will have the team at Blake's door right after dinner, and my buggy for yourselves as well. I can't change this note, madam, at present," he went on, scrutinizing his customer, "but you can give it to me again."

Grazely was satisfied that the lady had an honest

face, and besides, he saw a whole bunch of notes in her purse.

As she was about to leave, he suggested putting some nails and boards in the waggon, in case of an emergency, and allowing Hiram Watson to stay at the farm for the afternoon to help them.

Grazely was a very shrewd business man. He knew well the policy of throwing an apple where there was an orchard.

No man gave more dimes to the children in gratuity, or fewer dollars to their fathers in wages.

He got the name of being free handed, whilst at the same time he hired his labour cheaper than any man in the State. His favourite maxim was, "it is easier to make money out of friends than enemies."

CHAPTER IV.

GORE FARM.

Jane Halford's first thought the morning after their arrival, was how to reconcile her husband to his new surroundings.

She herself found her courage come back with sunrise. Determination returned with the dawn of a beautiful day. But she must think of him.

Knowing his great weakness for sport of any kind, she determined to make use of it in softening the shock of disappointment. He gladly accepted the suggestion, that he should go fishing, but she insisted that he should not go alone. "Get the landlord to go with you, or you'll be lost in the terrible woods," she said.

"Why, Jane, one would think I had never seen a trout stream or angling rod before. I cannot get lost if I follow the stream."

"Yes, but how will you know when you'm going up or down?"

"Goodness alive, the water can't run up hill," he replied, laughing, as he hurried away to make preparations.

Mr. Blake, nothing loth to be out of hearing of the jibes about the new railroad, got ready his tackle and went with him.

In spite of their promises to be back in good time, they kept everybody waiting a full hour, causing Mrs. Halford much uneasiness.

At last they appeared bearing a fine catch of speckled beauties. William was breathless in his praises of the sport. Mr. Blake was generally conceded to be the most skilful angler in the district, but his guest had fairly beaten him, and in consequence was pleased with himself and everybody else. Indeed, he talked and laughed as gayly as if this were not to be one of the most fateful days in his life. In his enjoyment of the sport, he lost sight of the grim necessities of everyday life. He forgot that he had left the primrose path forever, and that his inheritance was toil.

Soon everything was ready. The waggon with its load of trunks and sundries, was at the door. Mrs. Blake insisted on donating a day or two's cooked victuals just to be neighbourly, and the landlord himself vowed eternal friendship for so good a sportsman as Halford.

Both the buxom daughters, Sally and Julia, had little presents for the baby, and they all made promises to visit the farm at an early date.

Everybody was so kind, so friendly, and so thoughtful, that the strangers vowed the people of Grazely's Mills to be the kindest mortals under the sun. This very kindness acted as a buffer between them and their new surroundings, making an impression upon them, never to be forgotten.

To cap the climax Christina Langtry climbed up on the waggon, explaining that her ma sent her to mind the baby, and keep them company for a day or two. In honour of the occasion, dressed in her Sunday best she perched herself on the highest box. Her magenta stockings and copper-toed shoes dangled in mid-air, while she luxuriated under the shade of a faded parasol, and waited for the excursion to start. She was evidently proud of her projected trip to the country. She was a mark of envy for the other juveniles of the village.

Before leaving, Mrs. Halford ran into the post-office and grasping Mr. Langtry's hand said, "I are only a stranger here, but if us can ever do you a good turn we'm not forget this day."

As they drove up the long incline to the west, behind Mr. Grazely's spirited roadster, Mr. Halford was quite gay.

"The greatest fishing on earth," he said. "Never saw anything like it. If Ponsonby were here he'd go wild. And the game! why I saw scores of partridge and hares. It is as good as having an estate of one's own. Better, because there are bears and wolves as well." Thus he rambled on, talking about his fishing rods, and his guns, with almost boyish enthusiasm, seeming to forget the errand he was on.

But the young mother was abstracted and thoughtful. It was an important hour in her life, and she felt the gravity of the situation all the more keenly, because he did not. Occasionally heaving a deep sigh, she kept a sharp look out for the clearing.

Nothing but forest, forest, forest, and yet they must be nearing the farm, for it was said to be only three and a half or four miles from the village. When they reached the upland, they could, through occasional gaps in the trees, catch glimpses of the broad valley behind, and the village nestling by the river.

Mr. Langtry told them it was the first clearing to the right hand side of the road, but so far there was nothing but virgin forest. For a time they drove slowly along a narrow, level stretch of road, where the trees formed an endless canopy overhead, and they began to think, there must be some mistake, when suddenly, they came to a gap in the forest and there in front of them was Gore Farm.

In the middle of a clearing, which was still dotted with stumps, stood a low, log house with one door, and one small window. At the end was a large chimney of rough stone, whose base widened out at the bottom, and gave an impression, that the house had been built to the chimney, instead of the chimney to the house. The only sign of paint about the place, was on the door, which had been daubed with bright red.

Either the artist had merely been cleaning his brush or the supply of paint had run out, for the lower third was untouched, and even the upper part had been treated with a partiality which could scarcely have been intentional. The bundle of rags which filled the space of a vacant pane in the window, and the bones of some dead animal in the foreground, gave the place a most diabolical appearance.

The young couple sat mute and motionless gazing at their future abode.

Had they left their home and friends, crossed the trackless ocean and travelled thousands of miles for this? This dungeon of desolation, this wretched hovel, this field of weeds and stumps! Must they cast their lot in this dreary wilderness where they would see no human face, and hear no voice but the sighing of the forest trees, or the howling of wild beasts? Must they immure themselves in this vast, leafy tomb, and bid the world good-night?

The horse stood champing his bit, impatient to be moving, but the driver kept a tight rein and sat in a dazed condition, scarcely knowing what to do. A sickening, dreadful despondency came over them, which seemed to chain them to the spot and hold them speechless.

At last the sound of the waggon coming up behind broke the spell.

Holding her baby tighter to her breast, the young mother clasped her husband's hand. In a moment her frame was shaking with sobs, and the big tears were coursing down her cheeks. Poor creatures! From their dreams of an American Eldorado they had a rude awakening.

But they must dry their tears, for the big, fat, shining bays are coming up behind, and Christina is singing a rollicking song about "gettin' out de wilderness," a very anti-climax to their despair.

Alongside the ugly slash fence Mr. Halford led his

beast till he reached an opening, then turned into the clearing, carefully picking his way between the stumps.

The teamster followed in his tracks, the load swaying and creaking over the rough, uneven ground in such a way as to force the songstress to abandon her vocal efforts and concentrate her energies in the direction of hanging on.

The house, or rather hut, contained three rooms, and, thank goodness, had a huge fireplace.

Immediately after the light was let in the young wife's mind was engaged in planning her future household. When she got her own furniture she would place a cupboard here, a table there, and further over she would hang a picture or an ornament.

Is there not an inspiring constructiveness in planning and decorating even the humblest home? Born in the little maid who arranges her play-house, it seems to grow from year to year and reaches a climax when the young wife first feels the inspiration of her own fireside.

Is it not a sort of coronation which proclaims her queen, and free from the glitter of pomp and power? It kindles in her heart a glow which sheds its light on future generations, and blossoms into patriotism. Every sweep of the broom put strength in Mrs. Halford's arm; every rug she laid upon the rude floor gave fresh elasticity to her step, every pot and pan nestling in its corner gave a fresh hope, and every dish consigned to its rude shelf chased away a fear.

Christina and the teamster were both very helpful. The latter had surely kept bachelor's hall, he was so handy with everything. Once or twice she bantered him about it, but the stoical Mr. Watson never laughed and seldom spoke. He only worked and whistled.

William sat outside minding the baby and was surprised to hear his wife's musical laugh. "Strange creatures are women," he thought, "beyond all comprehension. Crying one minute and laughing the next."

Before long three busy pairs of hands brought order out of chaos, and cheerfulness out of gloom. When the logs were crackling on the hearth and the white cloth spread for supper, the young wife hummed little snatches of song in the very gladness of her heart.

Never would she forget the little evening meal in which they all joined.

The glossy bays were contentedly munching their oats from a box at the open door, a bird was singing and swinging near its nest on a tree at the window, and the long, soft shadows of evening were putting their fairy-like touches on the far off wooded hills; the baby was drinking contentedly at Nature's font, the kettle was singing on the hearth, and years afterwards the young mother looked back to that hour as the happiest of her life.

Oh, gilded palaces and stately mansions, ye are beggars both whose bread doth turn to stone!

How little ye know of the happiness of humble homes!

CHAPTER V.

TWO AND TWENTY YEARS AFTER.

Perhaps the only class of people who have many opportunities of seeing the beauties of sunrise, are those who enjoy them the least.

The farmer in every portion of the civilized world, is forced by the nature of his calling, to work during his busiest seasons from daylight till dark, and when he rises from his bed in the grey dawn of the morning, yawning regretfully over the shortness of his slumbers, he is not usually in a frame of mind to enjoy the beauties of nature.

His first waking hours are often tinged with bitterness at the drudgery and monotony of his everyday life.

When Sunday comes, it is welcomed as a day of rest, and both in town and country the weary toilers take advantage of the opportunity, and sleep till the sun is high in the sky.

Yet the early riser on a balmy June morning is surely repaid for his trouble, when sunrise is a perfect song of nature, full of glorious promise.

At least, so thought a young man who was driving rapidly eastward this particular Sunday morning, on one of the principal roads leading to Levisville, a thriving New England town.

The rolling hills and fields of shaded green, the woods where spring had woven such wondrous charms in leaf and blossom, the sparkling dew, the balmy, scented air, the awakening songs of birds and changing tints of cloud and sky—all took part in transforming this weary, work-a-day world into a land of beauty and bliss.

As our traveller neared the top of a long incline, known locally, as "the mile hill," the bright sunshine glistened on the wheels of his newly painted buggy, brought more clearly into view his finely groomed grey horse, and showed the driver to be a young man of about five and twenty.

He was dressed in a neatly fitting coat and trowsers of grey tweed, a spotless white vest, and a sailor-shaped straw hat, with a broad black band.

The whole turnout had a spick and span appearance, even to the shining black harness, which sat so becomingly on the glossy sides of his dapple grey steed. The care bestowed, both on his equipage and his person, indicated not that this early riser was out to enjoy the beauties of nature, but that there was a lady in the case. His closely fitting gloves, spotless linen, and smoothly shaved chin, gave him a clean and cool appearance, and, fortunately for his toilet, the dew still held in control the dust of the broad, white road.

Reaching the top of the hill, he came to a full stop, either to rest his beast, or to enjoy the panorama before him.

Away to the eastward, the road ran down the incline and narrowed into a white line, till it seemed to reach the sky, while as far as the eye could reach, lay beautiful rolling fields dotted with farm houses and buildings. Here and there were patches of woodland, and through the valley a rippling stream sang its gurgling song, glistening and glancing in the morning sun.

With the exception of a few cattle and sheep grazing quietly by the roadside, not a living object was in sight.

Our traveller was evidently deeply impressed with the view, for, removing his hat, either out of sentiment or to enlarge the area of his vision, he stood motionless in his vehicle, gazing away into the distance.

Just while he is in this position, we have an excellent opportunity of scanning his features, and of discovering what manner of a young man is this, who is such a lover of nature as to apparently forget the errand which was causing him such haste only a few moments before.

One could see at a glance that he was no Adonis. His features were too prominent and well marked. Yet that first look convinced you that he was "somebody." His face bore the stamp of intellectuality in a high degree, and his jet black hair, combed straight up from his massive forehead, gave him a peculiar air of command.

Although somewhat overshadowed by a pair of heavy eyebrows, his grey eyes were clear and keen, but not unkind. The heavy black mustache which adorned his upper lip did not hide the lines of firmness about his mouth, and his square chin only emphasized his air of determination. A strong face full of character and individuality, though pride and passion were a trifle too apparent. His form bore the same characteristics as his face. He was tall, large-boned and muscular, but too angular for symmetry.

Like all other human beings, David Gordon's character and countenance had been largely influenced by his surroundings, and if one could read aright, his life had not been a path of flowers.

Away back on the road which he had just travelled, lay the town of Gowanstone where, since his boyhood, he had fought the wolf of want and managed to support his widowed mother.

Enterprise, economy and determination, had at last given him a victory over his lowly estate.

People said that Gordon was on a fair way to get rich. His nature did not fit him for the subordinate position of journeyman miller, but he had borne with "slings and arrows of outrageous fortune" until he was able to lease the Gowanstone Mills and become master instead of servant. Not only this, but, now that he had a competency, he had decided that in the near future, he would take unto himself a wife. So on this bright Sunday morning, he was on his way to see the object of his affections.

For a long time he stood wrapt in admiration. "What a glorious view it is! I never get tired looking from this hill. It seems to expand one's soul. No wonder that Scotland and Switzerland are famous for their patriotism. There's inspiration in these hills."

Suddenly he remembered his errand. Reseating himself in his vehicle and spreading the light rug over his knees, he said softly, "Come, Dan, old fellow," and away he went down the grade at a rattling pace. Even Dan seemed to enjoy the situation. The gay arch of his shapely neck, and a coyness about the set of his ears, denoted exhilaration of spirits, while the clatter of his hoofs, and the deep hum of the buggy, furnished a suitable accompaniment to the snatches of song in which his master was now indulging.

David Gordon's heart was full of happiness, for every turn of the wheels was bringing him nearer to Marian Halford. It was two whole weeks since he had seen her, but it seemed to him an age. The very thought of her made his heart beat more quickly, and his cheek turn pale. In fact, there was, for him, a positive intoxication in her presence.

On this particular morning she was to drive out to meet him, but with a lover's eagerness he had started too early, and would probably reach his destination before his lady love had finished her morning slumbers.

For a whole hour he was in a constant state of expectation and excitement. With Dan's steady, swinging gait, mile after mile was passed with monotonous regularity.

It was now nearing eight o'clock, with not a vehicle in sight.

At last, a cloud of dust on a distant knoll set his heart going. David was no fop, but he hurriedly re-adjusted his neckwear, smoothed his hair, and brushed a speck of dust off his coat sleeve. Grave and reserved in manner, he always tried to hide his emotions, but his cheek *would* turn pale in spite of him.

As he neared the approaching vehicle he found to his annoyance and disgust, that his excitement had been all in vain, for it contained, instead of her, whom he thought the most beautiful creature in the world, a farmer and his spouse going probably to morning services some distance away.

"What's the use of wearing my heart in my mouth, when the chances are she is asleep yet.

"There is another rig coming, but I'll not be fooled twice."

"Six miles to Louisville" said a showy mile post, covered with advertisements. This caused him to give up all hopes of meeting her, when suddenly he spied a vision which sent his heart bounding into his throat.

There she was at last, with her little brother and younger sister, driving a fine big sorrel in a canopy topped surrey, and while she held the reins her companions waved their hats, and shouted at his approach.

David, of course, had no eyes excepting for the driver. The enchantment of the divine passion was upon him. Love, with its magic wand transformed her into something more than common clay.

Yet, even the severest critic would admit that there was some excuse for his raptures. She had an oval face, with a peach-like complexion, a mass of fluffy light brown hair blowing from beneath a dainty straw hat, and a pair of bewitching eyes, whose colour it was impossible to determine.

There was a subtle attractiveness about her face, which was not all beauty, a something which puzzled and excited curiosity. Her features were not regular enough for typical beauty; indeed, in some respects they were contradictory. The austerity of her brow denied the hint of sensuousness about her beautifully curved lips, and the faint dimple in her cheek contradicted the droop at the corner of her upper eyelid. Her eyes were the greatest puzzle of all. Generally they were full of tenderness, but at times one could detect a tiger-like flash lurking in the dark blue which turned them almost black.

It seemed impossible to form any idea of her inner nature from her face when in repose. Force and power were there, but in an indefinable shape, which seemed full of hidden possibilities.

But when she smiled her countenance lit up with a benevolence and generosity which silenced criticism, and carried confidence by storm.

Yet, when the smile faded the original problem repeated itself, and one could not help watching and waiting for the lights and shadows of this shifting conundrum.

No wonder that David was beside himself, for not only did she smile upon him, but the colour in her cheek deepened. As she tightened the reins to check the speed, her shapely arms and shoulders threatened destruction to her tight sleeves, while her bodice gave the impression that there was no room to spare.

It was evident that Dame Nature had been unusually kind, having given her not only a beautiful face, but a splendid physique. The pure, rich blood mantling in her neck and cheek gave that complexion which only health can bestow. One felt impressed by her physical completeness.

She was the first to speak. "Good morning, Mr. Gordon," she said archly. "Are you going far? You are quite an early riser."

"Yes, and wait till I tell you, Mr. Gordon," exclaimed Nelly (a bright girl in her teens), "if I hadn't woke her up, she would have been snoring yet."

"Please shut up, Nelly, you know I don't snore. You'll horrify Mr. Gordon."

Fred, a lad of ten with a voice as hoarse as a raven, here broke in with, "Well, she does, 'cause I slept with her one night and——" Marian's gloved hand suddenly covered his mouth, and they all broke into a hearty laugh.

David in the meantime had calmed himself sufficiently to speak, and he remarked after looking at his watch that he *was* a trifle ahead of time.

"You are certainly no laggard," she replied laughing. "I would have been earlier too, but this is a strange horse, and we had to get Watson to hitch him."

"Yes, I see, and a new surrey too. That was why I didn't know you, till you were right upon me. He is a fine-looking animal. Is he speedy?"

"He ain't nothin' else," responded Fred. "I bet he can beat your Dan all the same."

"He *is* a splendid traveller," said Marian with a confirmatory nod. "Mother paid a big price for him. Turn him around and we'll have a little spin," she added enthusiastically.

Gordon sprang out of his buggy, and shook hands with all. He longed to kiss one fair shapely hand, but of course there were too many pairs of eyes looking on, and he had to content himself with giving it a squeeze.

"What, run races on Sunday? That would be a terrible thing for a good churchwoman, like Miss Halford, let alone a poor heathen like me," said David with an air of mock humility.

"Cowardy, cowardy, custard," shouted Fred. "We'd beat you so bad you would think you was standin' still."

Marian's smile of confidence as she looked at her new steed, added to Fred's crowing, rather nettled David.

"Do you really wish it?" he asked.

She made a little grimace, which he seemed to understand, for he jumped into his vehicle and gave the word "Go."

Gordon thought at first he would have no trouble at all, and that he would go only fast enough to amuse them, but to his surprize and chagrin, the sorrel shot ahead of him like a rocket, and before he had time to realize his position, the surrey was fully twenty feet ahead. This would never do, so he urged Dan into it neck and crop. Away they went, leaving a great cloud of dust behind them.

Marian was evidently no novice. Gordon began to fear that he had met his match, both in horse and driver, for, urge as he would, they were still ahead.

His faithful grey had the reputation of being the best horse in the county, and to have him beaten by a changeling like this sorrel was to disgrace him forever.

"I'll wear the sorrel out. He's only a spurter at best," said Gordon to himself. "Ha, he is weakening already. Come, Dan, old fellow. Show them what blood will do. Steady now."

The rigs were fairly dancing along the highway with the wheels almost touching each other. An inch closer would have been disastrous to one or both. Every face was pale with excitement, but no one thought of danger, though more than once the hubs of the wheels crashed against each other.

The grey was now gaining inch by inch. In a moment they were even, neck and neck, nose and nose. Marian's face turned a shade paler as she saw herself gradually losing ground, for now Gordon's back wheels were nearly opposite her front ones and soon he would pass them. But not if she could help it.

The road up to this point was perfectly smooth, but here was a stretch where one-third of its width had been freshly gravelled, and the rough part was on Gordon's side.

There was still room for both in the smooth portion, but with defeat staring her in the face, Marian resolved to crowd her opponent into the rough piles of gravel.

He shouted for room as they approached, but she pretended not to hear. In a moment Gordon's buggy was bumping and bouncing over the knolls and lumps, and the sorrel again shot a full length ahead.

"Keep on, by heavens, and I'll pass you yet," he shouted defiantly as he made to cross the road behind her. But Marian foreseeing this possibility still managed to keep directly in front of him, for a few moments, and then held up her hand in token that the race was over and won.

"Whee," shouted Fred. "Better trade your grey off for a yoke of oxen. And we had the heaviest load too."

Nelly stood up and swung her hat with delight, but Marian did not take any part in the rejoicing, for she saw that David was looking black as a thunder cloud.

"I did not think you would get angry at a little thing like this," she said, elevating her eyebrows.

"It was the most disgraceful, bare-faced piece of jockeying I ever saw. I did not think you could be guilty of such dishonesty. If you were a man I would thrash you for a cheat."

The hot colour flashed over her face, and her eyes took on a deeper hue. You are complimentary."

"I am more," was his hot reply, "I am truthful."

This was too much. She pressed her lips tightly to keep the moisture from her eyes and turned her face away.

She knew that she had acted unfairly, but even that could surely not excuse his rudeness.

The horses were now walking along side of each other, fairly steaming with perspiration. Marian was not prepared either to defend her action, or to accept his affront. Nelly and Fred were both afraid to speak and the situation was very much strained.

"Ah, there is the side road," she said to herself. "I'll turn down and leave him to himself."

As the sorrel broke into a trot, the grey followed suit; but what was Gordon's surprise, when suddenly the surrey swept round the corner, leaving him to go on or turn back as he saw fit.

"Good God!" he said to himself, "I have offended her beyond forgiveness. This is a hint for me to go home, and by heavens I will go. I only told the truth. I can't be hypocrite enough to apologize, when I really meant it."

He stood still for a few moments, while the battle of love and pride was raging in his heart, then slowly but very deliberately turned his vehicle around.

A moment more and he would have started for

Gowanstone, but lying on the road just at the corner was a dainty embroidered handkerchief, which he recognized as Marian's. For a moment he hesitated, and that moment was probably the turning point in two lives. Had he ever started homewards, he would never have stopped till he reached his own door, but this trifling piece of white silk was the feather which turned the scales. He mechanically got out to pick it up, and its delicate perfume brought back a rush of tenderness. Hearts were trumps again.

Once his mind was made up there was no further hesitation, so he turned down the side road, and started in pursuit.

Miss Halford was driving very slowly now, and in a very uncertain frame of mind. The more she thought over it, the more guilty she felt. "I was really in the wrong. He would have been a spiritless man, who would not have been vexed. But then he needn't have been quite so rude." What about her hospitality though? Clearly it was her duty to go back, and she was looking for a place to turn around, when she heard the clatter of hoofs coming up behind, at a whirlwind pace? In spite of the narrowness of the road and the risk of upsetting his vehicle, Gordon turned out, and passed without slackening his speed. In a moment he was in front of them, and jumping out he grasped the sorrel's bridle rein.

"For God's sake, Marian, let us not quarrel over a trifle. I have come now, not so much to apologize for my words, as the spirit in which they were uttered. My rudeness was out of proportion to your injustice. Marian, you know I would gladly give my life for you. There is nothing under heaven consistent with honour, that I would not do for you. At the same time I would fight for justice, or even a fragment of it, against all the hosts of heaven and hell. Here is my hand, for Nelly and Fred too."

But Fred was not yet ready for peace. "You're a blamed crank gettin' so mad about us passin' your old side-wheeler. Mally ain't goin' to get in your buggy, she'll go to Murrays with us and let you flicker. If I was her I'd sit on you."

The unconscious humour of Fred's attitude and remarks, brought forth a smile, which warmed into a laugh, and came like a flash of sunshine through the clouds dispersing all the mists of misunderstanding and ill humour. There is no logic like laughter. It is the sunshine of the soul, towards which turn the flowers of charity. By its warmth the best elements of our natures are drawn to the surface, while the dregs of discontent are driven to deeper depths.

Marian could not help admiring the manliness of David's attitude as he apologized for his own shortcomings without excusing hers. There was no pretence of humility, but a fierce earnestness which told her he meant every word he said.

She knew that this man loved her with every atom of his strong nature, but both his tone and manner told her, that not even for her would he sacrifice a principle. Never did he appear to more advantage in her eyes.

"David, your rudeness was not half so bad as my meanness, and I can more easily forgive you than myself, so we will say no more about it."

"From what Fred has just said, I infer that you originally intended riding home with me. Show me that you forgive me by getting into my buggy." Seizing her hand he kissed it, (glove and all), almost pulling her out.

As she sprang to the ground he could not help admiring her figure, in which strength, ampleness and grace seemed equally combined; a very type of physical womanhood.

In a few moments the vehicles lost sight of each other, David returning to the broad road, while the others went on to the southwards.

For a time after they were alone neither of them spoke. They both felt ashamed of the part they had played.

At last, to break the painful silence, David asked if it was safe to leave the two youngsters alone with the strange horse.

"Oh, yes," replied Marian, with a smile, "both Fred and Nellie have driven him before. We all seem to take after mother in that respect. We take to horses like ducks to water. I often tell mother that her forefathers must either have been gypsies or jockeys. She thinks more of a good horse than most women do of their fancy work. Fred could ride nearly as soon as he could walk, and mother lets him have a horse whenever he wants one. Besides," she added, reddening guiltily, " I guess we have taken the wire edge off the sorrel already." While she was speaking the perfume of her presence kept stealing over him till with a sudden impulse he threw his arm around her neck and kissed her passionately on the lips.

Only a short distance away was a low log house by the roadside, and Marian was horrified to see old Mrs. Dorris sitting on the door-step looking straight at them.

"Oh, David, shame! Mrs. Dorris saw us kissing. Oh, dear, what a story she will have for mother next wash-day."

"I couldn't help it, darling, it's too bad, but never mind. What do I care for her?"

" Yes, Mr. Selfish, but I care. She knows me well, and she will tell it all over. You forget, David, that I am near home here. Why, that's the very house we lived in when we first came to America."

" Never mind," he said, dropping the curtains of his buggy top. "Your mother shall know all about it before I leave Broadview. I am going to ask her for her big daughter, and if I have not disgraced myself too much, I was going to ask a question of yourself, but I am both ashamed and afraid after my churlishness."

"You have less to be ashamed of than I have," she said, with a deprecatory smile as she gave him her hands. "I was too anxious to win. I admire a person who can hold principle above all else, but I can't seem to do it myself. I suppose I am too much of a savage."

He kept her hand in his, and pulling off her glove, he slipped a heavy gold ring on her finger. Before she was aware of what he was about he fastened a gold chain with a pendent locket around her neck.

Looking carefully around to see that she was not

being observed, Marian gave her reply by returning his kiss.

As if knowing that his driver had no attention to spare upon him, Dan kept up his swinging trot without pretending to notice that the reins were trailing in the dust.

Mrs. Dorris still sat on her doorstep and watched the vehicle as far as she could see it.

"So that's Marian's intended! Well, well! I seed him goin' past time and again. High-strung like herself. He'll have to be a good one to match Marian Halford. She'll have her own way, like her mother before her. Not that I have anything ag'in the girl, she is always friendly and civil with me. Lem," she cried to a decrepit looking individual, who came behind her in the doorway, " Marian Halford's just passed with her young man, and he was actually kissing her before my eyes."

"Hee, hee, hee," chuckled her husband. "What will Grazely say till that when he hears tell o't? She'll better luk out or her pride will have a fall."

"Shut your mouth, you idiot. She is not the kind of a girl a man will trifle with. Grazely, faugh! He's old enough to be her father. Jane Halford will never gain her point there. That's a match, or my name's not Sara," and, as if to close the subject, she slammed the door and went back into her hut, enviously wondering why happiness is showered upon some, while misery and squalor is the lot of others.

CHAPTER VI.

BROADVIEW AND ITS PROPRIETOR.

Perhaps we had better digress a little, and indulgently leave the lovers to themselves, while we renew some old acquaintances, and note the changes which have taken place during the past twenty odd years.

About two and a half miles from Levisville, to the

left of the road, as you approach the city from the west, stands a two-story brick house of liberal dimensions. A large square building, erected without any architectural pretence, and with nothing to break the general plainness of its appearance, but brown window shutters and a broad verandah. Evidently, it had been erected by some one of a practical turn of mind, who thought that stability and imperviousness to winter winds, was all that could be desired.

The surroundings, however, furnished what the building itself lacked, and gave evidence that the present inmates were not devoid of artistic taste. A spacious, well-trimmed lawn sloped gently towards the highway, ornamented here and there by trees and vines.

Beds of roses carefully arranged and tended, dotted the green sward, while on the east side, between the lawn and the driveway, was a beautiful cedar hedge, trimmed with mathematical precision.

Rows of maples lined each side of the lane, and ornamented the front, facing the roadway, almost hiding from view a plain-looking stone fence with its large, white gates.

About a hundred and fifty yards to the westwards, were the stables and outbuildings, nestling at the side of a huge barn, with its massive stone foundations and large checkered doors.

Everything about the place denoted affluence. Indeed the barn with its aggressive bulkiness, seemed to be continually asserting itself; a very Podsnap of plebeian architecture.

The broad smooth fields, rising gradually to the northwards, formed a suitable background for the picture, and gave rise to many an outburst of admiration from the passers-by. If anything more were needed to give additional charm to the surroundings, it was amply furnished, by the long stretch of woodland to the west; a miniature forest, whose stately elms and spreading beeches hid a score of shady nooks and dells, echoing with the songs of birds.

There was a friendly, coaxing appearance about those trees, which lured you into their shades. Could they have spoken, they might have told many a tale of plighted vows and stolen kisses.

To the practical minded, the bush suggested more prosaic thoughts; the value of its timber for fuel or lumber; the protection it afforded from the northwesterly blizzards of winter; or its usefulness for pasture during the hot, dry months of summer.

In warm weather, the cattle shared its delights with the feathered tribes. The tinkle of the cow-bell mingled with the song of the robin and the ripple of the woodland stream, where the lowing herds were wont to stand knee deep, and pass the drowsy summer days in dreamy contentment.

Scores of visitors and Sunday strollers made this a rendezvous for their pedestrian trips. Out to Broadview and back became a regulation distance for the swell turn-outs of the city. The level stretch in front of the bush, about a mile in length, was a favorite spot for spurting their roadsters, and opposite its far end was the famous Woodlawn race track.

The good people of Levisville were very proud of their model farm, with its generous hospitality. Broadview was always exhibited to strangers, as one of the sights and appurtenances of the city.

The fertility of its soil, the extra quality of its buildings, the convenience of its streams, and its close proximity to the city, made it the most valuable place in the county, and its three hundred broad acres were estimated to be worth, at least, thirty thousand dollars.

Yet this handsome estate had commenced life very inauspiciously under the name of Gore Farm, whose old log-house with its huge stone chimney, still stood at the further end of the bush.

Gore Farm had passed away with Grazely's Mills, while Broadview and Levisville had prospered together. As if to keep the alliance intact, the owner of these fair acres held deeds of all the land on the northside of the highway, for a stretch of three miles from the city limits.

Mrs. Halford, or Jane Halford, as she was called by those who were envious of her worldly success, was a very rich woman, but was just as fond of the almighty dollar as ever.

Her wealth had made her ambitious, but it had never changed her habits of economy. She was just as willing to ride into town in a market waggon, with her produce, as to loll in a carriage behind a pair of prancing bays. She always kept the finest vehicles and best horses, but did not always use them. When she was in her market waggon, she consoled herself with the thought that everyone knew she had better at home. She had a large share of pride, but it was not of the kind which is gratified by display. She might have lived in affluence and idleness the rest of her days, but that would have been contrary to the ruling spirit of her life.

She still carried on the dairying industry, which first started her on the road to prosperity, and which, together with looking after her tenants, kept her time fully occupied.

Mrs. Halford had few friends and no companions, nor did she ever attempt to enter Levisville society. Inwardly conscious of her own illiteracy, she refrained from mingling with those who would be most likely to notice it. Indeed, she had made very diligent efforts to repair her defective grammar, having succeeded to the extent that she could avoid mistakes when strictly on her guard; but when particularly interested or excited would unconsciously drop into her old habits.

Her bearing and manner were so full of lady-like dignity, that her misused verbs and pronouns were the more noticeable, causing many to wonder at this remarkable contrast between her manner and her speech.

The mistress of Broadview might have known that the jingle of her dollars would not only have excused such deficiencies, but would have turned them into attractive peculiarites.

But the frivolities of fashion had little attraction for her. She preferred a chat with her banker or man of business to a gossip with one of her own sex. Not that she was so unnatural or unwomanly as to dislike gossip. No indeed, but her old friend, Mr. Grazely, who lived about half a mile cityward on the opposite side of the road, could give her the cream, the kind of news and gossip which was the most important, and her washerwoman supplied her with the skim milk of ordinary scandal, which although less palatable was more profuse.

Mr. Grazely knew whose place was under mortgage, or whose goods were under chattel; who was living beyond their means, and who was making money; how much Mrs. So and So spent for a ball costume, or to what extent some potentate's wife liked her toddy.

Like Mrs. Halford, he had a mania for land. This kindred feeling, which might probably have created rivalry between two men, only made them closer friends, and taught them to play into each other's hands.

Some years ago, Mrs. Grazely (formerly Sally Blake) died in the pangs of child-birth, leaving him the care and responsibility of raising three small children.

Since that time, Grazely had depended largely on Mrs. Halford for advice; in fact she had become the sole arbiter of his household difficulties.

Housekeepers he found to be unsatisfactory and expensive. Some broke too many dishes, used too much tea, or put too much shortening in the pies, while others "clouted" the children, or were uncleanly.

One day he came to the conclusion that he must have a wife, and, as usual, took Mrs. Halford into his confidence.

"Your daughter is beautiful, healthy and strong. I would be only too proud, if she would consent to be a mother to my orphans, yes, indeed."

Now the ambitious mistress of Broadview had often thought of this herself, and was not ill pleased with his suggestion.

She pretended, however, to be surprised. Well now, I don't know. I am sure I have never thought of such a thing. Marian have had a high education as you know, and if her does read French or play a piano, her can milk a cow or cook a meal, with anybody. If I do say it myself, as should'nt, there are not a finer looking woman in the county.

"You might have said in the state," rejoined Grazely, with a nod of encouragement "yes, in the state, or the country either for that matter. Yes, indeed."

The widower never was good looking, even in his youth, and years of grasping avarice had not improved his countenance. Although only about fifty years of age, his face had become quite narrow and pointed, while from the loss of his front teeth, his nose was begining to salute his chin. What he most feared was the rivalry of some younger suitor, and he felt it his duty to warn his friend of the danger in that direction.

"What do you think of that young man from Gowanstone (Mr. what's his name) that comes to see your daughter?"

"Well, you know, Mr. Grazely, the cat may look at the queen. You can't blame the young men for fancying Marian, when the older ones do."

The widower did not quite like the innuendo, but he laughed it off. "Ha, ha, ha! That's one for you. You don't often miss a chance But you know I am not quite fifty yet, and your daughter is what?"

"Twenty-two."

"Oh yes, I remember she was a baby when you first came. Well, I'm sure there is nothing unusual in such a match, no indeed, no indeed!" and the widower blew his nose significantly. "You see," he continued, "she might take a fancy to the young man, and then——"

"No danger," interrupted the mother. "Her have had much handsomer admirers and refused them."

"So I have heard, so I have heard," repeated Grazely, nodding his head.

"Yes. There were Mr. Lennox, who has money past him, and are a perfect gentleman, Harry Benson, the city clerk, Dr. Roddick, and Mr. Gregg."

"Splendid offers, splendid offers," said the widower laconically, as he tapped the floor with his cane. "Gregg is a sound man financially, but then one can't always tell, no indeed. Perhaps your daughter's affections have already been bestowed," he continued, clearing his throat.

"I am sure that are not the case, Mr. Grazely," she stammered, as she stooped to pick something off the floor. "Her couldn't have without me knowing it."

Mr. Grazely fidgetted in his chair a few moments before speaking. "How did your daughter become acquainted with this young man?"

"Her were visiting at Gowanstone last fall, but it are nothing," she went on with a wave of her hand.

The widower shook his head doubtfully. "He has been here pretty often. Might be the dark horse, you know," and his cane came down with a note of warning like a lodge master's gavel.

"Why, you are getting jealous already. It are too soon for that. Ha, ha, ha!"

"Well, but one can't be too careful. No, indeed!" and the cane gave three taps more.

"If you think it best, the miller will be stopped," she replied, dropping her voice to a confidential whisper. "But you know Marian are headstrong and I must go careful."

"Just so, just so."

"You spruce up a bit and I will see that her don't lose her head, in the meantime, there's my hand on it."

The houses of Grazely and Halford were to join hands, acres were to marry acres, and the westward growth of the city would be under the thumb of this alliance.

CHAPTER VII.

ADAPTATION.

PIONEER life in America had strangely modified and moulded the character of William Halford. We are accustomed to saying that man is the creature of his circumstances and surroundings, yet it is doubtful if we ever thoroughly realize how much our environments have to do with developing our good or bad qualities.

Virtues and vices are, in many respects, like our muscles; they grow and strengthen by exercise, and shrivel from want of use.

Had William Halford passed his maturing years in the heart of a great city, enjoying its pleasures and allurements, he might have become a reckless spendthrift, or a drunkard. Previous to his coming to America, the necessity of thought or action for anything but pleasure had never entered his mind.

Fortunately, his solitary life in the forest forced him to think, and the rugged resistances of nature compelled him to act.

The destructive streak in his nature found vent, not only in hunting and fishing, but in felling the giants of the forest. The characteristics, which would have made him a brave soldier, stood him in good stead in his pioneer life.

He forgave his chopping axe because it kept company with his gun. His angling rod and traps were antidotes to the plow and the sickle.

How odd it is, that our weaknesses or our foibles are sometimes as valuable as our virtues.

Nothing but this love of sport made it possible to turn a thoughtless dandy of the primrose path into a moderately good farmer.

Not indeed, that he ever worked very hard, or ever assumed any responsibility; for he readily recognized from the first, that "the grey mare was the better horse," but he was reasonably attentive to anything which involved decoration or construction, and his bump of order prompted him to keep everything tidy and in its place.

In their pioneer days his wife had worked with him shoulder to shoulder. She was even more than his equal in physical endurance, and often helped to sow and reap while her baby slept or played beneath the friendly shelter of a bush or tree, under the protectorship of a collie dog.

As soon as possible, Mrs. Halford's early experience in dairying was put to full account. In this direction she was particularly successful.

The coming of the railroad revolutionized their whole system of farming. They became rich in leaps and bounds. The price of land went up to double or treble its original value. Jane Halford, with her cool clear head, was a good speculator. When people rushed to sell for ready money, she bought and held. When everybody else ran, she stood still. Yet she took some great chances, and once pawned her husband's gold watch and diamond breast-pin to pay a margin on some land.

The village of Grazely's mills lived only two months after the boom. It was swept out of existence, leaving the town of Levisville in its place.

Chimneys and church steeples took the place of towering elms. The whippoorwill's song gave place to the shrill whistle of the locomotive.

No longer the cow-bell clanked in the main street, it had long since been supplanted by the tinkle of the street car.

Instead of the ox-cart slowly dragging its way to market with its load of lumber, hourly processions of cars went rushing and roaring down the valley, carrying off the giants of the forests to build the cities of the new world. No longer did the gaudy sign at Blake's swing in the breeze, or the pigs wallow by the water trough.

The jovial landlord of the Bay Horse had long since gone to his reward, surrounded by the reptiles of his own imagination. Sally left home to become Mrs. Grazely, and Julia eloped with the stage driver for parts unknown. Mrs. Blake outlived her husband only two years, and at the time of her death, it was a disputed point between the doctors, as to whether she died of a broken heart brought on by grief, or apoplexy from over-eating.

Langtry, the potentate, was shorn of his glory; his versatility lost its market. Too proud to accommodate himself to his changed surroundings, he fought a gradually-losing battle till finally he settled on one of Mrs. Halford's farms.

Mrs. Dorris, the professional midwife, sank to the level of a common washerwoman.

Phil Snider languished in a poor-house.

All the old landmarks had gone. Most of the pioneers had either been crowded out, or succumbed to the grim reaper. Grazely and the Halfords seemed to be the only ones who caught the wave of prosperity, excepting, perhaps, Harry Bowles, who was now the proprietor of a circus.

Even the Halfords had their little financial crisis. One evening, about a year after the coming of the railway, while attending a social gathering in the town, Mr. Halford took a little too much brandy and soda and, under its generous influence subscribed five hundred dollars to the new English Church.

Although struggling at that time under a heavy load of mortgages, and holding together a great deal of property with a small capital, his wife was either too proud or too honest to repudiate the debt. The property was all in her own name, but she paid the subscription.

Then there had been a scene between them, which neither of them had ever forgotten. From that time forward Mr. Halford had become an abstainer.

He was passionately fond of children, and for miles around he was known amongst the juveniles as "Uncle William."

Every door was open to him. In every home he was a welcome guest. He could talk politics to paterfamilias, discuss a pudding or a pie with a housewife, or romp with the children.

His pockets were always full of candies and small coins. By every child in the district, he was regarded as a legitimate subject for plunder.

He had excellent taste in all matters of a decorative nature, so much so that many a proud housewife consulted him on the shade of a carpet, or the colour of curtains.

His eye for the beautiful was supposed to carry him even into the mazes of millinery, and the young ladies were fain to ask Uncle William how he liked their hats,

He was always very particular about his own personal appearance. Even at work he would as soon have thought of going without his boots, as without his collar and tie.

With him it was a point of honour, never to be caught *en deshabille*, and when he raised his hat to a lady his hair always looked as if it had just been brushed.

Summer and winter, Saturday and Sunday, he shaved just as regularly as he washed his face, and would have considered himself an aborigine if he had neglected his tooth brush.

The neighbours used to say in jest, that he got up through the night to comb his hair. Many of them vowed that if his house was on fire he would clean his teeth before giving the alarm.

But these little foibles only gave him a warmer place in their hearts, more especially as they saw that such was largely due to habit, training, and instinct.

We appreciate most of those friends or acquaintances who furnish us with something to laugh at or find fault with. It surrounds them with an atmosphere of charity and good humour, which makes us more friendly in our criticisms and more generous in our eulogies. It seems to disarm jealousy and envy.

Many a man's best friend is his peculiarity. Wily politicians have been known to affect some peculiar or ridiculous article of attire, in order to divert harsher criticisms.

Oftentimes, when the hat has been the target the head has escaped.

Uncle William, however, was entirely free from any such craftiness, for tidiness was a cornerstone of his character.

Of late years the idol of his heart was his daughter, Marian. Fred and Nelly both got a good share of parental love, but his eldest daughter was the apple of his eye. There was a generosity and breadth in her nature, so far beyond his own, that he almost worshipped her, and every day he discovered some new trait in her character.

He knew nothing of his wife's intentions regarding her, and if he had, he would at once have taken sides with Marian. He generally allowed Mrs. Halford her own way in everything. Though he might make suggestions, he never thought of interfering in her plans. But around the liberty, happiness, and welfare of his daughter he drew a line which none dare cross, not even the mother who bore her.

CHAPTER VIII.

A CHILD OF NATURE.

EVEN in early girlhood Marian Halford gave unusual promise of beauty and physical development, but to offset this, her mental proclivities were generally regarded as being very erratic, causing people to predict that Jane Halford would find her daughter hard to manage.

From the very first she was a rebel at school. More than once she led her schoolmates in open mutiny, and often played the truant.

When whipped by the teacher, she rarely cried like other girls, but took her punishment in stolid defiance.

Yet when others, and especially the little ones, were being chastised, she hid her face to cover the tears, or closed her ears to shut out the sounds. Once when her little sister Nelly was being punished very severely for some trivial offence she sprang at the teacher, and snatching the rod from his hand, threw it out the open window.

Her school life was filled with disgraces and irregularities of this kind, yet she learned rapidly, not by industrious plodding, but by fits and starts. Sometimes she was slow to grasp a problem, but once she got an inkling of light, it all came to her like a flash, and she saw in a moment what others took months to comprehend.

Nor was her antipathy to school altogether due to her frequent punishments, but rather to its cramped and narrow atmosphere.

She revelled in the woods, whose shady nooks were transformed by her youthful imagination into fairyland. Even in her infancy, she was accustomed to the blue sky. Pebbles were her playthings, and bushes her friends. Under their shelter she built houses of sand, made mud pies or went to sleep in the lullaby of whispering leaves. As far back as she could remember, the blue dome was the roof and the green sod the floor of her dwelling. The love of out-door life was firmly implanted in her nature. Her childhood had no companions but birds, barnyard fowls and her dog. She loved the dear old trees. They were her friends. The rustling of their leaves was music to her ears. They seemed to tell their tales of joy and grief; of dark and lonely nights with cruel, howling winds; of bright and sunny days when feathered songsters sat upon their boughs and sang the songs of love.

Her imagination was at once her weakness and her strength. Often in the woods she forgot her cares and sat for hours in dreamland.

Sometimes she peopled the dells with fairies, and sometimes with demons. Here she felt the keen exhilaration of the hunter, and the shrinking terror of the hunted; the savage joy of the tiger, and the horror of its victim.

Again, the lilied banks were turned to sculptured halls, on which the flowers and shrubs were men and women, whose lives she filled with joy and grief; with love and hate.

Sometimes they were gladiators thirsting for each other's blood, combatants in an imaginary arena where she gloated with the victor, and despaired with the vanquished.

Sometimes she felt the cunning of the thief, and sometimes the candour of the honest, while for some little flower which bloomed alone in dark seclusion she had sympathy and even tears.

The birds and squirrels became her pets and learned to know her voice. The cattle loved their young shepherdess, and gave obedience to her word and touch. There was something in her face or form which taught the dumb animals to trust her; something which stamped her as their friend.

This daughter of earth and sky seemed to feel the very pulse of nature in her veins, and was in touch with all its moods. She loved to lie upon some lonely bank and watch the drifting clouds or twinkling stars. She loved to see the lightning flash or hear the thunders roll, and often as a storm approached, she stole out to the forest, to watch her giants battling with the winds or hear the storm howling through the woods.

When about fourteen years of age, circumstances arose which were destined to influence her whole future life, and possibly her character.

Mr. Langtry had for some years been a tenant of the old Gore hundred. Though he was always behind with his rent, Mrs. Halford generally forgave him a portion of his indebtedness, out of gratitude to himself and his daughter Christina, who was a great favourite at Broadview. The son Charles was now a handsome, overgrown boy of sixteen, but he was of little use on the farm. Between the inexperience of the father and the indolence of the son, the affairs of the Langtrys were sadly neglected.

Charles cared for nothing but music. Outside of the old melodeon of their palmy days, the only instruments within his reach were an accordion and a harmonica, but these he played with astonishing skill and wonderful effect.

He and Marian first became companions and friends during their early school days. Always willing to do battle in her cause, he was the champion of her youth. He gave her fruit, brought her flowers, and often slyly expended his hoarded savings for candies which he kept in reserve for little offerings.

They walked to and from school together, and many a time he carried her through a snow bank, or walked in front of her to break the fierce cold wind.

In the summer days they wandered through the fields and woods together, herding their cattle, or hunting for flowers, and often they sat in the moonlight, and he played while she sang.

Mrs. Halford, accustomed to seeing them together, and forgetting that they were growing past their childhood, left them continually in the way of temptation.

One sultry summer evening they had occasion to cross the stream where the cattle watered. He had often carried her across before, but this evening was so warm that she determined to wade.

She took off her shoes and stockings, and pulling her skirts to her knees, with the innocence of a child, she stepped half-laughingly, and half-timidly, into the water.

He offered to assist her, but no, she *would* go alone. He crossed rapidly himself, and waited for her on the opposite bank, laughing at her timidity. In spite of her cautious efforts to select the shallow spots as he had done, she suddenly stumbled into a deep hole which forced her garments nearly to her waist.

"Wait! I'll help you," he shouted as she gave a little cry of fear. But something in her companion's eye made her blush, and abandoning her skirts to their fate she wept for shame.

He caught her in his arms and carried her across. As he set her down upon the bank he knelt beside her and kissed away her tears.

That night was kindled in their hearts a glow which awakened deeper motives and emotions. A flame in whose fantastic light imagination revelled, a passion new and strange, which gave them hopes and fears, tears and smiles which took possession of their souls, and in their youthful ignorance passed unchallenged either as love or lust.

Mrs. Halford, intent on her race for wealth, blind to all that was going on, left these two healthy, rich-blooded creatures to the mercies of warm sunshine, continued companionship and opportunity, till at last by the merest accident she discovered the serious extent of their intimacy. Great heavens! she was frozen with horror. Why had she not foreseen this? Was disgrace to turn all her gold to dross and her acres to ashes?

Yet in spite of the fact that she had left her daughter

to be the victim of circumstances, Mrs. Halford tried to justify herself before her own conscience. Never having known a mother's loving care herself, she scarcely knew that in omitting that companionship and counsel so necessary to the budding years of womanhood, she had failed in her duty.

Little did the youthful lovers know that their secret had been discovered, though they both wondered why they were so suddenly separated, and why Marian was sent so unexpectedly to live at the rectory for a few weeks.

This beggar's son was no match for her daughter, at least, so Mrs. Halford thought. As soon as she was satisfied that her daughter had escaped the sting of maternity, she thanked God for his leniency, and gave orders to the bailiff to sell the Langtrys out.

In spite of the intercession of neighbours on behalf of the delinquent tenants, and the personal appeals of Mr. Langtry himself, the sale went on, and the Langtrys were homeless.

A purse was gathered and presented to the sufferers, to keep away the wolf of want, and the strange part of it was, that Mrs. Halford herself munificently subscribed fifty dollars toward it, ostensibly for Christina's sake, but really to assist them in getting out of the neighbourhood.

To do her justice, money was no object in this case, indeed, if necessary, she would have given ten times that amount to have driven them from the district.

She succeeded in accomplishing her object, for, unable to bear up under the social disgrace, the Langtrys left without leaving any trace of their whereabouts.

Mrs. Halford was well on her guard. She intercepted several letters to her daughter, bearing the Boston postmark, and consigned them to the flames unread.

But she must send her daughter somewhere out of all reach, and one day she surprised her husband by telling him that she had arranged to send Marian for a four years' course to the seminary at Montreal.

Her father preferred an American institution at

Boston, Philadelphia or New York, but Mrs. Halford convinced him that Montreal was the best.

Thus it came to pass that Marian received a splendid training, not only in matters pertaining to general education, but in those graces which adorn womanhood.

Her mother, at any other time, would not have dreamt of incurring the expense, but now that she had put her hand to the plow she would not turn back.

Mrs. Halford seemed to have stumbled on the very plan of action best suited to the circumstances, for had Marian ever dreamt that her mother knew her secret, or had she suspected that she had been separated from Charles on purpose, she would probably have defied her mother's attempts at interference and gone to her lover.

As it was, she thought that he had forgotten her and she was too proud to make any complaint. But many a night she wept and moaned over her lost love, and the enthusiasm of youth was forever gone.

Her mind, previously raw and untrained, grew and expanded under the gentle influence of her teachers, and visions of a higher and nobler life inspired her with hope. Her past life, with its want of restraint and refinement, was a continual rebuke to her. She felt that, like Topsy, she had been left to grow, and she fully realized all that her mother had left undone.

One Clara Hawke, of Gowanstone, who happened to be taking a musical course at the seminary, became her constant friend and companion. Marian's surplus emotions found vent in Clara's melodies.

Music became a necessity to her. Although her own playing was far below her ideals, it acted like a safety valve in relieving the tension of her soul, seeming to take the place of her girlish love for young Langtry, a passion, which, as years rolled on, she felt that she had outlived. She came to look upon it as an experience which would guard her from the snares and pitfalls of life, and would give her a clearer insight into the character of any man who might seek her hand.

When she came back to the farm she gladly entered into the work, and for a time, with her cows, her fowls and her lambs, she was contented and happy. The familiar scenes, at first, brought back both painful and pleasant remembrances, but *work, work, work* was her panacea for all evils. In fact, she felt that she could not live without it.

Attracted by her beauty and her prospects as an heiress, many suitors and admirers came to Broadview but they failed to excite in her even a passing interest. Finally she met the young miller of Gowanstone, and although she did not fall in love with him at first sight, nor was she sure she was in love at all, yet he rekindled her interest in the opposite sex. She puzzled herself a good deal over her feelings towards him. She seemed to care for him more than for any one else, excepting her own people, but she was not sure that she really loved him.

Her feelings towards him were entirely different from her infatuation for Charles Langtry, but then in those days she was a savage.

She saw that Gordon loved her. She admired his genuine worth and sterling honesty. But, in spite of all this, David would probably have shared the same fate as her other suitors, had it not been for the importunities of the widower Grazely, backed up by tiresome innuendos from her mother.

As soon as she discovered that her mother was trying to coerce her, her defiance was up in arms.

"I shall never be bought and sold, and if David Gordon asks me, I will be his wife."

If parents would only stop to think how impossible it is to coerce love, and how any attempt of this kind is apt to drive young natures in an opposite direction, they would change their tactics.

Mrs. Halford, in endeavouring to force her daughter into an alliance with the widower, was simply throwing her into Gordon's arms.

"The best laid schemes of mice and men gang oft aglee."

CHAPTER IX.

AN UNWELCOME GUEST.

THE swallows were twittering and careening round the big barn, and the cattle were lowing at the further end of the lane, as David and Marian drove up to the gate at Broadview.

"Oh, dear," she said, fidgeting in her seat, "it is past milking time. This is the first time in years I have been late. I do hope mother won't notice it."

But just a moment later a woman came out of the back door with some pails on her arm, and sitting down beside a dun-coloured cow she commenced milking.

This process, however, the animal seemed to resent, for with a preliminary switch of its tail, it gave a kick and sent the pail flying behind it.

Marian laughed softly. "Mother is having trouble with Daisy." Then she shouted, "Wait, mother! let me manage her," and, jumping out of the vehicle while it was yet in motion, she ran to where the animal was calmly looking round at the battered pail.

As David approached he raised his hat to salute Marian's mother, "Good morning, Mrs. Halford," he said.

"Good morning, Mr. Gordon," came the reply in doubtful tones. What could her daughter see in this penniless nobody. Was it for such as he that Marian was late, she wondered.

But she must not forget her hospitality. "Just tie your horse to the post there. William are not up yet, and Watson are taking a stroll through the fields, but he will be back soon and put your horse away."

Time had dealt very gently with Jane Halford. Although nearly fifty years of age, there was not a streak of grey in her coal-black hair, and scarcely a wrinkle in her brow. Her cheek and neck still retained their smoothness. The roses of youth had not yet faded.

She turned her large, luminous eyes upon Gordon, seeming to look him through. Referring to the incident of the pail she said, " I are a little out of practice since the girls have grown up. Won't you sit down," she added, offering him a stool.

" No, thank you," he replied, " I am tired sitting so long in the buggy."

She reseated herself with a sigh, and gave a calculating glance at the group of cattle, while he stood leaning against a post, looking awkwardly about him.

Mrs. Halford did not care so much about her daughter being late so far as the milking was concerned ; but Marian always gave her cows the preference over everything else. In four years, nothing had ever made her forget milking time, till this beggarly miller came along.

Had she been late for any other cause, her mother would have thought nothing of it, but she knew where Nelly and Fred had gone, and readily guessed that Marian had gone with them to meet Gordon.

" I shall put a stop to this fellow's trips this very day. It are time this folly were ended."

Marian now appeared carrying more pails. She had donned a light blue sun bonnet, and a large white apron. A stray curl was blowing across her forehead, her dress was tucked up displaying a neatly turned ankle, and her lover thought she looked more enchanting than ever.

Daisy recognized her at once, and gave a satisfied moo-o-o-o, at the same time reaching out her nose to meet her mistress' hands.

After a little patting on the neck, and rubbing on the forehead, a process which the animal seemed to enjoy, Marian set to work, and for a time there was no sound but the tinkling of the milk into the pail.

Casually looking in the direction of Mrs. Halford, David was thunder-struck at the sullen expression of her face, and the tigerish look in her eyes. Heavens, there was his ring flashing on Marian's finger, and his chain still around her neck.

Just then the daughter arose, having finished her first cow. At a glance she took in the situation. She seemed staggered for a moment, and her hand unconsciously sought her neck, but she soon recovered her self-possession, and when she raised her eyes to meet her mother's, the look that flashed between them showed that each understood the other.

Patient resistance and self-reliance were in the daughter's face ; fierce determination in the mother's.

Each recognized it as a declaration of war ; a trial of strength and skill between them; the opening of hostilities, whose end neither could foresee.

To hide his embarrassment Gordon led his horse away to the stables, without pretending to notice this by-play but he was inwardly alarmed at the prospect of war between two women of such force of character. It was as if two ideal gladiators had saluted each other in the arena, before commencing the conflict of their lives.

When he returned Marian was still at work, but her mother had gone.

To give herself further freedom and coolness, her bodice was unbuttoned at the neck, and her sleeves rolled up to her elbows. Her sun bonnet was pushed back, and her head was pressed against the cow's side, while she sat plying her busy hands and gazing abstractedly into the pail.

The rich colouring of her pink-white neck and cheek contrasted oddly with the sun-browned tint of her shapely arms, while her half-stooping, half-kneeling position accentuated the graceful outlines of her figure.

She did not seem to notice him as he approached.

He was about to speak, when he was certain he saw a tear drop from her cheek.

Out of respect for her emotion he remained silent, and, seated on a stool near by, was content to watch the shapely form, whose delicate outlines and hidden strength reminded him of velvet and steel.

When she finished her cow, she rose and smiled at him, but the telltale moisture was in her eyes. "What are you looking so serious about?" she said with a

AN UNWELCOME GUEST.

forced laugh. "*I* was so annoyed at being late that I forgot to leave these off, and mother of course knows all about it. It's too bad. It will make trouble between us. But I suppose the course of true love never did run smooth," she added, smiling through her tears.

"It is a shame for me to bring such trouble upon you, darling. What can I do?"

"Oh, never mind," she replied, drying her eyes. "It had to come some time. As well now as again."

"Shall I go and tell her now?"

"If you like. I don't know, really, what is best. Somehow I feel we shall have bad luck to-day," she went on, shaking her head. "Mother is awful when she is angry; not rough, you know, but very cruel. Our racing, you see, has brought us bad luck."

"Pshaw! Marian; luck is only superstition. Besides, I am proud of the privilege of telling your mother that I love you. No man need apologize or feel ashamed of loving you."

"Good," she rejoined with a smile. "You are preparing for your interview by practicing on me."

David shook his head.

"No. My compliments may sometimes be clumsy but they are always sincere. No mortal man could help loving you, darling."

"If you come here and stoop down so that they can't see us from the house, I will give you a kiss for that. Bring a pail with you."

He threaded his way through the group of cows, and sheltered by Bella's friendly form, he took the milkmaid's face between his hands and reached into her sunbonnet for the proffered kiss. "By heavens! Marian, I *shall* win you, nothing but death can defeat me," he whispered as he took a few extra. "I'll go now and see your mother. Give me one more."

"No, no. Be careful, David, somebody might see us from the fields. No, I won't. I'll throw one after you, though, if you like. Go, now, and carry this pail out."

* * * * * *

Mrs. Halford sat at the kitchen window nursing her

wrath. Had the devoted lover seen the various expressions which flitted over her face, his confidence would have been shaken.

Her life, in spite of its financial success, had been embittered by disappointments. Her children, she thought, did not love her as they should. They showered their caresses on their father, but gave her only lukewarm affection in spite of all she had done for them.

Had she not been a good mother to them? Had she not planned, and schemed, and worked, in order that they might not be paupers? Had she not educated her eldest daughter, regardless of expense, and how was she requiting her?

It would be almost impossible to describe her feelings towards Marian. Since her daughter's return from the seminary, a quasi-independence had grown up between them. By tacit consent, Marian had gradually taken charge of the household, as well as the dairy. Her mother would not now have the temerity to interfere in matters pertaining to these departments. Indeed, keen calculation had proved to Mrs. Halford, that her daughter's management of the dairy was even more successful than her own, and her methods of housekeeping were more satisfactory and economical.

She admired her daughter's devotion to duty, and was surprised that even the seminary had not spoiled her for the farm. When she first heard that Marian was learning to read French, and play the piano, she made up her mind that her usefulness was gone.

But when she came home, and went to work of her own free will, her mother was overcome first with surprise, and then with jealousy.

Mrs. Halford was satisfied that her daughter should exceed her in education and refinement, but that she should outshine her in everything else was hard to bear.

No holiday function ever made Marian neglect the cows. Her father often teasingly told her that she preferred a cattle fair to a presidential reception.

Her mother envied the facility with which Marian could hurry home, and cook a meal or milk cows, in her silk or satin, without seeming to soil her hands or ruffle a feather.

But Mrs. Halford had another grievance of a still more serious nature. Her daughter was supplanting her in the affections of her other children.

Fred and Nellie always went to Marian now with their little troubles, instead of to her. It was Marian this, and Marian that. Her comings and her goings were watched with loving interest by all; and one word against her was a signal for household mutiny.

Fred and Nelly hovered about their sister and sat on her knee as if she had been their mother. Indeed, they *never* had shown a tithe of such tenderness to their maternal parent.

To make matters worse, William seemed lately to prefer the company of his daughter to that of his wife.

No woman ever loved a husband more truly than Mrs. Halford, and she suspected that the refined atmosphere of her daughter only served to show her deficiencies more plainly; and lower her in the estimation of her husband.

Mrs. Halford had an iron will, which she was at times accustomed to enforce; yet with a silken thread, her daughter could disarm her. There was a subtle something about Marian with which her mother could not cope, and in no respect did the mother feel that she was the reigning spirit of her own household.

No wonder then, that her feelings towards her daughter were not unmixed with jealousy.

Yet there was a strong resemblance between them. Marian seemed to be but a revised edition of her mother.

Mrs. Halford's large black eyes had given place to the deep blue orbs of the daughter; but there was the same luminousness about them.

The jet black hair, square chin, and firm mouth of the mother were supplanted by the softer outlines of the daughter, but the difference was only in degree.

Marian's hair was much lighter in colour, her chin more rounded, and her lips more full. The greatest difference was in the expression, which, in the daughter seemed to be a compound of her mother's pride and gravity, and the cheerful benevolence of her father.

Mrs. Halford had, without doubt, given her daughter a wonderful inheritance of beauty, health, and stature. She had indeed given her everything, but that sweet motherly sympathy and affection, which is surely the very refinement of woman's noblest emotions.

The result was that they breathed a different atmosphere, and were entirely out of touch with each other. Up till to-day, she had not thought that Marian had any serious intentions toward Gordon. Her daughter's tactics now took her by surprise.

She did not believe that Marian cared more for the miller than any of her other suitors, and she thought that the developments of to-day were due to contrariness.

Mrs. Halford was convinced that the infatuation for Charles Langtry still remained and was the real reason why so many good offers had been rejected. Now she had evidently accepted this beggarly mechanic out of pure spite.

Gordon, indeed! "A pauper and an infidel."

CHAPTER X.

AN INTERVIEW.

SELF reliance was one of the salient points in Gordon's character, but it was not without some apprehension that he walked into the kitchen where Mrs. Halford sat.

The moment he crossed the threshold, she raised her eyes, and looked at him with a stern air of inquiry.

"Would you please favour me with an interview, Mrs. Halford, on a very important subject?"

"Certainly," she replied, bowing coldly, "just follow me into the parlour, if you please."

With a dignified and impressive manner, she led him

into the room, raised a window, opened the shutters, and placing a chair where the light would fall upon him, she seated herself in a darker corner of the room.

He was her legitimate prey, and she would appease her wrath, by torturing him. With a sigh that was intended to betoken uneasiness, she said, "Well," and waited for him to proceed.

David felt as if he had walked into a lion's den, but he retained his composure remarkably well.

"You have no doubt noticed the attention I have been paying to your daughter, and have formed some opinion as to my intentions."

He waited for a reply but it was only

"Well!"

It was a hard matter to speak of the tender passion, in the presence of this human iceberg, so he decided to make a short story of it. "I have asked Marian to be my wife, and she has consented. Now I have come to asked your consent."

"And have you set the day for this grand affair?" she asked, with a cruel laugh. "Are it not customary for a gentleman to ask the parents first? Do you consider it proper to gain a young lady's affections before her parents have time to find out if you are suitable?"

"I admit you are right there, Mrs. Halford, but you have had ample time to guess my intentions."

"I are not good at guessing," she retorted, with an ironical laugh, "but if *you* be, then there are a good chance to guess mine."

This brought David to his feet, and sent him marching up and down the room.

"I don't see anything to laugh at, Mrs. Halford. It is a very serious matter to me."

"And me also, Mr. Gordon. I were only laughing at your—well now, I forget the proper word, but it means cheek."

"Good God! you can't mean to insult me in your own house. I have often heard of the hospitality of Broadview, but this is cold blooded discourtesy."

This was a tender point, and she scarcely knew how to answer, so she started on a new tack.

"How dare you mention the name of your Maker, you who are an unbeliever! Do you deny that you are an infidel?"

"Yes, I do deny it. An infidel is a man who is unfaithful either to himself or to others, and you can ask in Gowanstone if David Gordon's word is not as good as his bond."

"I am not saying a word about your business character, but—," and she pointed her finger at him—"you have dodged my question."

"You, yourself, would be called an infidel, if you lived in Constantinople," retorted David. "It is only a matter of geography."

"Do you believe in the Bible?" she demanded in a tone which showed that she intended to corner him.

Gordon, who had been pacing the floor now stopped in front of her, with his head thrown back, and his thumbs in his vest. He dearly loved an argument, and was getting warmed to his work. "You evidently do not know the nature of your question. If you mean whether I think it is all literally true, I answer no, and I make bold to say neither do you. Not even our greatest divines believe that Joshua stopped the sun, or that Jonah was swallowed by a whale."

She felt that she was losing ground, that she was being put upon the defensive.

"Those things are lessons for us to take good out of, and not to speak light of," she said in a forbidding tone.

"I don't wish to make light of them, Mrs. Halford. Even a fable or fairy tale, which contains a lesson or moral for the good of mankind, is worthy of respect. It is only narrow minded dunces who do not know the meaning of allegory, who shout infidel at a man who is not hypocrite enough to pretend that he believes impossibilities."

Mrs. Halford's eyes flashed, and springing to her feet she struck an attitude of defiance.

"How dare you insult me? How dare you hector me, in my own house? Now go," and she pointed to the door.

Gordon saw that he had been too severe. Instead

of following the direction of her finger, he grasped her extended hand in order to restrain her, and by a sudden impulse raised it to his lips. After all, she was Marian's mother.

This sudden change of front completely nonplussed Mrs. Halford. She stood for a moment almost stupefied. Had David been the wiliest of diplomats, he could not have made a more successful coup.

Here was a mark of respect she had never before received, not even from William ; a token of homage to which she was a perfect stranger, and then, she was a woman.

Before she recovered from her confusion, he led her back to the sofa, and sat down beside her.

"Accept my humblest apologies for my seeming rudeness, but I can assure you, on my word of honor, that my last remarks were not intended to be personal, First let me say, that towards any form of religion, I have not the slightest antipathy. I was brought up an agnostic by my father, who was as honest a man as ever breathed the breath of life. He lived and died, worshipping no deity, but Right. Yet, I am not so bigoted as to think that he could not have been mistaken."

Mrs. Halford had now recovered her self-possession, but her hauteur was gone. "Will you please explain what an agnostic are."

"He is simply a person who does not know, and admits that he does not."

"You claim there is no God," she said with grave severity.

"Indeed, I do not," he replied firmly, "I only say that I don't know, and that nobody else knows."

"You may not know yourself, but you have no right to say that nobody else knows. You cannot see with my eyes, hear with my ears, or think with my brains."

David was somewhat staggered at the force of her reply.

Before he had time to respond she went on with a wave of her hand, "It *are* no use for us to argue it. My daughter cannot marry you, at least, not with my consent."

"Stop for a moment," said David excitedly, jumping to his feet. "Your daughter loves me, and——"

"I don't believe it," she broke in with an air of decision.

This was a cruel shot; a blow beneath the belt that he was not prepared for, and he sank into a chair, toying nervously with his watch-chain.

"We shall leave your daughter to judge of that," he replied in a subdued voice, as soon as he recovered himself. "But pray let me go on. I have leased the Gowanstone mills with a capital of two thousand. I have good business prospects, a strong arm, a willing heart, a clear conscience and a good reputation. Your daughter would not have to work half so hard as she does at home, and——"

"Stop!" said Mrs. Halford, bridling at this hint. "What work my daughter does are of her own choosing. Work are needful to a woman like her, and you can't say her is broken down with it or her growth stunted."

The idea of there being anything stunted about Marian, would have made him smile at any other time, but the situation was all too serious. "I did not intend to be offensive," he explained. "What you say about work being a necessity, is no doubt true. But leaving that aside, I wish to say that, as my wife, she would be at liberty to attend divine service, as often as she chose. I believe in religious liberty, and I should not interfere with her worship in any way."

"No, Mr. Gordon. It can never be, and you had better make up your mind to it at once. I shall not forbid your coming, but you are a gentleman, and *us* had better not meet too often. So now, good day."

When David reached the open air and bright sunlight, his brain seemed to be on fire. He walked, or rather stumbled, to a shady spot on the lawn, where he would be alone.

His spirit was broken, and his emotions stirred to their very depths. He wanted to collect his thoughts, and rearrange his scattered faculties. He had often smiled inwardly at Mrs. Halford's verbs and pronouns, but he found that if she lacked in learning, she did not in intelligence. How cruel and terrible she seemed, and yet, (perish the thought) how like Marian in many ways. Heavens! What an angel his own mother was. Would he go home and —— here a pair of soft hands were clapped over his eyes from behind.

"I'll keep them there till you look yourself again," said Marian, who had stolen upon him unawares.

"I can guess the quality of your news, but never mind, come down to the pear tree, where the vines are, and you can tell me all about it."

He related the story of the interview, as nearly as possible, but omitted his gallantry in kissing her mother's hand. "What hurt me worse than anything else, Marian, was that she said she did not believe you loved me, and I am sure she meant it."

"What! was she cruel enough to say that? Well, that means an extra kiss for you," and putting her arm around his neck, she saluted him on the cheek.

"You asked me this morning to set the day and I asked for time. Now you can have me whenever you like. Mr. Gordon," she continued in mock heroic tones, while her eyes shone with a peculiar light, "I wish to make you an offer of marriage, to formally ask you to be my husband."

David made the only reply that a lover could under the circumstances, and taking her in his arms covered her face with kisses.

"Now, Sir Knight," she exclaimed, freeing herself from his embrace, "remember that faint heart never won fair lady. We can afford to wait. In the meantime, I shall promise not to elope with Mr. Grazely, who has the honour of being your rival," at which they both broke into a hearty laugh.

"But now, darling, how am I ever going to come here again, when I know I am not welcome? In fact I must be going now," and he made as if to start for the barn to get his horse.

"What!" she exclaimed, "let you and Dan go away hungry, and bring bad luck on the house? No, sir," she continued dramatically, "not for Venice."

"You shall have dinner here as *my* guest." A bright spot burned in either cheek, and the blue of her eyes was very dark. "After dinner I shall convey you on your way, No, that is improper. You shall drive me to Mr. Murray's, where I shall meet Nelly and Fred. 'A rose by any other name would smell as sweet.'" She put her arm through his and escorted him to the house, gaily humming some snatches from the "Lady of the Lake."

CHAPTER XI.

RETROSPECTION ON WHEELS.

ON his long drive homewards, David had ample time to reflect on the experiences of what had been the most eventful day of his life.

Half in jest and half in earnest, Marian had maintained that their crosses were a punishment for racing on Sunday. "You know the old adage about a Sunday well spent bringing a week of content, and the Sunday profaned bringing sorrow. Well, I am superstitious enough to *half* believe it."

The bitterness of his interview with Mrs. Halford was more than compensated for by the delightful part of his drive home, on which Marian had accompanied him. He smiled as he thought of her insisting on having the buggy curtains lowered before he was allowed to put his arm around her waist, and how her eyes scanned the horizon before she permitted a kiss.

But in spite of everything, his mind would revert to the phrase: "you are an infidel." Was he never to hear the last of that distasteful word, which had been a curse to his life, a destroyer of his happiness from childhood up. Why had his father not contented himself with being like other men? Why had he left him an inheritance which was like a mill-stone round his neck?

He could remember, when a little boy, sitting on his father's knee and singing: "Oh, happy day, when Jesus washed my sins away." He could recall the church and the Sunday school he used to attend, and never could forget the horror with which he first heard of the lake of fire and brimstone.

David never knew the reason why his father suddenly left the church, and instead of sending him to Sunday-school, took him for strolls in the woods and fields.

He remembered how old Mr. Bayley used to come on Sunday evenings and read books about religion, especially "Paine's Age of Reason." John Gordon had gradually grown more pronounced in his views, until he became an aggressive atheist, who would wrangle with every customer that came into his shop, where he plied his trade of shoemaking.

Nothing but fair dealing and excellent workmanship procured for him the custom trade upon which he depended for his bread and butter.

The clerical influence brought to bear against him, both in his social and business capacity, finally embittered him to a point at which he regarded all church goers as either fools or hypocrites. Thus he continued till he died, leaving his widow and twelve-year-old-son with little or nothing to support them.

One event of David's school days, (which was a sample of the persecution he had to undergo) was stamped indelibly on his memory. His schoolmates held aloof from him, as the infidel's son, for both parents and pastors warned the children against his companionship.

But at the examinations he generally had his revenge, for they could not prevent him from learning so fast that he distanced all his competitors.

On this particular occasion he had entered the lists for the proficiency prize of the county. A school function was being held, at which the prizes were to be distributed, and the town fathers and mothers had gathered in honour of the occasion. Fortunately, David's father was absent, or subsequent events might have been more startling.

After an opening address by the chairman, and the usual speech-making by ubiquitous wiseacres who never miss such opportunities of ventilating their ignorance, the prize list was commenced.

The excitement was at fever heat, for no one as yet knew the results.

The Rev. Mr. Inglis took up the list, and with aggravating slowness, read: "County proficiency prize, donated by Mr. Johnson Snell, public school inspector, is a handsome writing desk, awarded to David Gordon."

A murmur ran round the room at this announcement. The winner was the observed of all observers. "Each pupil will please come forward as his name is called."

In spite of his revamped coat sleeves, and the patches on his trowsers, David marched proudly forward to receive his prize.

After handing him his trophy, the chairman adjusted his spectacles and glared at him with a forbidding expression. Then in harsh, rasping tones he asked: "Are you infidel Gordon's son?" Immediately there was a hush in the room. All eyes were turned upon the boy to see how he took this rebuke. The hot blood rushed over his face, the patched knees trembled, and a great singing noise came in his ears. After several times swallowing the lump in his throat, he raised his head and answered as bravely as he might: "No, sir. My father is John Gordon, gentleman, and citizen of the United States of America."

A distinct murmur of applause greeted the latter half of this declaration, causing the reverend gentleman to wax wroth at the prospect of having the tables turned upon him.

In a voice pregnant with holy wrath and self-righteousness, he shouted, "What! *your* father a gentleman, eh, after denying our Saviour? Why, he is worse than the savages that——"

But the sentence was never finished, for in a second the boy's form was on the dais, and a vamped coat sleeve sent a fist crashing through the left eye of the chairman's spectacles. Before any one had time to realize what had happened, he darted through the back door and was gone.

A moment later he was seen running through the school-yard, his prize in one hand, and a cudgel picked up for defensive purposes in the other. Once out on the street he looked behind him to see if he were being pursued, and then walked home hatless and defiant, feeling in his heart that he had bid good-bye to the school forever.

Meanwhile the uproar in the audience was indescribable. Several sympathetic deacons rushed to the reverend gentleman's assistance; maiden ladies looked horrified, and dignitaries looked grave, but the human part of the audience bent over the desks and shook with smothered laughter.

The teacher endeavoured to restrain his pupils, who in various ways were exhibiting the delight which juveniles invariably take in a row or confusion in school.

The secretary of the board got up on the desks, and shouted for order. He might have succeeded, had there not been in this, as in nearly every other audience, somebody who invariably commences to laugh where the rest leave off.

Jake Fetterley's voice was only suitable for outdoor purposes, and when his guttural *haw, haw, haw*, resounded from the back benches, a posse of policemen could not have restored order.

"Sarved him right," said Jake, in a sort of horse-whisper, which was only intended for his next neighbour, but which was discernible through all the din. "This hain't Roosia, but the Yoonited States of America. The kid war sound on that pint. Haw, haw, haw! The preacher had no biziness steppin' outern his traces. Haw, haw, haw! Old Glory's the stuff when fair play is on deck. This is the land of the free. E plurybus yeunum."

When order was finally restored, the prize list was proceeded with, but the bulk of the audience dispersed, for all interest in the affair was now over.

Everybody wanted to get outside to have their laugh out and talk it all over.

To make matters worse, one of the local papers next morning had an account of it, written up in true

Arkansas style, much to the disgust of Mr. Inglis and his congregation, who insisted that the boy should be expelled from the school.

David was summoned before a magistrate's court and fined five dollars with costs. The father paid the fine, and sent David back to school, but he was refused admission.

Then a suit for damages was entered by the shoemaker, and carried from court to court till he finally won. But his property was all squandered in law costs, and the worry brought on brain fever of which he died.

Then came the days of gloom and grief, followed by the funeral, when great crowds came to see a man buried without church rites. David could remember the looks of horror and pity bestowed upon him and his mother as they stood by the open grave. To cap the climax, sermons came from several pulpits describing the tortures of the damned and the horrible death of the infidel.

Looking back over his past life, David felt that he owed nothing to Christianity but hatred and revenge. Had it not persecuted his father when living, and slandered him when dead. It had taken from him many opportunities of preferment and promotion, embittered his whole boyhood, and now it threatened to come between him and the woman he loved? For in spite of Marian's explanation in regard to Mr. Grazely, he still believed that his heterodoxy was the basis of Mrs. Halford's refusal.

For many years the hatchet of religious prejudice had been buried.

In his struggle for existence, he had almost forgotten that there had ever been any strife. But to-day Mrs. Halford had opened the old wound by throwing at him the detestable word, infidel—a word which for ten years had been a stranger to his ears.

So deeply was Gordon absorbed in thought that he did not notice he was nearing home till Dan, coquetting with his bridle, drew his attention as the lights of Gowanstone hove in sight.

CHAPTER XII.

MOTHER AND SON.

"WEEL, Davie, I'm gled ye're back. I was kinna wearyin' on ye," said David's mother, appearing at the side door of the cottage as he drove into the yard.

" It's too bad to keep you waiting, mother, but I was thinking deeply all the way home, and Dan sodgered on me a little." Young folks are very selfish where their pleasures are concerned, and jumping out, David commenced to unhitch. " But I am glad you stayed up," he continued, " for I want to have a long talk with you."

Mrs. Gordon lifted the lantern so that the light would fall upon his face, and looked at him with concern.

"Oh, it is nothing serious, mother," he laughed as he stooped to kiss her. " Just run in till I put Dan away, and then I'll tell you all about it."

Mrs. Gordon was one of those comfortable looking women, whose kindly face and generous figure, give them a motherly appearance. She had the kind of countenance that one instinctively trusts. All simplicity, candour and common sense. Sixty odd winters had frosted her hair, and wrinkled her brow, but had not destroyed her comeliness. Her face did not denote any great mental power, but a nice balance between the rational and the emotional, the kind of woman from whom you would expect wholesome companionship and sound advice.

Sorrow, the great purifier, had softened her heart. During her sojourn in life she had many trials. Two of her dear ones had been carried out at once with a malignant form of scarlet fever, and one boy of ten was drowned while bathing.

In his latter years Mr. Gordon had been very irritable, and overbearing. Yet, she loved him dearly to the last.

The struggle for existence, until David was able to earn something, and their utter loneliness after her husband's death, had aged her very rapidly.

Now she had only her baby left, and he was all in all to her. That something unusual had occurred she was certain, but her curiosity did not prevent her from getting his tea ready, nor did it cause her to omit the cold mutton and apple pie of which he was so fond.

She always told him that such things were "ower heavy for his stummack gaun tae bed," but she invariably gave it to him, nevertheless.

Very soon David made his appearance, and hanging his overcoat on a nail, sat down at the outspread table, in what he thought was the coziest little kitchen in the world.

His long drive had made him hungry, and for a time he devoted himself to his lunch, without thinking that his mother was burning with curiosity.

"Your cooking is the best, mother," said David. "From porridge up to pies or puddings, nobody can suit me like you, not even the best hotels in the city."

"Toots, laddie, there's far better cooks nor me. Ye hae been at yer mither's table a yer days, an ye're kinna partial wi custom. Then ye ken hunger is guid kitchin. But ye hinna telt me yer news yet."

"I suppose you can't guess. Well, I proposed to Marian to-day."

"Aye, aye, I jaloused it, for I ken ye've been maist gyte aboot the lassie this while back."

Without replying to his mother's remarks David went on: "She has accepted me, and promised to be my wife."

"She could na dae onything else, Davie, she'll ne'er hae a better chance, I'se warrant."

"Now, mother, you think the woman is not born who is good enough for your Davie; but," he continued with a shake of his head, "she is far above me in every way."

"Dinna talk sic nonsense, boy. She's nane aboon ye. But I'm gled for yer sake ye hae made it up. I could see when ye brocht hame bits o' ribbin and wither't roses, that yer heart was set on the lassie. I hae seen ye sittin for hours wi her letters, or glowering at her picter. She's a braw lass if the pictur disna lee, and guif she's as guid as she's bonnie, she'll dae."

"Yes, mother, is'nt she just beautiful, such glorious eyes and the figure of a queen. Oh, but just wait till you see her."

Mrs. Gordon smiled indulgently but shook her head. "Dinna be sae daft, laddie. She's a braw woman, nae doubt, and fit to be the mither o' strappin weans, but she'll hae her fauts like ither fok."

David did not reply; but went on devouring the remains of his cold mutton and finishing his tea.

"She'll maybe hae ower heigh notions for a workin' man's wife. The lassies noo a'day dinna like tae fyle their hauns wi wark."

"Oh, but she is not like that, mother," said David pushing his chair back from the table. "With all her lady-like appearance, she milks cows, cooks and washes dishes. Not only that, but she is an expert butter maker. She carries two big pails of milk as if they were feathers, and she is just——well, it is no use. I can't describe her. Just wait till you see her."

His mother smiled dubiously at his raptures. "Weel, weel, I'm gled she kens something aboot housekeepin'. Ye micht be able to keep her like a leddy, but there's a guid wheens ups an' downs in the worl', an' ye canna tell what may happen ony o' us. Hoo does her feyther like the notion?"

Now David had never explained to his mother how matters really stood at Broadview, and he proceeded to show why it was the mother's consent which was most important.

He gave her a vivid account of his interview with Mrs. Halford, omitting again his own act of gallantry, which he felt had been thrown away. When he told her of the taunts about his religion (or rather the lack of it), her face flushed with excitement, but she never interrupted him.

"Now, mother, how am I ever going to go back, when I am given to understand that I am not welcome? How and when am I going to see Marian again?"

"Never ye fear, Davie. If the lassie's fond o ye, she'll fin' a way some gate. Maybe the dochter has a kennen o' the mother in her, and will no ding ower easy. Does she look like the auld woman?"

David scratched his head. Here was a sore point. "Well, she does, and she doesn't. She is trimmer built and smaller in size than her mother. She has the same voice, the same walk, and many of the same ways. But Marian's face is ever so much gentler, and kinder. It is only when she is angry that she resembles her mother, and then she is the very picture of her."

"And, so she garred ye bide for dinner, and her feyther sat wi' ye. Whaur was the *mither* then?"

"I don't know. I never saw *her* afterwards."

"Aye, aye. Weel, she gied ye her tryst and cam a bit on the road hame. It looks tae me as if the mither was feart for her. Humph—weel, dinna fash yer heid aboot it. If her heart is in the richt place ye hae naething tae fear. But stop a wee. Maybe the mither wants her for some ither lad."

David laughed. "The *lad*, in this case, mother, is over fifty. Marian tells me that her mother has it all planned to marry her to old Grazely."

"Aye, aye! Is that the way o't? An' whatna like is this Grazely chap?"

"He isn't a *chap* at all, mother. He is a widower with three children. He looks to be about seventy-five. He's a regular old screw, and land grabber. He and Mrs. Halford own most of the property at the west end of the city."

"Dinna fash. She'll manage her mither some gate, if I'm no mista'en A lass that's tryin' tae win her lad wad cheat the deil. 'Deed I was gae gleg mysel, when yer feyther an' me was sparkin'. I hae min' o' yae day I joakiet ma feyther, and gaed doon the Clyde wi' Jock. He was gae braw that day wi' his bottle-green coat an' brass buttons, an' a wheen o' the lassies were makin' sheep's een at him. Aye, aye. An' I cam' hame that nicht wi' a face as lang as yer airm." Here the old lady smiled and wiped the moisture from her eyes.

"If I had been him, mother, I would ..ave run away with you," responded her son, as he reached over to kiss her cheek.

"'Deed we hadna' muckle to run wi'. Yer feyther had naething but his day's wage, and that wasna' very big. But we bidiet our time. They say toom sta's mak' bitin' horses, but we got on as weel as them that had mair." Here the old lady seemed lost in thought and finally heaved a deep sigh. "Maybe I shouldna' be plannin' and puttin' a dochter against her mither. If ma ain wee Jennie had been spared, I wad likiet her tae hae dune ma biddin'. Ise tell ye yaething, that auld age is nae match for beauty or young bluid. When I was young, I wad hae gaen throo fire an' water for yer feyther. Keep up yer heart. Ise warrant ye'll see her by this day fortnicht. Hae ye no min' o' the sang, 'tho' feyther an' mither an' a' should gae mad, whistle an' I'll came tae ye, ma lad?'"

Through the wrinkles in her face there shone the enthusiasm of girlhood. The frost of sixty winters had not chilled the memory of love's young dream. Jumping up, David caught her in his arms, and swung her around him gleefully.

"Aye, aye!" exclaimed the old lady, panting for breath, "ye'll soon forget yer auld mither. Ye'll no hae room in yer heart for twa, but I'm no blamin' ye. I was e'en as bad mysel."

After giving vent to the exuberance of his spirits, David sat down and took up the topic on which he had been thinking all the way home.

She listened attentively for some time in silence, and then placing her hand on his head she replied:

"David lad, I'm no able tae guide ye in thae things; ye maun een read, and think for yersel, as yer feyther did afore ye, but I wad na fash sae muckle about it as he did. He may hae been richt, or he may hae been wrang, but ma ain conscience tells me, if we dae what's richt, we hae naething tae fear in this worl, or the next. Ye feyther was worriet tae his death by the prejudice of his neebors, but he was gae an dour himsel, an I whiles thocht he gaed ower far. Yae thing, I ken, he tried to be richt, an' that's a great deal." She stopped, and rubbed her hand over her forehead. "It's ower big a question for ma auld heid, but I hae a notion it'll a' come richt onyway. I hae thocht that them that's fit tae leeve, is fit tae dee. Take nae side, but try an fin' aot what's true, and dinna be feart wher truth leads ye, for it maun aye be richt. Noo, laddie, awa tae yer bed, ye ken ye'll hae tae be at the mill in the mornin'. It wanna dae for ye tae be slack, noo that ye're maester yersel."

David went to bed, but not to sleep. The question of whence and whither had taken possession of him. It seemed a hopeless task for him to attack a problem which centuries of preaching and teaching had still left in sad uncertainty.

Were religions merely a reflex of the character of the people? They surely could not all be true.

But there must be some reason why the most intelligent and progressive nations on earth had accepted the teachings of Christ. There must be some reason why his precepts had stood the test of eighteen hundred years.

This was the one fact he could not reason away, the one idea that jarred upon his preconceived opinions.

At last his brain became weary and he went to sleep thinking of the woman he adored.

CHAPTER XIII.

GOWANSTONE.

NEARLY every town or city has a social atmosphere peculiar to itself; a character which is developed not only by its citizens, but by its industries, its geographical position, and its surroundings.

This peculiarity is more noticeable in smaller places, where every individual is under the scrutiny or espionage of his neighbour; where closer social and business relations accentuate the salient points of character.

The reader will have little interest in the physcial features of Gowanstone, but a few words by way of outline will be neither unnecessary nor out of place. Its very existence was based on the water power of the river, which ran through its centre, almost parallel with its main street. Mill dams alternated with business blocks all along one side of its principal thoroughfare, which was about a mile in length. One or two other streets crossed this at right angles, but they were very short, and mostly devoted to private dwellings.

The Gowanstone Flour Mill was situated on the northwest corner of the two principal streets, directly opposite the largest hotel in the town. The mill itself was a thing of patches and shreds. It had been changed and repaired till scarcely a vestige of the original building remained. But it had recently received a coat of dark red paint, and this, partly covered with white dust, gave it an air of venerable respectability.

Immediately to the west was a break in the buildings, where a fine green lawn, about fifty yards in length, adorned the nearest bank of the mill-dam, and enclosed a red brick cottage, belonging to the mill property, where David Gordon and his mother resided.

Several other manufactories were strung along the main street, taking their power from the river behind, but the great feature of the place, the industry which dwarfed all others, was the Excelsior Iron Works.

This extensive concern had been erected some ten years previous, and was the industrial nucleus of the town.

Not only had the iron works changed the physical features of the place, but its proprietor had brought about a social revolution as well.

Mr. Jamieson had been for years, and still was, the most notorious man in the district.

He was a pronounced and aggressive atheist.

The first Sunday after the arrival of his family into their spacious residence on the hill, his children actually played pull-a-way and went boating.

The good people on their way to church were horrified by such desecration, and expressed surprise that a thunderbolt did not destroy them on the spot.

No sooner had the citizens become accustomed to *this* horror, than he organized a brass band amongst his employees, and made special arrangements for them to play on his terrace on Sunday afternoons.

No wonder that David Gordon's heterodoxy was forgotten, in the presence of Jamieson's enormities; no wonder that his light faded in the lurid glare of the iron-founder's misdeeds.

The clergyman in his pulpit, earnestly fishing for the souls of men, often caught sight of Jamieson landing a speckled trout or snaring a sucker.

The iron founder was for a time the talk of the whole country side but he did not heed it; in fact he rather liked it. Every week the local papers were searched for some fresh enormity. No one would have been at all surprised to have met him arm in arm with Satan himself.

The local clergymen were in a very trying position. If they allowed this to go on unnoticed they were confessedly neglecting their duties, and if they attacked the offender, his artisans left them empty pews and slender purses.

The men all liked Jamieson. He was a model employer who treated his workmen like fellow creatures. Nine-tenths of the artisans of the place were his employees, and they would not countenance anything which seemed to strike a blow at their bread and butter.

Tom Greer, one of his principal foremen, always maintained that as Jamieson gave everybody the privilege of going to heaven in his own way, he was, in all fairness, entitled to a choice of the various routes to hell. Like the bulk of the workmen, he believed that his Satanic Majesty could be depended upon to attend to his duties as stoker without any prompting or coaching on their part. Furthermore, if Jamieson was to scorch and roast for all eternity, they considered that he ought not to be molested here on earth.

Gradually the social atmosphere began to change, because people saw that instead of being struck by lightning or swallowed by an earthquake, the iron founder flourished like the proverbial green bay tree.

Agnosticism became respectable. It drove the finest turn out, wore the best clothes, and gave the biggest dinners.

Then again, Jamieson was noted for his generosity. Every tramp or indigent for miles around came to regard him as their patron saint.

On one occasion the Congregational church was sadly in arrears to its pastor, and matters were at a deadlock financially, when Jamieson came to the rescue with a cheque, and turned clouds to sunshine.

This was noised about so diligently, that he soon became a shining mark for delinquent and impecunious church committees. He invariably bought tickets for all the soirées, and when his daughters attended church, to show off their new dresses, the collection plates always knew the difference.

How was it possible then for the pulpits to attack Mr. Jamieson? Where was the sense in killing the goose that laid the golden egg?

If the hardened sinner could not be persuaded to secure his title to mansions on high, it was some satisfaction to know that his dollars were following the straight and narrow path to righteousness. If not the soul, why then the shekels.

Mammon was the God of Gowanstone, and Jamieson its prophet. The bread and butter interests of this life triumphed over the joys of the next.

Bigotry had its mouth closed by *greenbacks*, and religious intolerance was fast becoming a thing of the past.

One would have expected that Jamieson would have been a great friend of Gordon's, and that their heterodoxy would have given them a common ground. But although people classed them together in this respect, their opinions differed as widely as night and day.

The iron founder was a conclusionist. When he formed an opinion, that settled it with him, but Gordon's mind was of that type which is continually undergoing a process of evolution.

David's sole companion was Dr. Bennet, one of the

oldest settlers, a man twenty years his senior. For many years the doctor was viewed with suspicion, not because he was ever known to express any heretical opinions, but because he did not go to church. Once, when asked to give the reason, he replied that Monday was wash-day, and before Saturday night he was always minus a clean shirt.

A small, active man, with a bald head, clean shaved face, and piercing eyes. Abrupt in manner, and incisive in speech, Dr. Bennet was always ready with a reply, and there were few who cared to bandy words with him.

He never laughed, and seldom smiled, and as for weeping, no one had ever seen him shed a tear; in fact, they did not believe there was such a thing in his whole anatomy.

Whether he had been disappointed in love, or had never experienced the thrill of the tender passion, nobody knew; but he remained in single blessedness. His entire household consisted of himself, his maiden sister, and a little dwarf of an hostler, whose name was Dennis. The same Dennis was rather a curiosity in his way. Nobody knew where he came from, or who his parents were. He had no companions but his horses, and only spoke in monosyllables. For this reason, if for no other, he suited the doctor's purpose admirably, being the less likely to tell tales.

The eccentric physician and his man often drove for weeks together without exchanging a word, though they understood each other perfectly.

Indeed, the doctor's position in his vehicle made conversation very difficult, for he invariably occupied three-fourths of the seat, and sat with back to anyone who rode with him.

One day David accompanied him on one of his visits to a patient, some miles away, and while *he* was slyly struggling for a share of the seat, the doctor was enlarging on the merits of a magazine article. Suddenly the wheels struck a stone.

Whether the jolt suggested some new train of thought to the old man's mind, David could not guess, but his discourse came to an abrupt termination, and during the rest of the journey he never uttered a word.

On the way back, by some odd coincidence, the buggy wheel struck the same stone, and the doctor commenced his discourse, exactly where he had left off.

Sometimes he would stop and chat with a neighbour or a patient, but just as often he would pass his most intimate friend without noticing him.

In spite of his supposed want of sentiment, the doctor was a very benevolent man, and never refused his services even to the poorest. With him the prince and the pauper received equal attention.

The working classes loved the doctor, and though they often made fun of his peculiar ways, they kept a warm spot in their hearts for one who so often relieved their sufferings without hope of reward.

If people paid their bills, well and good; if not, he soon forgot all about it.

In spite of his lax methods of business, he gradually acquired considerable wealth, for he lived frugally and his wants were few. He had a peculiar analytical way of discussing even the most trivial topics, a characteristic which followed him both in his professional and social life.

He dearly loved to analyze his fellow creatures, and was continually on the lookout for fresh specimens. Every character he met must be labelled, and placed away on the shelf of his memory.

The question with him was, not whether the character was good or bad in the ordinary sense, but whether there were any distinctive features which he had not previously observed.

The more difficult and complex the human problem, the more attraction it had for him. A burglar was as interesting as a bishop. Indeed, every specimen was welcome in his collection, save the dull and the ordinary.

The only dissipation in which he indulged was his evenings, when he invited a variety of specimens, and enjoyed the result of their social contact.

He was a sort of character-chemist, who delighted

in mixing social ingredients, and watching the various reactions which took place.

He noted with keen interest the attraction and repulsion which human beings exerted upon each other, just as one might play with loadstone and magnet.

Some of them would mix as gently as water with the syrup in his cough mixtures, others would foam and fizz like the ingredients of a seidletz powder, while still others would remain as distinct as oil and water.

On Gordon, the doctor bestowed a friendship which very few enjoyed. Knowing him from his infancy, and having been familiar with the physical qualities and surroundings of his parents, he had inwardly predicted what sort of a man David would become.

His expectations, so far, had been fully realized, and consequently the young miller was an object of special interest to him. In him, he had a living example of the correctness of his theories.

If the good people of Gowanstone could have taken a peep into the doctor's specimen cabinet, they would probably have endorsed all the labels, excepting those upon their own backs.

The only ones we *can not*, *do not* estimate fairly, are ourselves. In his rows of classified humanity, the doctor himself was conspicuous by his absence.

Why was it so, when *he* should have been the first? Why? Because he was human.

CHAPTER XIV.

"WHEN THE CAT'S AWAY, THE MICE WILL PLAY."

ONE day David came running in from the mill with a letter in his hand, and caught his mother in his arms.

"You were right, mother, as you always are. Here's a letter from Marian, telling me that her mother has

"WHEN THE CAT'S AWAY THE MICE WILL PLAY."

gone away on a two weeks' visit. To-day is Saturday, so you can put an extra touch on my collars."

He was all impatience during the day, and all fidgets at night. He could not sleep for thinking of her, and long before sunrise he was off.

Marian, of course, expected him, but it was only six o'clock in the morning, when she was awakened by the sound of wheels on the gravel driveway, and peeping through the shutters, she saw him tying his horse to a post.

"The foolish fellow, to come so early. Why, he must have got up in the middle of the night."

She hurriedly threw on a morning wrapper, put on a pair of slippers, and ran down to open the door for him.

It is only the beauty of perfect health which can bear inspection *en deshabille*, but no toilet was necessary to give Marian a bright eye and a rosy cheek.

As she opened the door, the fresh morning breeze blew her thin gown against her limbs, betraying the outlines of her figure, and exposing the bare ankle of a stockingless foot.

The impulse to catch her in his arms was almost irresistible, but she foresaw the possibility, and eluded his grasp. "Back, you rascal! can't you see I'm *half* asleep yet and only half dressed? My face is'nt even washed yet. The *idea* of coming so early," she added in a bantering tone, "and having me come down like a scarecrow."

"You don't seem to scare me," he remarked, trying to get closer.

"It seems not," she replied, getting on the opposite side of the kitchen stove, "but there is one offence a lady does not readily forgive; and that is, coming upon her before she has her war paint on."

"Nonsense, Marian, you don't need any cosmetics. *You* would look beautiful in sackcloth. War paint indeed! Faugh! I wouldn't give a pin for beauty that needs burnishing. Vanity, vanity!"

"Ah, ah! And what about yourself? Why, one of your famous countrymen, Rob Roy, would never be caught without his harness."

An open stairway led from the kitchen to a hallway above, and while she was talking, she was slyly preparing for her escape. But her tactics were discovered by the watchful eyes of her pursuer, and he caught her warm, throbbing figure in his arms, just as she was about to mount the stairs.

"For shame, David! let me go. I shall be angry in a moment."

"Give me a kiss then. Just one," and a scuffle ensued. His struggles, however, were futile, for her strength was almost equal to his own, and she was more lithe and supple. Finally he got her rosy face between his hands, and was about to imprint a kiss upon it, when, with a sudden movement, she landed him on the floor, and ran up the stairway with a triumphant laugh.

"Serves you right," she cried teasingly, leaning over the banister above. "Go and get your sackcloth now. You will need it."

"I think I have done penance enough already," he replied ruefully, as he brushed the dust from his coat.

"No, you have only just commenced. You've got to go to work and light that kitchen fire. I have half a notion to make you get the breakfast."

"So I will, if you will promise to eat it"

"Thanks, but I am not yet weary of life. No, you just light the fire, and while you are about it, save some ashes for a repentant lover."

"A humiliated one, you mean. The idea of being dumped on the floor is not pleasant to a Hielandman. I think you might let me off now."

"You forget, sir, that the Cornish were always great wrestlers. It is a hereditary accomplishment. Your defeat was excusable though, for you've not had your porridge yet."

"Come, get to work now," continued his tormentor. "But perhaps you had better put Dan in the stable first; that is, unless you are going right back;" and shying a stray cushion at his head, she fled to her room.

It was not long before the whole house was astir, and Marian appeared in her usual milking costume.

Meanwhile David's fire was blazing merrily, and she complimented him on it, remarking that his lady love must surely be in good humour.

"I hope she is," he replied as he followed her into the yard, where the group of cattle were awaiting her.

"Am I not forgiven yet, dear?" he asked in a repentant tone. "Don't be too hard on me. I was so hungry to see you, and you looked like a peach ready for eating. Can't I have a kiss yet?"

"What, right here? Well, only one, and be quick about it," she added as she placed her stool behind one of her cows, and held her face up to him. "There, there, now, that's stealing. I must get to work and no more nonsense."

"How would it be, Mally, if Mr. Gordon helped you to milk," cried Fred, coming forward in search of some mischief. He was in reality jealous of David for absorbing the attention of his sister, and felt that he owed him a grudge.

"I wish I could help. It looks easy enough. I feel certain I could do something at it," protested David.

"Very well," replied Marian, with roguishness in her eyes. "Run in and tell Nelly to give you a bonnet and an apron."

In a few moments he returned fully equipped for the occasion, with Fred and Nelly at his heels, shouting with laughter.

Marian gave him her stool, while, kneeling behind him, she took his hands in hers, to give him the first lesson.

She tried again and again to make him go through the motions, but he was a veritable dunce.

Indeed, poor David scarcely knew what he was doing, for with the pressure of her warm bust against him, and her breath fanning his cheek, he was completely mesmerized.

When she saw that he was really paying no attention to his task, she sent a stream athwart his nose, to the great amusement of the two spectators.

"I'm afraid, instead of a milker, you will make a milk sop of me," groaned David, wiping the milk from his eyes. "I was——." But he did not finish the sentence, for a white stream shot into his throat, and in his struggle for breath he fell off the stool.

"It's a calf he is now," roared Fred with the tears running down his cheeks, while Nelly held her sides with laughter.

"Come, I'll help you up," said Nelly, winking at her sister, and in a moment a relentless lacteal shower was pouring down his neck and ears, till he was forced to take to his heels, amid shouts of laughter.

"I'm not much of an astronomer," ejaculated Gordon, wiping his face in his apron, " but I ought to know something now of the milky way. You've ruined my collar and tie," he added ruefully."

" It's a pity about your tie," laughed Nelly. " It's a tartan too, just as if people wouldn't know you are Scotch, and the porridge looking out of your face."

"Indeed, I wouldn't quarrel with some going into my face this very minute," said the sufferer. "Only if I got it the way I got the milk, I'm afraid it wouldn't agree with me. However, it seems I can't help Marian any, so I'll go and help you, Nelly, to make the porridge, for I'm as hungry as a wolf."

After breakfast Marian brought some of her father's neck wear and proceeded to repair Gordon's shattered toilet. The tie was a cream silk with blue spots, and as she carefully adjusted it, she exclaimed dramatically, " Now, Sir Knight, there are my colors. See that you do credit to them."

During this pleasant operation, David experienced the thrill which her touch always gave him. He was just snatching a kiss, when Mr. Halford came into the room. Gordon was so embarrassed he did not know where to look. Marian turned as red as a peony but soon recovered herself.

" Good morning, father. I was just fixing Mr. Gordon's collar," she said with a look of mock innocence.

" Yes, I thought I heard the button snap," and they all had a good hearty laugh.

Mr. Halford knew little or nothing about Gordon, but his daughter's wishes were his. If Marian preferred him, why that settled the matter, as far as he was concerned.

Gordon, on the other hand, had never had a fair opportunity of improving Mr. Halford's acquaintance, and he determined to make the most of the present occasion. After breakfast they walked over the farm together, discussing crops, stock, and other commonplace topics. Fortunately, David's politics suited his host. Under the influence of a kindred feeling, their acquaintance ripened considerably.

After a while they returned to the lawn in front of the house, and there they commenced an animated discussion.

It seems that in his youth Mr. Halford had been a great cricketer, and for many years after coming to America, had mourned the loss of his favourite game. He tried several times to organize a club in Levisville, but the popular craze for baseball forced him to abandon the idea, and fall in with the national game.

The love of the sport had grown upon him till it became a hobby; in fact, Uncle William had been, for the past five years, honorary president of the Levisville Stars.

Here again was a common ground for enthusiasm. David was not only an ardent lover of the game, but for years was an active member of one of the local leagues. The discussion had only continued a short time, when Fred scented game in the atmosphere, and hurried out to take part in the discussion.

The boy fairly revelled in that freemasonry of sport, which places youth, adolescence, and old age on an equal footing. Often, he and his father would sit for hours, discussing the points of a game.

Is there not a wonderful charm in thus bridging the gulf of time? Is it not a blessing that through all the struggle for place and power, beyond all the mad race for gold, we still have in our hearts a spot fresh and unsullied by the ravages of time.

The gusto with which Mr. Halford described the last match was good to see. Kelly's jump for a foul; Rosenbaum's circus catch at second: and Walker's throw from deep centre, were themes that brought forth the greatest enthusiasm.

Marian caught occasional glimpses of the trio on the

lawn, and was delighted with her father's cordiality to David. She saw him slap Gordon on the shoulder and grasp his hand.

Then Fred, who had been lying on his stomach, with his heels in the air, suddenly jumped to his feet, with a look of surprise.

Something strange or startling had been discovered.

To satisfy her curiosity, Marian ran to the front window, where she could hear what was being said. Her father was speaking.

"Two home runs off Glendenning in one game. By the lord Harry, you must be a slugger. Why, Glen has one of the best records in America. God bless me, man, why didn't you tell me you were a ball player?"

"Well, I have not played at all for the past two years, besides I never was much of a player excepting at the bat. It was only my extra batting average that gave me a place on the team."

"What is the real secret of batting?" queried the old man.

"Simply to keep your eye on the ball. A great many don't really see it after it gets within six or eight feet, and they only strike where they expect it to come."

"It ain't in the way you stand, then," said Fred, who stood by with both mouth and ears open.

"Well, there's something in that too, and in quickness of motion, but the great secret is in the eye."

"It's a pity it's Sunday," murmured the boy, taking a ball from his pocket, and looking at it caressingly. Gordon had grown wonderfully in Fred's estimation. His jealousy was sunk in the nobler sympathies of sport.

With him, no earthly potentate equalled the man who could throw curves, or find them.

"It's no use talking, Gordon, you've simply got to stay over for the game to-morrow," exclaimed Mr. Halford. "God bless me, man, it's for the Championship of America."

In spite of all the expostulations, however, Gordon decided to go home, as he originally intended. He would not leave his mother in suspense over night for all the games in the world.

At dinner Mr. Halford related to Marian how he and Fred had tried to persuade David to stay over for the game.

"What! Of course he will stay," and she gave him a coaxing look.

David was sorely tempted, but he avoided her glance. He explained that his mother would expect him, and that he had some orders to give his foreman.

Some strange presentiment told him that this decision would be of life-long importance.

Often the most trivial circumstances affect our future destiny, opening a new era in our lives.

From the making of our toilets, to the meeting of some one on the street, or the missing of a train, we can all look back and mark some spot where a trivial nothing changed the current of life's events.

But the trouble of deciding in this case was taken out of his hands by an imperious young lady. "Fred, you saddle a horse and go to the station operator with a message. Nelly, get Mr. Gordon some paper and a pencil to write his telegram. Mr. Gordon, don't spare a few words for the sake of being explicit. We'll hurry it off, so that your mother will get some one to stay with her to-night. Hurry, Fred, get your horse and be sure to pay for a special delivery."

"Ha, ha, ha!" laughed Mr. Halford, "you can't stick Marian. She can outgeneral us all."

And so it was settled.

CHAPTER XV.

A LUCKY HIT.

IN spite of all that may be said to the contrary, in spite of all the evil associations which may be incidentally attached to it, there cannot be any doubt that true sport, genuine sport, has a wholesome effect on the human mind.

That it supplies opportunities for gambling and dishonesty is quite true, that it has often led indirectly to moral, physical, and financial suicide, cannot be disputed; but surely this is not the fault of sport itself. As well might we condemn the medicinal use of liquor, because drunkenness still exists.

In spite of the disrepute of the turf, there are still thousands of the best people in the world who continue to enjoy the races. There is something inspiring in those exhibitions of the power and speed of the noblest of the lower animals, and not even the presence of bookies and ring toughs prevents the attendance of culture and refinement.

Athletic games, however, are admitted by the most prudish to be comparatively free from the gambling element which follows the turf. A quoit field or a curling rink is considered a legitimate place for a gentleman; a spot where the freshness and buoyancy of youth is renewed; where mirth and gladness warm the hearts of grey-haired boys. Even a clergyman may appear in a cricket field without loss of caste. Indeed, if he excels in the game, it rather adds to his popularity.

In America there is no dissenting voice in classing baseball as the greatest game on earth. In fact, to speak disparagingly of it is a mild sort of heresy.

All through the forenoon, the good town of Levisville showed signs of suppressed excitement. Every incoming train deposited its cargo of spectators, and on every street corner were knots of people discussing the possibility of the coming contest. Bulletin boards in front of the newspaper offices announced that the great struggle for the championship was to commence at 2 P.M.

Broadview itself was full of expectancy. Mr. Halford and his guest did nothing all forenoon but discuss baseball, while Fred, with boyish eagerness, packed some lunch in a paper bag and started on horseback for the seat of war. Marian, who took little interest in the game, insisted on remaining at home to keep house and have tea ready for their return. Nelly was quite an enthusiast over the sport, but preferred to deny herself the pleasure of watching the game, to leaving her sister alone.

David and Mr. Halford started in good time, but before they reached the grounds the grand stand was packed. Uncle William's prestige, however, as president, preserved for him and his guest a seat immediately behind the netting known as the back stop.

The home team were dressed in white uniforms with red stars on the breasts of their sweaters, while the Crescents were in blue. When the Stars made their appearance, a tremendous shout of applause greeted them. The "big wig" forgot his dignity, the stately dame her pose, the blooming belle her beauty, and the withered spinster her austerity. Boys and girls, young and old, rich and poor, all shouted themselves hoarse for their favourites. Even thieves and pickpockets forgot their cunning, and joined in chorus with policemen and judges. Self, or selfish interest was forgotten, jealousy and hate were laid aside, and for a time this motley crowd became a common fraternity.

There was the usual delay at the outset, broken by shouts and catcalls from the bleachers. Impecunious urchins ornamented every telegraph pole or other point of vantage where they could steal a look at the game. Clinging to their perches, they could defy all and sundry, including the fat policeman, whom they kept in hot water by their repeated invitations to "hurry up." "Play ball there! what's eating you!" and similar salutes came from these aerial outposts, while the rythmic tramp, tramp, tramp of a thousand feet, showed that expectation was at fever heat.

Finally, the Stars took the field. Dempsey, the home pitcher stepped into his place and the umpire, in stentorian voice, shouted, "Play Ball!"

The first five innings on each side were very uneventful. The game, so far, was errorless, and though neither team had scored it was plain to all that the visitors had the advantage.

Several of the blue jackets had hit Dempsey freely, and came within an ace of scoring, but the Stars had been nearly all slaughtered in the striker's box. The home team were doing splendid fielding, but they could not hit Carey's tortuous balls. One after another they were retired with monotonous regularity, till "three strikes and out," became a continuous song. Only two of their men, Brooks and Donelly, had ever touched his curves or reached first base, and the grand stand was in agony. How they hated the villain Carey. The ladies detested "the ugly, bow-legged thing." In spite of the police, apple cores and banana peels were fired at him from the crowd, and a blossoming telegraph pole inquired of the redoubtable twirler if his nether garments had to be cut out with a circular saw? But all this did not "rattle" the renowned wizard of the diamond. He would stand for a moment smiling fiendishly at his victim, or winking at the bleachers, then suddenly, as if by magic, his arm would swing from his side, and the ball in its spiral spin, would flash past the batter and land with a smack in the catcher's mit. In the seventh inning, and in *their* last, the visitors managed to score, but up to their last turn at the bat, not a single Star had ever crossed the plate.

The strain was something terrible. "Damn that villain, Carey! Can nobody hit him?" groaned Uncle William.

"I think I could hit him," said Gordon. "I haven't touched a bat in two years, but I have been studying his delivery, and I understand the signs that he makes to the catcher."

"That's all right," retorted the old man, peevishly,

"but that won't save the game. We've just got to sit here and suffer. Why, it's awful!"

Just about this time an untoward accident happened, which made matters even worse for the Stars. Carey, who was batting, hit short, but he ran like an Indian, and in order to prevent his being thrown out, he sent his head full tilt against the first baseman's stomach, knocking him senseless. Poor Brooks had to be carried off the field, but the crowd had the satisfaction of hearing Carey called "out."

All hope was, of course, gone. The score stood two to nothing in favour of the Crescents, with one of the home team's best batters disabled. "The thing is impossible. The game is gone," said many who were about to leave the grounds, when something unusual caught their attention.

Uncle William was running towards Manager Tracy of the Stars, shouting and calling like mad. The general impression was that the excitement had been too much for the old man, and that he had taken leave of his senses. Out of curiosity, however, they would wait and see what he was about. The home team had to select a new man in Brooks' place, and Tracy was about to call out the name, when Uncle William caught him by the arm and dragged him apart. Panting for breath aud pale with excitement, the old man could scarcely speak. "I've got—man—regular slugger—put him on." The manager smiled sadly, and shook his head. "Greenhorns are no use here, Uncle William!"

"Greenhorn be—hanged. This fellow—knocked—home runs—off Glendenning in one—game. He's—been—watching Carey's curves—all—afternoon."

Tracy gave a low whistle, and shut one eye. "By gad! we'll risk him. Keep mum, though."

"Come, Tracy, trot out your man, and let us finish the slaughter!" shouted Humphreys of the Crescents.

"Gordon is the man."

"Easy now, this name is Gregory!"

"The name is wrongly spelled," replied Tracy, calmly. "He'll be ready in a minute."

"Looks like a plant, Reggy, my boy!" growled

Humphreys. "Your men must be as bad with the pencil as the stick! But never mind, trot him out, you can't play ringers on me. I guess I know every professional ball player in this country."

Meantime there was a great commotion on the grand stand. "What's up now?" "They're taking somebody off the stand!" "By George, they're going to play the fellow with the grey clothes!" "Yes, they're bringing him out!"

The knowing ones guessed that Uncle William had a card up his sleeve, and winked at the crowd to keep mum. David saw that resistance would spoil all, so he jumped over the railing, and shed his coat, vest and boots. Uncle William was so excited that he did not wait to roll up Gordon's sleeves, but, with a jack-knife, cut and tore them from the shoulders, amidst the laughter of the crowd.

But the audience had little faith in the new man; for his arms were white as milk. Humphreys looked him over, and laughed. "Yes, you can have him and welcome!"

Before going to bat for the last time, the Stars held a short consultation as to the best method of finding Carey's curves. David told them what he had learned by continual watching, and warned them of the nature of the signals.

The very first man who went to bat made a scratch hit and got safely to "first." The next got his base on "balls." The spirits of the crowd began to rise, for Donelly, the heavy hitter, came next, and if he hit hard, he might probably bring in the other two, and thus tie the score. Cries of, "Smash it, Jimmie!" "Bring them in!" came from the bleachers, but alas, poor Jimmie ticked a foul, which landed in the catcher's mit, amid the groans of the spectators, and one man was out. A number of visitors, who were in sympathy with the Crescents and who were assembled at one corner of the grand stand, here rose to their feet and gave "three cheers for Corkscrew Carey, the wizard of the Diamond." The next batter retired on three strikes. All hope was lost. "Gordon to bat," shouted the scorer, as David stepped forward to meet his fate.

A LUCKY HIT.

With his trousers rolled up above his ankles, his suspenders tied about his waist, and the remains of his shirt sleeves dangling from his shoulders, he formed an odd contrast to the players in uniform. He created quite a sensation, drawing derisive hoots from the *claquers* of the Crescents. To calm his excitement he took some time in selecting a bat. "Take a fence board," shouted Carey with a laugh. "Jasper wants a rail!" But David was too old a player to let such salutes annoy him; he pretended not to notice them.

The moment his feet were in the striker's box the ball flew past him, and the umpire shouted "Strike one!" Tracy here protested on the grounds of illegal delivery, but his claim was disallowed. "Ball one!" as David dodged his head to miss one that whizzed past his ear and was calculated to intimidate him. "Ball two!" as the dust flew off the plate, and the crowd shouted, "Good eye, old man!" "Ball three!" brought a cheer.

Carey began to feel puzzled. He had calculated that the new man would be an easy victim. All the other batters stood sidewise to him, stooping slightly over the plate, but Gordon stood straight as a statue, facing his antagonist with his bat on his right shoulder.

In order to gain time, and restore his confidence, the pitcher now resorted to that dramatic sort of by-play so often used to intimidate the batter, and decoy the unwary base runner. Marching up to the batsman he looked him carefully up and down, ostensibly to see if he was in his legal position. David still stood like a statue, with his hair straight up from his forehead, and only smiled at the inspection. During the hush which momentarily passed over the crowd, an urchin astride a crossbar in mid-air cried, "Take a good look, old man. That's goose egg Gordon." This salute brought down the house, and David's hearty laugh brought back all his usual self-confidence.

"Perhaps we'd better get him a balloon," suggested Carey.

"Not necessary," replied David, "the ball will do me. Put it over the plate if you dare!"

Those who heard Gordon's reply gave a cheer, and the crossbar shouted, "Corky's cake is dough!"

The pitcher then held a short consultation with the first baseman, and to further keep the batter in suspense he threw the ball around the bases. Then, as suddenly as the rules would permit, he sprang into his position and sent the ball whirling towards the plate. The umpire was about to call, "Strike two!" when suddenly the long bat flashed through the air, and away went the ball towards the blue sky, landing just inside the right field fence. The pent-up enthusiasm, broke loose. The air was rent with cheers and yells, as Gordon ran his bases and brought in the two Stars. But stop, look! look! Gordon has not yet reached third base, and Wilks, the long-thrower of the Crescents, is almost upon the ball. "Go down, Gordon, go down, go down! Run, run, fly!" shouted the crowd, wringing its hands. "Two to one he don't get there!" shouted Humphreys. A hundred handfuls of greenbacks were shaken in the air, while men tumbled over each other to take the bet. The audience rose in a mass with clenched hands and bated breath, women trembled and fainted, and boys with bulging eyes, scrambled and fought their way to the shoulders of the seething mass. Gordon must reach home before the ball, or the pennant is lost. "Quick, quick!" shouted Tracy, "hand him a wet sponge, he begins to stumble. Keep back! Keep back! Give him air! Let Bolter run him in. Steady, Jim! Don't crowd him or he'll fall! Good boy, Gordon, make ready for your slide! There's a thousand dollars at the plate!" Heavens! the ball is coming like a rocket. In a second it will reach the pitcher. "Keep back!" shouted the umpire, running towards the goal, as the great mob swayed to and fro with excitement. Look, he's almost there, but the pitcher wheels, and the ball is flying towards the "blue jacket" at the plate. "Heavens! he has fallen, and all is lost!" A moan of anguish swept the vast assembly. No, no, he has the fraction of a second left. With a convulsive movement the fallen man throws himself toward the stone slab, and when the catcher with the ball in his hands alights on the fateful square, the fingers of Gordon's right hand are under his feet.

Never did electric button or train of gunpowder explode such a volley of sound as went up from ten thousand throats.

They did not wait for the umpire's stentorian shout, of "Safe." The crushed fingers were enough. The mob went mad with joy. Hats, canes, and bouquets filled the air, and exultant spectators stumbled over each other to get another look at the victor. Hark! There go the city chimes. The shouts of victory have been heard from afar. Tower after tower clanged forth its song of gladness. Locomotives screeched, whistles blew, and the big gun on the hill added its deafening boom to the great chorus, for the Levisville Stars were Champions of America.

CHAPTER XVI.

AFTERMATH.

When Gordon recovered from his momentary loss of consciousness, he was being carried on the shoulders of the mob, who with songs and shouts were moving in procession towards the heart of the city.

"Where's the old man? Let's elevate him," and in a few moments, Mr. Halford's form was also in mid-air.

He was still swinging his top hat, and shouting like mad, while tears of joy were running down his cheeks. Down through the main streets went the mob, carrying everything before them in their wild enthusiasm, till finally they deposited their captives on the balcony of the city hall, and called on them for a speech.

Gordon thanked the crowd for their appreciation of his efforts, but explained that probably it was only his luck, and not his skill, which won the game.

This statement brought shouts of "No, no!" from every quarter, and for the sake of peace he had to qualify it. He then paid a tribute to the almost errorless playing of both teams, eulogized the umpire's fairness, and concluded by telling them that, before tomorrow's sun set, the name of Levisville would be heard throughout the length and breadth of America.

Uncle William started several times with, "Gentlemen and fellow citizens," but could get no further.

"It's no use, boys," he exclaimed, wiping the moisture from his eyes; "I can't talk."

This brought three cheers for Uncle William, and cries of, "he's all right."

Just as the crowd was dispersing, the mayor and some prominent members of the city council swooped down upon the now illustrious pair.

"We'll have bands, fireworks and torchlight processions," shouted Mayor Harrison, whose tongue with its lightning rapidity usually created a feeling of dizziness. "A banquet for the boys, with you two as honored guests. What! no clothes, eh?" he exclaimed looking at David's half-dressed condition. "Anderson, you bolt for Dunlap's. Dress suit and hat for tonight, remember. No cheap John botch, but a Fifth Avenue outfit. Skip, now, and bring the cutter here.

"Pretty sore fingers, eh? Look, Dennison, there's Dr. Meldrum. Call him up.

"What! your watch gone, too? Well, never mind. By the living, we'll get you one as big as an eight-day clock. Rendal, snatch that telephone and call up Grant, the jeweller. By Jove, there's Webster! Very man I want to see. Say, Dave, you've got to put up the lush to-night and no mistake. See to it, now, or by the jumping Jehosaphat, we'll massacre you. No bank barn business, but the real McCoy, with all the fixings, music and all. And say, Dave, look here, no cold tea, but stuff that's fit to put down a white man's neck. Keep moving! Hello! Is that you, Grant? Well, get your skates on. Best ticker in the shanty there, and have some engraving done. Yes, of course, right away, now. What do you take us for? An ox-team?

"What to put on it? Oh, yes. Say, Gordon, what the devil is your other name? All right!

"Hello, Grant! Put on it, 'City of Levisville to D. Gordon. Play Ball.' Capital B. of course. Yes. Wait a minute. Say, Jenkins, where have you been hiding yourself? By the powers of dynamite, if you don't get around and look after the toot-horns, and fire-crackers, we'll build a fire under you. Scoot now!

"Hello, Grant! Hustle there, now, if you want to die a natural death. Yes, the date, of course, and a big star. Chain? Why, yes. Everything goes, and a seal as big as a walnut. Expense? Good heavens! we're no Sheeneys. Look here, Scotty, this ain't Aberdeen. This ain't no ten cent town, and when we take snuff everybody's got to sneeze. See?"

Marian and Nellie had just finished their milking that evening, when Fred came galloping along like the wind, swinging something over his head.

The clanging of the city bells had given them the news of victory, but they little thought that their father or Gordon had anything to do with it. At first sight, they did not recognize in Fred's banner David's coat and vest, but when he got half way up the lane Marian spied a familiar handkerchief hanging from one of the pockets. For a moment she felt dizzy, but the look of exultation on the boy's face reassured her.

"In the name of God, what's wrong?" The only answer was another cheer and another swing of the coat.

In a moment Marian was at the horse's head. Grasping the bridle in one hand she pulled the rider off with the other.

"You young rascal, if you don't tell me at once, I'll twist your ears off. Give me that," and she snatched the garments from his hand. "What's wrong? Do you hear?" she cried, giving him a preliminary shake.

"Blame it all, there's nuthin' wrong," replied Fred, sulkily, "the boys won the game."

"We know that already. I suppose you wouldn't care if everybody was killed so long as your side won. Is Mr. Gordon hurt?" she demanded as she gazed at the soiled and trampled clothing.

"No, it was Brooks got hurt, and David took his place. Gee, whiz, you'd oughter seen him swipe Carey," he added with a burst of enthusiasm. "He nearly pounded him out of the lot. David's fingers is a little bruised, that's all."

"He was fighting then," she exclaimed in horrified tones, while her two companions burst into a fit of laughter.

"Say, Mally, you're greener'n grass. You'd ought to be ashamed if you don't know more'n that. He was playing ball, don't I tell you, in Brooks's place, and he played for keeps too. Nell knows what I mean. Don't you, Nell?" he continued, turning to his younger sister, who inherited her father's love of sport, and who understood the language of the diamond.

"Tie that horse up and tell me all about it," exclaimed Marian. "Remember, no ball slang, but plain English."

Fred started to tell the story, but paused to drag from his pockets a pair of tattered shirt sleeves and a watch.

"What in the name of conscience have you got there?" she asked, catching the torn linen.

"Well, them's his sleeves, of course. You know Dad was in such a hurry he just cut and tore them off."

"Surely father and David must have taken leave of their senses. Such goings on I never heard of. It's a good thing you got the sleeves, for those are valuable sleeve buttons. The watch was his father's. Now go on with your story and no more interruptions."

When Fred commenced his narrative, Marian was seated on a milking-stool and he stood beside her, but before he got half way through he was sitting on her knee with his arms around her.

"So Carey couldn't scare him," she repeated as she gave him a squeeze.

"No, sirree. He dared Carey to put it over the plate, and then Dad cheered like sixty."

"I wonder if he lost his necktie," she asked as she took the buttons from the empty sleeves.

"That one of Dad's, you mean?"

"Yes, the one with the blue spots."

"No, he didn't, 'cause I mind of it blowing round his neck when he was runnin'." Fred wondered why his sister gave him such a hug just then, but he did not ask any questions, for he dearly loved her caresses and often asked to sit on her knee.

"What will Mr. Gordon do without his clothes?" asked Nelly.

"Dear me, he *will* be in a terrible plight," responded Marian. "I think I shall clean them up, and you can take them back, Fred."

"Well, you don't have to, for Bill Hinks, what sweeps out the city hall, told me that Mayor Harrison was goin' to rig David out all new. He said for me to take the clothes home. They're goin' to have a big blow-out, with fireworks and everything, and they all said that Gordon and Dad would own the town to-night. Won't you go in, Mally, and see the fireworks?"

"No dear, I think I'll stay at home, but you can take Nelly with you."

For a long time after they had gone, Marian sat out on the verandah and watched the rockets shooting into the sky. She was proud of her lover to-night, and why should she not be? She loved courage, and if Fred's account were true, David had proven himself as brave as a lion. "He did do credit to my colours. He did *not* part with them. I believe I love him more than ever."

In spite of all this, however, she felt gloomy and low-spirited. A dread lest something should happen her father destroyed the pleasure which otherwise she would have felt.

For many years he had not touched liquor of any kind, but she was afraid that the excitement and conviviality would be too much for him.

About eleven o'clock, her brother and sister returned, but she could learn nothing from them to relieve her uneasiness. They had no opportunity of speaking to their father or David, who were on a balcony addressing the crowd. The last they saw of them was when the mayor presented David with a gold watch. Then there was nothing but bands and fireworks.

Her anxiety increased more rapidly when the family had gone to bed, when the house became wrapt in silence.

She walked to and from the gate a score of times. She cleaned her lover's coat and vest. She went over to the stable to give Dan an extra feed, knowing that Gordon would start for home as soon as he could. She polished her tinware in the kitchen, and had the table spread, ready to give them a lunch. Twelve o'clock—one—two—said the pitiless time-piece on the mantle, while to make matters worse a thunder storm was brewing in the west. At last, when weary with waiting, and worn out with suspense, she heard the welcome rumble of wheels on the gravel.

As she opened the side door the light fell directly on the vehicle, and poor Marian saw at once that her fears were only too well grounded.

With the reins in his bandaged hand, Gordon was supporting with the other the collapsed and almost prostrate form of her father.

"Tie the horse for me, dear, and then call Watson. This is no sight for you," said David in a low voice, as he drove close to the door.

She shook her head sadly, while the tears streamed from her eyes, but she never spoke. She tied the horse, while David steadied the unconscious man and lifted him from the vehicle. She motioned David to take her father by the feet, while she lifted him by the shoulders. Then they carried him into the house and laid him on a lounge in the parlour, when she ran for cushions and pillows to make him comfortable for the night.

"Marian," said David solemnly, "not for all the games or glory in the world would I willingly have brought this grief upon you. I was ashamed to bring him home to you in this plight; it took all my courage to do it. As soon as I got an inkling of his condition I took him away to a private room in the hopes that a sleep would revive him. I would have given that hand," he continued, holding out his bandaged member, "to have spared you this pain. I got a doctor to see him, and waited till I could wait no longer, hoping that he would be able to come home in his senses. Darling," he went on, dropping on his knee before her, and reverently kissing her hand, "forgive me for my thoughtlessness."

She leaned over and kissed his forehead. "It was not your fault. You knew nothing of his weakness. Was he like this before the whole assembly?"

"No, dear, he was talking and laughing when I coaxed him out. Nobody knows anything about it excepting the care-taker, who helped me to bring him out the back way."

"You don't think there will be anything in the papers about his condition? If we can only keep it from mother. She is so fond of reading the papers."

"I don't think there is any danger, Marian. All the newspaper men and half the company were in the same plight. Jones, the wit of the Standard, had a fellow propping him up as he took down his notes. It was champagne, and they drank it like water. No dear, newspaper men, with all their Bohemianism are gentlemen, who would consider anything of that kind *infra dig. Noblesse oblige.*'

Marian sat bathing her father's head with eau-de-cologne, occasionally holding a bottle of smelling salts to his nostrils.

"Won't you call Watson and let us put him to bed?"

"No, David, I shall not allow any one to see him till he is himself again. Poor Nelly and Fred would be broken hearted if they saw him in this state."

She kissed the sleeping man's face with exquisite tenderness. "I must cover up his faults as he would mine. We all have some weakness, vice, or imperfection, and I suppose this is his."

"Yes, I suppose so," responded David with a sigh.

"Dr. Bennet maintains that we all have a "pane out," that the difference is in its being seen. But now I must go, dear, for I hear the thunder coming nearer."

"*Must* you go, David!"

"Yes, I have given my word, and that means go every time! I wired mother not to worry, if I was late, but that I would be home before morning. I hate to break my word. A person had nearly as well break his neck. If a man's word cannot be depended on, what does he amount to?"

When David sat in his rig at the door, ready to start, and Marian kissed him good bye he tasted the salt drops on her cheek.

"Don't cry, darling," he said in a low soft whisper, kissing away her tears, " he will be all right in the morning. Good night." He had only gone a few yards down the lane, when she called him again through the darkness.

Her voice trembled as she spoke. She was thankful that he could not see her face. " Did he say anything bad or out of place," she inquired.

" No, dear, nothing coarse or vulgar. I don't think there is anything low in him. But——" and here the speaker hesitated, "in reply to a toast he told the assembly that I was his future son-in-law."

At that instant there was a sharp peal of thunder followed by a great dash of rain, and Dan, full of impatience, sped down the lane into the black night.

A vivid flash of lightning gave them a glimpse of each other, as David turned into the highway.

She was leaning against the wall in the shelter of the verandah, with a face like marble, while he stood up in the pouring rain, throwing her a kiss and waving in his wounded hand the blue spotted necktie.

CHAPTER XVII.

A DISAGREEABLE SURPRISE.

Ten or eleven days after the events narrated in the last chapter, Mrs. Halford was seated in the morning express, en route for home.

For the space of two weeks she had been free from the cares of business, and she felt revived and strengthened by her holiday.

She had a good appetite, a vigorous digestion, and slept soundly at night.

These are, after all, the very pillars of happiness and contentment. It is the man with weak digestion who has qualms of conscience, and gloomy forebodings.

Perhaps had Mrs. Halford been a confirmed dyspeptic, she might have had some presentiment of the trouble in store for her.

Or had she possessed the fondness for her daughter which some mothers have, she would probably have dreamt about her.

Many a fond mother's dream has seemed to give a forecast of fate, has forestalled the news of trouble, sickness or death among the loved ones.

We are accustomed to smile at such things, but who knows how far it is possible for sensitive organizations to be affected by the events and circumstances surrounding those near and dear to them? May there not, after all, be some reasonable explanation of those things which are now either considered as supernatural or set down as mere coincidences?

In these days, when animal magnetism is opening such wide fields of investigation, are there not thousands of possibilities, as yet unheard of? Why should distance debar currents of animal magnetism, any more than it does electricity in its popular form? Does it not seem possible that, when two human creatures have a powerful attraction for each other, the atmosphere may be used as a medium, just as ordinary electricity uses the wire? Is not the earth itself a huge magnet? May not the very ground we tread upon convey the electricity of human beings?

May it not, after all, be a question of the strength of animal currents measured by affection, and modified by sex?

Truly may we say with Hamlet:

"There are more things in heaven and earth, Horatio, than are dreamt of in our philosophy."

Whether she lacked in affection or sensitiveness, Mrs. Halford had certainly no forebodings.

She had only received one letter during her absence, and at the time it seemed rather unsatisfactory, but she had not thought of it since. She had also been out of the reach of a daily newspaper. She knew nothing of what was going on at home, but she was satisfied that no news was good news. On the previous night she dreamt that the big barn was on fire, and though she awoke in a great fright, she was not at all fanciful, and she attributed her dream to errors in diet.

At present she was quietly contemplating the fleeting fields through the car window, comparing them with her own broad acres at home.

Nothing she had ever seen in her travels equalled the sloping fields of Broadview. She inwardly congratulated herself on her good fortune and prosperity.

As she drew nearer home her mind became more and more infused with business calculations. Rent, interest, and mortgages required her attention; besides, there were changes and improvements to make. Thank goodness, she had no household duties to worry her. Marian could be depended on for that. Her former responsibilities connected with the dairy had also been assumed by her daughter, leaving her mind free to cope with her larger business interests.

She began to feel tired and drowsy. Like many others she wondered why it was that a few hours on a railway train exhausted her so much.

Who has not experienced that same feeling? How often do we see the participants in a pleasure excursion looking as gloomy as pall bearers? Do we not often need a holiday most just after taking one?

Is it bad ventilation, the noise, the motion, or is it from the conflicting currents of attraction and repulsion which strangers exert upon each other.

The same exhaustion may be noticed after social gatherings, where the presence of a certain individual will destroy all our pleasure and give us the kind of feeling we experience when we find flies in our soup.

Laying aside all this, however, there seems to be another disagreeable feature in travel from which there is no protection, and which we must suffer in patience, viz., the travelling bore, the assiduous creature who infests railway carriages, and inflicts himself upon a suffering public.

Anxious to attract attention, they invariably talk in loud, lively tones, in order to convey to all the impression that the real importance of life is centred in them. Any one who does not know *them*, or is not cognizant of *their* affairs, is in the most pitiable darkness, and out of charity they are in duty bound to let people know who they are.

Mrs. Halford, sitting with her eyes half closed, did not notice a dapper little man who strutted into the car with grandiloquent air and slammed the door behind him, while his eye roamed over the seats in search of fresh victims.

Mr. Reid, a small dry goods dealer from Levisville, was fairly shining with etiquette and peanut politeness.

As soon as he discovered Mrs. Halford his face wreathed with smiles. Touching her on the shoulder to draw her attention, he went off with a bang.

"Ah, how do you do, Mrs. Halford? Just getting back from your holidays? I've been down to New York buying goods. Must keep up with the times, you know. Fine weather, isn't it? Great season for the farmers. Hope you enjoyed your trip? You're looking well. I'm feeling well, myself. Never felt better. Oh, by the way, must congratulate your future son-in-law. Fine fellow, Gordon. Boys all wild over him that night."

His voice faded into a cackle and even the roar of the train left her ears.

For a moment she lost consciousness. When she came to her head she was leaning on the sill of the open window and Mr. Reid was holding a cup of water to her lips.

She had fainted; she, who believed that such things were mostly pretence.

But she must not let her fellow townsman guess the cause of her distress.

Something very strange had happened at home, of which she had never been told.

"I always get weak and dizzy riding on the train," she explained to Mr. Reid.

She wanted more information, but must not let him suspect her ignorance.

"Yes, it were a great time, but I never saw any of the local papers."

"Dear me. Very lucky. Got an *Echo* in my overcoat pocket. Carried it ever since. Happy to oblige," and soon the paper was forthcoming.

On the front page in double leaded headings were the following:

"LEVISVILLE ON TOP.

THE STARS ARE CHAMPIONS.

GORDON'S GREAT DRIVE SAVES THE GAME.

A STALWART WITH THE STICK IS HALFORD'S SON-IN-LAW.

FUN AND FIREWORKS GALORE."

This was too horrible. The paper fell into her lap and for a time she could read no more.

By some villainous plot Marian had outwitted her; had taken advantage of her absence to cheat and deceive her.

But she would have her revenge for this black treachery. Not another night would her daughter spend under her roof unless she humbly went on her knees and promised to undo what she had done.

"I'll make her suffer. I'll humble her pride, the hussy," and she ground her teeth with vexation.

But she must know all before she reached home, she must not seem to be taken unawares. She took up the paper again and read till she came to where Uncle William in his speech announced Gordon as his future son-in-law. Then she tore it into fragments and tossed it out of the window.

"So, so. William got tipsy. That low beggar have put the words in his mouth. Well, it are only so much more her will have to account for."

She sat looking about her like a caged lioness, beating her foot upon the floor, as was her custom when in a passion.

She did not doubt for a moment that the whole affair had been planned to outwit her. Indeed, the *Echo* misled her. The statement of the *Echo* read as if Gordon were a member of the Stars and a resident of Levisville. There was no hint that his taking part in the game was accidental. In fact, the paper made it appear as if President Halford had merely held him in reserve, like an ace up his sleeve, to scoop the backers of the Crescents.

She had no doubt that the dinner and the champagne which her husband drank were a part of the treacherous programme planned by Marian and carried out by Gordon.

In her rage she forgot many things; that the dinner itself was unforeseen; that Gordon knew nothing of her husband's weakness; that Mr. Halford's enthusiasm over the game was extreme; and that Marian would suffer any anguish or torment rather than expose her father. She might have known, in fact she did know, that her daughter, loving her father as she did, could not possibly have been a party to such a plot. But her pride and anger swept away all else.

With eyes closed and teeth clenched, she sat nursing her wrath till the train pulled into Levisville depot,

CHAPTER XVIII.

"WHEN GREEK MEETS GREEK."

MR. HALFORD was at the station to meet his wife, and was in a very anxious frame of mind. He expected that she had seen the Levisville papers at least a week before. He hoped that time had cooled her anger. The post-card of the previous day, announcing the time of her return, contained the usual love to all and showed no sign of wrath.

Yet he felt that he had reached a crisis in his life, for Marian had told him, not only of David's rejection, but of her mother's efforts to coerce her into a marriage with the widower Grazely.

"By heavens, Marian, it shall not be. There shall be no coercion. You are free to choose whom you may, and your choice shall be mine."

"Father, dear, don't quarrel with mother. Think of poor Nelly and Fred. It will be enough to know that I have your sympathy. Nothing can ever come between you and me," and she laid her cheek against his.

"Your mother and I have got along well together. She is a clever woman. She has been a good wife and a good mother. But she must not go too far. I like peace, but not at the price of your happiness."

He feared that the incoming train would bring matters to a climax, and was not surprised when, instead of the usual embrace, his wife merely shook hands with him. Not a word was spoken, but she gave him a look more eloquent than words.

She did not care to say anything to him, she was reserving her wrath for her daughter.

On the way from the station she did not even ask him how they all were, or how matters were progressing at the farm, but sat with compressed lips and clenched teeth, till the vehicle pulled up in front of the house,

Fred and Nelly were at the door to meet her, but Marian, who instinctively felt a storm approaching, was trying to discover, from behind one of the window shutters, the state of her mother's mind.

Mrs. Halford did not lose a moment. She sprang lightly from the buggy and, after hurriedly kissing Fred and Nelly, walked rapidly into the house. Hurrying through the kitchen and dining-room into the parlour, and throwing her cape and bonnet on a table, she said to Nelly, who was following her, "Tell Marian I are waiting here to see her."

The parlour was always a blue room for serious matters. Nelly knew that a storm was at hand. Indeed, she begged her sister not to get angry with her mother.

In a few moments Marian appeared. She stood for an instant at the door, with pale face and glistening eyes, then came bravely forward and offered her hand.

Mrs. Halford was sitting looking out of the window, but as soon as she saw her daughter she sprang to her feet. Pointing her finger at her she hissed, "Back, you traitor! You miserable, sneaking vixen! Pack your traps, and leave this house forever."

"Oh, mother, for the love of God, hear me."

"No, you hussy, them as act lies can tell them." Then taking two steps forward she hissed something in her daughter's ear.

The taunt, whatever it was, brought the tiger-like gleam to Marian's eyes, and she made as if to spring upon her mother, but checked herself and sank into a chair, in a torrent of weeping.

"Yes, weep! You ungrateful wretch! I'm wring your heart, till there be no tears left."

Marian sat sobbing with her elbows on her knees, and her face buried in her hands. Her tears had cooled her anger, leaving only her better nature. But she felt that she and her mother must part. If her father knew the words that had been spoken the peace of Broadview would be gone forever.

She would take all blame upon herself and preserve peace between her parents.

Rising to her feet, she went with bowed head towards the door, and then turning with a gentle expression on her face, she said solemnly, "Mother, may God help me to forgive and forget this day."

Reaching the kitchen, her grief broke out afresh, and catching her sister in her arms she rocked her to and fro in the agony of the moment.

"Oh, Nelly darling, I'm going to leave you forever," she cried with tears streaming down her cheeks.

"I'll go too," sobbed Nelly. "I can't live without you, Mally; who'll cure my headaches, and kiss me when I'm pettish?" and the poor girl clung to her sister, while her frame shook with sobs. "Can't—I—go—with—you? Oh—oh—Mally—don't go—don't—don't——."

"Oh, but I must, darling. Mother and I can't get along."

"Where—are—you going—Mally?"

"I don't just know, dear; let me think a few moments." With her sister's head on her bosom, Marian sat a few moments, deciding her own fate. "Ah, I know now. Run and send Fred to me."

Meantime, Mrs. Halford sits like one in a dream. Through the half open door she can see into the kitchen. What a sight greets her! What a vision for a mother! She cannot bear to look. She closes the door to shut out the sounds of weeping.

"Hark! Marian have gone upstairs. Yes, her is packing up. God, what have I done? I thought her would go on her knees to me. Hush! There are Fred going up the stairs two steps at a time. Heavens, how he are weeping."

Now they were in the room together and oh, the outburst of grief. Fred was fairly shouting through his sobs and his mother could hear him. "I—won't—stay—with—her. I'll tell—her—that too."

Mrs. Halford put her hands over her ears to shut out her baby boy's impeachment. "He loves his sister then even more than his mother. So does Nelly."

But where was William? Would he too take sides against her? A horrible feeling of guilt and loneliness came over her. At that moment, she would have given all her wealth to have recalled her words.

But her pride she could not, would not, sacrifice. Matters must take their course.

She darkened the room, locked the door and partly opened one of the shutters, to watch the progressive steps in her daughter's departure, each one of which seemed more terrible than its predecessor.

Why, there is Fred on a horse galloping down the lane, and he turns towards the city, while Marian, all dressed, is going over towards the barn.

She opens the great checkered doors and enters through a cloud of dust. In a few moments Mr. Halford comes out and is making towards the house, but Marian overtakes him and holds him by the sleeve. Now she has her arm around him and is talking earnestly, while he is expostulating.

Finally, she triumphs, and he enters the stable. " Heavens! he have gone to hitch up," groaned Mrs. Halford, at her window. But she seemed helpless to stay the fatal step.

Marian ran over to the meadows to see her cows, to take a last look at their peaceful faces. At the sound of her voice the animals started towards her, some running and frolicking, others walking sedately.

She jumped over the fence to meet them, and busied herself patting their heads. Bella, her pet, crowded up and licked her hands. The gentleness of the poor brutes started her grief afresh. She leaned against the fence, weeping freely, while the cattle, not understanding her unusual actions, looked on in silent wonder.

Then the fowls greeted her as she crossed the barnyard. The hens, ducks and geese all flocked about her, and some of her pet chickens flew up on her shoulders.

What delight she always took in feeding them. Each one of all that flock was like a personal acquaintance. Now she was feeding them for the last time.

" My God! murmured her mother, " the animals all love her. It are truly wonderful."

Suddenly Nelly makes her appearance, dressed in her very best.

What could this mean? Was Nelly going too?

No, there is Mr. Halford with the small buggy that only carries two. He is going to take Marian, but where?

There is a fresh outburst of grief between the two sisters as the father straps a large valise on behind the vehicle.

Now they are started down the lane, Nelly walking alongside, covering her sister's hand with tears and kisses. Finally, they start at a rapid pace citywards, leaving Nelly sobbing at the gate. Clouds of dust and clumps of trees hide them occasionally from sight, but when they reach the top of the little hill Marian waves her handkerchief as a last farewell, and her heartbroken sister drops in a heap on the grass.

Mrs. Halford stifled a groan, and started pacing the room. She longed to go into the fresh air to relieve this choking feeling, but she was afraid to meet Nelly. She crept quietly up to her own room, where she would be out of reach.

When she looked out again Nelly had gone from the gate, and all was still. What could it all mean? Where was Marian going?

The baker's waggon came up the lane, and her daughter (for she had only one now) ran out to get the usual complement of bread. This was a load off her mind. It meant that Nelly was going to get supper for the men.

But where was Fred all this time? Had her baby boy deserted her too? She watched the road wearily for the first sign of his return.

At last he came cantering up from the city and, as soon as he reached the yard, he slid off the horse's back with boy-like agility, and called loudly to his sister. His cap was pulled down over his eyes and his face was swollen with weeping.

As twilight comes on, Fred goes down to the gate repeatedly, and is evidently watching for some one. It cannot be for his father, because he is looking in the opposite direction.

Ha, there is a vehicle coming at great speed from the west. Fred runs out into the road.

"What! That looks like Gordon's beast," said Mrs. Halford to herself. " No, this are dark coloured. It looks like the rolling gait and trim ears. Ha, yes, it are Gordon."

The horse, black with dust and perspiration, goes to turn in at the gate. Fred stops him and Gordon jumps out.

Together, they pull the long grass at the roadside, and commence rubbing the animal down, talking excitedly all the while.

A moment later Fred runs to the house and hurries back with Nelly, who is carrying an umbrella and some wraps.

Then, and not till then, did Mrs. Halford understand it all. They would be married at once. Marian had wired Gordon and was probably waiting for him at the parsonage.

The rumbling of distant thunder and the signs of an approaching storm seemed to be in keeping with the condition of her feelings.

Humbled and outwitted, despised and deserted, she threw herself down on her bed and groaned with the anguish of self-accusation.

CHAPTER XIX.

THE HONEYMOON.

ONE of the most popular delusions of either ancient or modern times is that the honeymoon is the happiest portion of married life. It may be so in some instances, but as a rule it is surely the most trying period of our existence.

Presupposing that love and intelligence are prominent on both sides, it seems impossible for two people with any great force of character to have their lives so closely bound together, without temporary and recurrent explosions of temper or temperament.

We must become attuned to each other, like the instruments of an orchestra, before harmony is produced.

Occasionally the process of adaptation may require only a few months, but oftener it takes years, and sometimes a lifetime.

Ignorance in this, as in every other phase of life, is the greatest enemy of happiness. In the majority of marriages, two young, thoughtless creatures are thrown together, without their having the faintest idea of their proper sexual and social relations, or without their having stopped to think of the responsibilities they are about to incur.

Owing to the prudishness which regards sexology as an unmentionable subject, they are left in ignorance of the laws of nature, and those principles of self-abnegation which must always be the foundation of happy homes.

With all our education and religious training, can we not feel, in the evening of our lives, that we are just becoming fit to live; fit to be husbands and wives, fathers and mothers? Indeed, we are fortunate if then we have weathered the storm of passion, and arrived safely in a sheltered spot where we are at peace with ourselves and the world at large.

It is generally presumed, that if a pair truly love each other all difficulties will disappear, and all storms will be weathered. Fortunately for humanity, this seems to be true to a large extent, but marriages of convenience are as frequent as ever.

There is no sign that we are about to be emancipated from the slavery in which tender maidens and beautiful women are practically bought and sold. Is not the reception room of to-day simply a refinement of the ancient slave market, and beneath all the glitter and gloss of title or wealth, is it not just as hideous?

It is true that in many of these cases there is more than the average intelligence, but this cannot take the place of that mental and physical affinity which we call love.

The reader who has become acquainted with our young couple will feel confident, that even if the bride does not have the affection for the bridegroom which she might have, that their united honesty of purpose and high self-respect will steer them clear of the shoals which wreck many lives.

Both were proud and passionate, but on the one hand was his ardent love, and on the other that universal sympathy and benevolence which under favourable conditions grows with contact, and makes the wife more of a lover at forty than in the first flush of her bridal days.

She, herself, had precipitated the marriage and he had gladly accepted the situation, in spite of her declaration to him before the ceremony took place.

"David, a short time ago, in jest, I asked you to be my husband, but now I ask you in earnest. I have told you that my love for you lacks in something, I know not what; but I love you sufficiently to place my future in your hands. I feel that I shall grow to love you more and more. But do not take this step without consideration. I know that *you* love me fondly, truly, but to the extent that this has been brought about by extraneous circumstances which should have no consideration in sacred matters of this kind, to that extent I may wrong you and myself."

"Darling," he replied, "I know you do not wear your heart upon your sleeve, but I also know that you love me enough to marry me for my own sake, and not for a home. Not another word, dear. You are showering happiness upon me. I shall feel that you are all my own. It seems too good to be true," and taking her in his arms, he gazed at her fondly and whispered in her ear, "My own dear wife."

To her dying day, Marian would never forget the scene enacted at the parsonage. The stuffy little study with its pictures and hangings, the lurid glare of the red hanging-lamp, the ticking of the mantel-clock, her father's trembling hand, Nelly's pale face and Fred's sobs were stamped upon her memory with letters of fire.

Once the thunder rumbled so fiercely that the clergyman was forced to suspend the ceremony till it had passed.

Then came the wait at the station for the ten o'clock

train. A great wave of fear swept over her as it came thundering in, and the hour had arrived for separating the ties of a lifetime.

How they wept and clung to her as she mounted the car steps, while poor Fred shoved his " bank " into her ulster pocket. When the coaches began to move the boy ran along the platform, shouting, that he would bring Bella and the guinea hen too. Her last look from the window showed him standing on the end of the platform, sobbing as if his heart would break.

David took tickets for Boston, first because they had no time to form any particular plans, and secondly because he had important business there.

She had no trousseau and he wore his every day suit of Halifax tweed. But Boston was the place to supply this deficiency, and David vowed they would never go home looking like a runaway couple from Gretna Green.

Every woman takes a pleasure in adorning herself, and Marian was no exception to the rule. It is at once the privilege and duty of the sex; as natural as for the bird to preen its wings.

When dressmakers and milliners had finished their task, and she blazed forth in all her beauty, he exclaimed, " Good heavens, Marian, what a beautiful woman you are. It makes me almost afraid of you !"

" If that is the case, I shall go and take them off. It *does* seem almost too grand for me; besides it is awfully extravagant."

" Nonsense, dear ! When we have a beautiful picture, a masterpiece, we do not begrudge a suitable frame. You were certainly intended for a duchess, and you shall always dress well as long as I can afford it."

In their round of pleasure seeking and sight seeing, she had scarcely time to analyze her feelings.

David was all kindness and attention. He added fondness to love, and love to duty, till she felt at times that he was tiresome.

But she always had a means of escape from emotionalism by introducing some topic for discussion,

Then his company became a wholesome pleasure. Oftentimes, she had a "good cry" when she was alone, but she never allowed him to see her in this mood, for he did everything that mortal man could do to entertain and amuse her. She could not seem to strike a balance in her sentiments. Sometimes she was quite happy, and at other times the most miserable creature on earth.

But every day his step became more familiar, his face more handsome, his voice more musical, and his caress more welcome. She felt that her affection for him was growing rapidly.

Their holiday was just becoming enjoyable. Besides being lovers, they were now comrades, and all barriers of reserve had vanished in the light of mutual confidence, when a peculiar and unlooked-for incident destroyed the harmony and peace in her heart, and brought their stay in Boston to a sudden termination.

On the second Sunday after they became husband and wife, she induced him to go to church. Already they had one or two friendly discussions on religious topics, and Marian, feeling that her husband had some wrong impressions of the average service, wished to have him see and hear for himself.

Since his boyhood he had never entered a church door, and he seemed to have forgotten that the church had made some progress in that time.

The day was intensely hot, so Marian chose the nearest Anglican church. To David it was a matter of indifference. They were all the same to him.

It was a novel experience, however, and as they seated themselves, she smiled at his embarrassed appearance. He sat bolt upright in his seat, and did not know what to do with his hands. Occasionally a deep sigh or long drawn breath betokened his uneasiness.

She, herself, felt nervous and distraught, for what reason she could not tell. She was half inclined to ask David to go somewhere else. The air seemed stifling. It was a beautiful and commodious edifice, and, though the attendance was not large, yet the ventilation might be at fault.

The eloquent Mr. Cosgrove was away on his holidays, and his substitute must be rather disappointing, she thought, since the congregation was so small. She was about to nudge David on the elbow and propose going elsewhere, when suddenly her eyes fell upon the pulpit. For a moment the church span round like a top. Her heart stood still. There, before her eyes, with his pink cheeks and fair curly hair, was Charles Langtry, her girlhood lover. In his hands was the very prayer book she gave him when they plighted their troth. Excepting his surplice, he looked just as she had seen him in her dream the previous night.

She dreamt that they were rambling through the woods at Broadview as of yore. They came to a little bank where the daisies grew. He plucked her one, but as he gave it to her it stained her hands with blood. She awoke in a dreadful fright, and the memory of it had haunted her all day.

She grasped David's hand and it seemed to fortify her, but she looked around, and longed for some excuse to make her escape. Thank God, the reverend gentleman had not seen her. But, somehow, she felt that he would, nor could she refrain from occasional glimpses at him.

When he arose to commence the services she looked up, and their eyes met. They seemed to look into each other's souls. All the memories of the past were crowded into a moment. She clung to her husband as a drowning man would to a straw, her face turning white as marble. The Rev. Mr. Langtry, with a look that ever afterwards haunted her, staggered back and sank into his chair.

For a time she scarcely knew what transpired, but when her senses came back the churchwardens were holding a whispered consultation, while the pastor sat with his face buried in his hands.

Finally one of them came forward, and announced that the afternoon services would be postponed, as the reverend gentleman was prostrated by the heat.

That evening she told David tearfully that she was tired of sight-seeing and that she wished to go home,

"Very well, dear, just as you say," and he sent the following telegram to his mother :

"Home Tuesday, four o'clock. Send hack to station. All's well."

CHAPTER XX.

THE HOME COMING.

THOSE who wish to have their vices ventilated need only run for office or get married. Over our graves the world will pronounce eulogies and benedictions, and even ascribe to us virtues we never possessed.

"*De mortuis nil nisi bonum,*" is no doubt a very good axiom, but if it could be reversed so as to read, "of the living speak nothing but good," the sum of human happiness would surely be increased.

Once let it be known that you have chosen your mate for the voyage of life, and your dear neighbours immediately apply their magnifying glasses to your shortcomings.

But the good people of Gowanstone had not been fairly treated.

Concurrently with Gordon's baseball fame, came the news of his engagement, as announced in the Levisville papers.

His victory of the "diamond" raised him greatly in the estimation of the sterner sex, but his success in "hearts" made him very unpopular with the ladies.

The mothers of marriageable daughters were up in arms at Gordon's slighting the home market. They would have evenings and leave him out in the cold; and the young ladies themselves would cut him dead.

Silent contempt was to be his portion all round from the fair sex, but behold, he had gone and got married before they had an opportunity of inflicting upon him the punishment he so richly deserved. Mrs. Grundy had not only been defied, but she had been cheated out of the time-honoured privilege of unearthing some scandal about the bride.

Gordon had never had even the decency to announce his marriage, but left people to find it out for themselves.

The news of its having been a runaway match, and whispers of a quarrel with the mother, were the only crumbs of comfort to be had out of the affair, and these were picked over as critically as cakes at a picnic.

"Elopements are out-of date. They are low and vulgar," said Mrs. Mills, the banker's wife.

"I shan't call on her," protested the judge's better half.

"Nor I," said another.

"She is said to be the most beautiful woman in the State," remarked Mrs. Ainsley, who was too old to be jealous, but not too old to amuse herself at the expense of her companions.

"Who says that?" demanded Mrs. Baker, the sheriff's angelic spouse.

"Sydney Dillon, no less," was the authoritative reply.

"Sydney is getting altogether too impertinent," snapped Mrs. Carroll, whose pink cheeks had for years been a mark of envy. "I don't see why he should be any better judge than any one else. He only pretends to be."

"Yes, but people all believe that he is, just the same," retorted Mrs. Ainsley.

"I don't believe he ever said it," broke in Mrs. Baker defiantly.

"Thank you, Mrs. Baker; let me compliment you on your politeness. I am trying to be truthful in my old age, and you are becoming polite. One is never too old to learn. Sydney, however, told me himself."

Sydney Dillon was the Beau Brummel of Gowanstone. He was the great local authority on all questions pertaining to the rules and usages of society. No criticisms were genuine without his signature; very few had the temerity to differ with him, on questions of taste.

He was clerk of the registry office, and only a young man. Nobody knew how he came to be recognized as the pet patrician of the town, but there he was, and from his lofty eminence none could dislodge him. His verdict was,

"Gordon is a lucky fellow. The old lady will come round all right. They always do. Besides, she is worth running away with herself."

When the telegram announcing the bride and groom's arrival came to Mrs. Gordon, Sen., the news spread through the town like wild-fire, for the telegraph operator was a young lady.,

Next afternoon, when the Pacific express came thundering into Gowanstone, the platform was crowded with townspeople, who happened to have business at the station.

The predominance of ladies who expected parcels off the train was truly astonishing, and each one pretended to be surprised when they heard that the young couple were on the incoming train.

Of course, they would have a look at the bride, now that they were here; but it was a matter of no consequence.

When David saw, through the car window, the crowd which had collected on the platform, his cheek turned pale with excitement. He knew enough of human nature in general, and of Gowanstone in particular, to expect a great deal of adverse criticism.

But one look at his wife brought back his usual confidence. "Raise your veil, Marian," he whispered, "you needn't be afraid to let them look at you. Just wait till you see me do the honours."

Something in the subdued murmur and the expression on the faces of the crowd, as they alighted on the platform, told Gordon that his wife had scored a decided success.

She had wonderful self-possession. Her smile, as she looked about her, was entirely free from embarrassment, and her careless, graceful attitude, as she waited for David to give his orders to the porter, gave the impression that she was accustomed to admiration and homage.

Spiteful femininity saw at a glance the futility of trying to belittle such beauty of face and form. The criticisms became comments.

With the most slavish assiduity did David guide her footsteps to the carriage, and hand her in. Had she been a princess and he a page, he could not have been a more devoted attendant. This was all the more noticeable when the onlookers knew that Gordon was usually very reserved and undemonstrative.

To cap the climax, just before leaving he arose in his seat, and lifting his hat, said : " I thank you all for this mark of respect to Mrs. Gordon and myself," and throwing a handing of small silver among the juveniles, they drove off in triumph.

"I didn't know you were such an actor, David. You made them all stare. You shall have a dozen kisses for your diplomacy."

"Who wouldn't be brave for a woman like you? I'd go through it all ten times over for that reward," he replied, looking at her with fondness and admiration.

She pinched his arm. "Be careful of your manner now, as we go through the town. Sit up straight, and not too close. We might as well finish the act," and she laughed gaily.

The hackman, no doubt with a desire to show off his fares, went out of his way to go down the main street.

"You bow and nod to your acquaintances in the usual way," she whispered, without turning her head, "and I shall try to look as though I were admiring the street and the buildings, without seeing the people."

"Not quite so stiff and formal," she murmured, as he raised his shining silk hat to some one on the street. "Don't look quite so serious. There, that is splendid."

Everybody in town seemed to be on the street. It was almost like a fair. But Marian looked about her with easy indifference and appeared to be rather amused than otherwise.

At last they reached the house, and as they stopped at the neat, brick cottage, she felt instinctively that she would like her new home.

THE HOME COMING.

The greeting which David's mother gave her was the brightest spot in her home coming.

The old lady was almost frightened as she gazed at the beautiful stranger, but when the young wife smiled kindly, her heart went out to her at once. At a glance they seemed to read each other's souls, and in a moment they were in each other's arms, kissing and laughing through their tears.

Holding her at arm's length, the old lady scanned her carefully with a serious look. " Ye're as bonnie a bride, lassie, as ever graced a guid man's hame, but I'm feart ye're ower gran' for puir folk like me and Davie. I hae na muckle tae hansel yer hame-comin', but I'se gae ye ma blessin'."

David here caught his mother in his arms, and swung her gleefully around him.

" Toots, the laddie's daft. De ye ken, lassie, he gied me a sweeng like that the nicht ye gied him yer tryst. He's been clean gyte aboot ye, an aye tellin' me hoo bonnie and guid ye were."

Gordon took hold of his mother's ears and threatened to pull them if she told tales on him, while Marian smiled indulgently and fondly on them both.

" He used tae like his auld mither the best, but I'm feart ma neb is oot of jint the noo. Aye, aye. And so you came doon the main street. I'se warrant a wheen o' them wad be gae gleg at finin' faut wi' yer dress or yer bonnet."

" Don't you remember the song, mother," interposed Gordon :

> "It wasna the bonnet,
> But the heid that was in it
> Gar'd a' the folk talk
> O' Rob Rarison's bonnet.'

" That's the first time I ever heard him speak Scotch," said Marian, addressing the old lady. " I love the accent, it sounds so honest. You'll have to teach me, mother," she continued, taking the old lady's hand in hers.

The word, mother, brought the tears to Mrs. Gordon's eyes.

' Weel, I'll jist ca' ye Merran, as if ye were ma ain dochter," replied the mother, kissing her. "But come awa' ben the hoose. I'm keepin' ye here when ye're baith tired and hunger't."

"Come awa', come awa'. Toom stomachs make cauld hearts."

CHAPTER XXI.

A VACANT CHAIR.

IT is an old saying, that we learn most from our mistakes. Failure has always been more instructive than success.

The reader will not wonder that Mrs. Halford's quarrel with her daughter left her a sadder and a wiser woman.

The ordeal through which she had passed was an unusually painful one, and it had taken the sharp edges off the salient points of her character.

Not only had she to face her own conscience, but to quail before the accusing looks of her husband and remaining children. Since that memorable day William had never been the same to her. She fretted and grieved over the possibility of losing his love, and mourned the absence of his kisses which were as dear to her as ever.

The gap at Broadview was almost indescribable. The atmosphere of home had vanished. Their dwelling for a time became simply a lodging-house.

From the milk-pans in the kitchen to the cattle in the fields, everything about the place seemed to cry out "for a touch of the vanished hand, and a sound of the voice that was still."

For some days after Marian had gone the gloom was almost unbearable. Indeed, had she been laid away in her grave she could not have been mourned for more deeply.

For the first time in her life, Mrs. Halford questioned herself.

Had she really done her duty to her daughter in early life? Her error in allowing Marian's intimacy with young Langtry to go too far was not remedied by their separation. Indeed, she was not now certain whether it were not the greater mistake of the two.

She was forced to confess to herself, that in severing the youthful ties, her motives were based on self-interest, and not on her daughter's welfare. It was pride and ambition which made her stoop to questionable methods in keeping them apart and not any real unfitness on Charley's part.

Deep down in her heart she felt that she was not only responsible for her own error, but she had probably driven her daughter into a graver one.

She would rather have seen her daughter the wife of Charles Langtry than in her present position, for she had a firm impression that Marian's love for him was not dead.

Mrs. Halford was a woman who had religious confidence in the laws of nature. In fact, without knowing it, nature was her God.

Her religion partook largely of the physical. It was directed principally to bodily welfare, and no one was more conscientiously devout.

None of her family had ever suffered from a single day's illness, and she had very little respect for doctors or drugs. Indeed, she regarded sickness as a sin, for those who treated their bodies properly, had, she thought, no cause to be ill.

With her, good health was religion, and strength was piety. A mother who fed her children on dainties, neglected to see that they were properly clad, or allowed her daughter to lace too tightly, was the unholiest of sinners, even though she attended prayer meeting three times a week.

Her neighbour's wife might instil into her children the principles of virtue and morality, she might be loving, gentle and kind, but if she neglected dry stockings, clean flannels or the bath-tub, she was a heretic of the worst type.

Following out this physical line of reasoning, there was one feature of her daughter's intimacy with young Langtry which kept coming up before her.

Marian's face and form had developed astonishing beauty at that time, in fact, she had seemed like a rose bursting into bloom. She remembered that her daughter had grown more shapely, and that she had become more sensible and woman-like. It looked as if Marian's physical nature required an early marriage, and if so, was not the young man her proper mate.

Had she taken grave liberties with nature's laws, and assumed an unholy responsibility? Judging by herself, and the powerful affinity she had for her husband after their love had been supplemented by physical union, she believed that the tie between Charles Langtry and her daughter was one which nothing but death could destroy. Their union was surely based on the laws of nature. " Whom God hath joined together, let no man put asunder," was a passage which gave her many qualms of conscience.

Marian's absence threw a lot of additional responsibilities on her shoulders. Nelly had neither the strength nor the skill to fill the vacant place in the dairy, and skilled help had to be employed. She was forced to take up her housekeeping again. Every day revealed to her something she had forgotten. It was like the unravelling of many tangled threads, she neither knew where to begin, nor where to leave off.

Then the dealers commenced to complain of her butter. They said it was falling off in quality and losing its delicacy of flavour. Day after day, it was the same story.

She discharged her butter maker, and undertook it herself. She scrubbed and cleaned everything within reach. She inquired into the feeding of the cows, and bade Watson be on the lookout for weeds of any kind, but all in vain.

The dealers at last refused it, and the day that Watson brought home the rejected butter was a black day for Mrs. Halford.

For nearly a quarter of a century her stamp (a sheaf

of wheat), had never been changed. During that time it had been a mark of purity and worth.

Other brands might be as good, but *it* had the reputation, and many of the retailers would have no other.

Time had brought many changes, but Broadview butter had always been queen of the market. In fact, it was the corner stone on which the estate had been founded, and to-day it was disgraced forever.

What could have gone wrong? Mrs. Halford had made good butter for many a year, and why not now? She did everything in her power to discover the source of the trouble, but without success.

Fred and Nelly were dumfounded. Watson shook his head, and Martha Briggs declared it was bewitched. They all felt helpless in the presence of the mystery.

What could Mrs. Halford do? There was no creamery within reach, and the milk market in Levisville was already over supplied.

She must sell off her cows. There was nothing else for it. But this meant a great sacrifice, for cattle were below par in price, her appliances would go for half nothing, and her whole system of farming would have to be changed. It was wantonly throwing money away. She was certain that by applying to her absent daughter, the mystery would be solved, but to do that she would have to sacrifice her pride, and that was even dearer to her than her money.

The night that followed the rejection of the butter found her walking the floor for hours, and when she sought her pillow she had arrived at no decision.

Retribution was overtaking her already. One cow had died, a valuable horse had broken its leg, and the butter had been rejected, all in the short space of two weeks.

In sending her daughter away Mrs. Halford seemed to have struck a blow at her own prosperity.

Just what she would have done, it is impossible to say, but next morning Nelly took the matter in her own hands, by asking for a week's trial of the dairy.

"Well, Nelly, it are only fair you should have a chance. It are really strange how it have baffled me. If you can make it succeed, it shall be worth your while."

She little dreamt that at that very moment Nelly had in her pocket a letter of advice from Marian, or that Fred, with a sample of the rejected butter, had made a night visit to Gowanstone to consult her. The letter ran as follows:

"DEAR NELLY:—You can imagine my surprise to-night when we were roused long after midnight by a hammering at the door, more especially as we just got home this very evening.

"When David, who went to the door, told me it was Fred, I got a terrible fright, for I thought something very serious had happened. Indeed, for that matter, it is serious enough, and I can imagine how mother felt when the butter came back.

"Fred and his chum are just eating a lunch, and they wish to get away as soon as possible, so I will confine myself to the matter in hand.

"You can be sure of one thing, that the trouble is not due to anything tainting the butter, or to any uncleanliness, for mother would attend to that.

"The flavour suggests to me either that the cream is being ripened too long, or that there is too large a proportion of old milk.

"If my taste was in its usual form I think I could tell, but you know I am two weeks out of practice. Besides, the best time to taste butter is just before dinner, when you are hungry. I have always found my taste keener then, and by practising you will, no doubt, have a like experience.

"Fred tells me that Winkle is dead, Daisy has been sold for kicking, and Curly has gone dry. These were all extra milkers, so I can see just how the trouble has arisen.

"He tells me that mother waits till the creamers are full, just as I did. But don't you see the conditions are different, for not only are three good milkers cut off, but the yield of milk per cow is at least a third less during this dry, hot weather.

"Consequently, it takes so much longer to fill the creamers, and the cream gets too ripe. The more I study it over the more certain I am that this is the principal trouble.

"Churn every other day, just as I did. Get father to buy you two fresh cows, and until then leave out the milk of two old ones.

"Then, I see the butter lacks in texture; it is too brittle. That means not enough working. Don't work it too much or it will go off in flavour, but give it, say, one-third more.

"If, as Fred says (and no doubt he is correct), everything else is absolutely as I left it, then go ahead without fear of failure.

"You are a brave little girl, Nelly. Don't be afraid. There is no element of chance in butter-making, and if your system is correct you will succeed as sure as sunrise. Fred is nagging me, so good-bye till Sunday, when I expect you all. Tell father I will have some apple dumplings and some kisses for him.

"Your loving sister,
"MARIAN."

"P. S. Fred promises to write me about the butter to-morrow night. Don't change the brand. Its good name cannot be worn out yet.

"Stick to it, you dear little brick, and you will soon redeem the good name of the 'Sheaf of Wheat.'"

CHAPTER XXII.

MOTLEY AND MONARCH.

"COME up this evening, Gordon, I have a treat in store for you," said Doctor Bennet one day as he came running into the mill. "I have picked up a half-crazy professor of phrenology, whom you will be delighted with. He has some odd ideas on theology, and I have invited Jamieson to make a background for the conversation." He smiled, and rubbed his left arm in anticipation of a pleasant evening.

"Stag party, you know. Small and early. Just the four of us. We'll have dinner at eight."

"I shall only be too glad to meet anyone with original ideas on any subject. Is it the old gent with the short trowsers and the white plug hat who has been distributing pamphlets around town?"

"The very man," replied the doctor. "He is as crazy as a loon on some points, and a perfect giant on others. His principal phantasy is that he has the only proper theory of the earth's formation. He goes deeply into astronomy and geology with a gusto that is really refreshing."

David looked smilingly at his friend's expressive face, and asked how he had picked him up.

"Oh, by the merest chance. I heard him spouting in Carrol's drug store the other night. I took him up to the house, and after an hour or two spent in discussion I became quite infatuated with him. Do you know," and here the speaker's voice dropped to a confidential whisper, "I believe I have at last found a living example of the *dual existence* theory," and his eyes flashed with animation.

"Like a school boy over a new toy," said Gordon laughingly. "Well, I'll come and see this prodigy of yours. Men are your books, doctor."

"Yes, and the best ones," he replied as he turned on his heel and was off in a twinkling.

A few days previous, one of the millers met with an accident to his foot, and to-day Gordon was taking his place. Besides attending to his own duties, he was obliged to handle sacks and wait on customers. He was busy at work, when a shadow in the door-way attracted his attention and caused him to look up. Behold, it was the professor himself, with a bundle of pamphlets under his arm.

David could scarcely refrain from smiling at the stranger's grotesque appearance. His clothes were worn threadbare, and his hat was such a one as might adorn a habitué of the race-course. His fingers and soiled shirt-front fairly glistened with cheap jewelry, and his necktie was of a decidedly violent colour and pattern. His waistcoat, which was not ample enough for his increasing corpulency, was left unbuttoned at the bottom, his trowsers scarcely reached his ankle below, and there was a distinct line of separation between them and his vest at the top. This, with an exaggerated Prince Albert coat fairly glistening with wear, completed a make-up which the street gamins christened the "cartoon."

David would have laughed outright, only that something in the man's face prevented him. There was an indefinite expression in his large, steadfast eyes, which made it impossible for you to tell whether he was looking at you, or away past you in a fit of abstraction. A more perfectly shaped head David had never seen, but the lips were thick, the mouth too prominent, and the heavy, grey mustache made it appear to protrude still further. He was a man of apparently fifty odd years, and although his hair was almost white, he still had a vigourous and robust appearance. He was tall and well built, excepting that he was inclined to corpulency.

Waiting till Gordon had finished tying a sack, the professor raised his hat and bowed, displaying at the same time a bald, shining crown.

"Let me introduce myself," he said. "I'm Professor Senger, a professor of phrenology. I have here a twenty-page pamphlet on that subject; the most complete ever written. Tells you how to choose a profession, wife or habitation. Really, sir, you can't afford to be without it. Only twenty-five cents."

"No, thanks," replied David. "I am too busy for anything of that kind to-day."

"Well, sir, I'll make you a present of it. I am endeavouring to bring my ideas before the public. Why, sir, our whole educational system is wrong, root and branch. The present system begins at the wrong end. Instead of developing the young mind, it actually stunts growth. But they won't take time to read my works, though I *boil* them down till there is not a waste word in them. Well, it will be *their* loss. They can't say that Senger did not give them a chance. Why, sir, I spent my last shilling on this pamphlet, entitled,

'Senger's System of Education,' and right here in this town of intelligent people I have only sold one copy."

David seated himself on a sack and pointed to the work around him.

"Ah, work, eh. Well, the time is coming when those who have work will be considered fortunate. Labor will have to go a begging before long. Here's a pamphlet, called 'Labour and Capital,' a magnificent treatise in small bulk. Just the thing for this age of displaced labour. Only twenty-five cents."

Gordon was going to send his visitor to the right about, when it struck him that probably the man was in want, so he took out some money and paid for the pamphlet.

The transformation that came over the professor's face was good to see. It was as if winter's gloom had passed into summer sunshine.

David watched him for a moment, and then asked him his price for one of each.

The professor fumbled excitedly in his pocket for a pencil, and after some figuring exclaimed, "Why, sir, I'll give you the whole series for one dollar and twenty cents, a great bargain."

David handed him one-twenty-five, and told him to keep the change.

"No, sir, thank you all the same, but exactness is the first principle of honesty, and any departure from that principle is dangerous." As the stranger ran out to get the change, David looked over his list of purchases. "Mind and Matter," "Problem of Life," "Phrenological Synopsis," "What is Life?" "Senger's Hypothesis of Sound," and half a dozen others on like subjects.

When the professor came back, and the change was properly made, he shook Gordon warmly by the hand. "I don't mind telling you, sir, that I am fond of a good dinner, and now I have the wherewithal to procure it. I shall also be able to purchase some paper and pens for my afternoon's work."

The eagerness and joy in his face as he spoke fully repaid David, apart entirely from the pamphlets.

"What time is it, please?"

"Ten minutes to twelve."

"Ah, then, I shall go," he exclaimed eagerly. "Fate cannot harm me, I shall dine to-day. Excuse the warped quotation, sir, Good bye and thank you." With the air of a Chesterfield he backed through the door, and then ran towards the hotel with the eagerness of a hungry boy.

"A strange creature, truly," thought David. "He has the air of a gentleman, and the attire of a jockey."

The pamphlets were as strange as their author. Above the chaos of the writer's thoughts were flights of genius. In the same paragraph with childishness and charlatanism were visions of the infinite; glimpses of the eternal. He seemed to have a tremendous grasp of large problems, and none at all of small ones. His thoughts seemed to be a confused procession of prizes and blanks. The pamphlets seemed to remind David that gold is often buried mountains deep, or mingled with the slime of rivers.

"Truly Dryden was right when he said:

"'Great wits are sure to madness near allied,
And thin partitions do their bounds divide.'

"Surely nature makes mistakes as well as mortals, else why such waste of talent, why such 'sweet bells jangled out of tune'?

"Why is light wasted, while humanity suffers in semi-darkness, and why are diamonds given to demons to trample under foot?

"What good can a man like Senger do to his fellowmen? None whatever. Life is only a breath between the cradle and the grave.

"All is vanity and vexation of spirit."

CHAPTER XXIII.

AN EVENING AT THE DOCTOR'S.

When Mr. Jamieson and David arrived at the doctor's that night, the professor had not yet put in an appearance, and the host was very uneasy. "There's two things I am afraid of, either that he won't come at all, or that it may be the fool instead of the philosopher who does come. But we will just have to take our chances on it."

About half an hour after the appointed time, the door bell rang, and the doctor with a smile of satisfaction on his face, admitted his guest. But the professor was so changed that David scarcely recognized him. A heavy grey wig had taken the place of his shining baldness. His linen was spotless, his ample coat of broadcloth had a rose in his buttonhole, his jewelry had disappeared, his flashy necktie had given place to one of plain black, and his countenance had an entirely different expression.

Who says that the tailor does not make the man? or that the quality of our clothing does not react on our characters? Nearly any man can respect himself in a full-dress suit. Even Swelldom has its virtues.

What surprised David still further, was that Senger did not seem to recognize him, for when the host went through the form of introducing the professor to his guests he bowed to David as to a perfect stranger.

The doctor's eyes fairly sparkled with delight when he saw the puzzled look in Gordon's face, and he gave him a nod which meant, I told you so.

Very soon dinner was announced, and the professor humbly apologized for keeping them waiting. When they took their places at the table, the host placed Mr. Senger where the light would fall on his face, while he seated himself directly opposite.

From every day common-places the doctor brought

AN EVENING AT THE DOCTOR'S.

the conversation round to the desired topic, by telling the professor that he was in a nest of freethinkers.

"Good," he exclaimed, "it is the only atmosphere that intelligent people can enjoy."

"Glad to hear you are one of us," said Jamieson, "we infidels here catch it pretty severely sometimes."

The phrenologist slightly elevated his eyebrows, as he swallowed a mouthful of soup, but vouchsafed no reply.

"Perhaps Mr. Senger is not an atheist, like yourself, nor even an agnostic. He may be a Christian," interposed the host.

"How in the name of conscience, doctor, can a man be a Christian and a freethinker at the same time," queried Jamieson.

The professor looked up for a moment. "Agnostics and atheists are not always freethinkers; indeed, the most bigoted man I ever met was an atheist."

"How do you make that out?" demanded the iron-founder, considerably ruffled.

Mr. Senger shook his head. "Bigotry and narrowness are qualities of mind independent entirely of religious beliefs. The orthodox bigot regards the agnostic as an inferior animal, while he on the other hand regards all church-goers either as fools or hypocrites."

"Are you a Christian, then?" asked David, speaking for the first time.

"I try to be," replied the professor with a smile, "but I doubt whether I shall ever succeed. I'm afraid that to be a real good Christian we must start a generation or two ahead. It is hard enough now-a-days to find a man who loves his neighbour enough to help him along, let alone one who would sacrifice everything for his fellowmen."

This reply checked the conversation, and for a time there was silence. Disgust and disappointment were so apparent in Jamieson's face that David bent over his plate to hide a smile.

But the host would not allow the proceedings to lag, so he set the ball rolling again by asking Mr. Senger what he thought of agnosticism.

With a placid smile, the professor replied that it was a logical position as far as theology was concerned. "But," he added, with a doubtful shake of his head, "very illogical as far as religion is concerned."

This was too much for the iron-founder, who immediately exploded. "What's the use of talking such d——d rot, Mr. Senger? Just as if theology and religion were not one and the same thing."

The doctor rubbed his arm with delight, at seeing the debate waxing warm, but the professor only coloured at the vehemence of the last speaker, and seemed inclined to drop the discussion.

"Would you mind explaining the distinction between the two," said David, who was now very much interested. "I only ask for information."

The professor laid down his knife and fork, and held up his left hand in front of him, with his fingers extended.

"Religion, I take it, is composed of the fundamental truths, principles, and sentiments of human life," and he closed his first finger. "Theology is a theoretical explanation of the unknown, founded on superstition, and varied by race, conditions, and climate." The second finger closed. "Religion is founded on truths we know. Theology is a guess at what we don't know."

The fingers were all closed now, and his explanation seemed to be ended, but he went on. "We know that truth is good, and love is good; that faith and hope are helpful to ourselves, and that charity is a boon to our less fortunate fellow men. Man knows these things by experience, hence these tested truths are the foundation stones of religion."

"Yes, but how do you apply your original statement as to agnosticism?" asked David.

"Oh, very easily. To be agnostic towards what is unknowable or incomprehensible is at once candid and honest. In fact, to that extent we are all agnostics; but to claim ignorance in the face of facts and truths is surely downright prejudice. No man who in his childhood ever sat upon his mother's knee, who ever felt her tears and kisses on his cheek, or nestled in her warm unselfish bosom, can consistently be agnostic towards a religion based on love and self-sacrifice."

This touch of eloquence probed them all in a tender spot, especially Gordon, and their hearts unconsciously applauded while their lips were silent.

"How does that argument apply to Christianity?" queried the doctor, who only spoke when the conversation lagged, and was much more intent on watching his guest than the discussion.

Mr. Senger looked at his host in mild astonishment. "Why, the life of Christ was an embodiment of the eternal principles of religion."

Mr. Jamieson here broke in. "Yes, but Christ may have only been a myth. There was Christna, Buddha, Confucius, and all the rest of them. Why, the world has had a host of Saviours."

The professor frowned and looked steadily into the iron-founder's face.

"We have as much evidence of the existence of Christ, as we have of Julius Cæsar, or Charlemagne, so we may lay that point aside. You say the world has had other saviours. What then? Supposing you were poor and in want, and the Doctor should come to you with ten dollars; then after a while Mr. Gordon should come with fifteen; and after a still longer period, when you were in suffering and misery, I should come with fifty, would the last half hundred be any the less useful? Is the electric light any the less a boon to mankind because a tallow candle cheered the homes of our forefathers, or does it prove that they were imbeciles for using the best light they had? Because the religion of one age crystallized in Brahma, and another in Buddha, each does not disprove the other. Each, in itself, furnishes us with the most overwhelming evidence that religion is as eternal as the stars, and that, through all the ages there were god-like spirits who shot out of the darkness and ignorance with messages of love and truth for mankind."

By this time the others had finished eating, but the professor was still as busy as ever, plying his knife and fork, and they out of courtesy pretended to eat as well.

"What is your opinion of the Trinity? Do you regard Christ as the son of God?"

"Yes, let us hear how you explain anything so ridiculous as one in three and three in one. Let us hear how you get around that," demanded Jamieson.

The professor smiled patiently, although he was getting tired of being cross-questioned. "It is very simple. It is only the phraseology that is misleading. I do not regard Christ as the son of God in the sense that you or I might have a son, but in the sense that he was a personification of the attributes of God. Perhaps I myself am wrong, but that is how it appears to me. You know we are getting into theology," he added with a smile.

"What about the Holy Ghost?" protested Jamieson in sarcastic tones. "Perhaps you believe in ghosts too?"

Mr. Senger hesitated a moment, scarcely knowing whether to laugh or get angry, but with a wave of his hand he went on, as before.

"I don't really like the word, ghost. It conveys a wrong impression to many. It produces a sort of mental confusion. If you will kindly allow me to read in its place, Holy Spirit, or to further simplify matters by construing the word, holy, into such words as high, pure, and noble, the meaning may be more apparent. No one who reads the life of Christ can doubt that his mother was imbued with the highest, noblest and most perfect sentiments, from the time of his conception to the time of his birth. The doctor here can readily understand that."

"Upon my word," exclaimed David, "you are hard to corner! Your Christianity is the most simple, and most reasonable I have yet heard of, but perhaps you are taking great liberties with orthodoxy."

"Perhaps so," replied Mr. Senger. "I have no guide but my own conscience, no authority but the Bible, and no light but a deep seated love and reverence for Christ. Very likely, however, some of our learned divines might regard me as a heretic, though I feel assured that if Christ were on earth to-day, he would not, excepting in the sense that I am not able to live up to my own ideals."

"Let us hear your opinion of the pentateuch next," said the doctor, "and then we'll change the subject," for he saw that his guest was being wearied.

The professor shook his head. "I shall not attempt to defend or explain the cosmos of the various nations of the earth, not even that of the Hebrews."

"I don't see how you can claim to be a Christian, when you don't believe in the Old Testament," roared Jamieson, bringing his fist down on the table with a bang that set the dishes rattling.

Mr. Senger elevated his eyebrows and smiled faintly. "It is not a question of believing or disbelieving. I read the Old Testament, as I might read Buckle's History of Civilization.

"We learn the methods, manners, and morals of a truly wonderful people; the most enlightened people at that time on the face of the earth; indeed, there are a hundred things which, even in this progressive age, we might admire and copy. Why, to read and understand the Bible is an education in itself. It is like an inexhaustible spring; the larger the vessel we take to it, the more we carry away. There are times when my understanding is clearer than at others, and I often find the most wonderful depths in apparently simple passages. You must remember, Mr. Jamieson, that any translated work loses half its beauty and force in the translation. Fortunately, I learned to read Hebrew from a Rabbi (who, by the way, was the most intelligent, broadest, most benevolent and most charitable man I ever had the good fortune to meet), and the Bible is always my best companion and friend."

The doctor now rose from the table, and they all adjourned to the library, where the wines and cigars were handed about. The professor politely declined both, explaining that a man who ate so heartily as he did had no use for stimulants.

His eye fell upon a beautifully illuminated copy of Omar Khyam's Rubairyat, which he picked up and commenced thumbing over.

The rest smoked on in silence, each waiting for the

other to speak. Finally the doctor asked Mr. Senger if he were an admirer of the Persian Astronomer Poet.

"Yes, I am an ardent admirer of his masterly style, and yet not a follower. He is certainly one of the best exponents of his particular school of thought."

"What is that?" asked David, who had not read it.

"Oh, eat, drink and be merry, for to-morrow we die."

"And is that not good philosophy?" inquired the doctor.

"No, it is very faulty. No philosophy based on selfishness can ever be good for humanity. True happiness can never come to the man who lives only for himself. Indeed, he who lives only for the gratification of his senses, treads a path that can only lead to satiety and ennui, misery and suffering. The man of pleasures is the man of pains.

"Happiness," continued the professor, "must consist of something more than relates to ourselves. Our lives must reach over into those of others and be influenced by them. We must maintain our interest in the affairs of every day life, and keep a spot in our hearts, fresh and green, where our sympathies and emotions never grow cold. Our purest and most lasting joy is in giving joy to others, in throwing the sunshine of sympathy across their paths. The last two verses of this magnificent poem condemn its philosophy——

> "'Yon rising moon that looks for us again
> How oft hereafter she will wax and wane;
> How oft hereafter rising look for us
> Through this same garden and for one in vain.
>
> And when like her, O Saki, you shall pass
> Among the guests star scattered on the grass,
> And in your blissful errand reach the spot
> Where I made one, Turn down an empty glass.'"

Soon after reading these lines the professor passed his hand over his forehead and yawned heavily. He closed his eyes, and sat for a few moments as if fast asleep. Indeed, they thought he was asleep, when suddenly he arose and looked hurriedly about him.

"I think, gentlemen, I shall go home. I have some writing to do in the morning, a twenty-four page pamphlet on the chemistry of light. Splendid thing. Explodes all other theories. Good night."

As he was about to open the door, the doctor grasped his hand, and under the pretense of shaking it, drew him where the light shone full in his face. When the door closed behind him, the host came back to his remaining guests in transports of delight.

"Splendid specimen, truly wonderful! His pupils changed in a few moments. Yes, even the cornea deepened in colour. An entirely distinct cerebral current."

"What do we know about corneas and pupils, doctor? That's all Greek to us," exclaimed Gordon. "Why, it is ten o'clock. We must be going too."

"Your professor is only fit for a lunatic asylum," protested Jamieson. "The man is crazy."

"There's method in his madness though," observed David. "I wouldn't mind having another night with him."

"You can have him all, for me," growled the ironfounder. "He's neither fish, flesh, nor good red herring."

When they were leaving, the doctor whispered in Gordon's ear that they would have the professor another evening all to themselves.

But, alas, they were doomed to disappointment, for the doctor, with a heart-broken look, came into the mill next day with the news that the professor had suddenly disappeared.

CHAPTER XXIV.

A BROKEN PANE.

MANY couples claim to have gone through life without a harsh word, without a single cloud to mar the sunshine of their married life. Others again admit having quarrelled in order to enjoy the process of making it up, and to bring flashes of tenderness from the dull monotony of everyday life.

The great majority of husbands and wives, however, find that storms, great or small, come in the ordinary course of events. If each quarrel brings with it a lesson or a moral, if it succeeds in stamping some new truth upon our minds, in giving us further insight into each other's characters, or into our own, then these matrimonial disturbances may be said to have some redeeming features.

Marian was coming home from a shopping expedition one afternoon, when just at the corner, opposite the mill, was a strolling violin player. The fellow had a forlorn look about him that appealed to her sympathy. He was evidently an Italian, from his swarthy complexion, and his age might have been anywhere between twenty and thirty. His clothes were worn and shabby, but neither dirty nor ragged. He was very delicate and sickly-looking, but there was something refined about his general appearance. While she was approaching, he was playing the "*Miserere*" from "Trovatore," and, in spite of the crowd of loafers which surrounded him, she stopped to listen to the beautiful plaintive tones which spoke to her heart.

The instrument seemed to be a living, breathing thing, which told, with throbbing heart, its tale of sorrow.

Surely, she thought, such human emotions, hopes, tears and smiles, must come from wood which had felt the throb of life.

When the musician saw the lady listening, he seemed

to feel the inspiration of her presence. His head dropped to one side, his eyes instinctively closed, and leaning against the brick wall, he poured forth his soul in sound.

He selects another theme. Slowly he commences. The deep soft "purple hum" of his base string lays a background, and with a rising inflection spreads it out, till a few staccato notes, in the upper register, draws an outline between earth and sky. Gowanstone vanishes like magic, and in its place are green fields and shady woods, while here and there, in rippling tones, comes a stream. A few fortissimo notes clear the sky and show the brilliant glare of noonday sun, while the rapid, swinging bow strikes out in bold relief the trunk and branches of a tree, which little whispering slurs bedeck with foliage. Hush! the voice is changed. There's something living coming now, which is approached with care and caution. It is a human form, asleep under the tree. A toil-worn, rugged face, pinched with poverty, marked with grief and care, a face which might be taken to represent the toiling millions of to-day. From calm and placid sleep the face changes and becomes radiant with joy. The sleeper dreams. His little hut beyond the hills becomes magnified into a mansion beautified with vines and flowers. His rags are turned to robes, and the very air is roseate with joy, when suddenly the double stops cruelly throw a glare of sunlight on the sleeper's face, and his dream of joy is over. Again he is a peasant whose heritage is care and toil.

The loafers ceased their jokes, and wondered what it was that made them feel so sad. What weird magic was in that slender wrist and trembling fingers, which made them ashamed of their coarseness?

Marian was weeping softly while he played, and as soon as he had finished, she stepped forward and emptied her purse into his hand.

"Come with me, please. Come to my house and play for me." The fiddler put his instrument in its bag, and grasped a crutch behind him. "What! are you lame? Poor fellow! Well, here, lean on me. Let me carry your violin." In a few moments she was walking arm in arm up the main street with a tramp fiddler.

Poor Marian forgot that the world was looking on, forgot that David's office was just across the street. She did not notice the fashionable Mrs. Mills and the spiteful Mrs. Baker driving past in their carriages. She did not see the jeering looks, or hear the smothered laughs of her neighbours. Indeed, in her flood of sympathy, her very individuality was swept away, and she scarcely knew who or where she was.

She took him home to play for Mrs. Gordon the old Scotch airs she loved so well. She gave him food, and was about to give him wine when he refused it, explaining sadly, that not only had liquor cost him his position, but had been the cause of the accident through which his leg had been broken. She took his name and gave him her address, telling him to write her when in trouble, and, if possible, visit her again.

To this little drama, however, there was a painful sequel, for David from his office window had seen his wife defying all the proprieties, and standing weeping in a crowd of loafers. Then to see her going up the street, carrying the greasy fiddle-bag, and supporting the low fellow's arm, was enough to make a saint swear. When he saw the people on the street making fun of her, he fairly ground his teeth with rage.

"It is nothing but damned gawkishness. Anybody else would know better. By God, I don't know how she could make herself so ridiculous. It will be the talk of the town."

Not knowing the depths of his wife's nature, he could not understand such barefaced, downright defiance of Mrs. Grundy. He was in a terrible temper all afternoon, and he felt that it would not be good for him to meet his wife. She had touched him in a tender spot. He could not bear to have his pride humbled. To make matters worse, one of the bins burst and wasted a quantity of wheat, while by the carelessness of one of his men, a valuable machine was broken. When he came in to supper, he was in a very explosive frame of mind, but he waited till his wife had laid the dishes away, before he commenced.

"What in the name of common decency, made you stand at the corner this afternoon, like a gipsy among a crowd of loafers?"

Marian turned pale, and replied faintly, that she did not know she had done anything wrong.

"I did not say you did anything wrong, but I do say it was d—d foolish." Mrs. Baker and Mrs. Mills will make you the laughing-stock of the town."

She was so unconscious of wrong-doing, and his rebuke was so unexpected, that she knew not what to say. She sank into a chair with a look of pain and wonder in her face. The fact that his wife did not reply made David still worse. He paced the floor like a caged lion.

"You acted like a tomboy, all through," he continued, "chumming with a greasy low tramp." Still no reply, no excuse, or no apology, and still his temper was getting hotter. He would make her speak. He would cut her to the quick.

"By heavens, I won't have such work. If you have no regard for yourself, you've got to have for me. Do you hear? I won't have such loutishness."

She was roused at last. With flaming eyes and burning cheeks she drew herself up to her full height, and stood facing him.

"David Gordon, you are a ruffian and a rowdy to bully me like this. A tyrant is always a coward. Have you no heart? Is there no music in your soul to sweep away your vain and sordid self? Are you but a mass of flesh and bones whose spirit never rises past its common wants? Look you, sir. I had rather be the muddiest piece of clay deep in the waters of some stagnant pool marked with the trail of slimy reptiles, than be a living, conscious creature who never felt the mingling of the soul with all the elements of earth and sky. I'd rather be the dead limb of a tree whose neighbouring branches would bud and blossom to cover up my ugliness."

David was completely overwhelmed both by her radiant beauty and her unconscious eloquence. She seemed to have risen above the common clay in majesty and power.

A glimpse into the wonderful depths of her nature awed him with its vastness. Before he had time to speak she left the room. He listened to her footsteps as she ascended the stairs, and he noticed that she did not go to the apartment they usually occupied, but to a private chamber.

She had scarcely gone when old Mrs. Gordon, who lived in separate apartments, came in with a look of reproach on her face. "Davie, yer door was open, and I couldna help hearin' ye baith. Man, but ye hae the clink o' yer feyther's tongue, and many a sair heart I had wi't.

"Merrian, puir thing, her heart is ower big for yae body. The music, Davie, was far past common. I gar'd myself believe I saw the heather hills, and wee bit neucks and braes where often on a simmer's nicht, I dauner't wi ma lad. Aye, and the burnie pirling doon the glen, where wiles us lassies wat oor feet when comin' frae the schule. Yon woman, Davie, is far ayont you or me. Ye maun guide her wi' a gentle haun.

"Noo, awa' up the stair and make it up wi' her. Dinna aye be wondering what this ane or that ane will say. I wadna' gae her sic a sair heart for a' the fo'k in Gowanstone."

To the old lady's surprise David broke down and wept. "I must look small in her eyes, mother. She will never think the same of me again."

His mother looked at him tenderly. She caressed his head against her bosom, and almost choked herself to suppress her own tears. "Oh, laddie," she said, sorrowfully, "I'm feart ye sharp tongue 'ill gae ye mony a sair heart, as weel as her. It was the only faut yer puir feyther had afore ye."

"She'll never think anything of me again."

"Toots, mon, ye ken little aboot a woman's heart. I looed yer feyther nane the less for a' his fauts. We hae mair patience wi' men's fauts than they has wi' oors. Rin awa', noo, and tak ma blessin' wi' ye. If she daes gae ye a bit cut wi' the tongue, keep mind ye deserve it."

"Marian, I have come to apologize," said David, entering the room where his wife lay, apparently half asleep on her bed. "Won't you forgive me?"

"Leave the room now, I wish to be alone."

"But, Marian, wait till I explain."

"No," she replied, "you thought I was a tomboy, and I thought you were a gentleman. We were both mistaken. The ruffians, it seems, were not all on the corner. Those were only the ones who wear no disguise."

David jumped to his feet. "Marian, I have offered you my apology and you refuse even to listen to it. I will make amends suitable and proportionate to the occasion, but I give you fair warning that not even for you shall I cringe or crawl. I am ashamed of my temper. I am sorry for the injustice I have done you. I always told you I had an abominable temper which prompts me to say things I am afterwards sorry for. I deeply regret that for a time I forgot what was due to you as a lady, as my wife. If this will suffice, here is my hand. If not I shall be inclined to believe that you never have loved me." There was a ring of defiance in his tones as he walked over to the bed and held out his hand, but she neither moved nor looked towards him. "Very well," he continued, and was about to leave the room, when his mother entered.

She did not speak a word, but took her son by the hand and led him to his knees at his wife's bedside. There was a sacredness in her presence which overawed them both, and the big tears which ran down her cheek made them forget their quarrel. Marian's beautiful snowy bosom was partly uncovered, and the old lady placed her son's head upon his wife's beating heart.

Gently she took Marian's arm and placed it round his neck, then without speaking a word she closed the door behind her, and left them sobbing in each other's arms.

CHAPTER XXV.

MARIAN'S DEBUT.

The estimate which the world places upon us depends largely upon ourselves. It is not what we are, but what we appear to be, that is the basis of society's valuation. A man with very ordinary talents, who is high in self-esteem, is almost certain to outshine his competitor who has more ability and less assurance. One of the many things we are apt to take on trust is our fellow-creatures. Gravity is successfully used to cover ignorance. Those who look wise and say nothing get credit for knowing a great deal more than they do. Self-confidence is even better than gravity. How can we expect our neighbours to have confidence in us, if we do not have it in ourselves?

Marian made up her mind that there should be no more quarrels with her husband for lack of observing the proprieties, or standing on her dignity. She saw that he was anxious to have her recognized by those who were considered the aristocrats of the town and she adopted a new attitude towards them.

When she met these luminaries, she wore an air of calm, dignified superiority. She did not affect that retaliating expression which is so often spitefully overdone in circumstances of this kind. Her face and figure gave her wonderful advantages in a warfare of this nature, and her careless way of looking right past them without seeming to notice them was terribly aggravating to her adversaries.

Mrs. Baker had tried to fasten upon her the appellation of the "barnyard beauty," but lately she had revised her nickname and Mrs. Gordon was now "the Sphinx," because she took no notice of them. This went on for some time until they became piqued at her silence, and considered it a distinction to be noticed by her, the more so as it was one which very few enjoyed.

Her first conquests were Sydney Dillon and Mrs. Ainsley. Having gone this far, victory was in her own hands. Before long, Mrs. Baker was glad to get an answering bow from her. Everybody got the impression that Mrs. Gordon considered Gowanstone society not good enough for her, and though they protested that she was no better than any one else, yet they had a dim impression that she might be, after all.

A trifling incident one day made her triumph complete. Mr. Dally, cashier of the First National Bank of Levisville, drove over to see David on business, bringing with him his wife. She was well known in Gowanstone, and was supposed to have more than the usual supply of blue blood in her veins. She had been a school friend of Marian, and now paid her a visit to renew her acquaintance. When Mrs. Dally learned the social position of the Gordons she exclaimed:

"Dear me, what impudence! Why, your mother could buy out the whole lot of them. Just wait, we'll fix them. Mr. Dally, you know, has the strongest political pull in the State. Just watch how quickly they will come to time. Have you got a little carriage of your own? You have. Good! You drive me around while I make flying calls on a few of them. You shall sit in the buggy, and when they invite me to stay I shall tell them I am spending the day with my old friend, Marian. By the way, what a lovely parasol you have. Just lend it to me and they will think we have one alike," continued the little woman, laughing merrily. "They'll come to time, the boobies. I'll wager a pair of gloves they will all call in a week."

Mrs. Dally proved a true prophet, for the procession of callers commenced the very next day. One had been suffering from a cold, another had been detained by company, and still another had been from home. Each and every one had an excuse to offer for not having called before, expressed the hope that Mrs. Gordon would not stand on ceremony, and begged her to call any time.

David was vain enough to be pleased with this new

turn of events, not that he cared a pin for the pleasures of society, but he wanted such recognition as would satisfy his pride. Soon after this he brought home a card of invitation to a ball at Jamieson's. He and his wife were to be publicly admitted within the charmed circle of the upper ten. Not, indeed, that the iron-founder was the real *crème de la crème* himself. He was a member under protest, as it were, who had purchased his way in ; but there he was, nevertheless, and there he was likely to remain as long as his purse held out.

Of course it was to be a swell affair. That went without saying. Everybody was expected to be in full dress. David was not at all displeased at this feature, for he had the elegant outfit with which the mayor of Levisville had decorated him on the evening of his baseball victory, and then he would have an opportunity of showing off his wife.

"Just wait, Marian, till they see your neck and shoulders—oh, you may pooh, pooh, and claim that it is only my imagination, but I tell you that they are just heavenly. You are afraid to go that way? Ashamed? Pshaw! Why, half of them will look like anatomical specimens. You'll feel comfortable enough when you see them, excepting that they will give you gruesome visions of the skull and cross-bones order. They can dress and dress ; they can exhaust all the artistic skill on earth, but none of them can match nature's adornments."

From the time of its announcement till the affair came off, Jamieson's ball was the talk of the town, especially amongst the fair sex. The little flutter of excitement which preceded it was a boon to the dressmakers.

The iron founder's gatherings were always on a large scale. He had the biggest rooms, the most brilliant chandeliers, the most elaborate decorations in town, and his *menu* was more delicate and expensive than that of any of the others.

His decorations were always on too gorgeous a scale, according to Sydney Dillon's opinion, but Jamieson did not recognize his censorship. To that extent he was a social rebel.

To offset this, however, he generally secured, by hook or crook, some social or political lion as a leading attraction. These gatherings, though strong in numbers, were supposed to be somewhat "leaky" in quality; people from the common herd were invariably present. He actually, on one occasion, invited his foremen mechanics; and at another time the whole assembly was poisoned by the presence of a servant girl. The omnivorousness of Jamieson's social tastes was always a sort of bugaboo, but people became accustomed to his democratic notions and suffered in silence.

That night, before going out, David called his mother to look at his wife before putting on her cloak and wraps. For some moments the old lady did not speak. Then, shaking her head doubtfully, she said: "Merrian, lass, I'm feart it's no richt tae let fok glower at yer bonnie neck and shoulthers. It canna be richt tae mak men forget their ain wives. Fashion was surely invented by the deil."

"I'll put on another waist, then, mother, if you say so."

"Indeed you won't," David protested. "If you do, we will stay at home. If we can't go like others, we shan't go at all."

"Toots, lassie, dinna heed an auld body like me. The worl' is ower far ahead o' ma time noo. Deed, I like tae look at ye mysel'. Awa' ye go, and mind ye dinna get yer death o' cauld."

Before they reached the house they could hear the strains of the band crashing through the open windows. Here again custom had taught Jamieson's guests to prepare for an ordeal which they not only suffered without protest, but often feebly applauded for appearance sake.

He always procured for the occasion the best orchestra which money could obtain, but in order to still further outshine his social rivals, his own brass band must be on hand, to open the proceedings and give to the affair a certain amount of military éclat. The shining steel helmets, glistening brass instruments, and scarlet-faced uniforms of fifty men, had a picturesque effect upon the assembly, which was practically out of the reach of his competitors. But in spite of all his vanities, Jamieson was a hail fellow. He liked to go about extracting approbation from one and all, but he gave good value in return, and whenever a fresh consignment of popularity was purchased, he always paid the highest price. He was generous to a fault, and generally took pleasure by giving it to others. Therein lay the great secret of his success as a host; the reason why his evenings were the most successful of any. His soldierly attention to the smallest details left nothing undone, consequently his programme of proceedings went on with a smoothness which was the envy and wonder of the town. The doctor always maintained that Jamieson had missed his calling. He should have been a field-marshal.

When Marian entered the room, she was greeted with a perfect hum of admiration. A score of eyeglasses were immediately brought into play.

In a few moments the gentlemen, young and old, were raving about her, while the ladies were pale with envy. It was no use trying to belittle her any longer. The wisest of her envious rivals tacitly acknowledged their defeat with good grace. They determined to be friendly with her.

Her eyes! Her hair! Her mouth and her smile; then such a figure and such a bust! Why, they were fit for a goddess!

Judges, senators and congressmen jostled each other in securing an introduction, while Sydney Dillon was heard whispering to a friend that she made all the other ladies in the room look small or wrinkled.

Marian had never been at a social gathering of this kind in her life. She had no experience to guide her. At first, she felt a slight inward trembling as the cool air came in contact with her bare arms, but when she saw scores of others, whose nakedness was far more extravagant than her own, she recovered her self-possession.

At the seminary she had taken lessons in deportment, but had quite forgotten them.

"I shall just be natural; be myself. I shall act just as I do at home. Why should dress make any difference? Besides, I cannot be pent up with stiff conventionalties. I could not breathe in an atmosphere of artificiality. If I have the instincts of a lady, I shall not need any veneering, and if I have not, the varnish will only make vulgarity more vulgar. I shall not try to palm off cheap etiquette for good breeding, nor polished ignorance for intellectual culture. I am not very sure of myself at best, but whether I be patrician or plebeian, pretense will not help me."

Without knowing it Marian stumbled on the very first principle of good breeding. Her manner on this occasion was pronounced by Sydney Dillon to be perfect, though she violated the proprieties by giving him two dances.

David was also a novice, but he had self-confidence enough to carry him through. Indeed, his mother always maintained that he had "a kenin owre muckle o' Hielan' pride in him."

There were none of the guests who enjoyed the proceedings more thoroughly than did Dr. Bennet. He sat at the far end of the room, smiling and nodding to all, inwardly delighted with the fine variety of specimens.

There was Mr. Halton—the druggist, rather amusing, always happy, perfectly satisfied with himself. If he broke one leg, he would pat himself on the back, because he had been clever enough to save the other.

Sheriff Baker—clean slate, whitewash, as the ball players call it.

Mrs. Baker—fine head for a burglar. Dying with envy and hating everybody. Grand specimen. Should have been a hangman.

Judge McKim—all wool, but not quite the yard wide. Mrs. McKim—dear little kitten with extra claws.

Congressman Bates—born anarchist; down with everything that's up.

Mr. Shefford—indifferent banker. Rascal himself,

and thinks everybody else is. Believes in nothing but Mr. Shefford. Too much caution for a criminal, and too little courage for a detective. Splendid gambler for small stakes.

David Gordon—egotistical, narrow and conscientious. Make good preacher.

Mrs. Gordon—" Ha! that's her, eh. Heard a good deal about her, but never saw her."

His eyes gleamed and he fidgetted in his chair. He took a pinch of snuff and wiped his glasses.

"Great specimen, genus homo, feminine gender. Under lip a trifle heavy, fond of eating, fond of pleasure and of the opposite sex. Fine mother for big men."

Just then she happened to turn her face towards him with a smile upon it. "Wheew! wild pitch! Try again! Great frontal development, both breadth and depth. But the eyes; yes, and the whole face. Humph! a puzzle."

He rubbed his left arm; helped himself to another pinch of snuff, and for a time never took his eyes off her face.

But she was not allowed to sit long, for her card was nearly filled. The doctor himself was so captivated that he asked her to sit out a dance with him. He drew her into conversation, and watched her as closely as decency would permit, but in the end he was as far from a solution as ever.

His usual methods of analysis had failed. "Strange combination. Wonderfully magnetic. Could feel it myself. Felt as if I wanted to sit on her knee and kiss her. Humph! confound it, she has deflected my mental compass."

These were the reflections of Dr. Bennet on his way home that night. "I'll cipher her out yet," he said as he savagely dug his umbrella into the sidewalk, " but I shall try it at long range after this."

CHAPTER XXVI.

PURER LIGHT.

There was one thing which had recently become a cloud on Marian's happiness and a rebuke to her conscience.

The summer had again come and gone. More than a year had passed away since the memorable scene in the parlour at Broadview, yet her mother had sent no token of forgiveness.

Nelly, Fred and her father were constant bi-weekly visitors and they never came empty-handed, but the something she longed for never came.

None of them ever mentioned Marian's name in her mother's presence for fear of creating further disturbance, and, often as they had been over, Mrs. Halford had never asked after her daughter's health.

Marian longed for a reconciliation, but as she had been ordered from home with maledictions on her head, she thought it was her mother's duty to make the first advances.

But the insult which had been hissed into her ear was the hardest blow of all. Whenever she thought of it her cheek flushed with shame. The secret which she thought buried forever was no secret at all. Her mother had known it all these years. Why, then, had she not kept it to herself.

As she looked back over the past Marian saw through the whole situation. She understood why the Langtrys had been sold out, and why she was sent to Montreal. She even guessed that her mother had intercepted her letters.

Well, it was all over now, and perhaps it was all for the best. One thing of which she was glad was that, on the memorable day of the quarrel, she had said nothing disrespectful to her mother, consequently, she had no harsh words for which to apologize. The feeling that justice was on her side had heretofore satisfied her, but within the past few months her inward consciousness told her that her duty lay beyond the line of justice into the realms of charity and forgiveness. When her father, brother and sister visited her, when they were seated round her board she often said to herself, "Poor mother, how lonesome she must be! Her life must be a joyless one."

Her natural tendency towards benevolence was probably increased by the knowledge that she was soon to become a mother.

"God knows, perhaps I shall need some day the indulgence and forgiveness of the child unborn.

"Twenty odd years ago mother probably felt as I do now. I'll go and write this very minute. I'll never let the sun go down on my wrath again. Poor mother can hardly write her name, but she will answer somehow."

Now that she had made up her mind to do it she was all eagerness and haste.

She ran into the old lady's rooms and almost frightened her with her impetuousness.

"Losh, Merran, ye gied me a gliff. I thought there was something wrang. Are ye weel enuch!" she continued in a confidential tone of voice as she scanned her critically. "Yer een are rid wi' greetin'."

"Yes, but they are wholesome tears," replied the young wife. "I'm going to write home to mother and ask her to come and see me. Will it be right?" The old lady wiped the moisture from her eyes.

"Ah, Merran lass, the wee thing has open't yer een. Yes, write to yer mither, puir body. Put awa a' yer pride, and gang tae her as ye wad hae yer bairn come tae yersel some day. We mauna judge ane anither ower sair. We canna haud up our heids and say that ane's black and I'm white, when we're a' taured wi' the yae stick. It disna dae for fo'k that bide in gless hooses tae cast stanes, an' I'm thinkin yae body's hoose canna lauch at anithers in that respec'. Aye, aye, make a clean breast o' 't. There's little use carryin' aboot a pooch fu' o' stanes, when we daurna cast them."

Following out the old lady's advice she wrote as follows:

"DEAR MOTHER:—After our long estrangement, I scarcely know how to begin this letter, but now that I am writing, I wonder that I never did so before. For months past I have been longing to see you and, just to-day, not many minutes ago, I made up my mind to ask your forgiveness. Let me confess that, for a time, I harboured thoughts of revenge and retaliation. Your cruel words stung me to the quick, but I know you did not mean it when you called me "light skirt." You only said it in a temper. I have often said and done things in a temper that I was sorry for a moment afterwards. It was hard to have you think ill of me; to have you think I was unworthy of being your daughter. You know I was young, warm blooded and full of imagination; and I had not learnt the lesson of controlling my passions. You will believe that for a time I tried to do right, young as I was. Surrounded by temptation in the form of music, moonlight, and lack of restraint, I might even then have succeeded, but that I had to resist myself as well as him.

"Well, it is all over now, and I only refer to it so as not to leave a single cloud between us, and when we meet again we may look into each other's eyes. You will be glad to know that, so far, my married life has been a happy one. Whatever faults my husband may have, he is a good, moral man, and I am glad to know that the father of my child is clean and pure in thought. A strange feeling came over me to-day. I felt as if I wanted to lay my head on your breast and have a good cry. I know you must have felt like this before I was born. Something seemed to tell me that I had never loved you as I ought to. David's mother, the dear old soul, told me to tell you everything, so you will not laugh when I tell you that I took a great longing for that custard you used to make. I tried to make some to-day, but it hadn't the right flavour. It seems silly to mention it, but I dreamt last night that I ate a whole bowlful, and I have been thinking about it all day. You can send the recipe with Fred on Sunday. Couldn't you come over yourself soon? I know you will come when I am sick, won't you, mother?

"I know you don't like writing, but you can answer me somehow, so that I will know your heart is still warm for

"Your repentant daughter,
MARIAN."

"The letter must be posted immediately. This is Thursday and I will get a reply on Saturday. Oh, dear, it seems long to wait. I shall register it, so that no one will get it but herself. I feel better now," and she gave a great sigh of relief.

Nothing seems more conducive to happiness than a noble duty, nobly done. In a short time Marian was at her piano singing the "Crookiet Bawbee" for David's mother. She was so cheerful that evening that her husband remarked it as soon as he entered the door.

"I wrote home to mother to-day asking her forgiveness."

David was completely thunderstruck. He threw his hat on the table and stood looking at her in astonishment. "For God's sake, Marian, have you gone crazy? How could you be such a hypocrite, when you know you had nothing to apologize for. I detest even *mock* humility."

This was too much for poor Marian. She fairly ran from the room in a torrent of weeping.

David saw that he had been too severe. He followed her and caught her in his arms.

"Forgive me now and kiss me. Oh, but you must. Now again. There, now sit down here on my knee and tell me all about it."

He took his handkerchief and wiped her face and eyes.

"My tongue is too sharp, darling. Mother says it 'clinks like airn.'"

Marian looked up triumphantly. "Well, mother said I should write, so now! And I am sure she ought to know better than you."

"Oh, she should, should she? Ha, ha, ha! Well, I'll give up trying to understand women after this, but I suppose you coaxed her into siding with you?"

Marian was touched at this insinuation, and made an effort to free herself.

"Oh, no, you don't get away like that. Here, now, another kiss. That's right. Now, darling, you know as well as I do that you had nothing to apologize for. Your mother simply drove you out."

"Yes, but, David, I can see that I never loved mother as I ought to."

"What on earth has that got to do with it? She repudiated all guardianship and control over you, and how, in the name of common sense, can any one think you did wrong in acting for yourself? I'll stand up for justice at all times, but no humbleness for me. I always detested Uriah Heep."

Marian was really vexed now, but David only held her the tighter. "I hope you don't compare me with him. It's mean of you to insinuate such things. I never cringed or crawled to anybody. Let me go or I will strike you."

"I really wish you would," he said with a laugh. "Here," and he held out his cheek. Smack! "Here's the other now," and she treated it in the same way, but followed it up with a kiss, and broke down crying.

"It's mean of you to tease me like this when you know I am so peevish and childish. Because I act like a baby you needn't treat me like one."

"Now, dear, if you cry I'll get cross. It is the silliest thing a person can do. It was your mother's place to come to you. She acted the part of a tyrant, and let me say, right here, that no tyrant shall make a footstool of my neck, at least, not while I am alive. 'Wha sae base as be a slave?'" he quoted from the soul-stirring song of "Scots wha hae."

"Don't talk too harshly about mother or you and I shall quarrel."

"You may be sure, Marian, I shall tell the truth, even at that risk. A spade is a spade. Your apology to your mother has not my approval."

She sprang to her feet and walked across the floor

without speaking, but David continued, "Right is right and wrong is wrong. No one can make it otherwise."

Marian was roused now. "You talk of right and wrong as if they were sacks of wheat. What I may think right, you may think wrong, and vice versa. Who is to be judge? How can you set yourself up as an arbiter? Are you not human like the rest of us?"

He made as if to answer, but she went on. "The first thing a man or woman does, when they commit a misdeed, is to justify it in their own conscience. The robber, the burglar, the libertine, and the drunkard, all have a thousand excuses and conscience-salves for their misdeeds. Even Torquemada and Robespierre were moral men in their own estimation."

"A very good argument, my dear, but no sophistry will do away with conscience."

"Yes, but I have tried to show you how elastic and uncertain conscience is. Wasn't that fat fellow in Shakespeare's play an example? Falstaff, I mean, who did not know right from wrong."

David hesitated a moment. He felt that he was getting the worst of the argument, and wanted time to frame his reply. His wife had long since discovered his love of argument, and latterly, in all their little tiffs she found that an intelligent discussion was always like oil on troubled waters. Even when she worsted him, he was a thousand times better pleased than when she remained silent, for his deep sense of justice always recognized a point when it was made. He honestly felt that he was being cornered, but at last replied that there surely must be some fixed basis of right and wrong, or justice could never be meted out.

"Granted. But are there not times when we should do more than justice?" she asked.

"No," he replied. "Justice is sufficient. It is the only ship in which humanity can safely sail."

"What, then, would become of acts of kindness, love and charity? Did the mother who bore you measure her actions towards you by the iron rule of justice? Were the deeds of *Wallace*, to whom you have just referred, inspired by bare justice? Your ideas, David, are too cold. There must be something above us, on which to lean for sympathy and guidance."

"All very good, if your imagination is vivid enough. Everyone is entitled to all the comfort that can be got out of such delusions."

She came and placed her hands on his shoulders. She could scarcely find words to express her meaning. She started to speak several times, and stopped. Finally she said, "David, don't you see that if reason is all in all, if knowledge is everything, people would only be *clever*, they wouldn't be *good*?"

"Well, I will be satisfied with bare justice in this world, Marian, and I will takes chances on the next."

She shook her head. "I don't know. I would be afraid of bare justice. I would want a little charity and mercy thrown in to balance the scales for me. I know that there is lots of bad in me."

"Why, Marian, you are getting morbid. You are not going to commit highway robbery? You are not yourself to-night. Come, dear, we'll drop the subject. The tea is getting cold and I like neither cold tea nor cold love."

CHAPTER XXVII.

A TOUCH OF NATURE.

THE world is not peopled with heroes and villains, as works of fiction would have us suppose. The words good and bad, moral and immoral, are only relative when applied to individuals. In the worst desperadoes have been found the finest traits of character, and the dazzling splendour of genius is often marred by dark unsightly scars, like spots upon the sun. Every garden has its reptile and every marsh its flower. Into the lives of our greatest and best a skeleton may come, and in its chamber grim and gaunt it mocks and waits—a herald of decay. And, then, we know that virtues themselves are largely relative; that even they may turn to vice in some surroundings, while vice itself has often raised a barrier between men and their doom. Ambition has prompted high and noble deeds: it is the propelling power of progress, and yet how often has it led to crime and degradation, to the prison or the gallows. The avarice which prompts the miser to hoard his gold often stays the drunkard's downward course, and the steadfastness and perseverance which bring prosperity to the peasant may, when armed with power, turn to persecution and tyranny. Does not the cunning of the thief become the tact of the ambassador; and the daring of the highwayman, the bravery of the soldier?

May not the generous shilling sometimes supplant the just one, and would not generosity in a millionaire be extravagance in a mechanic? May not the fondness of the husband blend with the sensuality of the libertine, and is there not only a paper partition between the selfishness of thrift and theft?

But there is one virtue which stands alone apart from its surroundings and shines like an eternal star. 'Tis love, and love alone, which is a jewel in any setting, incorruptible and unchangeable. It is the sun round which all other virtues must revolve. It is the magic light which changes baser metals into gold, and turns the poison of the weed to perfume in the flower. It makes patriots of partisans, philanthopists of philosophers, and poets of pessimists. No matter where our footsteps lead, or where our lot in life may chance to fall, if we but keep our faces towards the sun 'twill all be well.

The love of wealth had turned Mrs. Halford's face from the sun. She was groping in the shadowy paths of selfishness. The tenacity of purpose which brought prosperity to Gore farm turned to tyranny at Broadview.

It is true that from her quarrel with her daughter she took a lesson never to be forgotten, but as yet she lacked the courage to turn repentance into restitution.

The pride that defied the storm of adversity refused to surrender at the call of duty. She longed to hear from her daughter, and had she been able to write fluently she would have broken the ice long ago, but she was too proud to ask any one else, or even to let them know the altered condition of her feelings towards her absent child. She had been dreaming of her lately. Somehow she expected that something was going to happen. She caught herself thinking of Marian, even in her busiest hours, and on that very afternoon when Mrs. Gordon was inscribing her message of love, the mother at Broadview sat looking fondly at her daughter's photograph and shedding tears of regret. Next morning, after breakfast, she walked over to the field where Fred was ploughing. She was very anxious to hear how matters were at Gowanstone, but how was she to manage it? She had forbidden the mention of Marian's name. Therefore, how could she consistently inquire about her? She leaned on the fence and watched her baby boy ploughing his first field.

Latterly, Fred had grown and developed with astonishing rapidity. He almost refused to go to school where boys of half his size put him to shame. He preferred on this raw November day to speed the plough. With his head to one side he was watching the folding sod that rolled from off his mould-board, and occasionally glancing towards a pole at the farther end of the field. So intent was he on his work that he did not notice his mother till she spoke.

"Well, how are it going, Fred?"

"Oh, not so bad," replied the ploughman, bringing his team to a halt and looking back over his work. "Gilpin is too keen, he won't give me time."

"I suppose it are because him don't get driving enough." (Ha, here was an opening). "Did you not have him out on Sunday?"

"Yes, I was over to Gowanstone."

"I suppose they are all well," she said, in a careless tone, as she stooped to pick up something at her feet.

Fred looked sidewise at her for a moment before answering. He was so astonished at her question that he scarcely knew whether to answer at all or not. He picked up a stone from the furrow and tossed it into the fence corner. "Mally was not very well."

"Oh," exclaimed his mother, with her face still turned away. "It are not serious, I suppose?"

"I guess not," rejoined Fred. "I heard the old lady say that she worked too much at the sewing-machine."

Mrs. Halford's face became a shade paler, but she did not speak, and Fred, thinking the conversation was ended, went on with his furrow. She stood for some time leaning against the fence. "I knew it," she said to herself. "Poor girl, her will have to face her own trouble. If I could only meet her alone us would soon be friends."

The struggle between pride and *motherly, womanly* sympathy was raging in her heart.

Deep down in the lowest strata of humanity do we find the freemasonry of motherhood. Jealousies, petty spites and neighbour's quarrels are all swept away by the larger sympathies of sex. What a wonderful leveler the reproductive function is! . There is no royal road or primrose path. The pauper's hut is equal with the palace. Dame Nature smiles at vanity and pomp and power, and in the infant's wail proclaims the brotherhood of man.

Slowly Mrs. Halford bent her steps towards the house. She could not bear the yearning feeling that came over her. She almost felt like taking her fleetest horse and starting for Gowanstone at once.

As she neared the house Nelly came running out with a letter in her hand.

"Here's a registered letter for you, mother. I'm sure I know the handwriting and it has the Gowanstone postmark on it."

"Are it not addressed to me?" she asked in breathless excitement as she greedily snatched the letter and hurried to her own room.

For an hour she sat poring over this message of love. She could not read writing very easily but Marian had taken great trouble to make it plain. She read it again and again, each time grasping a larger and fuller meaning. When she came out into

A TOUCH OF NATURE. 173

the kitchen all the bathing and rubbing of her eyes had not removed the traces of weeping.

"Anything wrong, mother?" asked Nelly with concern.

"No, dear, only I have had a letter from Marian."

"And are you friends again?" gasped the young girl with eager face and flashing eyes.

"Yes, I think us are."

In a moment Nelly was running through the fields with the glad tidings to father and Fred, while her mother prepared to go into town to do some shopping.

About eight o'clock next morning Fred drove into the yard at Gowanstone, and Marian guessed at once that her mother had sent him for some special reason. The boy came in growling that he was "near dead" with hunger, and immediately went to the cupboard to help himself.

"Did mother send me a letter, Fred?"

"No—she didn't—" he growled between the bites, "but she sent a basket. It's out—in the buggy. She had—me up—at four o'clock—this morning—to come here. Don't see what—the hurry—was about."

Without waiting for Fred's last remarks she ran to secure her prize.

"I must be alone when I open it," she said to herself. "Dear me, how my heart beats. I feel almost like choking." Seated on the edge of her bed, with the door securely locked, she waited for a moment to let her agitation subside and then ventured to lift the cover of the basket.

First a tiny wool jacket, and a pair of little booties, trimmed with pink. Laughing through her tears she went on unpacking. Next came a powder box, a puff ball and some perfume. Then a layer of dainty lace-trimmed bibs and dresses, while at the bottom, protected by folds of snow-white flannel, in a beautiful and costly porcelain bowl was a dainty dish of custard.

"This is mother's answer."

What need of ink and paper when every tiny treasure spoke with a thousand tongues?

Three days later, after a night of anxious watching

and waiting, the little stranger came and a telegram addressed to Grandma Halford announced:

"A baby boy and both doing well."

In the dusk of the evening Marian's mother came into the room, pale and trembling. She was afraid lest her daughter should be excited like herself, and had her arrival announced an hour or two before she ventured into the sickroom.

But the face in the bed, though somewhat pale, was radiant with joy. "Oh, mother, darling, you have come at last. I never loved you till now."

Mrs. Halford dropped on her knees at the bedside and covered her daughter's hands with tears and kisses. She tried to speak but could not. The sobs checked her utterance. But, with her daughter's hand upon her head, she told in tears her tale of deep repentance.

The sacred light of motherhood shed its radiance on their souls and all the ghosts of jealousy and hate were buried beneath a common sympathy.

Time in its flight turned backwards and, in a humble chamber far away, a woman pressed to her breast a babe whose image shone in the young mother's face.

A tiny hand touched the chords no skill or art could reach and mother nature sang again her grand old song.

CHAPTER XXVIII.

"UNEASY LIES THE HEAD THAT WEARS A CROWN."

It is questionable whether a woman's best and noblest qualities are brought to light before she becomes a mother. Indeed, we often find maternity changing the giggling, frivolous maiden into a grave and thoughtful woman. It would seem that this completion of her physical destiny purifies her moral atmosphere and enlarges her mental horizon. There is surely nothing in this vale of tears to equal the tender look of a mother to her babe; that wonderful, mysterious tenderness, that glorious climax of love which painters and sculptors have for ages tried to reproduce. We never seem to tire of looking at the Madonna and child. Surely the infant Christ received inspiration from the inexpressible tenderness of the mother's gaze. It was the keynote of his life, a vision of the lofty position which mankind may yet attain. Is it not sad to think that men should hold themselves aloof from each other because their worship is divided between mother and son? To reverence the love and truth which shone in the mother's face is to worship Christ, the personal embodiment of that spirit which for eighteen hundred years has sung the glorious anthem of peace on earth, good will to men.

These were the ideas that flitted through Dr. Bennet's mind from time to time, as he visited his patient. Not that Marian's general health was affected, or that she required much medical attendance, but the doctor was endeavouring under these new circumstances to solve the mystery of his very important specimen.

Soon the roses were back in her cheeks, the blue of her eyes became deeper, and the outlines of her figure more generous. She had passed from spring into summer. She became more thoughtful, and her natural pride seemed to soften down to self-respect. Then, and not till then, did the doctor complete his analysis. Another specimen labelled "A Woman," and emphasized by italics, was placed on the shelves of his memory.

David, too, was changed. His hopes and aspirations assumed a more definite shape. His motives now inspired him to wider fields of action.

He wanted to be rich. Not for the comforts and luxuries it might place within his reach (for he was a man of frugal habits), but for the sake of power and prestige. He thirsted for the approbation of his neighbours, he wanted to be a man among men.

He resolved to drop the ordinary frivolities of life,

and, looking neither to the right nor to the left, he would make his way to the top of the ladder.

Competition every year was becoming keener and profits smaller, but in spite of this he adopted a more vigourous policy.

He purchased the mill, enlarged the building, put in new machinery and trebled its grinding capacity. Everybody said that Gordon was a rising man. His credit at the bank was excellent. He acquired the reputation of being particularly fair in his dealings. Close and exact to a fraction, he would render the last cent to a customer or take it himself; yet when appealed to for help in any good cause he was more liberal than many of his neighbours. His reputation for solidity became so thoroughly established that even Jamieson was slightly jealous of his business rival. But their lights shone in different directions.

The iron-founder was fond of the glare and glitter of society, while latterly Gordon avoided it. David liked to see his wife mingling with the best people in the town, but for himself he cared little for festivities or functions of any kind. Once having established his social status, he lost all interest in that direction.

He dropped into the habit of wearing a plain grey tweed suit, summer and winter, Saturday and Sunday; indeed, he often had little tiffs with his wife on the question of dress.

"How is it, David, you are so careless now? Nothing was too good for you when you used to come to Broadview."

"Oh, yes, I suppose I was daft then, but one gets over that kind of thing as they do the measles."

"You were nicer then than you are now. I liked your daftness better than your wisdom," was her saucy reply. "I just hate that greedy old mill where you bury yourself all the time. If it wasn't for baby and grandma I should die of loneliness. Since baby came you haven't been the same, David," she continued, while the moisture gathered in her eyes, "and when mother was here you hardly ever looked near us."

"Come and sit down, Marian, till I talk to you," he replied, placing a chair beside his own.

"I have seen the time when you wouldn't have me sit any place but on your knee."

"Well, come, both of you," he said, laughing. "There, I'll give you two and Davie two. Now, dear, you know that I am doing a very large business on a comparatively small capital, and I can only get through by close financing. I am just like a rope-walker, if I take my eye off my task for a moment, I am lost."

Baby was now clutching and pulling at his hair, and Marian seemed to be paying more attention to the little darling's movements than to his conversation.

"You little tyrant, you pull too hard. Ouch!" shouted papa, while the baby laughed and crowed.

"That's right, baby, pull his hair. He's a bad boy," said the mother, coaxingly cooing to the child, while her very soul shone through her eyes.

Gordon pretended to close his eyes while baby endeavoured to pull his scalp to pieces, but through his half closed lids he secretly watched his wife's face as she chirrupped to her babe, until he was lost in admiration and forgot to go on with the conversation. He inwardly vowed that her next photo should be taken with this expression on her face, an expression which in itself was an anthem of motherhood.

She flushed with pleasure as she caught his look and pinching his ear, said, "Well, go on, I am listening."

"Well, you must not think, dear, that I have forgotten you or Davie because I am so absorbed in business. Just wait a little while until the pressure is over and I shall be a model husband. I am trying to place you and Davie beyond the reach of want. But I must go now. I have some invoicing to do yet. Don't wait up for me. Just go to bed as usual. I shall not be through before midnight."

Week after week, and month after month, it was the same story. Gordon was only visible at meal times. In fact, he was becoming a stranger in his own house.

His mother gave him many hints of his worldliness. One evening as he was hurrying back to the mill, as usual, after working hours, she caught him by the arm as he was passing through the door.

"Can you no come and sit doon a wee. Come awa' till I hae a crack wi' ye."

"Well, what is it, mother?" he asked as he hurriedly seated himself, "I haven't much time to spare."

"I am feart, laddie, that ye are drappin' the substance and 'rinnin' after the shadow. Siller 'ill no buy ye warm hearts, an when ye're auld, like me, ye'll fin' that oot."

"Yes, mother, but you have no idea how hard it is to keep *even* in the race. When I have acquired a little more capital, I shall have more time to be sociable, but it is a neck and neck race at present."

"Aye, aye," replied the old lady, "but maybe yer e'e will grow as fast as yer siller. Keep min' o' that. When yer feyther and me were marriet, we had a wee bit hoose wi a but and ben. He used to say he could rax doon the lum and lift the sneck aff the door, but it was na sae sma' as that. Weel, I'm telling ye, that we were as blythe and canty wi' a bit ingin and a tattae scone, as ye and Merrian are the day wi' a' yer fixings."

"I know that happiness does not depend upon wealth, but you know I have put my hand to the plough, and I can't turn back. You know the old saying, 'Devil take the hindmost.'"

"I'm thinkin' auld Nick 'i'll hae his e'e on mair than the hinmost," remarked his mother with a shake of her head. "Tak care he disna hae a keek at yersel."

"Why, mother, one would think by your tones you had heard from auld Clootie himself."

"Toots, mon, ye ken I dinna mean ony deil in particular, for I'm thinking whiles that there's deils in us a'; but fo'k that's ower keen o' winnin' the race, are often tempted tae trip their neebors. They'll no aye stop to dae what's richt. They hinna time."

David's eye flashed. "You cannot mean, mother, that you doubt my honesty, or that anything would ever make me forget my good name."

The old lady grasped his hand and kissed it, then with the tears glistening in her eyes, she said : "Dinna be vext wi' me, Davie. Ye tak me ower short. Ye ken I would raether see the sods happiet ower ye than hae a stain on yer guid name. I was only gien ye a bit warnin'. I've seen a guid wheen ups and doons in the worl', and fo'k that gie themselves ower tae gatherin' gear, whiles get trippiet by lookin' ower far ahead. Ye maun min', Davie, ye hae a wife and wean. Ye maun keep their hearts warm and no' let them forget ye. A guid heart is better than a braw tocher."

"Well, but I intend to have both," he replied laughing and rising from his chair. Then in a more serious tone, he went on: "You all know that I love you, and would give my life for you, if necessary."

"Hoots, mon! We dinna want yer life, we want your crack, yer joke, and yer company. Come doon off yer high horse and be ane amang us. Ye hae the brawest wife in the state, and ma certes, gif some men were in yer shoon they wad mak an idol o' her. Then the bit wean; the bonniest, cleverest wee doo I ever saw, and yet ye mak little o' them."

He was about to go when she caught him by the hand and spoke in a whisper. "You and her has had nae castin' out, hae ye?" and she looked eagerly into his face.

"Oh, no," he replied, with a reassuring smile. "Only when her mother was here it seemed as if I wanted to keep out of her way. Marian maintained that I should not be so stiff with her mother and that I ought to forgive her, but it is time enough when she asks, and I don't suppose she ever will."

"The auld woman is gae and door. She's as proud as a peacock, but losh, mon, ye need na think ony the less o' Merran on that account."

"Neither I do, but somehow the old woman was like an iceberg between us, and I was glad when she went away. She and I are like fire and water. She can't play fast and loose with me. But now I must go," he added. "I shall try to be a better boy," and kissing his mother, he went back to his ledgers.

CHAPTER XXIX.

AN OLD ACQUAINTANCE.

THE winter winds were howling round the house. The air was filled with whirling, drifting snow, and Marian, thankful for the coziness of her quarters, had just put baby to sleep when the door-bell gave several sharp rings.

"Dear me, who can be out on a day like this? I have not had time to dress yet, and baby has pulled down my hair. I suppose it is only an errand boy from the butcher's or grocer's."

But Mrs. Gordon fairly cried out with astonishment when she opened the door and found a tall, clerical-looking gentleman before her, who, with a polite bow, exclaimed: "How do you do, Mrs. Gordon."

The voice sent a wave of hot colour over her face and left her deadly pale. Even with furs about his neck, she recognized Charles Langtry.

For a moment she felt dizzy. Her knees trembled. "Oh, Charles—I mean, Mr. Langtry—where did you —I mean, won't you come in? It is very stormy."

Her visitor stepped inside, shook some snow from the fur collar of his overcoat and removed his overshoes.

During this time a thousand thoughts and fears chased each other through her mind.

Why had he come? What could his object be? Was he pursuing her?

Not knowing whether he came in the guise of friend or foe, in peace or in war, she scarcely knew how to receive him. "Come into the parlour, it is warmer there. Pray be seated, and excuse me for a moment."

Reaching the kitchen, she sat down with beating heart to compose herself. It was so sudden and unexpected. It was as if the dead past had been resurrected, or a thunder-bolt had shot out of a blue sky. His presence still affected her as it used to, and brought back a score of fond memories, for which she now must blush. She ran to the cradle, and lifting little Davie in her arms, she devoured him with kisses. The touch of his dear little body brought back her courage and strength. "Pshaw! Why should I be so excited? He is a clergyman and a gentleman. If he ignores the past, surely I can," she thought. She smoothed her hair, changed her dress, pinched her cheeks to bring back their usual colour and, with baby in her arms went back to her visitor without a trace of embarassment in her face.

"What do you think of my boy? Isn't he a fine little fellow?" she said, bouncing Davie up and down, while he dug his little fists into his eyes and frowned by way of protest for his disturbed slumbers.

"He is really a fine boy. I'm very fond of children. Will he come to me," and he reached out his arms to take him, but Davie gave vent to a decided squall and buried his face in his mother's bosom.

"Dear me," exclaimed Marian, as soon as peace was restored. "I have not asked how you all are. I was so astonished to see you."

"You have not heard then that father is dead?"

"No, I did not. Well, well! He was not an old man."

"Oh no! It was not old age that killed him, but a broken heart. He tried many ways of getting on in the world but could not succeed. We had it very hard in Boston for a while," he continued sadly. "Christina worked in a ready-made clothing establishment, and I played piano in a dime museum. My first good luck came when I got a situation in the orchestra of a respectable Opera House, and there I remained till father died."

"And how is Christina?" broke in Mrs. Gordon.

"She is quite well, thanks, and, like myself, she still sticks to the maternal roof."

"And your mother, the dear old soul?"

"Is quite well and as jolly as ever. We are living at the upper end of Water street and you must——"

"What!" exclaimed Marian. "*You* living here in Gowanstone?" And her face turned as white as marble. "When did you move here?" she continued turning aside to hide her distress.

"About a week ago. I conducted the services last Sunday at Grace Church, but mother and Christina only arrived last night. You don't go out much, I see."

"Not lately, since the weather is so rough. I did hear that Mr. Sweetnam had gone, but I had not heard who had taken his place."

"I suppose you don't go to church very often, but your people used to belong to the Anglican church."

"And do yet," replied Marian. "No doubt you have heard that my husband is an agnostic," she added with a faint ring of defiance in her tones.

"Yes, and I am sorry that it is so, more particularly as I thought to get your assistance in choir work. But I have always heard Mr. Gordon spoken of as an honourable and upright man, who is well worthy of respect."

"Even his worst enemies could not deny that," said Marian proudly, while her cheek flushed with pleasure at his praise. "But he does not interfere with my church-going. Indeed, he often asks why I don't go. I think we all have the right to think for ourselves."

"Surely, else the world would not be fit to live in. Let me apologize for a thoughtless question. I was not seeking an opportunity of talking shop, or imposing my opinions and self-righteousness upon you. I hope my calling will never make me omit the behaviour of a gentleman. Besides you and I are too old friends to quarrel, even on so important a question. I am not one of those who think that a clergyman should be a privileged bore. But," he added in a different tone, "you must come and see us now that we are neighbours. In fact, Christina charged me not to leave without your promise to come in a week, if not sooner. She would have come herself, only that she is in a perfect fever to get the house cleaned and to get settled."

"Of course I will come. Tell her to expect me the first mild day. It is getting late in the season and we shall surely have spring soon. Why, yes, I used to be a pet of Christina's and mother used to say she spoiled me. She saved me many a whipping, and I have often thought since what an ungrateful wretch I was. I often scratched her face, and do you remember the day of the school picnic, when I tore her new muslin dress in a fit of temper and mother sent me to bed?"

Mr. Langtry joined in Marian's hearty laugh, and for a time they recalled many amusing incidents of by-gone days.

But this was dangerous ground, and Mrs. Gordon deftly turned the conversation by asking him if he still kept up his music.

"I gave it up as a profession only, although I loved it. I loved the intellectual brilliancy of the people with whom I came in contact. Indeed, I only wish I could move an audience with so forcible and wholesome an effect as some of the better brilliant lights of the stage. But it was my father's dying request that I quit the opera house and study for the ministry."

"Indeed! Why, that *was* too bad."

Mr. Langtry broke into a hearty laugh. "Spoiled a horn without making a spoon, eh? A very doubtful compliment, Mrs. Gordon," and again they gave vent to their merriment.

"I did not mean that," she protested. "I only meant that as a musician I know you have genius, while as a preacher of the gospel you may only have talent. In choosing a profession or calling one should follow the natural bent of one's mind."

"What you say is quite true. I am afraid I lack sadly in eloquence, yes, even in language; and yet," he added in a more serious tone, "if I could get my tongue to express my thoughts as fully as my touch, I might succeed, but language seems so bare and unsympathetic. I am never so devout as when I feel the ivory keys. My own personal prayers are mostly uttered by my piano."

Meanwhile Master Davie became very restless. He wanted something to replenish his inner man, and did not stop to consider that his mother had company. She tried to coax him in various ways by little toys, but he threw them away as fast as she gave them to him.

"She is more beautiful than ever," said Mr. Langtry to himself as he watched her cooing to her babe and stooping for the toys, "a very type of motherhood."

Little Davie was still unpacified and, as plainly as he could, made manifest his hunger. Toys and talk were all very well in their place, but they would not satisfy the craving of his vigourous digestive organs. Marian felt embarrassed, for she did not like to leave her visitor alone, and Grandma Gordon had gone to bed for a few hours with rheumatic pains.

The little tyrant, however, would not wait. He pulled and tugged his mother's dress-opening till she was forced to submit.

To cover their embarrassment Mr. Langtry seated himself at the piano, and in a moment the room was flooded with melody.

First came "Te Deum Laudamus," with a grandeur and power that thrilled every nerve; but this was only a prelude to his theme; a tuning of his thoughts; a stimulus to inspiration. His head is thrown back, his eyes are closed; and as the throbbing instrument gives its first great shout of greeting, the light of genius shines in his face. Like magic the listener is swept from off the earth into the regions of the clouds and stars, where in the deep ethereal blue the planets in their orbits spin. Above, below, and all around the endless dome of space, the sister worlds wheel their way about some dazzling sun, and meteors flash through endless azure fathoms to mingle with a million twinkling orbs, who, ghostlike, greet each other through eternal space and link their everlasting, noiseless motion with the awful stillness of the universe.

Peace, the everlasting, incomprehensible peace of God, sheds its halo on the fleeting worlds, and in the pure white light of countless suns there meet two human souls who, from yon grain of sand called earth, have come with fleshless forms to greet each other in eternity.

Marian sat sobbing in her chair until the music ceased. She understood his prayer in all its fervency and purity, and deep in her heart she joined in the supplication of " Lead us not into temptation."

For a few moments the stillness was broken only by the infant's satisfied grunts and gurgles as he enjoyed his delayed repast. Conversation was impossible. The piano had already told it all. It had given its assurance that the past was to be forgotten, its pledge of mutual assistance; and as they bade each other good evening it sounded like " Amen."

CHAPTER XXX.

" MULTUM IN PARVO."

That evening, when Gordon came in from the mill, his wife greeted him with a kiss.

" You can't guess who was here to-day. The Rev. Mr. Langtry, no less."

" Humph," said David in a cynical tone. " Making a pastoral call was he? Plucking a brand from the burning. That is the young man who has taken Mr. Sweetnam's place, I suppose."

" Yes. His people used to live at Levisville, and he called to renew acquaintance."

" Some literary light says, ' Bumble bees are biggest when they are first hatched.' I suppose he is going to convert every body off hand, and this call was to break the ice."

" No, David, I am positive that his visit had no such object. His people used to be tenants of mother's, and he was a schoolmate of mine. He called merely to let me know they were in town, and to invite me to call on them. I suppose you would not have any objections."

" Pooh, no! Why should I have any objection? Though, no doubt, they will be pitying you for being linked to such a benighted heathen as myself."

"David," she retorted, half proudly and half angrily, "they would not dare to say anything disrespectful of you, in my presence. Besides Charles Langtry is, by education and instinct, a gentleman, and as for his mother and sister, there are not two kinder souls in the world."

"Well, well, I suppose there are exceptions, but the cant of these fellows is what sickens me. They're sure to tell you how they were saved and, while they incidentally give the credit to Christ, they are careful to impress upon you the fact that their souls are bleached white, while yours is black as ink. They are purity and you are pollution. While, as a matter of fact, their inner lives as husbands, fathers, neighbours or citizens are scarcely up to the average of other educated men. Pshaw! I would as soon take a drink of castor-oil as listen to the sickening, nauseating palaver of them, with their everlasting sing-song self-righteousness."

"They are not all like that, David. Take them here in Gowanstone, and while one may be a little narrow, or another a little bigoted, and yet another very ignorant, they are all, as far as I can judge, inspired by good motives."

"Oh, they're not bad fellows here in town, but they are as jealous of each other as they can be, and as backbiting as they dare be."

"What! Then are not doctors, lawyers or rivals in any business or profession, just the same? Look at our two leading grocers. I have often heard you say that there were not two more honourable, upright men anywhere, and while they have a good word for every body else, they cannot speak civilly to each other; even Dr. Bennet hates his rival and says hard things of him. You can't expect men to be angels, even though they pretend to be, or because they wear black coats. Men's instincts are apart from their calling."

"Very good, Marian, but what I complain of is the pretence. The process of being ordained, they seem to think, remodels their whole anatomy, just as the magician by his wand turns baser metal into gold. The ceremony is supposed to sweep away the lusts of the flesh and take them so far beyond the average mortal that they are privileged to look down upon us poor animals, and hold up their hands in holy horror at our imperfections. However, it seems this new man is not of that stamp. McGuire was telling me the other day that the new pastor thinks more of a piano or a good horse than he does of saving souls. I met him on the street yesterday and I wondered who the handsome fellow was till I noticed his white choker. He seems to me more cut out for the army than the church; just about the stamp of a fellow for wearing fancy uniforms and flirting with women. He reminds me of the preacher who had to give up his sermon that Sunday in Boston."

Mrs. Gordon, in order to hide her confusion, held little Davie's face close to her own and pretended not to notice his last remark.

"So you and he were schoolmates," continued David. "Well, you will have an idea of what he is now. The boy is father to the man."

Marian laughed. "He was a great fighter at school. Not that he was quarrelsome, but he was always taking the part of any one who was being imposed on. He thrashed two boys as big as himself for stealing apples from my school-bag, and another time he fought for a whole hour after school with a coarse fellow who made insulting remarks to me. Indeed, he bears to this day the scar that he got in the affray."

"Oh! Mr. Langtry has been quite a son of Mars in his time. No wonder you take such an interest in him. Perhaps he is an old beau of yours. When a fellow is of no use for anything else they make him a preacher."

Mrs. Gordon's eyes flashed. She did not like his cynical tones.

"David Gordon, you are not like yourself to-night. Your language, tone, and manner are unworthy of you. If I did not know you were an abstainer, I would think you had been drinking."

He was about to speak, but she waived off his interruption and went on: "David, I have known you long enough to know that in your natural condition you are a gentleman. Something must have happened. Tell me what it is that has made you so unlike yourself."

The husband's face flushed with shame. He felt that the grosser elements of his nature had come to the surface. The reaction was so great that he buried his face in his hands and gave a great sob.

In a moment she was kneeling at his side. "Darling, please tell me what is wrong. I have a right to know."

"Sampson & Co. have failed and left me to the tune of three thousand dollars. The old rascal has been preaching, praying and donating to churches, while he was picking other people's pockets. I am ruined." Her face turned pale and her hand trembled. "Well, dear," she said, placing her chair beside his and drawing his head to her bosom, "money is nothing compared with honour."

"Even that will be lost," he groaned. "The banks will close on me in twenty-four hours, and I shall not be able to pay a hundred cents to the dollar. I shall not be able to look honest people in the face."

She sat caressing his head and smoothing his hair, while she gazed into the fire and tried to conjure up ways and means of coming to his rescue.

"How much would it take to save you?" she asked in a subdued voice.

"About twelve hundred, with extra vigilance and economy, would tide me over. It is all a matter of confidence. If the banks think my resources are exhausted, they will force me to liquidate."

"Mother can help you, and she *shall*."

"No, Marian, I could not accept assistance from that source. I would rather get assistance from a stranger, or go down."

"David, you don't know mother. Though she is an implacable enemy, she is a warm friend. I am sure she would give it gladly. Indeed, before I was able to be out of bed, she said that I ought to have had something when I was married, and not gone from home like a pauper.

"I told her about Fred shoving his little bank into

my pocket that night, as I got on the train. The toy was sitting on the bureau in my bedroom at the time. She picked it up, and looked at it for quite a while. She asked me if I had opened it, and I told her no, that I was keeping it as a love-token of Fred's. She laughed a little, and said that she would wager a good deal that father had a finger in the pie, as well. Don't leave it sitting about, she said; father would never let you go away empty handed. She locked it in the bottom bureau drawer, and told me to put it in the safe over in the mill, but I forgot all about it till now. I will go this minute and see what is in it."

"It would make no difference, Marian. I could not take your little gift, like a beggar. I have not got so low yet. I will try my life-insurance policies, and see what I can do with them."

"Shame on you, David Gordon, for your everlasting iron pride. If you refuse help from those who love you, you deserve to fall. Remember what Portia said to Brutus: 'Dwell I but in the suburbs of your good pleasure? If it be no more, Portia is Brutus' harlot, not his wife.'

"David, if your heart is not open to me, as well as your arms, then I am not your wife. You took me from home without a cent in my pocket. You bought the very clothes I should have had. Even the poor servant girl expects to buy her own trousseau, and contribute her little mite towards the general good. But there is little use in discussing it till we see what the trinket contains."

She ran up the stairs and brought down the little iron safe.

"Now, David, please open it, and remember that much or little, it is yours. Here, kiss me for good luck. Mother may have tampered with it too."

When the rusted screws which held the little iron door to its place were removed and the contents poured on the table, they were dumb with astonishment.

Mingled with the boy's silver, soiled and blackened by long contact with the coins, were a number of crisp one hundred-dollar bank notes, and underneath the pile, neatly folded so as to pass through the little slide, and bearing the scrawling and almost illegible signature, Jane Halford, was a cheque drawn in favour of Mrs. David Gordon for one thousand dollars.

CHAPTER XXXI.

A FRIENDLY CALL.

"WELL, Marian, you did come at last, you stingy old thing," was the salute Mrs. Gordon received from a tall, elderly lady who opened the parsonage door and caught her in her arms.

"And here is baby, the sweet little pet. You deserve a scolding for not coming sooner."

"Well, you know, Christina, I had to wait for a fine day to bring baby out. This is really the first fine day we have had for some time."

"Give him to me," said Christina, lifting him out of the carriage and devouring him with kisses, while Davie opened his eyes widely and stared at her presumption, but did not cry.

"Mother and I are not settled yet, we had so much cleaning to do. Oh, here she comes," and Mrs. Langtry came forward, waddling and laughing as usual.

"Well, aunty," said Mrs. Gordon, "have you a piece of pumpkin pie for me to-day, or a fried cake?"

"Indeed, I have both," replied the old lady, embracing her visitor. "I made some fried cakes yesterday, thinking you would come, and I put the same old twist on them," she said, laughing through her tears, "But come away into the kitchen; it is more home-like."

She was as fat and shapeless as ever, and shook when she laughed in the old familiar way. Care and trouble had sat very lightly on her shoulders. Her moon-like countenance was the picture of good humour.

"I see you are just as jolly as ever, Auntie. You don't seem to look a bit older."

"Mother won't die as long as she can laugh," said Christina. "Sometimes she is never serious for a single moment of the day. One night in Wentford, I took her to a concert, where a comic singer came out in character, and sang 'Laughing Farmer McGee.' I laughed heartily enough myself, but mother was past all bounds. I had to bring her away, for the audience was laughing as much at her as at the singer."

"Well, I'm just as far ahead as if I had been crying all the time," remarked the old lady. "There's no sense in always growling and complaining. Laugh and grow fat, you know," she continued with a nod, as she broke out again and compelled the others to join her.

"It's a wonder Christina doesn't get fat then when she's with you."

"She's fretting too much about 'the fellows,'" exclaimed the mother with a fresh outburst which carried them by storm. The idea of Christina being love-lorn was too ridiculous for anything.

When the mirth had subsided Christina remarked that both Charles and herself were born for single blessedness.

"Nonsense, Christina," said Marian, "just wait until some of the young ladies of Gowanstone get a chance at your brother. Why, I heard yesterday there were two or three angling for him already."

Christina shook her head. "He will scarcely look at a young lady. Both in Boston and in Wentford, there were a lot of nice-looking young ladies and one widow with both wealth and beauty, who set their caps for him, but he treated them alike."

"Perhaps he is too much absorbed in his studies to think of marrying," suggested Mrs. Gordon.

"No, indeed. It isn't that," replied his sister, shaking her head, "because he does not study much, excepting music, and he often gets up through the night for that. He plays cricket or ball wherever there is a club to play with, and he is fond of hunting and fishing, but," and here she dropped her voice to a whisper,

"I believe he must have been disappointed in love." The serious look on Christina's face as she said this was too much for the old lady, and for a few moments the room fairly echoed with laughter. They could not stop, and the picture of Mrs. Langtry vibrating in her chair, with the tears running down her cheeks, continually furnished fresh food for mirth.

"Really, though," protested Christina, drying her eyes with her apron, "I'm sure he's been in love, for the music he plays sounds like that. Do you remember the day he called at your place, Marian? Well, that night, when he came in after his constitutional (as he calls it), he played so sad and pitiful that mother and I both cried like babies."

Marian turned away to hide the tell-tale colour in her face, and went over to the window to look out, but she started back with a cry of fear and surprise. There, before her eyes, in the backyard in his shirt sleeves, swinging on a horizontal bar, was the Rev. Charles Langtry, whirling and spinning like a teetotum.

"My! I got such a fright," exclaimed Marian, beating a retreat.

"'Deed, I used to be frightened myself," said the old lady, "but we got used to it. He is at it every day for an hour. Sit here and watch him," she continued, "only we must not let him see us, for he does not like anybody to know about it. He put that high fence all round the yard so that the neighbours could not see him."

For a while they watched his evolutions, and at times, when a fall seemed imminent, Marian gave a little cry of fear. His face was rosy with exercise in the chilly wind, his heavy curls fell loosely over his forehead, and the muscles of his bare arms stood out like ropes.

The performer stopped for a moment to take his breath and tighten the broad belt about his waist.

"Watch him now," whispered Christina. "I know by the way he is rubbing sand in his hands that he is going to do his 'double-radius,' as he calls it. Yes, there he goes. Look!"

The gymnast made a running jump at the bar, and catching it by one hand he swung round with terrible velocity. With a sudden jerk the bar slid into his half-closed elbows while he kept on whirling as before. The armpits, groins, knees, ankles, each in turn, became the centre of motion. Suddenly the bar slipped back into one of his half-flexed knees, when with a wild swoop he turned a backward somersault and landed on his feet.

The performance was now over, for he was pulling down his shirt sleeves, gathering up his clothing and wiping the sweat from his brow. A moment later, when he came into the kitchen in his half-dressed condition and saw who was present, his eyes flashed with anger.

He bowed politely to Mrs. Gordon. "Allow me to apologize for the impropriety of mother and Christina in bringing you into the kitchen. You were probably an unwilling witness of exercises which must look ridiculous in one of my position and calling. They forget that I object to performing before an audience like a mountebank. You will excuse me for a moment till I make myself presentable. Christina, I should be very angry, only that I know Mrs. Gordon is a lady, and is sure to ignore what was not intended for her to see."

"Gracious! but he is vexed," said Christina, as the door closed behind him. "I did not think he would mind it much, on account of your being old acquaintances."

Marian rose to go, but they would not listen to such a proposition. "What? and we made the fried cakes on purpose. You surely would not treat your old aunty like that? Christina or Charles will escort you home if it gets dark before you go, or perhaps Mr. Gordon will come for you."

Marian laughed. "Oh, David knows I won't run away. Grandma will have his tea ready, and then he will be at the mill till ten or eleven o'clock."

"Well, just make yourself contented. Go into the parlour there till we get tea ready," pleaded Christina, "and Charles will play for you."

"Very well, Christina, Davie and I will amuse ourselves at the piano. Come, Davie." Putting the baby on her knee Marian seated herself at the instrument and, from sheer force of habit, played "Caller Herrin'."

She played with a great deal of taste and skill, for it was one of Grandma's favourites, and she played it almost daily.

When she had finished, Mr. Langtry entered the room in his usual clerical dress, and complimented her on her playing. "I see you have caught the spirit of the piece," he said. "'Caller Herrin'" is a perfect gem, but most people do not understand it. A great many have the impression that it is only a rollicking, reckless street song, but to me it is the quintessence of sadness. Through the outside veneering one can catch the smothered sob of a bursting heart. Stern necessity demands that grief be gilded with nonchalance, because the great big, selfish world cares little for our woes. The fishwife in order to get bread for her little ones at home must choke her sobs, and sing to sell her wares. She must mimic mirth to catch the ear of her customers. She must forget that the herring in her creel cost her a son or a husband; she must shut from her ears the sound of the foaming billows in which he went down: she must banish from her mind the vacant chair at home, and the ruddy cheery face that's gone forever. Oh it is sad, very sad. Why I once preached a sermon on that grand old song. I have had people laugh at me for saying it, but that music will live as long as civilization. Indeed it is a page from Scottish history. Besides, its peculiar phrasing has the fresh, breezy atmosphere of the sea."

"Mr. Gordon's mother would be delighted to hear you speak like that. You know she is Scotch. It was she who induced me to get several Scotch songs and selections. She is very fond of 'Robin Adair.'"

"No wonder! Its purity and depth of feeling is truly beautiful. The candour, simplicity, and lack of sophistication about Scottish music is really remarkable. It has no equal in this respect, and for that reason it is acceptable in every land and every clime."

"Will you play me 'Robin Adair?'"

"Yes, if I can remember it. I have not seen the music of it for some time, but if I do take some liberties with the original score I shall try to catch the spirit."

In a moment the very walls of the room seemed to be lamenting the absent one, and the figure of a pure sweet maiden weeping for her lover seemed to hover over the instrument. Oh, Scotland, land of brown heath and shaggy wood, how close to Nature's heart thy bards have kept; what secrets of the soul they must have learned to set them thus to sound.

"Won't you sing for me now?" he asked, "just that simple little song you used to sing, long ago."

He fumbled through a great pile of music and finally drew it forth. "Here it is: 'Some day I'll wander back again.' There is not so much in it, but you used to sing it well."

The rich colour swept over her face, and her lips were pressed tightly together while she glanced towards the open door, half hoping that Mrs. Langtry or Christina would come in.

She was going to make an excuse for refusing, but the accompaniment which came rippling from his finger tips seemed to overcome her reluctance.

Pushing her chair close to the piano she stood Davie upon it. Holding him by the hand, and clearing her throat of its nervous huskiness, she commenced. The familiar pitch and tone seemed to give her inspiration. She sang in splendid voice till she turned the last leaf, and then she broke down. There, after all these years, nestling in a corner to which it was pinned, lay the little piece of blue ribbon he had stolen from her hair on the night they waded the stream.

CHAPTER XXXII.

CROSSED WIRES.

"Sit down, Gordon, sit down. I can't diagnose your case in a moment. Every patient thinks that the name of his disease is spelt out in his face in gilded letters and all we have to do is read at a glance. We cannot jump at conclusions. We have to take the evidence, and then weigh it like a judge."

David Gordon, who had been impatiently pacing the floor of the doctor's consulting room with feverish anxiety, dropped into a chair, but he could scarcely sit still. He was pale and haggard looking, his eyes were sunken, and the lines of his countenance were expressive of distress.

"First, tell me how your mother is," said the doctor, wishing to throw him off his guard and to watch the expression of his eye.

"She seems better this last month," David replied, fidgetting in his chair. "She can't go about, but she is quite cheerful."

"Does she rest well at night?" inquired the physician, peeping at him through his eyebrows.

"Oh, very well," responded David, rising again and beginning to pace the floor. "She does not complain. But you say it is dangerous?"

"Yes, rheumatism is always dangerous when it affects the heart as it does in her case. But you tell me you are not feeling well yourself?"

"Doctor, if I don't get sleep I shall go crazy. Many a time lately it has only been the toss of a copper whether I blew my brains out or not."

"How long has this been going on?" was the next question.

"About three months. I have tried cold baths, light diet and active exercise. I used to get up through the night and walk a few miles. It used to help me but it does not now."

The doctor noticed that his patient spoke with unusual rapidity, and occasionally stammered over a word. " How many hours a week do you sleep?"

"Oh, I can't say. Not more than four or five at best, but these last three nights I have never slept a second."

" Does your wife know of this?"

" No. That is, she does not know how bad I've been. The fact of the matter is, doctor," he added in a confidential whisper, " my wife and I don't occupy the same room lately. I am ashamed to mention it, but, really, her presence, lately, seem to irritate me beyond control. Once or twice I woke her out of her sleep and scolded her for nothing. It is the strangest thing, too, but I am now positive of it, that I can sleep if she is away. Half a dozen times during the past year she has gone over to Broadview to her mother's, and I always slept well when she was gone. It's not imagination, doctor, for if I were forced to remain in the same room, I would positively go out of my mind."

The doctor saw that his patient was in a talkative mood, so he let him go on without interruption, while he watched the various expressions which passed over his face.

" My wife thinks I am turning against her, I know she does, although she is always patient and gentle with me. It's not that I don't love her. I can't explain it. It is not because she goes to church and sings in the choir; or that we ever quarrel about religion or anything else. But her very touch that once would electrify me or soothe me, as the case might be, is positively irritating now. There's one more thing I am going to tell you, though you may think it of no consequence. The other day I had a chance to cheat a man out of a hundred dollars and no one would have known it. Well, I did not do it, but," and here the sick man held out his finger by way of emphasis or warning, " I tell you I hesitated. Yes, I actually hesitated, and there was only the toss of a copper then, between roguery and honesty."

The doctor readjusted his spectacles and smiled blandly, but did not reply. He saw that his patient had not finished talking. "You may smile, doctor, but I have seen the time when ten times that amount would not have tempted me for a single second ; when the idea even would never have entered my mind. Then I am getting suspicious and can hardly speak civilly to anybody. I'm just like a man who has been drinking. Poor Marian. We're only four years married, and she thinks I've got tired of her, just as if any sane man couldn't see that she is a magnificent woman. For God's sake, doctor, tell me what it all means," he went on, throwing himself gloomily into a chair. "If you can do anything for me, say so, and if not, by heavens, I'll jump the 'big divide' before I become a damned rascal. A man has no business in this world if he can't act like a gentleman."

"Are you in business difficulties?"

"Not now. I have been pulling up ever since the Sampson failure, but it was neck and neck for a long time. You remember the big spurt in wheat. Well, I netted fifteen cents a bushel on my whole stock. Last week only I bought a twenty car lot of flour, and sold it at a quarter dollar advance."

"Phew!" whistled the doctor, "you *are* going it and no mistake, but remember your nervous system won't stand it."

"Hang my nervous system. If my lamp lacks oil, and I can't try a fall with other men, why I'd better go to breaking stones."

"You *were* on thin ice for a long time you say?"

"Yes, but I am all right now. A miss is as good as a mile."

"Not always," responded the doctor shaking his head. "The ball that passes too close, often kills by windage."

"Well, never mind, you haven't told me yet what is the matter with me."

"Neurasthenia."

"What in the name of goodness is that? Remember I never studied Greek."

The doctor, taking his patient by the hand, led him to the window, and pointed to the network of wires on the poles which lined the street.

"Do you see those wires? Well, just imagine them all in a tangle, and you will have an idea of what your condition is."

"Then, in the name of suffering humanity, give me something to untangle them."

"Very good; but remember medicine won't do it. The wires will have to be slackened, while they are being restored to order. Keep away from the mill for a month, and don't even look at the cover of a ledger. I'm going off for a little holiday myself, why not come along?"

"I heard you were going away in the morning. That is why I came to-day. I was anxious to see you before you left town."

"Just go home, pack up your traps, and go shooting with me for a couple of weeks."

"I don't think I would care for that kind of sport, Doctor."

"Tush, man, it is the bracing, soothing effects of the virgin forest you need. It is as soothing as a mother to her babe. Away you go now, and leave the question of sleep to me."

"I'm not at the bottom of the case yet," said the doctor to himself, after his patient had gone, "but when we are away together I shall watch him."

He was at a loss to know whether David's illness was entirely due to nervous exhaustion from business strain, or to deflected magnetism between him and his wife.

According to his theories there should be magnetic harmony between them, although the balance of power, he conceived, was largely on her side.

The repellent effect of Mrs. Gordon upon her husband at the present must be due to one of two causes. Either the exhaustion of business worry and strain had left his patient magnetically bankrupt, or his wife's affinity for him had been deflected. Perhaps both. This theory, however, presupposed the presence of a third magnetic influence. Surely Mrs. Gordon can not have a fancy for any one else. No, no; it's impossible. And yet, confound it, there is the evidence. Humph! there must be. They were surely well mated.

He was large boned and angular, while she was the opposite. His hair was jet-black and coarse, while hers was light and fine as silk. Even mentally they were adapted to each other. He was firm, and she forgiving; he rational, and she emotional.

The doctor's theory was that physical similarity repelled, both in love and friendship. The positive poles of a battery would never attract each other, and if brought into too close contact would have the opposite tendency. To him every individual was an electrical machine, attracting and repelling each other on fixed principles which were as yet unknown.

During their holiday in the woods the doctor (to use his own expression) put a ground-wire on his patient in order to restore the electrical balance and to procure for him a fresh supply of magnetic force from the mother earth.

Indeed, he himself felt the necessity of a restoration of that kind. He was continually dispensing cheerfulness and sympathy to his patients. Consequently, he was often left devoid of mental and physical energy till he secured another loan from the mother earth.

His investigation went on, however, in a leisurely way, and he came to the conclusion that Gordon's condition was at least not solely due to nervous exhaustion.

He discovered that his patient's brain was capable of an enormous amount of work; that his courage and self-reliance made him a very Napoleon of finance, who could live and thrive in an atmosphere of danger.

"No doubt this human machine when devoid of electrical force has lost its attraction for its mate, and now a new affinity has been formed, leaving it isolated. Mrs. Gordon is a noble woman, but—well, no matter, I can't help it. It gives me no chance to cure my patient, excepting for a temporary patch-up. Humph!"

CHAPTER XXXIII.

"THE LAND O' THE LEAL."

GRANDMA GORDON for many months had been an invalid. She was moved into her daughter-in-law's rooms, not only to facilitate attendance, but for increased cheerfulness and companionship. Her occupation was to amuse Davie, and allow Marian to go on with her household duties. She sat in her chair from morning till night, never uttering a complaint: indeed, she was almost as cheerful as when in perfect health. Her simple philosophy taught her that there was little use in repining, that cheerfulness was the best anaesthetic. She soon discovered that there was a lack of warmth between David and his wife, and contrary to the usual rule, she decided that the fault lay with her son. This was her only grief; the only thorn in her rose of contentment; but she deemed it wisest not to interfere. They appeared to have grown away from each other in a few months, but for what reason she could not possibly understand. She hoped for the best, however, and confidently expected that when relieved from the pressure of business, David would be himself again.

The old lady found a new friend in whom she rejoiced. Christina Langtry was now almost a constant visitor. She brought books, papers and magazines, and forestalled her every wish in fruit and other delicacies.

She seemed to know just when the invalid wished to talk, or when she preferred to be left in silence; while the old lady looked forward to her visits as the brightest hour in her day.

Mr. Langtry himself came two or three times every week, but never to discuss theology, or refer to the invalid's heterodoxy. His rendition of Scotch airs was joy and gladness to the heart of David's mother, and if he did not come on the day he was expected she invariably reminded Christina of it.

Gordon was not altogether pleased at the way in which matters had recently shaped themselves.

The Langtrys seemed to have taken possession of his home. Their comings and goings seemed to have become of more interest to his wife and his mother than his own movements. Marian not only went to church regularly, but was the leading soprano of the choir. The clergyman and his sister seemed to have brought into his home an atmosphere which was not congenial to him. Many a time he wished them at the other end of the earth. This condition of affairs went on for weeks before David ever had an opportunity of meeting his clerical visitor. At last one evening the reverend gentleman remained to tea and Marian was fearful of the consequences.

When her husband came in from the mill with his dusty grey clothes and his jet-black hair, he formed a strong contrast to his guest. One could see at a glance that these two men were cast in entirely different moulds. Had Dr. Bennet been present he would have enjoyed the antagonism, which was particularly noticeable on David's part.

With wonderful tact did Marian steer the conversation clear of dangerous topics, and the evening passed pleasantly enough. She was far more afraid of David than of her guest, for while the atmosphere of contention was congenial to her husband, it was distasteful to the clergyman. Mr. Langtry assisted his hostess in pouring oil on the troubled waters, deftly changing the subject whenever he saw any danger ahead.

As soon as David learned that Mr. Langtry had no intention or desire to cross swords with him he changed his attitude, and from that time forward they were quite friendly. No matter when or where they met the clergyman always carried a flag of truce, till Gordan began to feel more kindly towards him, especially for his kindness to his mother in playing so exquisitely the airs she loved so well.

He felt somewhat jealous, however, of the warmth with which his mother always greeted her musical benefactor, and of the freemasonry which seemed to have grown up between them. They would smile or shed tears over the same passages, and often they whiled away an hour in discussing the depths of meaning which lay buried in their favourite melodies.

David even took his mother to task for being so intimate with her visitor. " What, are you going to turn Christian, too, mother? Are you going to desert me and go over to the majority?"

" Toots, Davie, ma releegion is ower simple tae quarrel aboot, and ower long *set* tae change noo. I ken weel enuch yer feyther woodna hae likiet to hae a black-coat comin' sae often tae his hoose, but yon man is nane o' yer seeven by nine thinkers. He never speaks aboot releegion, but I ken by his music just what he's thinkin o'. Merran tells me that on Sunday fortnicht he preached a sermon that garred them a' stare. He telt them that he kent agnostics wha' were mair Christ-like in their ways than a wheen o' them that gaed tae the kirk. Yae day, him an' me got crackin' aboot Jeemison and hoo he sent turkeys and geese tae puir folk at Christmas, and claes tae them that were nakiet. Aye, and hoo he treated his workmen sae fair, considerin' their guid as weel as his ain. Weel, when we got through he said that if fo'k were to be judged by their fruits Jeemison was a far better Christian than maist o' them. He telt me himsel' that it didna matter what we ca' fo'k sae long as their hearts are warm and kind. I'm sure naebody can fin' fau't wi' that doctrine."

This was a time of sore trial for Marian, who was in almost daily contact with the lover of her youth. She never trusted herself alone in his company after the discovery of the ribbon, though it took a great deal of tact to prevent it without making her efforts noticeable. It seemed as if fate had thrown them together for some purpose, and that his music was weaving a web around her. But her boy was a citadel of strength to her. With him on her knee she could defy temptation. Day by day she prayed for assistance to school herself to the new order of things, to fortify herself against the attraction which the clergyman seemed to have for her and she for him.

Suddenly one evening the old lady took a sharp pain in her breast.

"Something has gaen wrang in here," she gasped, placing her hand over her heart. "I dout the doctor was richt, Merran, lass. Ye better rin and tell Davie. Hush, dinna greet. It had tae come some time."

When the doctor came, he took her wrist in his hand for a moment, then dropped it suddenly, and stepped over to the window without speaking a word. It was his way of telling them that all hope was gone.

"How long, Doctor?" asked David in a whisper.

"Only a few hours. Shall I tell her?"

"Yes, you had better, for I cannot," said David with a sob.

But "Granny" was quite prepared for the announcement. "Aye, aye, I jaloosed it," she murmured faintly. "Aweel, I hae dreed ma weird. I wad likiet tae hae been wi' ye a bit langer, but it canna be. Dinna greet, bairns," she continued as David and Marian knelt weeping at her bedside. "Bear up an' be strang. Ye hae life a' afore ye an' I hae gaen out ma time. Just bury me, Davie, aside yer feyther, withoot ony ceremony. It wad mak nae odds tae me, but if yer feyther was here, he wouldna like ony preachin' ower me. Maybe Jeemison wad let his band play 'The Land o' the Leal' at the grave before the sods are happiet ower me."

She was silent for some time and nothing but sobs broke the stillness.

"Bring me a drink o' cauld, cauld water, Davie."

As soon as he had left the room she took Marian's hand in hers.

"Merran, lass, bear wi' ma boy. He's kinna thrawn at times, but he's guid an' true for a' that. Yer heart is big enuch tae aye forgie him, and I'll leave him in your charge, lassie."

When her son returned she motioned him to kneel beside his wife.

Marian understood her. She drew David's face to hers, and they kissed each other tenderly. There they remained in each other's embrace, with their hands clasped about the wasted fingers of the dying woman.

After a time she seemed to rally and could talk a little better.

"Ye ance asked me, Davie, aboot the next worl', but tho' I'm deein' ye ken as muckle aboot it as me. I wadna like tae think I wad never see ye again. I dinna ken. I can only hope—that's a'. Bring wee Davie, the puir wee lamb, and let me kiss his sweet moo. Puir laddie, he'll be lonesome noo. He'll soon hae nae grannie tae play chuckie stanes wi' him. I hope he'll mak a braw man some day. He seems ower guid for this worl'."

After the first great outburst of grief was over, the dying woman said in a whisper, "Gang in an' play a bit for me, Merran; a wee bit, saft and low. Play 'Caller Herrin',' it minds me o' hame and the bonnie blue sea."

When Dr. Bennet came into the room after a two hours' absence, the scene that met his gaze brought the moisture to his eyes.

With the piano across the further door of the death chamber, Marian sat, sobbing, and sounding the last few chords of an old Scotch song. The setting sun sent a streak of light across the bed where David knelt with his head buried in the pillow beside his mother's grey and pallid face.

The big dog, Nero, was lying with his nose upon his paws, looking dolefully towards his master, while on the bed sat little Davie, sucking contentedly at a sugar stick, and playing with the hand of his dead "Granny."

CHAPTER XXXIV.

DR. BENNET'S SPECTACLES.

THE reader has already discovered that the great study of Dr. Bennet's life was animal magnetism and the relation of mind to matter. He detested mystery; in fact, he insisted that it was only another name for superstitious ignorance. His nature led him to seek an explanation for everything that came within his notice. He followed his path alone, and instead of reading books he studied men and women. He had nothing but contempt for spiritualists, who, with their seances, and their mystery, were debauching a noble science. Charlatans and mountebanks had made the subject almost disreputable, had driven honest, earnest thinkers from the field. He was willing to believe that there were germs of truth underlying such things as faith-curing and mind-reading, but that these so-called occult manifestations were dependent upon supernatural existences, he was at a loss to see how any sane person could believe. Just as natural phenomena, such as lightning, meteors or rainbows, were, during ages of superstition and ignorance, believed to be special manifestations of divine will and power for the benefit of the poor ignorant egotists who inhabit this grain of sand, so, in the ignorance of the present, the most simple and natural manifestations of animal magnetism were attributed to causes neither sensible nor scientific.

"I am convinced," he said to himself, "that in this field there are wonderful possibilities, and if new truths be discovered, we should, instead of surrounding them with mystery, place them on a scientific basis, and apply them in some way for the benefit of mankind."

He had an idea that love, the divine passion, was simply a current of magnetism between the sexes, depending upon both physical and mental conditions.

He believed that these currents were modified by physical peculiarities, such as the size and shape of the bones and the quality of the tissues. He thought that the outlines of the face, the shape of the head, and the colour and quality of the eyes and hair, were all reliable indicators of the magnetic peculiarities of each individual.

He conceived the idea, that thorough investigation would make it possible for us to measure with exactness the magnetic force of each man and woman, and give us certain grounds on which to base a natural marriage.

He was further convinced, from close observation, that the quality of brain currents, thoughts, motives and actions were largely influenced by surroundings and habits of life, and that what are known as dual existences were merely marked examples of this underlying principle.

A careful analysis of his fellow creatures convinced him that there was a duality in every nature. He found that under certain conditions and influences people's motives and instincts changed; the only question being the degree and quality of the forces necessary to reverse the picture. He was familiar with, *the devil at home and saint abroad,* the man who is all querulousness and tyranny to his own, and all affability and kindness to strangers. He saw the stimulus of strange faces bringing geniality and generosity to the surface in some natures, and sinking it in others. He had known the statesman forget his wife for some passing fancy, and the sneak thief remain the ardent lover of his faithful spouse. The respectable orderly citizen, when sober, often became a brawling rowdy when drunk, and the hard, grinding, selfish man of the world became a genial, generous gentleman, under the influence of wine. The music which inspired sentiment in some natures incited sensuality in others, and the same theme that perchance had prompted poesy and song had let loose the wild horses of passion which carried vestal virgins and virtuous wives over the brink of degradation and ruin. He found that the perfume of the flower brought love to some hearts and lust to others. That the touch of one hand gave attraction and another repulsion. He found that the nurse whose presence soothed some irritated others. He watched his patients become tyrannical or benevolent under different diets. He saw that feasting induced generosity in some, while fasting had the same effect on others.

He believed that in every man's nature was some secret spring which, if touched, would liberate some vice; and that our five senses were so many roots through which external influences brought forth the nobler or the baser qualities of our minds.

Discussing this subject with the doctor on one of his quiet evenings when they were alone, Gordon remarked that rational people regarded the whole field of occultism as fit only for harmless lunatics.

"You never made a greater mistake in your life, Gordon."

"You think, then, that there is room for legitimate investigation?"

"Room? Why, man, it is fairly bristling with countless possibilities. If students of occultism would drop sophistry and superstition; if they would cease talking and writing a lot of technical rubbish about imaginary spirits and influences; if they would stop looking to the clouds and study their fellow men, we would soon have the most astonishing results. So far it is only charlatans who have taken it up for the sake of revenue, but remember that at the bottom of all this trash there is an underlying truth, the magnetic influence which one individual exerts upon another."

"Supposing, then, that animal magnetism were thoroughly understood, of what use would it be?"

"I am astonished that you should ask, since it touches the very foundation of existence itself. Don't you see that a knowledge of animal magnetism would guide every man and woman in the selection of a mate with whom life might be spent with the greatest possible happiness, the least possible antagonism, and consequently, the most highly developed progeny?"

"Is not love a safe enough basis?" queried David, with a smile.

"Most assuredly, if we all understood the difference between love and lust, and did not occasionally confound love with admiration. A couple between whom there is not magnetic harmony cannot possibly live happily together. They may, by an extra amount of forbearance, go through life without any outward sign, but their happiness will be destroyed, their lives will be shortened, and their children will lack that sympathetic, enthusiastic animus of life which marks the fruit of wholesome marriages."

"What are your definitions of love and lust, or rather where does the difference lie?"

"You can't compare them. Lust is only the baser,

the physical portion of love. Love itself, is, as I take it, the mental, moral, spiritual and physical affinity of sex for sex. Love is at first entirely unconscious of the physical element, but in its growth, development and continuance, the physical portion plays an important, if not an essential part. If lust is spontaneous on both sides, it may be an evidence of magnetic affinity, and in some cases an excuse for marriage, but it is often artificially created by contact and opportunity."

"If all you say be true, Doctor, then the great majority of marriages are matters of blind chance, at least as far as women are concerned."

The doctor smiled. "Chance is a word I don't like, but if you refer to a woman who marries for a home, or to the marriage of state, there cannot be any doubt that it is simply refined prostitution, the only difference being in the price."

"You forget though, Doctor, that woman is placed at a disadvantage. According to the rules of society, she must wait until she is picked up, and if a wooer comes along who is fairly well-to-do, one man is as good as another."

"Don't make any mistake," said the doctor, wiping his glasses. "It is only the sexless, characterless woman who has no individual preference. The right woman seldom refuses the right man excepting for powerful reasons of expediency. I tell you, Gordon," he continued, with an emphatic gleam in his eye, "the woman who marries for any other cause than love is accursed of God. She is worse than the man, because she is endowed with higher duties and higher responsibilities."

Gordon laughed at the doctor's vehemence, and remarked that such a theory bore very heavily on royalty.

"I don't care whether she be duchess or dish-washer, patrician or plebeian, the same thing holds good. Just as surely as yon moon is now shining through that window, and by the same inevitable law that this planet turns on its axis, will she suffer the penalty on this earth, and nothing but death can protect her. The maiden, who loves not wisely but too well, and struggles bravely, after being forsaken by her whilom lover, to rear her child, is a pure and spotless heroine compared with the titled granddame who barters off her body for a consideration; and ten times over would I back her chances of happiness either in this world or the next against the polluted offspring of royalty. Tush! what does nature care for titles? Toys for children or tools for tyrants."

"Do you find many of these perfect marriages?" asked David with a doubtful smile. "You see into people's lives pretty thoroughly and have many opportunities of judging."

"Not so many as there should be," responded the physician somewhat sadly, "not so many as there might be if animal magnetism was thoroughly understood. Think of the lame, the halt, and the blind, of the criminals, maniacs and imbeciles who are the fruit of ill-mated marriages; and yet the world goes madly, blindly on. If to-day kings and princes had to eat the same food, wear the same clothes, and live under the same circumstances as the poor, the majority of our rulers would be demons or imbeciles."

Gordon broke into a hearty laugh. "What keeps them from being so now?"

"Why, their surroundings, of course, and an occasional wholesome marriage. Take the finest blood horse from his palace stall, his pure, fresh air, his good, clean, well-regulated food, his well-timed rubbing and grooming, turn him out to a straw stack surrounded by filth, exposed to cold and wet, and he will soon become the veriest plug in the barnyard. Kings and queens, with all their splendid surroundings, should be the noblest and best of our race, and *would* be, were it not for the loveless marriages of state."

"You are very democratic, Doctor, you think that one man is as good as another, provided the surroundings are equal."

"No, you have mistaken me. You might as well (to continue the simile) say that one horse is as good as another. No, no. If we are to have an aristocracy, let it be one of heart and brain. Instead of hanging orders and stars on some titled booby, like jewelry on a gypsy, let mother nature put her stamp upon him. Her stamp of gentility is the only genuine one."

The doctor arose, and going to a cupboard brought forth wine and cigars.

"Never mind wine for me," said David, biting off the end of a cigar. "A smoke seems to loosen my tongue and bring my ideas more quickly; but one glass of that wine would make me a perfect villain. Not that I would be intoxicated, in the ordinary sense, but I would feel that I was a lower, coarser type of a man; and I might say and do things I would not think of when in my ordinary condition."

"Another case of dual existence," remarked his host with a peculiar smile. "You are like Professor Senger in that respect. I suppose you remember him?"

"One does not easily forget a man like him," responded Gordon, "but the duality in his case was surely not distinct, for when you invited the fakir to dinner it was the philosopher who came."

"No, indeed, Gordon, it was the philosopher to whom the invitation was given. I will admit, however, that the fakir's hunger was appeased when the philosopher ate his dinner. You remember he did not even recognize you after having met you in the mill a few hours before?"

"Quite true. But don't you think there is more than a physical relation between the two conditions?"

"Practically speaking, there is little more," replied the doctor.

"But what brought about the change? It was neither whiskey nor tobacco, for I remember he neither smoked nor drank that night."

The host leaned back in his chair a moment, and watched the smoke that curled up from his lips.

"Did you notice that he had a large mouth, full lips and an eater's jaw? No? Well, there lies the explanation of it all."

"You don't mean to say that eating does it?"

"Indeed, I do," replied the doctor with an emphatic nod.

"Good heavens!" exclaimed Gordon, "you can't

mean to say that a man can get intoxicated on roast goose?"

"That's the very thing I do mean. *Why there are thousands of people, who from over-eating, are never sober.*"

David got up from his chair and walked the floor, laughing.

"Look here, Doctor, if you go on like this, I shall think there are wheels in your head."

"Sit down, man, sit down," said his host, snappishly. "You don't suppose that I have studied this subject for twenty years, only to have it laughed out of court. What is alcohol," he demanded, "but a distilled extract of some food product? Every man who consumes more food (either in quantity or quality) than he requires simply converts his body into a distillery. Every particle of unassimilated food floating in the circulation is a poison as toxic as alcohol."

"Is that really so?"

"It is a positive fact," replied the doctor. "I have not given you the proper pathological terms, but roughly speaking, that is what it amounts to."

"*Well, well, well!*" exclaimed David, pacing the floor, with his thumbs in his vest, "this beats anything I ever heard of. But, hold on. You don't mean to say that what he ate that night could have done it in so short a time? Although I remember now he devoured as much as the three of us put together."

"No, I don't mean you to infer that. But he had previously been having a number of hearty meals in quick succession, for I took the trouble to inquire at the hotel, and found that such was the case. Food will not intoxicate as fast as liquor, for in the latter, the distillation is done in advance, but the effect comes just as surely," and the speaker, drumming his fingers on his desk, looked defiantly at his guest.

"Let us go back to the horse," he continued, as he wiped and readjusted his spectacles. "If you keep your horse in the stable eating oats, and not giving him sufficient or proportionate exercise, he will soon go wrong in either body or brain. In nine cases out of ten he will lose his head with intoxication, and will probably smash everything to pieces at the first opportunity. What is known as fieryness, in that case is merely intoxication. Just keep that in your mind, and then take notice that in the human family it is the worker that gets the straw and the loafer the oats."

"You mean to say that if the professor were properly fed he would always be the philosopher?"

"Exactly," replied the host. "In fact, I have proven it. I never told you (because I was ashamed of my negligence), that I had the professor in tow once since you saw him. About six months ago I received a letter from the lost man, a letter which was a perfect marvel of beautiful philosophy and delightful candour. He was living, or rather, existing, in an obscure street in Boston, and had just recovered from an attack of typhoid fever, brought on, no doubt, by his over-eating. I wired to a friend of mine, Dr. Tuck, giving him carte blanche in providing for the professor's creature comforts. I had several beautiful letters during his convalescence, but would you believe it, he was only five weeks on liberal diet when I got a scrawl referring to a conversation we had when we first met. He wanted money to get his ring out of pawn, and to publish more of his infernal pamphlets. Next day, came a telegram from the doctor, saying that his patient had suddenly disappeared, and that no trace of him could be found."

"And have you not heard of him since?" inquired Gordon.

"Not a trace," replied the doctor, with a sad shake of his head. "I employed Pinkerton's people, but as yet they have not struck his trail."

"It's pretty hard," remarked David, "for a man to remain in hiding very long in these days of steam and electricity."

"He is not hiding at all, and that makes the search all the more difficult. A criminal with a definite purpose is not hard to find, but the fellow who goes about without any particular motive is very difficult to trace; at least, so the detectives tell me. His disguise is perfect, for besides his clothes and wig, there is the expression of his face. If he is in luck one day, and out of it the next, he will change as often as a chamcleon. No, Gordon, I have missed the opportunity of my life. I shall regret it as long as I live. Well, good-night," he added, as David rose to go. "Better quit smoking. It makes you a better guest but a worse patient. Come over any evening. It will keep you from fretting about your mother. Good-night."

CHAPTER XXXV.

A DIFFICULT PROBLEM.

"I WON'T take 'no' for an answer, Marian. I can't allow you to bury yourself alive. Come now, go and put on your wraps."

"I really cannot, Christina. I have no heart to go out, since Grandma died. Besides, mother is here now and I couldn't go out and leave her."

"Well, bring her too, of course. Your mother and I were always great friends. Charles was just remarking last night that you never came over now."

Marian flushed a little and turned her face away. She wished to change the subject. "Oh, how is your mother, dear? I heard she was ill."

"She is better now. She was in bed only half a day, but she does not seem quite so jolly," replied Christina, seating herself on Marian's knee, and putting her arms around her neck. "Come, now," she continued, tugging gently at Mrs. Gordon's ear, "Come. I'll pester you till you do. Go and tell your mother to get ready, and I'll amuse Davie. Come to Aunty, dear," she went on, picking up the little fellow. "Aunty's got candy for Davie. Oh, you want to dance? Well, here we go."

While Christina was racing up and down the room for the amusement of Davie, she ran full tilt against Mrs. Halford, who had just entered the door.

"Why, how do you do, Aunt Jane," exclaimed

Christina, using the old familiar name, and holding out her hand.

Mrs. Halford's face turned a dull red, but Christina pretended not to notice it.

"You've not changed a bit, Aunt Jane. You are only a young woman yet."

The mistress of Broadview always had a warm side for Christina, but she did not expect so kindly a greeting from an evicted tenant. When she had time to recover from her surprise, her face softened, and in her kindliest tones she said, "Why, it are Christina," and she did what she would do for no one else outside of her own family, kissed her on the cheek.

This woman of the world admired the pure whiteness of Christina's soul, and loved her for her guilelessness. She often said that if there were only one Christian in the world, that one was Christina Langtry. Next to, or perhaps equal to her own children, she loved the faded spinster, whose face was a type of simplicity and kindliness.

When Christina freed herself from the embrace, Mrs. Halford sank into a chair, and sobbed quietly into her handkerchief, while her companion knelt beside her and clasped her hand between her own.

But Mrs. Halford was not one to give away long to such weakness. Drying her eyes, she said: "It reminds me of old times to see you again, Christina. I thought of the day us went out to Gore farm and you sat on the boxes. How are your mother?"

"Nearly as well as usual. I have just been trying to coax Marian to come over a while this afternoon. She has just gone upstairs to dress. But you must come too and see mother. It will do us good, I know."

"Thank you, Christina, if Marian are willing I shall go too."

When Mrs. Halford was smoothing her jet black hair and preparing to go out, she was busy with her thoughts. When she first heard of the Langtrys coming to Gowanstone it gave her a great shock. She was superstitious enough to think that their settling in Gowanstone, of all the places in America, was something more than blind chance. At first she suspected that Charles had followed her daughter, but, on inquiry, she found that Mr. Langtry himself could not possibly have had anything to do in deciding his location. For a time she comforted herself with the thought that David's being an agnostic would socially separate him and his wife from the young clergyman and his people. It was only recently she learned that the two houses were not only on visiting terms, but in close friendly relations. She suspected that Charles' frequent visits during the old lady's illness were prompted partly by his old time passion for Marian.

"If they love each other yet it will be terrible. Are this the hand of fate? Why could him not have gone some place else?"

At any rate, she determined to face him and his mother to find out whether her daughter still loved the companion of her youth.

The reception at the parsonage was everything that could be desired. Not a trace of embarrassment was visible on the good-natured countenance of the hostess. She took Mrs. Halford's hand as familiarly as of yore, and they chatted and laughed as freely as if there had never been a shadow between them. But when Charles came into the room the atmosphere suddenly changed. All the friendly warmth vanished. Mrs. Halford could not help admiring this handsome man with the complexion of a woman and the figure of an athlete.

As he removed his broad-brimmed hat she was surprised to see that his hair was as fair and as curly as ever. This, with his cleanly shaved face, gave him the appearance of a beautiful big boy.

His manner was certainly that of a gentleman, and something about the easy gracefulness of his form reminded her of Marian.

When introduced to Mrs. Halford he bowed and gave her one look that told all. Her knees trembled, but only for a moment, because she had prepared herself for this, and she managed to blurt out some commonplace about the weather. When he shook hands with Mrs. Gordon the anxious mother could not see his face, but she was certain that her daughter's colour deepened. As he stood face to face with Marian, Mrs. Halford could not help thinking what a splendid couple they would have made. She realized that only for her interference they would have been husband and wife.

She heaved a deep sigh as she thought of the great responsibility she had assumed and wondered how it would all end.

But she had a stern duty to perform, a task which she must accomplish. She must watch the words and actions of these two attractive creatures, who had once been all in all to each other. She must find out whether her daughter was in any danger, and if so, how it best could be avoided.

In spite of all efforts the conversation lagged and the situation became somewhat strained, until Christina suggested that her brother and Mrs. Gordon should sing a duet from one of the anthems which the choir had been practising. When Mr. Langtry sat down to the piano, little Davie climbed up on his knee and Marian stood close by reading off the same copy as the player. They sang beautifully together. Their voices seemed to blend like the colours of an autumn sunset. Even Mrs. Halford was carried away by the music and she applauded warmly. For at least half an hour they sang together, and as the beautiful woman stood beside the handsome man, their very forms seemed to tell Mrs. Halford that they were drawn together by some powerful influence.

Finally little Davie became restless, and in trying to climb from Mr. Langtry's knee to his mother's arms he almost fell. Both stooped to catch him at once. Their faces touched and for a moment the fair curls mingled with the glossy light-brown hair.

One look at Mr. Langtry's eyes told Mrs. Halford that he still loved her daughter, and as to Marian, why did the rich, warm colour suffuse her neck and brow? Why did she breathe more deeply? Why did she hide her face by smothering her boy with kisses, and for what reason did she develop such a sudden desire to look out the window?

Everything told the mother that her daughter was unconsciously standing on the edge of a precipice. It was some comfort, however, to think that he was a clergyman and a gentleman, while she was a lady and a mother. With her child in her arms, Marian soon recovered her self-possession, and when she turned from the window there was not a trace of embarrassment in her face.

But the tale had been told. Mrs. Halford passed a sleepless night. It seemed as if her sin against nature had found her out. Would Marian always be in a position to defy temptation? Would she always be able to fight the passions of herself and the lover of her youth? Might not opportunity and temptation combined come upon her unawares, or catch her in a moment of weakness?

A quarrel or estrangement must be brought about between the two houses, so that they would cease to be on visiting terms. The young clergyman and her daughter must be kept out of each other's company. Marian would have to quit singing in the choir, and attend some other church. But how was all this to be attained? For hours and hours, she tossed and turned in her bed, trying to conjure up some plan or plot to accomplish her object. At last, it suddenly struck her that she ought to get him out of Gowanstone altogether, and, if possible, out of the country. Ha, she would procure him a more lucrative appointment in some foreign country and would be doing him a service in that way. She would send him, bag and baggage, out of all reach, and then she would feel safe. But how would she go about it? She must take time to think it over. Yes, she would sleep over it. If it were properly applied she felt certain that the key to the whole situation was the Almighty Dollar.

CHAPTER XXXVI.

THE DEEP, DARK VALLEY.

CAN anybody tell why it is that troubles and misfortunes never seem to come singly? That they do come in groups most of us know, to our sorrow, but probably very few have ever tried to discover why it should be so. Perhaps if we looked deeply into the matter we might find traceable causes or connecting links between them, and, what at first sight appears to be a coincidence might be a natural sequence. When all our energies are absorbed by one misfortune are we not naturally apt to neglect the most important affairs of everyday life? When cavalry, infantry and artillery are eagerly pressing forward the rear is often left unguarded. Again, may not a whole group of misfortunes have indirectly a common cause? Society as well as the individual is very careless of evil so long as it is not apparent on the surface. "Out of sight out of mind."

One night little Davie awakened his mother by his strident breathing and feverish restlessness. She listened for a moment in horror, as if she could scarcely believe her ears. Every breath seemed to cost him a great effort. When she held the light to his face her heart stood still.

She ran to her husband's room, with a great outburst of grief. "Oh, David, hurry. Run for the doctor, quick. Davie is dying. Hurry, oh, hurry," she moaned as she hurried back to the little sufferer again.

She picked him up in her arms and carried him excitedly about the room. The poor little darling could hardly speak, but when he saw his mother sobbing and weeping he tried to say: "Davie tick, mama kye," and reached out his hand to soothe her. "Davie give mama candy."

"Oh, oh, oh!" she cried with bursting heart, "to

think that I slept while he suffered. Oh, Davie, Davie, mamma's little darling! you can't get your breath! Oh, this is awful! Will the doctor never come?"

After what seemed a long time, David returned with the doctor. The mother's face blanched with fear as she awaited his verdict. "Is there any danger?" she cried in agony. "Oh, Doctor, will he get better?"

The physician did not reply until he had examined the little sufferer thoroughly. Marian kept her eyes fixed on his countenance for the first glimpse of hope or despair.

"Inflammatory croup, and very severe at that. The little fellow is dangerously ill, Mrs. Gordon."

The mother snatched the child greedily in her arms and burst into a fresh torrent of weeping, while the father turned pale and staggered into a chair.

"Bear up, Marian, all hope is not gone. Is it, Doctor?"

The physician shook his head. "He has what you might call a fighting chance. The only way to make sure of these cases is to catch them when the first brassy cough is heard."

The poor mother fairly groaned. "Oh, my stupidity and carelessness. I heard that cough three nights ago. But he did not seem to be ill. Why, he played about all day yesterday. I was busy cleaning out poor Grandma's rooms and I thought he had just caught a little cold. But there," she continued, as she dried her eyes, "I am done weeping. Now for your orders, Doctor. If nursing and attention can save him, he shall live yet, please God."

Before Dr. Bennet left the house, Gordon asked him what he thought had caused the trouble.

"Exposure or damp surroundings," he replied categorically. "A damp cellar is particularly bad."

David's lips turned white. "Good heavens, our cellar is so wet, that I had to put a floor in it, to keep our feet out of the mud. Come and see it."

With the aid of a lantern they made their way to the foot of the stairs. In the dim light, the dark walls glistened with moisture. As he sniffed the foul damp air, the doctor exclaimed, "Humph! Here is the cause, right here, and," he continued, pointing to the water which shone through the crevices between the boards of the rough floor, " here is where your mother's rheumatism came from as well."

Gordon staggered against the wall, holding up his hands as if to ward off a blow. " Don't, Doctor, don't, for pity's sake. I see it all now. Mother used to tell me that those who strove only for wealth were generally overtaken by misfortune. 'Them that's ower keen o' winnin' the race often forget tae dae what's richt. They dinna tak time.' When I was increasing my water power and raising my mill-dam I never thought of my cellar. This is terrible. I feel like a murderer."

The doctor, for a few moments, seemed to be lost in thought. " Really, Gordon, I feel culpable myself. I should have thought about this before. When Mr. Gowan lived here the cellar was as dry as powder. I forgot that you raised your pond. I can't conceive, though, how a man of your intelligence could allow such a state of things to exist. If you had been some ordinary lout, without brains, I should have inquired about the cellar before this. Well, we have both been guilty of culpable negligence ; you before the fact, and I accessory to it. Humph !"

The doctor's candour sent a flash of light through David's soul, and for the first time in his life he caught a glimpse of his real, hideous self.

As daylight approached the sufferer's breathing became easier, and when the physician came back the second time, he pronounced his patient a little better. " But don't build on it too much, for there is generally an improvement in the morning."

On his way home Dr. Bennet communed with himself on this lesson in life which Marian and her child seemed to teach. " Talk about martyrs and heroines. That woman would allow herself to be torn to pieces for her child, and take a savage joy in the suffering if it would relieve him. Well, well, Motherhood is a martyrdom from beginning to end. First she undergoes suffering and risks her life in order that her offspring may see the light. And then she sits for hours and hours, days and days, weeks and weeks, watching and waiting for the glow of health, or the ashy grey of death. Muscles may ache, pulses may flag, nerves may throb with pain, and the brain be numbed by continued strain and exhaustion, yes, even reason may totter on its throne, but round the watcher's pale and haggard face there flits the twin angels of love and duty. For every hero who has given up his life for the petty quarrels of kings, or lay in pools of gore for glory's sake, a thousand mothers have died by inches at the bedside of love, where the greatest, grandest joy which God could give would be the privilege of offering up their lives for those they loved.

"Let poets sing of glorious scenes, where glistening banners greet the closing eyes of dying heroes, where shouts of victory fill their ears and tears of comrades fall upon their grimy cheeks, but give me the heroine of hearth and home, who in the lonely watches of the night suffers in silence for future generations, who, drop by drop, and year by year, ekes out the ebbing energies of life upon the cross of motherhood."

The doctor had scarcely reached home, when Gordon overtook him. "If there is anything on earth," he gasped, "to save that child, I want it done. Don't spare expense. I would give all I own and a thousand times more to save him. You are my friend, Doctor, as well as my physician. I shall leave it all with you."

Gordon tried to keep himself busy. He *could* not, dare not stop to think. But in spite of all, his mother's words kept ringing in his ears. He could not bear to remain in the room and witness the suffering he had inflicted upon his child. He patrolled the little pathway between the mill and the house like one demented. He went to the sluice-way, lowered the dam and shut down the mill. He telegraphed to Mrs. Halford and went to the doctor's every hour, with tidings of the little sufferer. Before evening several men were wheeling gravel into his cellar, through an opening in the wall. It was like locking the stable after the horse was stolen, but it seemed to give him a certain amount of relief. All day long he never sat down for a moment, and his spirits hovered between hope and despair.

Christina came and quietly took charge of the household without question or comment. She knew that there was little cure in condolence, she was satisfied to be useful in her humble way. She could cook food, keep on fires, heat water, and hurry to the nurse with every little appliance that was wanted. Without hope of reward or fear of blame, she always fell into line like a soldier on duty. No commanding officer was needed to point out her place. She knew it by instinct.

Then came Mrs. Halford, who assumed the duty of receiving or answering the scores of inquirers who besieged the door.

Her nature was well fitted for this sort of police duty. A multitude of people had suddenly developed a great affection for the little sufferer, but this did not give them admission to the sick-room, and the only satisfaction that callers had was a glimpse at the furniture or a caustic remark about the untidiness of the house.

It is astonishing how fond people become of us when we are about to depart this life: how those who would never assist us when living will weep over our graves. Outside of relatives the one who saturates the most handkerchiefs is invariably the one who never before had a good word for the departed.

Society rituals all impress upon us the duty of visiting the sick, but it would be well if they would qualify that motto by adding the words, "when one can be of any service."

Mrs. Halford, in her sombre way, rather enjoyed the opportunities it gave her of quizzing people. Instead of gratifying the curiosity of her visitors, she generally satisfied her own.

Marian never for a moment left her child. Neither food, sleep nor the entreaties of others would induce her to slacken her vigilance on behalf of her darling. Neither David nor Mrs. Halford could bear to remain in the room, but Christina during each night sat beside the anxious mother to give the comfort of companionship. Worse, gradually worse, the little patient grew until, on the evening of the third day, Wilberforce Russel, the surgeon specialist of New York, Dr. Delamere of Levisville, and the attending physician all agreed that the only hope lay in tracheotomy. The very mention of it horrified Gordon and Mrs. Halford. "What, butcher the child? Cut his throat? Never! Let him die in peace." Marian alone remained firm. "David, the child is surely safer with their skill than our ignorance. Just listen to the poor little darling's struggles for breath. They all say he will get relief, anyway."

Then came the horror of the operation, the trio of doctors with their cruel, shining knives, the odor of chloroform, the white sheets and pillows on the table, and the sponges ready to wipe away the blood of the little lamb. "I must be firm. I must do my duty," the mother said to herself, as she leaned against the wall for support. But the room spun around her and she remembered nothing more till she found herself on her knees by her husband's side, asking him to pray. She clamoured bitterly against being excluded from the sick-room, but the doctors reminded her that she was only flesh and blood. They insisted on her remaining out of all hearing.

She caught glimpses of Christina carrying towels and hot water, from which she knew that her trusty friend had taken her place.

In an incredibly short space of time Dr. Bennet came into the room to tell them that it was all over, and that the little patient was quite conscious and breathing quite easily.

The mother almost flew to the sick-room. Thank heaven, the struggle for breath was over, and the only trace of the operation was a silver tube peeping through the bandages on his throat.

When the strange doctors had gone and everything had resumed its accustomed quiet, Dr. Bennet touched David on the shoulder. "Get your hat, Gordon, and come for a little walk till I get the fumes of chloroform out of my head."

They walked for some time in silence down a side street in the cool night air. Then taking David's arm in his, the doctor said: "Well, we have given your boy ease, Gordon, but we have not saved his life. You will have to break it gently to your wife, but wait till she gets over the shock of the operation."

David trembled and staggered like a drunken man, but his companion slipped his arm about his waist and held him tighter. "He'll live for two or three days in comparative ease. After all, if people could look at things as philosophically as you and I can, life itself is little more."

CHAPTER XXXVII.

A STRANGER IN A STRANGE LAND.

A LIMITED express on one of the great American transcontinental routes was speeding its way westward, with its burden of human freight, and the long trail of dust and smoke in its wake gave evidence of its bird-like velocity. The palatial coaches swinging along behind the gigantic locomotive will never rest from their tireless flight till they greet the sunny slopes of the far-off Pacific. There, the soil of travel and the dust of a continent will be washed from their glossy sides, and the smoke of New York rinsed off by the waters of the Golden Horn.

It was a fine morning in June, and, in one of the berths of the sleeping car Metapedia, a young man was lying, gazing at the fleeting landscape with its kaleidoscopic changes. Fences, fields and forests, hills, hollows and hamlets, were madly chasing each other in the opposite direction, while an occasional tall chimney or church steeple suggested some larger town along the line of flight. Sometimes the monotonous roar would strike a deeper note as they swept over a bridge or viaduct, while ever and anon a clashing sound or fleeting shadow told of a wayside station or a sister train speeding in an opposite direction. To the tired eyes and aching head of the traveller, everything seemed going but himself. The mother earth appeared to have slipped a cog and taken a dizzy notion to spin round like a top. Of course, he had been taught that the earth revolved on its axis, but he never fully realized it till now. Nor had our traveller been trifling with flasks or demijohns, but he had passed a sleepless night, and the motion of the train produced a sort of nausea which resembled sea-sickness. He was not in the best of spirits when he boarded the train at New York, and the weariness of travel only added to his dejection. Yet he had seen many things which interested and amused him. He was a stranger in a strange land, but, with unusually keen perceptive faculties, he had taken note of many things which others might have passed unseen. He had already gathered the impression that the Americans were a strange and wonderful people. He saw young and old of both sexes undertaking long journeys without the slightest perturbation. On his car alone were several examples.

A little Miss of ten was going on a visit to her aunt at San Francisco, a boy of seven was on his return trip from New York to Omaha, and a beautiful young lady, without chaperone or companion, was booked for some point far West.

Then how quickly everybody got acquainted with each other. Several of his fellow-passengers had the audacity to quiz him as to where he came from, where he was going, and what his business was, just as if they had a right to know. But these Americans seemed to like that sort of thing. People who never saw or heard of each other before, and probably would never meet again in this vale of tears, mingled and chatted with the familiarity of old acquaintances.

They were only fifteen hours out from New York, and already the occupants of the Metapedia were like members of one family.

The little Miss had become very affectionate with an

elderly gentleman who revelled in a foghorn voice, a broom-straw chin-whisker, and wire-like hair. She was continually sitting on his knee and calling him Uncle Jake. The fellow with show-bills sticking from his pockets fraternized freely with the clerical gentleman, a card-sharp was arguing politics with a senator, and the beautiful young lady was like a loving daughter to the fat woman with the asthma.

The sleeping car itself was a sort of revelation to him. The idea of a person being packed away on a shelf, with nothing between him and a whole car full of strangers, was not an agreeable one. Somebody might rob him or throttle him as he lay helpless in his berth. It was like tempting Providence.

But one after another, his fellow passengers disappeared behind their respective curtains, the beautiful young lady as well as the rest.

Fortunately, he had secured a lower berth, which he could ventilate by opening his window, and thus avoid the danger of being asphixiated. Excepting for his repugnance to being undressed, and the novelty of his position, he was soon fairly comfortable.

But the rushing roar of the train and the rhythmic rattling of the wheels underneath him made sleep impossible.

What if something were to break or give way while he was minus his trowsers? Death would come sometime, and a person had only to go through it once, but the possibility of being tossed through the air in his night shirt put him in a cold sweat.

After a while he became accustomed to his position and ventured a peep into the aisle. All was quiet. Not a soul in sight, nothing but a narrow passage between two rows of dark curtains and the lamp burning dimly at the top.

Truly, these were strange people. With no protection to themselves or their valuables they were apparently sleeping as soundly and contentedly as if they were in their own beds at home.

The whole arrangement seemed preposterous; a tempting opportunity for thieves and villains of all sorts. Of course, there was the porter, but he was nowhere in sight, and, then, he was only a negro. Long and deeply did he ponder over this object lesson of American civilization.

Another peep through his curtains showed rows of boots and shoes strung along the aisle. Away at the other end, lying beside Uncle Jake's huge pedal envelopes, were the boots of the little Miss; a swollen looking pair which probably belonged to the fat woman were embracing the card-sharp's gaiters; the senator's lanky calfskins were laughing at the lumpy corn-curing foot-armour of the judge; and there, not two feet away, like flowers in a field of weeds, were the dainty, tan-coloured boots of the young lady.

Something about the whole situation tickled his sense of humour, and he almost laughed aloud. The amount of self-reliance indicated by the rows of boots was both amazing and amusing.

His attention, however, was soon centred on the dear-little tan-coloured triumphs of St. Crispin's art, that were modestly blushing at his gaze.

What a charming suggestion the dainty instep and ankle gave to the faint creases which marked the gracefully sloped enlargement at the top.

He listened for a while to make sure the owner was asleep, then gently lifted one of them, and gazed at it caressingly. He had heard that American girls had large feet, but here was a flat contradiction of that idea. Even Cinderella's slipper, he thought, could not compare with the graceful curves and outlines of this coy and candid piece of foot-wear.

Ha! there was a button hanging loose. Yes, it was nearly off. Would it be any harm for him to keep it? "She would only lose it anyway," he thought.

He slyly pulled it off, and slipped it into his trowsers pocket, feeling as guilty as a thief, but quieting his conscience by the promise that he would give it back to her in the morning. Besides it would give him an excuse for introducing himself to her. Hark, there is some one coming. In a moment his little treasure was deposited beside its mate. Then the black porter carried them off and he was left disconsolate.

For hours he lay awake, listening to the song of the wheels, wondering whether they ever got tired. He dozed over at last, but soon was awakened by a bright light glaring through the window and a perfect Babel of sounds outside.

The train had stopped for the first time during the night, and a glance through his window at the sea of coloured lights and moving cars showed him that they were at some large depot.

Inside, the squall of an infant here and a cough or a yawn there told him that the bulk of his fellow passengers were awake. He took another peep into the aisle.

The porter, evidently without any request, was placing a glass of water underneath the young lady's curtain, and our traveller caught a glimpse of the shapely hand and lace-trimmed sleeve which reached out for it.

In vain he kept watching to see her curtain move again, but the empty glass rolled out into the aisle, and all was still.

Then he lay for a time listening to the clanking of hammers on the wheels and the shouts and bustle outside, when his attention was drawn to a conversation immediately under his window.

"How did you make out," said a voice, which he immediately recognized as Uncle Jake's.

"Smashed him all to pieces," replied his companion in a confidential tone. "Why, he got so rank they had to take him out of the box."

"Wall now, dew tell. Any trouble to find him?"

"Just a little. Half a dozen died pounding the atmosphere at first, but after that we battered everything to pieces."

"Haw, haw, haw," laughed the hoary headed old villain. "They'll hev to bury him now. But did'nt they get on to you?"

"No!" exclaimed the other in a deprecating tone, "they couldn't find me with a detective agency and a search warrant. Three shots finished more than half of them. We'll simply massacre the whole outfit when we get them out to Denver."

"Did you rake in much?" inquired Jake.

"Yes, about seventeen hundred, but mostly in fives and tens, though we tapped one old fellow for five hundred."

The voices were now drowned by the hissing of a locomotive which stopped immediately opposite his window, and when it moved away the villains had gone.

What desperate work was here? Was this the prelude to some terrible train-robbing tragedy? Evidently they were going red-handed from one plot to another. He had frequently read of the daring train-robberies of the West, and, sure enough, here it was in all its grim realities.

This Uncle Jake must, after all, be a desperado of the worst type, in spite of his grey hair and kindly face. He had simply been laying his plans by getting into the confidence of all around him. "So they are going to spring their plot at Denver. Well, we shall see about that. We won't reach Denver for twenty-four hours or more, but I will notify the conductor first thing in the morning."

The train again began to move. Coloured lights and sundry noises were left behind, and the familiar voice of the wheels told him that the "Limited" had again resumed its tireless flight across the continent.

He was almost asleep again, when, to his horror, he heard the voices of the two desperadoes immediately in front of his berth.

His hand involuntarily clutched the vest containing his valuables, and his heart leaped into his throat.

"He's in here some place," whispered the elderly villain, "but I don't know whether he's top or bottom."

An attempt was made to pull his curtain aside, but he clutched and held it fast.

"Durn his picter, he's tuk the bottom," said Jake in a hoarse whisper, and they both gave a smothered laugh.

"Keep still, for God's sake," grumbled the other. "You'll bring the conductor and porter after us and ruin my game. You exchanged berths, you say. Here, give me a leg up and nobody will know I'm here."

He could hear them laughing, sotto voce, up above, and in spite of all the whispered remonstrances of his companion, Jake's haw, haw, hâw! would break out till someone across the aisle would growl at him to shut up. Occasionally, he could catch snatches of their conversation. "Go you ten to one, Jake, that I'll stand him off with a shillin' and dodge the 'con', too."

Soon he heard them snoring, these hardened votaries of crime, sleeping as contentedly as a pair of innocent babes. After all, America's freedom had its drawbacks. Jack was not only as good as his master, but the desperado's dollar placed him cheek by jowl with purity and innocence. Sleep was, of course, now out of the question. He quietly slipped on his nether garments and vest and lay there awaiting developments. Perhaps the snoring above him was only a ruse to throw people off their guard.

At any rate he would remain where he was and guard the chamber of youth and beauty. He would watch his Cinderella's berth. She must not be molested.

Hour after hour he lay looking through his window till the sun was well above the horizon. But anxiety, loss of sleep and the continuous motion gradually made him deathly sick.

He ceased peeping into the aisle, he lost all interest in his burglars; in fact, he would not have cared much if the train had jumped the first embankment. At last in sheer desperation he crawled out of his little prison and staggered along to the smoking apartment. All was still. The rosy sun was peeping through the back door of the coach, the lamps were still burning dimly in their sockets, and the coloured porter was snoring on a pile of cushions.

CHAPTER XXXVIII.

A NEEDLE IN A HAYSTACK.

The traveller was soon revived by the kindness of the porter. That functionary was on the alert in a moment, taking him in charge with professional adroitness.

He bathed his head and fomented his eyes and forehead with towels wrung out of hot water. Then, with a knowing wink, which, however, was lost upon his patient, he brought forth a foaming drink of Bromo-Seltzer "dat he kep' foh de purpose."

When this was followed by a cup of hot coffee and a sandwich, the young man felt quite restored. After giving his attendant a silver dollar for his trouble, he ventured to ask who the young lady was that occupied the berth opposite his, but he could get no information, excepting that she was to get off at Chicago, the next stopping place.

This was bad news, indeed, for he already felt a sort of protectorship for her, if not something more, and now she would disappear from his sight forever.

However, he must not let anything overshadow the duty which devolved upon him of notifying the conductor of what he had learned during the night.

"When shall I see the conductor?" he inquired.

"Not till we leave Chicawgo, sah. Den a new conductah comes on."

"How can I see him right away?"

"By goin' through six coaches and a baggage cah. If you like, sah, I'll carry de message," continued the coloured gentleman, no doubt scenting a fresh fee. "De passengers am all in bed yet, and de aisles am full of baggage."

After some hesitation the traveller took the porter

into his confidence. He not only told him all, but pointed out the berths where the villains still slept. With an eagerness worthy of his official position, the negro rushed from the car without waiting for the end of the story, and so the matter was off his mind.

Maurice Fletcher felt sad and homesick. Four weeks ago that very morning he had watched the spires of Liverpool sink into the sea, and bade his native land good-bye, perhaps forever. With a good business education, and a dozen ten-pound notes, he had come to America to carve out, if not a fortune, at least a future for himself. Left an orphan in early years, he could remember nothing of his parents, but their place had been kindly filled by John Thurston, his guardian, who was to him a loving father. When he was leaving home Mr. Thurston had placed a very important matter in his charge. He was to make a thorough search for some parties who had left England twenty-six years before for some foreign country, which was more likely to have been Australia than America. Acting, however, on the supposition that they had come to America, he had searched ship registers and immigration records for two weeks. He had advertised in a number of leading dailies, had gone North, South, East and West, on the strength of a similarity of names, and yet not only had he failed to get a clue, but so far had not been able to get a situation.

His pound notes had been changed for American dollars, and these, in turn, were disappearing with a rapidity that was alarming.

For the present, at least, he had given up the search, and was on his way to Denver, with a letter of introduction to one of its leading citizens.

He took a package from his pocket, looked at it fondly, and commenced to read.

After a few fatherly sentences about his own welfare and future, the letter ran as follows:

" But there is another matter, dear Maurice, which I would like you to take in hand, viz., to locate the heir to an estate of which I am sole executor. First, let me tell you the story and then you will more thoroughly understand your chances of success.

"Twenty-six years ago this month, a young man named William Halford (a son of the old squire's), left England as we supposed for Australia, at least a young man answering to his description sailed for Sydney about the time of his disappearance, in company with a young woman whose description we could not obtain.

"Halford was supposed to have taken with him a young woman named Symonds, the adopted daughter of the old lodge-keeper.

"About seven weeks previous to their departure this young woman gave birth to a child, and there was no reasonable doubt that Halford was the father of it.

"The 'squire was ill at the time, and when he heard the scandal he sent for his son. Just what passed between them is not known, but the result was that the son was disinherited, although, for that matter, it was no great loss, for the 'squire was really bankrupt at the time.

"Now comes the odd part of it. When the 'squire's second wife died she left her property to this child of Jane Symonds. You remember, of course, that Lady Mary had no children of her own, and that all the younger Halfords fairly detested their step-mother. But William, or Will as he was always called, was a favourite with her, and she took his part in the time of trouble.

"Now, instead of leaving her property to young Halford, as you might have expected, the will directs that, failing this child, the property falls first to Jane Symonds and then to Halford.

"A most extraordinary will, you think, and yet there were natural reasons for it which none but myself know. Jane Symonds was really an illegitimate child of Lady Mary's, and it was through her that the old lodge-keeper and his wife adopted this Jane when ten years of age.

"Lady Mary, it seems, had in her youth loved, not wisely but too well, a colonel of the hussars, who abandoned her as soon as he found she had no fortune.

"She was, as you have no doubt heard, a most extraordinary woman, and in spite of the 'squire, who, by the way, was rather afraid of her, she visited the young woman during her illness, bought clothing for the child, and no doubt furnished the money which took the young couple abroad. They were not married at the time of their leaving, but no doubt were soon afterwards, for though Will Halford was wild he was the soul of honor.

"The 'squire, of course, knew nothing of the parentage of Jane Symonds, and he raved and swore that it was nothing but contrariness which prompted his wife's kindness to the young mother.

"He drove Symonds and his wife off the place. But Lady Mary built them a house on her own land and assisted them in other ways. This property now constitutes the entire estate. At the time of the old lady's death it was worth, perhaps, about two-hundred and fifty pounds, but the recent discovery of coal in the vicinity, and the location of the railway depot adjacent to it, has raised its value to easily ten times that amount.

"The interest, heretofore, has been absorbed by the cost of advertising in Australia, and the search is still going on there.

"But it occurred to me that possibly we have been wrong in taking for granted that the young couple who sailed for Australia at that time were really the parties we are in search of. At the time of her death Lady Mary seemed positive that they were in Australia, but she herself may have been mistaken.

"Be this as it may, the enlarged interest and increased value of the estate warrants me in commencing a search in America, and I have thought I could not do better than (for a time, at least), place the matter in your hands.

"The enclosed two hundred pounds is to be expended legitimately in advertising and searching for the heir, or rather heiress, for the child was a girl.

"While you are engaged in this you will have enlarged opportunities of becoming acquainted with the customs and manners of the American people, and will probably see business opportunities which might be suitable for you.

"I may tell you in advance that I do not expect you will succeed in finding them, but I feel certain you will enter an honorable and useful career, and I have no misgivings as to your future.

"Enclosed find a letter of introduction to a Mr. Tracy (a son of my most intimate friend), who is, I believe, an influential man in Denver, and will, no doubt, be of great assistance in securing you a situation.

"And now good-bye, dear boy, and God bless you. I am sorry your own little capital is not greater, but remember, in prosperity or adversity that although I am no longer your guardian, I am still
"Your friend,
"JOHN THURSTON."

"N. B. In another package are tintypes of the lost couple and letters to be delivered to them if found. Advertise for 'Jane Symonds' as well as for 'Jane Halford.' He may have deserted her. If your funds run low, keep enough to cable me.
"J. T."

Poor Maurice turned his face to the window to hide his tears. Then he noticed that the train was slackening its speed. The engine was whistling and calling for room on the great network of rails which surrounded them in every direction.

A number of the passengers were preparing to take their leave, and among them was the young lady, looking bright and fresh from her morning ablutions. On her feet were the dear little boots which he had caressed but a few hours before. He had a feeling that he ought to get off and go with her to the end of her journey, wherever it might be.

At last, with clanging bell, the train glided slowly into the great depôt and he followed her out of the car. For a few moments she stood on the upper step, looking over the sea of faces. Having at last caught a glimpse of the right one, she waved her handkerchief and disappeared in the crowd, while he went sadly back into the coach with a lump in his throat, and stealthily kissed an oval button.

There was great shouting, hurrying, jostling, and ringing of bells, but just as soon as the huge piles of baggage were loaded and unloaded, and a sumptuous dining-car was tacked on behind, a fresh iron horse was pulling them out of the interminable network tracks, to the main highway of steel, and the Limited after its short greeting to the great metropolis of the West, again started for the far-off Pacific.

CHAPTER XXXIX.

JAKE FETTERLY'S CONVERSION.

THE most surprising, and yet often the most simple of all occurrences, are those which are usually classed as coincidences. Somebody whom we had forgotten or had not seen for years happens to take the same train, boat, or car; to stop at the same hotel; or to turn the corner of a street at the same time as ourselves. If we are not accustomed to travelling much, we will say to ourselves, "What an odd coincidence!" but if our business, occupation or calling necessitates much going about, we will be apt to pass it by unnoticed, or perhaps make the remark that we never go to any place without meeting somebody we know. Nor is it to be wondered at in this age of cheap transportation, telegraphs, telephones and newspapers. Man is a migratory animal and is continually becoming more so, as the facilities and inducements for getting about are cheapened and multiplied. In America every man talks to his next neighbour in car, boat, or hotel; each finds out about the other as much as he cares to know, and people in this way pick up acquaintances with the most astonishing rapidity.

Had Maurice Fletcher been as communicative as the average American it is quite possible that before this he might have been successful in his search. But he was distant in his manner. He scarcely ever spoke unless spoken to, and then only in monosyllables.

A Wilkins Micawber sort of policy is of little use in America, or indeed anywhere else. One must exert oneself continually.

Next to the newspapers, the best advertising mediums are our talkative, sociable, company-loving fellow men.

The loss of Maurice's loadstar at Chicago, and the sadness caused thereby, made him forget all about his robbers until the train was well under way, and then neither of them was in sight. They must have left the car while he was standing outside, breathing the fresh morning air. The berths were all closed up, and the coach had resumed its usual day appearance. The little girl had also left the car. She was no doubt with " Uncle Jake." Well, no matter, the conductor would soon be around, and Maurice would further unload himself of all responsibility in regard to them.

But the porter came first, and, with a curious gleam in his eye, said " Breakfast am ready in de dining cah."

The moment Maurice entered the breakfast apartment he saw that he had made some ridiculous blunder. Every eye was turned upon him, winks and nods went from one to another, while the head waiter, with a suppressed smile, motioned him into a seat, cheek by jowl with his train-robbers.

On Jake's knee sat the little girl enjoying her morning repast, while at his left hand sat the weasel-like fellow with the voice of villain number two.

The venerable rascal broke out with a loud haw, haw, haw, as soon as he set eyes on the young Englishman, and in a moment the whole car resounded with laughter.

Maurice's face turned scarlet. He fairly choked with anger, but he resolved to take no notice of them. He went on with his breakfast.

Finally Jake spoke up. " Look here, stranger, I want

ter 'pologize fur my want of perliteness, but the idea of Jake Fetterly holdin' up a train and taking up a colleckshun is a little too much fur me," and he broke out again, worse than ever.

"You don't have to use a gun when you want a loan, Jake," said the scrubby man beside him.

"Go easy, Carey. Don't throw another ball till he gets in his box. Here, stranger, gimme yer hand. Don't get yer back up at the boys fur havin' a little fun. They don't mean no harm. Durn it all, I wuz a tenderfoot once myself."

The offer was so genuine that Maurice could not refuse it, so he reached out his hand and Fetterly shook it warmly, exclaiming at the same time: "Here's to our better acquaintance."

A small, sharp-eyed, trim-built, well-dressed man at the adjoining table was next heard from. "You were quite right, stranger, to regard those men with suspicion. Fetterly stole the richest mine in Colorado, and Carey is a born 'base thief.' You only anticipated their promotion. Give them time."

"You scored that time, Reggy," said Jake, when the laughter had subsided, "but we mustn't spile the joke by rubbin' it in."

For a few moments there was silence, but Uncle Jake could not long contain himself.

Dropping his voice to a conversational tone, he said; "I ain't no slouch at readin' faces. I sed to myself, 'thar's a clean, fresh, wholesome young Britisher, all wool and a yard wide, but away from home for the first time.'"

Maurice good-naturedly admitted the soft impeachment, and added that he was only a few weeks in America.

"Well, what do you think of the country?" said the man called Reggy, wheeling round in his chair.

"That's right, tell us what you think of us," said another.

"Don't spring it on him all to once, boys, but jest let him tell his experience, as they say at camp meeting."

"It seems you all know something of my experience

already," replied the young Englishman, looking around him. This was the signal for a fresh outburst of merriment in which Maurice himself heartily joined, for although he still had no explanation of last night's dialogue, he knew that his mistake had been a ridiculous one. But he did not care to ask. He preferred to wait for light on the subject.

Reggy proposed that the joke be published in the newspapers. "It is really too good to keep," he added with a twinkle in his eye. "It could be filed away among the archives of the Denver Ball Club."

"I have not the slightest objection," said Maurice, "provided my name is withheld."

"That settles it then. A rose by any other name will smell as sweet, only we won't spare Jake and Carey."

"You haven't told us what you think of America yet," remarked a quiet-looking man at another table.

"Yes, yes. Let us have your opinion," exclaimed Reggy.

"I scarcely know how to answer you, but so far, I have been astonished by the enterprise, sociability, and self-reliance of your people. Before I came here, I fancied that America was largely a howling wilderness, but when I saw your great metropolis, New York, I had to confess to myself that even London seemed dull and dingy compared with it."

The enthusiasm on the faces of the listeners was good to see. From time to time they nodded and smiled, while Jake broke in with "dew tell."

"I was astonished," continued Maurice, "to see ladies and children travelling alone, but I can see they are just as safe as I am."

"Yes, and safer," exclaimed Jake, kissing the little girl's cheek, while the laughter broke out afresh.

"Order, boys," shouted the old man, "let the stranger go on with his yarn. He's got the floor."

"I am expected to look out for myself," continued Fletcher, "but I notice that every American citizen, is a *pro tem.* policeman for the protection of ladies and children in his company. This and the reception you are giving me would seem to indicate that the average American is a genial gentleman."

The pent up enthusiasm of his hearers now broke loose.

"Put it there, old man. You're the stuff. E pluribus unum," and other enthusiastic exclamations went round the assembly. To wind up with Fetterly rose to his feet and shouted, "What's the matter with the Britisher?" and the answer came in chorus, "He's all right."

The waiter here interfered, saying he was "'bliged to call the gentlemen to ordah."

"That's right, boys. We've got to cramp it down, but it's mighty hard. The eagle will screech when it's gettin' its feathers rubbed down. Haw, haw, haw."

"Perhaps the stranger has been reading Sam Slick," said a man at the opposite side of the car.

"Who's umpiring this game?" retorted Carey, looking severely at the speaker. "You can't call balls on him, with that curve on."

"No, sirree," exclaimed Jake, emphatically. "If he war given us taffy, he done it mighty slick, anyhow."

"I only gave you my impressions, as I received them," protested Maurice, "neither more nor less."

The waiter now came round to collect the breakfast checks, and Maurice's hand naturally sought his pocket.

"Stop right thar, stranger," shouted Jake. "You can't pay fur anything on this here car. This is the first, and mebbie the last time, we'll ever kick shins under the same mahog'ny. When the lion dines with the eagle, there hain't no fares collected, no, sirree. Waiter, trot out the slickest juice on the ice wagon, and we'll drink to the health of the Britisher. Hang it, boys, we're all cousins, and these fellows, what can't drink to the health of Johnny Bull, hain't no real blood relations of Uncle Sam. Blood's thicker'n water, boys, and long may the two greatest nations on earth chew off the same plug."

When they adjourned to the smoking apartment, Reggy brought in a plentiful supply of cigars, and the conversation was resumed.

"Wall, stranger," commenced Jake, "I won them cigars off the boss here, on you bein' a Britisher."

"How did you know?" laughed Fletcher.

"Know. Why, by the cut of your jib, of course, and the fresh colour in your gills. Why, I had a dead sure thing."

"Americans don't have complexions," explained Reggy. "But you'll soon lose yours, too, if you stay here long."

"Some thinks it's too much fancy grub," said Jake, thoughtfully, "others thinks it's the climate, but anyhow, it does seem a fact."

"Is it the water, do you suppose?" asked Carey roguishly.

"Not in this crowd, anyhow. We don't take enuff to hurt us, but say, stranger, gimme yer name and we'll have a little introduction all round."

"Maurice Fletcher."

"Good! Well, Mr. Fletcher, these here, are Corkscrew Carey, Jim Stratton, and Joe Slatter of the Denver Ball Club. Jake Fetterly, from anywhere is your humble servant, and last, but not least by a long chalk, is the worshipful Mayor of Denver City and captain of the said ball team, Mr. Reignald Tracy."

In a second Fletcher was on his feet, pale with excitement. "What, Reginald Tracy of Denver?"

"That's me, I guess," replied the little man, with a smile.

"Then, by heavens, you are the very man I'm going to see. I have a letter for you."

The whole group were thunderstruck at this unexpected turn of affairs. They eagerly watched the alternating expressions on Tracy's face as he read the letter.

When he had finished he grasped Maurice's hand. "Welcome to America. Why, boys, this is a friend of the family from England."

There was a shake all round and Tracy ordered a fresh consignment of juice. "The greatest luck I ever heerd of," said Jake, "but I always told you, boys, that a tenderfoot has the tallest luck. I've seed them time and again clean out the oldest head in the party," he continued, with a solemn shake of his iron-grey locks.

"Never mind about the situation for a week or two, Mr. Fletcher. You had better run around with us for another week, till the boys finish their tour. You can be our mascot."

"Indeed, I am almost tired of travelling. I have been for the past four weeks searching for the heirs to a small estate in England."

"And who is the fortunate creature or creatures?"

"The people I'm searching for are called Halford. They left England twenty-six years ago. William and Jane Halford."

"I knew a Halford back East," said Tracy, musingly. "but I don't just remember where. Oh, yes, now I remember. He was president of the Levisville Stars."

"I have found quite a number of the same name but never the right ones. However, I can show you their pictures. That is his wife."

"Hum! Rather fine-looking woman, but I never saw Mrs. Halford, so, of course, can't say. This picture does seem to resemble the old man a little. There's the mutton-chop whiskers, but this picture is of a young man and the Halford I know was an elderly man. I wouldn't say there is any real resemblance. Think his name was William, though. Might as well note it down."

The matter was dropped, and the conversation had drifted into other channels when the conductor came round for the tickets.

"Oh, say, Bill," exclaimed Tracy, "you used to live at Levisville. Do you remember old man Halford?'

"Well, rather," replied the official, in a decided tone, "he and his wife were the first foreign passengers I drove in on my new stage. What about him?"

"Well, this man here," explained Tracy, pointing to Maurice, "has been hunting all over the continent for a man named Halford and his wife. Here's a picture; see if it's the right man."

Expectation ran high. Every eye was on the conductor's face. Jake savagely bit off a fresh chew,

"It does seem like him," said Innes, "but I couldn't swear to him. Perhaps this ain't a good likeness."

"Well, try this," and the other tintype was slipped into his hand.

The official's face lit up like a flash. He fairly shouted, "Jane Halford, by the eternal."

The little group cheered with excitement; all but Jake. His hair stood on end. "Look here, boys, this thing is got serious. There hain't no sech a thing as chance or luck after this. God Almighty's got a hand in this game, an' he's called me down."

They were all dumfounded by the double coincidence, though none of them were so seriously affected as Fetterly. He solemnly vowed that something was going to happen the young man. He was either going to heaven at an early date, or to be made president of the United States.

"Straight goods, boys; it's a warnin' for all hands. We've got to quit stackin' the cards, and play sqar all round. This here is two strikes for Jake Fetterly. First was when the missus crossed the big divide with the baby. Yes, you may smile, Jim, but this hain't your turn at the bat. Mebbie it don't matter much if old Jake does fan out, but it won't be carelessness if he does. I hain't agoin' to fool away my last chance. I know you didn't mean no harm, Jim, 'cause I was a kid onct myself. Whin Bill thar first knowed me, I was a purty spry chap. Well, come to think of it, this is a mighty small world, after all, eh, Bill," and the old man heaved a deep sigh.

"You're right thar, Jake. If a man wants to get lost nowadays he's got to get off the earth. That's how I've got it figgered up."

CHAPTER XL.

THE SPIDER AND THE FLY.

ON the very spot which once was ornamented by Blake's hostelry and Langtry's store now stands the stateliest block in Levisville, with its rich façades, and polished pillars. Yet from a visitor's point of view the change was not altogether for the better. In contradistinction to the cheeriness of old, when canary birds sang in their cages and neighbours chatted merrily over their glass of ale, the place has now a look of gloomy solemnity.

Musty papers had taken the place of meat and drink, and Mammon had supplanted Bacchus. If one might judge by the faces and forms in their entrance and exit from the gloomy portals, neither happiness nor morality had gained by the transformation. The dark stone front seemed to absorb all the sunshine, and the inner offices, even at bright noonday, were lit with jets of gas. Neither food nor shelter, comfort nor cheer, kindness nor charity could be found here, for the entire building was occupied by gentlemen of the legal fraternity.

The architect, however, had been something of a humourist, for just above the massive doorway of the rotunda, in beautiful bronze effect, was Justice with her scales, but, either by mistake or motive, one eye was partly uncovered.

On the ground floor were the most elaborate and sumptuously furnished offices, and these were almost wholly occupied by one firm.

The plate-glass doors and windows, as far backwards as one could see, bore in beautiful gilt letters, the inscription " Slade & Co., Barrister & Solicitors, etc."

As far as the public were concerned, the whole firm consisted of Mr. Slade himself. He had a perfect army of understrappers, but all business of any importance passed through his own hands.

Magistrate's petty-court and police-court cases were not considered of sufficient importance for the head of the firm, unless the victim was a particularly juicy one. His apartments were like the modern departmental store, where you could purchase anything you wished. The dodging debtor went to one door for advice, and the pursuing creditor to another; the defaulter and trickster went to the right, and the widow scrambling for her stolen mite turned to the left. Fire-bugs and insurance detectives filled one aisle, financiers and kite-flyers another, and perhaps, within a foot of each other, with only a partition between them, was the wife entering a divorce plea, and the husband securing a counter action. Guilelessness and guilt, generosity and greed, candour and cunning, virtue and vice, law and licence, jostled each other in the shadowy passages, but "all roads led to London."

Nor was it always litigation that customers were in search of. If the big wig wanted to buy his way quietly out of some *scrape*, or the grandame wished to push an intrigue, Slade was the man to manage it.

Dame Rumour spoke in bated breath of transactions fearful and unholy. Many a crime and compromise were supposed to be buried in his vaults.

Yet no one could put their finger on anything that could commit the legal luminary, or stain his good name. If he *did* flourish on the edge of filthy pools of vice he took good care never to fall in. There was one crime of which he was never guilty—that of being found out.

In the money-*lending* department everything was managed with clock-work regularity and scrupulous honesty. No one was in danger of being cheated out of a cent—it would'nt have paid!

If you had money coming from Slade & Co., you could count on it just as surely as sunrise. This fact, alone, offset many a dark whisper. Vice can always thrive better in company with virtue.

On this particular morning the number of clients were fewer than usual. A long sitting of the high court was just over, and, no doubt, this was the calm that usually follows a storm.

Mrs. Halford had gone from one office to another, led by an usher who generally distributed untutored callers to the various departments. But she insisted on seeing Mr. Slade, and would not even mention the nature of her business.

It was no easy matter, however, to reach headquarters, for the outer offices, like satellites, were clustered round the one great centre.

Mrs. Halford had never before been under the necessity of employing a solicitor, for hitherto her transactions had been simple and straight forward, merely sale and purchase.

Her neighbour, Mr. Grazely, in return for many kindnesses, had done all her conveyancing, and given her all the legal advice she had required.

She had, however, a passing acquaintance with the great lawyer, and had formed a pretty fair estimate of his character.

After a good deal of waiting she was at last ushered into his presence, and as she looked around at the heavy, thick, double-padded doors, she guessed that here was the spot where clients told their secrets.

Mr. Slade was a small, thin man, slightly stooped, with a large nose and small piercing eyes, which through his spectacles looked like glass beads. His face was of a peculiar shape. It sloped gradually from his ears to his nose and chin like a wedge to its thin end. His lips were thin, and his mouth was large, but he had a fine head of dark hair and the pink and white complexion of a woman.

"Ah, how do you do, Mrs. Halford? Fine weather we are having," he said, as he wheeled round in his chair, and smiled blandly on his client.

She hardly knew how to commence, her business was of so peculiar and delicate a nature.

She expected him to ask the nature of her business, and give her a chance to open the subject gradually, but he only spoke on general topics, just as if her call was merely a matter of friendship. With his nose slightly elevated as though he scented mystery, he went on chatting as cheerfully as if he were entertaining a dear friend.

"Your people all well?" he inquired with an approving nod.

"Well, now I really might say 'yes,' at the present, but us buried a grandchild last week. He were my daughter's only child; a little boy."

Mr. Slade cared nothing for all the babies in Christendom, but he must thaw his client out. "What was the nature of the trouble?" he asked with well feigned interest.

"It were croup. The poor little fellow just choked to death."

"It must have been very hard for you and the poor mother," he remarked sympathetically, as he blew his nose with musical resonance. There must be something unusual, he thought, or she would "out with it."

He turned away for a few moments, pretending to arrange some papers on his desk.

This gave her confidence and she commenced.

"Well, now, Mr. Slade, I would like to get your advice about an affair which are not law altogether. I don't know whether it are quite in your line."

"A very cautious customer this," thought the lawyer, but he did not reply, he simply elevated his eyebrows and smiled blandly.

"I have an interest in a young man and I would like to get him a higher position."

"The young gentleman is fortunate in having such an ally as yourself, Mrs. Halford," replied the legal gentleman with great unction. "Might I venture to ask his calling or profession?"

"He are a clergyman. I want him moved into a higher position."

"Ah, indeed! That is rather a delicate matter," remarked Mr. Slade with an indulgent smile. "I suppose he is well qualified for filling a higher position, but lacks influence."

She hesitated a moment and coloured slightly. "Well, now, I are not sure that he is, but I should think that were not always needful."

"Oh, no, not at all! Promotion, like kisses, goes by

favour. Sometimes the greatest numskulls draw the largest salaries."

"He are at present a rector on six hundred a year, and if him got an offer of three or four hundred more he would likely take it."

Mr. Slade closed his eyes. There was more in this than appeared on the surface, but he would get it out of her yet. "Just where would you like to have him located, Mrs. Halford?"

"As far away as possible," she blurted out without thinking. She felt like biting her tongue the moment afterwards. The cat was out of the bag now.

The legal gentleman, drumming his fingers on his desk, pretended not to notice it. "Anywhere in the Union would do, I suppose, or would you prefer England or Australia?"

The glow on Mrs. Halford's face deepened. She worked her chair closer. "Do you think you could manage it in Australia?"

"Oh, certainly. It is only a question of cost, and," he added, after a short pause, "a little time, of course. I suppose the post of chaplain to some public institution would be suitable?"

"That are the very thing, because him are not just a good speaker."

"It will be much easier if he is handsome, presentable, and unmarried," remarked her adviser, fishing for more information as to his client's motives.

"Well, now, Mr. Slade, I don't think you ever saw a handsomer man. He are a picture to look at, and single, too."

"Ah, here is the motive at last," thought the wily lawyer. "She wishes to remove him out of the reach of her marriageable daughter. Some higher game in her eye." He leaned back in his chair with his eyes closed, evidently studying over his client's case, but in reality, trying to remember her financial rating. He touched a button which rang a bell in another room, and wrote a few words on a slip of paper, which he gave to the clerk who entered and disappeared like an automaton.

"Clerks are sometimes very careless, and though

mine are, perhaps, as punctual as any, yet I have to be continually on the alert for fear that important business may be overlooked. We will go on with our conversation. But, by the way, would you like a mouthful of wine?"

"No, thank you, I are a strict teetotaller."

"You are like myself, you feel that you have no need for it. Excuse me a moment, there is my bell."

A letter was dropped into a box at his door. He adjusted his glasses and read what purported to be a letter, but was in reality a statement of Mrs. Halford's financial standing.

Without moving a muscle of his face he filed the document away in his own private desk and turned to resume the conversation.

"You think, then, Mrs. Halford, that the young gentleman would prefer Australia? Of course, that would be the most expensive."

"How much would it cost," she asked, turning pale, "to get him a post at a thousand a year in Australia?" She clenched her hands as she awaited his reply.

"I could not say exactly," answered the lawyer evasively, "but somewhere in the thousands."

"How many?" she gasped in a hoarse whisper.

"Five, at least."

Mrs. Halford took a drink of water from the pitcher near by and moved over to the window, where she tried to look through the frosted panes out into the daylight. "Him would have to lose his position here to make all secure," she said in a hard voice, without turning her face.

"Certainly," replied Mr. Slade, "I have thought of that, as well."

"How long will it take to have it done with?"

"Three or four months."

"Will you guarantee the job for that money, Mr. Slade?"

"I will guarantee everything but the amount of his salary. However, if he accepts the situation, I suppose it will be satisfactory to you?"

"There are my hand, Mr. Slade. You shall have

your money this very day, and, when it are all settled, a little more."

"Of course, you know the sum stated does not include our fees," replied Mr. Slade, with a smile. "But we shall push the matter along with all possible haste. As for the money," he continued, "we don't need it very badly, but it is as well to have it. By the way, you know we lend a good deal of money. If you should be in need we would be glad to serve you."

"Dear me!" exclaimed Mrs. Halford. "I are not in need of money. I have sold all but the homestead and wish to invest, but the banks only give four per cent."

"Tush! that's no investment at all. We find no difficulty in getting six and seven, with good security. Of course, we only allow five on deposit. We must have our profit, you know."

"You pay five, then. Well, I shall call and see you again, Mr. Slade."

The lawyer passed his hand over his forehead and paused as if in doubt. "To tell you the truth, we are not particular about taking in any money at present. We have considerable now awaiting investment. But of course, we are here to do business and never turn away respectable clients. Now," he added, with a kindly smile, "if you will favour me with the name of the young gentleman and his present location, I shall not detain you longer."

"Dear me, I thought I had told you. His name are Charles Langtry and him lives at Gowanstone."

CHAPTER XLI.

CUPID'S CAPERS.

NELLY HALFORD had grown to be a very attractive young lady. She had a large share of what is commonly called beauty, although to be concise, perhaps the word pretty would better describe her fair hair, rosy cheeks, and dimpled chin.

Her figure, which was rather under the medium height, was neither plump nor spare, but lithe and well proportioned.

She had inherited her father's sunny ways and cheerful disposition, and, like him, was not given to fret and worry over those little troubles that rob us of so much happiness. Both in brain and physique she was of smaller calibre than her sister, but there was a delightful simplicity about her which was hard to resist. Like her father, she was a general favourite wherever she went. She was always welcome for the sake of the sunshine and cheerfulness that accompanied her.

She had been away visiting a lady friend at Chicago, but a telegram announcing the death of poor little Davie brought her hurriedly home, just in time to attend the funeral.

Marian had been brought over to Broadview to soothe her grief, and there she remained for a fortnight, restoring her exhausted nerves. Sometimes Nelly would weep with her sister, and sometimes tease her into a laugh about Mr. Grazely, who still visited the farm with his old time regularity, and with an eye for Martha Briggs. As in former days, Marian found work to be the great panacea for grief, and at Broadview she had many opportunities of securing those twin restorers, *labor* and *sleep*.

During her sister's visit, out of respect to her grief, Nelly had controlled the natural buoyancy of her spirits to an extent which showed her sympathy; but now that Marian had returned to Gowanstone, it could not be much harm to sing and laugh; so she went about with the abandon of a happy child. She was very sorry for poor little Davie and his bereaved parents, she had wept bitterly over the grave, but somehow the warm sunshine and the beautiful summer days made her feel glad.

"Where are you going, Nelly?" asked her mother, one afternoon, as she started out with a basket on her arm.

"Out to pick cherries, mother mine. It was a silly trick to plant fruit trees so near the road. I saw two tramps at the tree by the gate this morning. They broke off one of the biggest branches."

With a huge straw hat stuck jauntily on the back of her head, she went off singing as usual, and was soon standing on the broad stone fence, reaching and jumping for branches. So absorbed was she by her occupation that she did not hear a footstep coming along the road, nor notice a young man who was walking leisurely from the direction of the city. His coat was thrown over his back, and his vest was opened in front, to compensate for the intense heat of the weather, while from time to time he paused in a shady spot, and raised his hat to wipe the sweat from his brow.

When he spied the fair harvester perched on the fence, he hurriedly donned his coat, buttoned up his waistcoat, and readjusted his tie.

The big straw hat hid her face from sight, but judging from her form, she must be pretty. He was about to speak, when something arrested his attention and rivetted him to the spot. *There*, on the stone fence, partly hidden by the frills and laces of a white petticoat, were the tan-coloured boots of the Metapedia. In a moment, Maurice Fletcher's heart was in his mouth. The whole scene was suddenly transformed into a fairyland, the air was filled with joy. Yes, there was no mistaking them. The dainty little toe-caps and arched instep were stamped in his memory, and when she jumped for a branch he noticed that the second button from the top of the left boot had been supplanted by one of different shape and colour. He was to have the privilege of seeing her again. *This time he would speak to her, come what may. Here* he had her all to himself. He leaned against the opposite fence and feasted his eyes. How long he would have watched her it is impossible to say, for it was joy enough to have her in sight; but, suddenly, with a spring, she scrambled into the tree, and her ponderous headgear, striking a limb, fell over into the roadway.

As soon as Nellie had adjusted herself to her new position she reached out to look for her missing sunshade, when, to her horror, she discovered a young gentleman lifting it out of the dust and looking up towards her.

She coloured like a peony and hurriedly gathered her skirts about her ankles.

"I beg your pardon," said the young man, "but will you allow me to hand up your hat?"

"No, sir," she replied snappishly. "Please go away from there. I can manage myself, thank you."

Hidden by the branches, she had the advantage of seeing without being seen. She was overcome with astonishment when she recognized the foreign-looking young man who had been her fellow-passenger on her trip West. She knew him by his pink cheeks and by his clothes, which had an odd, but rather stylish, look about them.

"The sun is pretty hot," he pleaded. "If you won't allow me to hand it up I will leave it on the fence here, where you can get it. But you had better let me hand it to you or your complexion will soon suffer."

"You needn't trouble about it, sir. It must take you all your time to protect your own."

She took a peep through a gap in the leaves to see how he took her thrust. Instead of being embarrassed he was laughing and coming closer. The fellow was altogether too familiar. She must teach him his place. "How long have you been standing there?" she demanded in a severe tone. "No gentleman would be guilty of such meanness."

"I only just came to pick up your hat as you swung

into the tree, not a second sooner, on my word of honour," he replied, backing into the middle of the road.

In a moment Nelly regained her confidence. From behind her leafy screen she would tease the stranger out of pure revenge.

"I should think it must be hard to be an agent or peddler tramping about in the hot sun," she remarked.

She noticed him first colour and then smile.

"I am very glad to say I am neither."

"Perhaps you are buying fruit then," suggested the cherry-tree. This time she saw and heard him laugh.

"I see you are an American, too," he responded.

"Indeed, how did you make that discovery? Are not Americans nice people? Don't you like them?"

"Some of them are very nice. I think a great deal of some of them."

"Oh! I suppose it is safe to say you are not one. But you haven't said what you are paying for cherries."

"I might be willing to give all my earthly possessions for even one off that tree, but I am afraid my offer is too low."

"This fellow is getting gay again," thought Nelly. "He can't be so green as I thought. He has nice eyes and a real complexion. He is rather nice looking. I wonder who he is. But he is too bold."

The cherry-tree's silence, Maurice felt, was a punishment for his presumptuous gallantry, but of course he could not see her face.

He could see the little boots, however, and he had been taking them as a guide instead of her countenance. They seemed to laugh, smile, or frown as the occasion required, but now they were crushed unmercifully in the sharp angle between two limbs, and looked decidedly vexed.

The prolonged silence was a hint to him to take his leave, but he only moved to a shaded spot on the road and waited, in hopes that she would speak. Finally he could wait no longer. "Will you accept an apology for my foolish words? Such liberty was very unbecoming and very ungrateful for your kindness in permitting me to speak to you at all."

"Oh, you are not gone yet," exclaimed the tree, with well feigned surprise. "I did not really notice what it was you said, so it is of no consequence." The boots seemed to blush at this fib, but she went on: "It is a good thing your business is not very pressing, but I suppose you are not going far?"

Maurice smiled at the implied question, so characteristic of the country, where everything bore an interrogation mark. "I am looking for the residence of William Halford. Perhaps you can tell me where he lives?"

"Yes, sir. He lives right here. If you look between the trees you will see the house."

"Can you inform me if he is at home? I have come a long way to see him."

The little boots traded places and the toe-caps were turned with an air of inquiry. "No; father went into town this afternoon, but mother is home." Who can he be?

"Thank you. Mrs. Halford will do as well. I have a package here to deliver to her," he said, holding up a large envelope covered with red seals.

"Very well, you can take it to mother if you like, or you can put it in my hat there on the fence. It will be quite safe."

"I beg your pardon, Miss Halford, but I have come all the way from Cornwall, from England, to see your parents. I have been travelling and searching for them for weeks, and I cannot go without seeing them."

For a time the tree was still. Not a leaf or a branch moved. Nelly had heard her parents talk of Cornwall, and her curiosity was now aroused. "Are you a relative?" she asked, in a voice of subdued excitement.

"Not exactly a relative. But I am a friend of the family, and have very important tidings."

Nelly was fairly trembling with excitement now. None of the children knew anything of their father's or mother's antecedents. All questions in that direction had been rebuffed. Now, however, something startling was going to take place.

"If you will look the other way I will jump down and take you into the house. I hope you will excuse me if I have been uncivil," she added, in a serious tone.

"You have been more civil than I deserved, but won't you let me help you down?" he said, eagerly, coming towards the fence.

"No, you go back," she protested, "till I reach the gate-post, then you can help me."

After a short scramble, during which she noticed that he conscientiously kept his eyes in an opposite direction, she landed on the fence. "Now, if you please," she said, colouring and brushing back her stray locks, "but take the basket first."

He stood on a huge stone and reached up his hands to catch her, but either she jumped too soon or he had not sufficient footing, for the impetus of her spring threw him off his balance and he fell sprawling on his back, while she, like a kitten, landed on her feet.

For a moment she looked to see if he were hurt, and then gave vent to peals of laughter like a school-girl at play.

There is nothing like merriment to break down reserve. In a moment they were laughing together like old acquaintances.

"I suppose that is what they call being knocked out in the first round," he exclaimed, brushing the dust off his sleeves.

"Fred would call it muffing a fly," laughed Nelly, who was now cleaning the dust off his back.

"Who is Fred?" he asked with sudden concern, wheeling round to face her.

"You first tell me whether your news is good or bad, and if it will bring any trouble."

"The news is good," he replied, "and you will all be pleased with it. It will not cause any trouble."

"Well, what is it about? Has somebody that was lost been found? Is there any secret or mystery just discovered, or what?"

"Now, now, you must not question me any further. My news is for your father and mother. It would be a breach of trust to tell it to any one else. But you promised to tell me who Fred is. An admirer, I suppose. Answer truly, now."

"No, he is only my brother, but I love him very much."

"I am very glad to hear it. I was afraid he was somebody else's brother. I don't know how it is over here, but in England young ladies don't always love their own brothers the best."

"Indeed! Why, people must have curious ways and customs over there. But the young gentlemen are particularly diligent and clever, I hear. They are said to beat the world at playing cricket or eating pudding. I should have taken pity on you and offered you some cherries, but be careful, like a good boy, and spit out the stones."

"Don't talk about cricket," he said, helping himself to some luscious red jackets. "The whole country, here, is crazy over baseball. Why, I have heard nothing else, since the day you left the Metapedia at Chicago."

"The Metapedia? Oh yes, that was the name of our coach, going west. Come to think of it, I remember seeing a green looking Englishman there," and they broke into a merry laugh.

"If I had possessed courage, in proportion to my inclination, I might have spoken to you then, and saved myself a journey over half the continent. Just think of me hunting all over America for your people, and you sitting in the next seat."

"It is the strangest thing I ever heard of," she replied. "But come now, you can carry the basket, and I will take you to see mother. It is funny to think of you coming here," she mused, as they walked up the lane together. "One never knows what is going to happen."

CHAPTER XLII.

A LEGACY AND A LOVER.

Mrs. Halford had, for the past few weeks, been leading a very unhappy life. Not that she fretted much over the loss of her grandchild, but his death removed from her daughter a protection which seemed a necessity under the present circumstances. Then she had to expend a large sum of money for nothing, and such a direct loss was like an open sore. To make matters worse, on the day following her visit to Mr. Slade's office, she received an unexpected blow from another direction. She was looking over one of the great New York dailies, searching for some stock quotations and financial news, when her eye fell upon an advertisment which made the room spin around her. " If Jane Symonds, who left Boscastle, England, twenty-six years ago, will communicate with John Thurston of Tregoodwell, she will hear something to her advantage." She dropped the paper in her lap, and sat for a long time conjuring up a thousand memories of bygone days.

She knew John Thurston to be a registrar or clerk of the court where wills were proven, and her first impulse was to communicate with him by cable. But a few moments' calculation made her hesitate. What could it be? Some property left her, but by whom? The old 'squire might have repented, but then he was almost penniless. Anyway that was impossible, for he always called her a forward hussy. Would it be Lady Mary? She had some little property, but it did not amount to much. It couldn't be her foster parents, the Symonds, for they were poor and must have gone to their reward long ago. Most likely it was a small legacy from Lady Mary.

Next she wondered how long the advertisement had been running. She searched through several numbers of an earlier date, and still the advertisement was there.

But behold, further down on the same column was another which was even worse than the first. It was the same advertisement, but instead of Jane Symonds were the names William and Jane Halford.

The cold sweat stood out on her forehead, and she almost gasped for breath.

"It must be Lady Mary. It can't be any one else. God knows I don't even know who I are.

"Are it worth while to have my doings made public for the sake of a hundred pounds or so? What would Marian say if her knew her was a bastard? What would Nelly and Fred think? No, not for ten times the money would I be made a talk of. I shall not trouble writing."

But, stop, *any one* might see the advertisement, even her own family. She could stop her own paper but that would not save her. New York dailies were scattered over the continent like leaves of the forest, and somebody who knew her would be certain to see it. First she must find out the amount of the legacy (if such it were), and then she could judge for herself. In the meantime she must try to stop the advertisement. Perhaps, after all, there might be enough in the legacy to recoup her for her loss anent Langtry. She would consult Mr. Slade, and so on her second visit to his office she gave him another case to work upon.

She had just nicely recovered from the shock when, a few days afterwards, Nelly brought a young man into the room, whom she introduced as "Mr. Fletcher from Cornwall."

Mrs. Halford looked at him in a dazed sort of way, and dropped into a chair. "I knew no Fletchers in Cornwall," she said, huskily, as she scanned him from head to foot.

Maurice smiled. "I am of Irish descent, madam, but I was reared in Tregoodwell by my guardian, John Thurston. Did you know him?"

"Yes, I remember him were connected with making wills. Him were quite a gentleman in those days."

"And is so still," replied the stranger warmly, "and always will be;" he added with emotion, "to the last hour of his life."

"You have come from John Thurston then?" she asked with faltering voice.

"Yes, madam, I brought this package from him," and he held up the envelope with the red seals. "I was to deliver it to you or your husband. Now that I have discharged my duty, I hope I may be allowed to congratulate you on your good fortune."

"Have you forgotten your manners, mother? You have not offered Mr. Fletcher a seat yet," said Nelly, handing her visitor a chair.

"Mr. Fletcher will excuse me if I forgot myself for a moment," replied her mother with a deep sigh.

"Run, Nelly, and send Fred to Levisville for father. I shall not open this letter till him comes."

As soon as Nelly had left the room, she said in a low voice, "Mr. Thurston were advertising for us?"

"It was I who inserted the advertisment one for yourself, and the other for you both."

Mrs. Halford turned a trifle paler. "Do you know all that are in this?" she asked, looking at the ominous envelope.

"It was necessary that I should know all."

"Well, Mr. Fletcher, I see you are a gentleman. I am sure you will not repeat anything of this which you should not. Are it understood?"

"Here is my hand, Mrs. Halford. I give you my word of honour, as a gentleman, as a ward of my respected guardian, that I shall not to any one betray the confidence he reposed in me."

"Who are the will in favour of, and what are the amount?"

"If your eldest daughter is alive she is the heiress; if not, then yourself. The amount, according to my latest advices, is about three thousand pounds, though that is considered a low estimate."

Nelly now came running in, and seeing her mother's pale face and excited manner, asked if anyone were dead.

"No, dear, but Marian have come into a legacy of fifteen thousand dollars."

"Oh, isn't that splendid! Poor Mally, I am so glad. Maybe it will cheer her up. I will run and send a telegram," continued Nelly, clapping her hands and fairly brimming over with excitement.

"Wait till your father comes home, Nelly, and then us can see what are best to do. Mr. Fletcher will please stay for a few days till us find out how to finish up the business."

That night, when the first general rejoicing was over, when Fred was away visiting Clara Grazely, and the old folks were closeted over the important envelope, Maurice and Nelly were left alone.

"So you remember seeing me on the train, Mr. Fleteher?"

"I can remember nothing else. Why, I knew you to-day on the fence before I saw your face."

"Oh, oh, what a fib!" exclaimed Nelly. "Telling fibs is worse than asking questions, which you say Americans are always doing."

"It's not a fib," he reasserted, "it's a positive fact. I could have sworn to you."

"Well, I declare you are getting worse and worse. Do you know where liars go to, Mr. Fletcher?" she added warningly, "Why, I hadn't even on the same dress."

"No, but you had on the same boots."

"Oh, that's nothing," she replied, looking a moment at one of the toe-caps which was peeping from under her dress. "There are hundreds of pairs just like them."

"Indeed there are not. There is not a pair on earth just like them. They are the neatest shaped little boots I ever saw."

"Ha, ha, ha!" laughed Nelly, as she flushed with pleasure at his compliment. "You owned up to being Irish. It wasn't necessary. Any one could tell you had kissed the blarney stone. I am afraid, Mr. Fletcher, that veracity is not your strong point."

"Well, now, did you ever see anything like this?" he said, holding up a brown, oval-shaped button.

She looked at it for a moment in blank astonishment. Then, noticing the smile on his face she blushed a rosy red. "Where did you get that, sir?"

"I found it on the Metapedia. Your berth was right opposite mine."

"Oh, there's another. The button was only loose that night, but it was gone in the morning. I blamed the porter for rubbing it off when he polished them. You wicked thing, I believe you stole it."

Maurice laughed good-naturedly. "I did pull it off but it was only to prevent it from being lost."

"You are a terrible man, Mr. Fletcher. Why didn't you give it to me in the morning? I hunted a dozen stores in Chicago and couldn't get one like it. Please give it to me now."

"I would not part with it for a fortune," he responded. "It is my talisman, now."

"I don't see what you want with an odd button. The shoes themselves are not worth much now. The soles are nearly worn through."

"What? If they are for sale I will give you five guineas. Come!"

"Now, you *are* Irish, and no mistake. They were not worth quarter of that when they were new. What nonsense, to make me wear an odd button."

"That is how I knew you on the fence to-day. Second button from the top."

Nelly sprang up with tears in her eyes. "You are a mean, contemptible thing, sitting here and making fun of me. You told me on your honour, as a gentleman, that you were not standing there a second. I can't believe a word you say," and she left the room, slamming the door behind her.

CHAPTER XLIII.

A TEMPEST OF THE SOUL.

"DEAR MADAM:—Your husband's health is not improving. He has not consulted me for some time, in fact, I can see that some odd fancy has lately prompted him to avoid me. For several nights I have noticed a light in his study window, and I am certain from his appearance that his nights are sleepless. Yesterday morning at two o'clock, while returning from a night call into the country, I met him about two miles from Gowanstone, on the Elmwood road, walking rapidly in the opposite direction. I pretended to be sound asleep as I passed him, in order to spare his sensitiveness, but I am certain that he knew me. At seven o'clock the same morning I pretended to require some horse-feed, and went over to the mill. He was working as usual, but there was something odd in his manner.

"We shall have to decide on some further and more radical plan of treatment, and for that reason I wish you would return as soon as convenient.

"Yours, etc.,
"GEO. BENNET.

"N. B.—Make it appear as if you came back of your own accord, and throw as much affection into your manner as possible.

G. B."

This was the letter that brought Marian's holidays at Gowanstone to an abrupt termination, and gave her fresh cause for sorrow and distress.

She had regained her usual health, but her usual cheerfulness had given way to an air of resignation.

The solemn stillness of the woods had acted like a balm to her wounded soul. In her childhood's haunts she shared her sorrows with the trees and flowers; sat for hours listening to the rippling stream, or wandered over fields and hills to greet in tree and shrub some half forgotten friend. She renewed her friendship with the cattle. The fowls soon flocked around her as of yore. David had come to see her once, and it seemed to rekindle in their hearts the warmth which had latterly grown cold. She was just beginning to feel contented, when this new trouble arose. Was there to be another grave filled before the grim reaper passed her door? Had she not already drank deeply enough of sorrow's cup?

When her visit to Broadview was first proposed, Marian had protested against leaving poor David alone with his sorrow, but he had insisted on her going. "I am as much alone, Marian, in a crowded room, as in a dark closet. I seem to have a quarrel on with myself, and I prefer that the battle should have no spectators. No, you go to the farm, and when you come back I may be able to borrow some of your cheerfulness. I feel most contented with the roar of the machinery in my ears; it seems to suit the quality of my thoughts."

As a matter of fact, he wished to be alone. His nerve storms were coming back on him. He felt that he was too irritable to be a fit companion for any one. When alone, he could sit up, or go to bed as he chose, without disturbing any one, or being troubled with irritating questions as to his rest.

It would be hard to describe the state of his feelings as the earth fell with hollow thuds on little Davie's coffin. For days after the funeral he went about in a sort of stupor, scarcely knowing what he did. He had readily granted his wife's request to have the child buried with church rites. Charles Langtry had conducted the services, and like a true gentleman he endeavoured to make the proceedings as little objectionable as possible to the father. He studiously avoided anything which would be likely to hurt Gordon's feelings. The reverend gentleman's prayer was honest, sincere and simple, while underneath it all was a current of sympathy and good will. Summed up in a few words, it meant help for this life and hope for the next. Never did Gordon have less animosity towards Christianity, than when Mr. Langtry was presenting it in its simple, helpful, human form. And yet his thoughts were tinged with bitterness. Looking back on his past life, he was conscientious enough to condemn himself and the narrow selfishness of his motives, which had been responsible for his double bereavement. But his sense of justice was grievously offended. He deserved his own punishment ; indeed, he felt he was not suffering, perhaps, as much as his moral crimes called for, but why should his mother and innocent child suffer for *his* negligence ?

He did not stop to ask whether death was really a punishment or an evil.

He presumed that it was so because of the physical suffering usually attached to it, apart altogether from the question of what might be beyond the "walls and limitations" of this life. To him it appeared as if Nature were neither cruel nor kind, and that, in the eternal procession of cause and effect, saint and sinner seemed to share an equal fate.

" What cares disease for any quality of mind or soul ? It only flees before the vital force of physical life. The child of sin, born in the lowest dens of vice, reared in an atmosphere of villainy and crime ; the embyro murderer, whose only earthly goal is the gallows, might probably have resisted the fell destroyer which strangled my boy."

Davie had suffered. His mother had suffered. Both had undergone great physical pain and distress, for *his* sins. That was where the iron of injustice entered his soul. For justice, in whole or in part, in the actual or in the abstract, his soul was clamouring. He was always willing to gird on his armour in its behalf. He loved to think that for justice he would fight alone against all the hosts of heaven or hell, against all the arrows of ostracism, persecution, and contumely; through all the suffering, pain and anguish which might be heaped upon him. Down the deep valley of despair, surrounded by the darkness of eternal night, he would fight alone, and with the last ray of reason in his soul would, like Leonidas, leave his body in the pass. Like a shipwrecked sailor in mid-ocean, he looked in vain for land or for a friendly sail, but from the utter loneliness of his isolation, there came no cry of anguish or despair.

His property and all his worldly goods seemed turned to ashes. His dreams of commercial power and prestige were now a hollow mockery.

On the same day upon which she received the doctor's letter Marian surprised her husband by walking into his office and throwing her arms around his neck. He seemed glad to see her but his reception lacked enthusiasm. Every outline of his form betokened weariness and languor. His eye was lit with the dogged courage of despair.

He sat on his high stool, in his dusty clothes, poring over his books. Even his hands were beginning to look thin and bony, and as she noted the lines of suffering on his face a great wave of pity came over her. But she must not let him see it. She fought back her tears and choked down her sobs till she reached the doctor's consulting room, and then broke into a torrent of weeping.

"Oh, Doctor," she cried, grasping his hand and covering it with her tears, "what shall we do with David?"

Her tried and trusty friend turned pale and trembled as he felt upon his hand the warm tears and throbbing brow of the only creature on earth who ever stirred his emotions.

He quietly released his hand, and after clearing his throat and blowing his nose he commenced to outline his plans. He could not, dare not, tell her what he conceived to be at least one of the causes of her husband's illness. True or false, he must carry his diagnosis to the grave. He had devoted his life and energies to the cause of science, but not even for it would he cause this woman a moment's pain. Not even to save the life of David Gordon, nay, nor his own, would he put the blush of shame upon the cheek of this woman, whom, from his specimen cabinet, he had moved to a sacred little corner which never saw the light of day.

"Your husband, Mrs. Gordon, must go away from

business altogether for a few months. He must go far enough away to forget everything at home. He must go alone. He must have some special motive in going. He needs the stimulus of strange faces and surroundings. He must be so placed that he will have to exert himself in order to secure his own wants and creature comforts. His thoughts and brain currents must be entirely changed."

"But, Doctor, the poor fellow would die of neglect. You don't think there is any danger of him, do you?" she asked, in a half-timid, half-coaxing tone.

"No, he is not going to die, Mrs. Gordon, but we must take the strain off his mind. He is struggling against himself, and, unfortunately, is a lineal descendant of those ' kilties ' who, in the thick of battle, yielded only to death. Now we have the problem before us. If we can only solve it we shall succeed. Come back to-morrow and we shall compare notes. In the meantime think over it; sleep over it."

That evening David caught her weeping and alone. She was sitting by the window in the dusk. The gloominess of the semi-darkness was quite in tune with her frame of mind.

"Come, Marian, that won't do. Come and tell me your troubles. Come here, and sit on my knee as you used to. Come and tell me what you have been thinking about. That's right. It seems like old times to have you on my knee. Put your arm around my neck and kiss me. Now, what is it, dear?"

"You won't think me silly, David, if I tell you?"

"No, dear, why should I? Nobody can be more foolish than I have been."

"I was just thinking I would like to have a little baby to take Davie's place," and burying her face in his bosom, she broke into a fit of sobbing.

Her weeping was cut short by a sharp ring at the door-bell, and a telegram was handed in which read as follows:

"*To Mrs. D. Gordon*:—Unexpected news from England. You are an heiress. Will be over to-morrow. JANE HALFORD."

CHAPTER XLIV.

WAYS AND MEANS.

THE family council held at Gowanstone on the following day to discuss the situation not only included the whole family, but Maurice Fletcher as well. Who was to go and who was to stay at home was the great question of the hour. No two were of the same opinion. During the early part of the discussion, Marian sent out for Dr. Bennet, feeling that now was the time when his advice would be of most service. She knew that he would be delighted with the opportunity which presented itself of sending David off on the proposed trip. At first glimpse it seemed that, of course, Marian must go to England, seeing that she was the most interested party, and she hoped that the doctor would suggest David's going as well. Here, however, there seemed to be a hitch in the arrangements.

Mrs. Halford had made up *her* mind to go, and proposed that her husband should accompany her. This would leave Fred and Nellie at home alone, an arrangement to which they made a vigourous protest. If "father and mother" went, then Marian would have to remain at home.

"Why not leave Mr. Halford at home?" suggested Gordon to his mother-in-law.

"Oh, it are like this, here, David, I couldn't think of going without William."

"But why go at all, mother?" interposed Nelly. "You don't have to."

"Yes; mother ain't getting the money. I don't see what she has to go for," growled Fred.

The look which Mrs. Halford gave in reply to these remarks, made them all understand that *her* going was beyond all discussion, that it was already a settled fact.

Matters had reached a crisis when Dr. Bennet arrived. He first listened patiently to what each had to say, and then ventured his opinion.

"It seems already settled that Mr. and Mrs. Halford are going," he commenced with a caustic glance at Marian's mother, "and seeing that the young people here insist on Mrs. Gordon's remaining, I would suggest that Mr. Gordon go himself to look after his wife's interests. The closing of an estate is sometimes more troublesome than you might imagine. Mr. Gordon's business skill and acumen would probably be required. It is not necessary for Mrs. Gordon to go in person, as you might suppose, and as her husband would be acting for her, she would do well to remain at home to guard his interests. With the assistance of a bookkeeper and the experience of your foreman, your business, Mr. Gordon, would, I think, be safe in your wife's hands. Of course, you require some one with power of attorney to sign cheques, drafts, and other documents. I am not flattering Mrs. Gordon when I say that although she knows nothing of the business, she has more than an average share of common sense and judgment, and would sign nothing without fully understanding what she was doing."

"I think your arrangement, Doctor, is a very lame one, because the most interested party remains at home, while all the rest go. Besides, I could not think of leaving my wife alone. It would be downright cruelty, in view of all our recent troubles."

"Stop one moment, Mr. Gordon. I have another matter to consider," rejoined the doctor, "and that is your health. I had made up my mind that you must have a total rest from business for a few months, and I had decided on your taking a trip to the West. Here is an opportunity of killing two birds with the one stone; of securing your wife's legacy, and her husband's health."

"David," said Marian, catching a look from the doctor's eye, "Your health is certainly worth more to me than the money. I think we had better do as the doctor suggests."

"Why, Doctor," exclaimed Mrs. Halford, "her

couldn't be left here at Gowanstone all alone. I couldn't hearken to that."

"How would it do if I stayed at Broadview, and drove over two or three times a week?" asked Marian.

Nelly clapped her hands gleefully at this suggestion, while Fred slyly stole his arm around his sister's waist, and voted the arrangement as being "out of sight."

For the first time Mr. Fletcher spoke, and very modestly proclaimed his ability to fill the post of book-keeper. He further stated that he would be very glad to secure even a temporary situation, especially as he had nothing in view as yet.

Just how far his desire to be near Broadview prompted him, it is impossible to say, but Maurice cast his eyes toward Nelly while making the proposition, and if looks were any indication that young lady was not displeased.

Mrs. Halford, who felt that her own interests would be perfectly safe in Marian's hands, applauded the doctor's ultimatum, and when the little session was closed, everything was harmonious and satisfactory.

On the evening before their departure the doctor called in to have a final chat with his patient. "By the way, Gordon, now that you are going, there are two or three things I wish you to remember. Don't think of business; don't read any American newspapers. Then, most important of all, you must neither *write* nor *receive* letters from home."

"You surely cannot mean that to apply to me," exclaimed Marian, in consternation. "Why, I should die of loneliness."

"Yes, but I do mean it to apply to you. Surely you are not children."

"Well, but——"

"Excuse me, Gordon, but am I your physician or not?"

"Certainly you are."

"Then I shall expect you to obey orders implicitly."

Husband and wife exchanged glances of protest. "We might be both dead, and neither of us would know a thing about it," said Marian.

The doctor smiled at the Hibernianism, but shook

his head firmly. He knew that Gordon would insist on an explanation, and he was ready with it. "Don't you see, Gordon, that to think of your wife is to think of home; and to think of home is to think of business. If your *mind* is to remain at home, where is the use of going at all?"

"You forget, Doctor, that I am going on business, or I would not be going at all. The legacy is surely worth going for. You doctors are always thinking shop if not talking it. Your forbidding me to write to my wife is very unusual. For how long do you expect us to keep it up?"

The doctor scratched his arm for a moment. "I'll tell you what I'll do, Gordon. You write to me in seven weeks (not sooner), and if I am satisfied with the tone of your letter, then you may both write twice a day if you like."

"Is it a bargain?" and he extended a hand to each of them.

"I suppose it will have to be as you say," replied Marian, "but how am I to hear of him at all?"

"You can hear of him through your father and mother, but remember, no subterfuges. You may get all the news of him you like, but you must not be sending little messages to him or anything of that kind. I must keep the wires cut around him. Now, Gordon, you can go where you like, and see what you like. When you are tired of one place, go to another. Boating, lawn-tennis, music halls, gymnasiums, walking, fishing or fighting. I don't believe that an occasional 'bout' would do you any harm. Now this is all the medicine I ask you to take, and I give you *carte-blanche* as to time and dose. Forget everything. Forget that such a place as Gowanstone is in existence. Forget your own name if you like, but don't forget that copy of Chaucer, and the black-thorn you promised me. Good-bye."

CHAPTER XLV.

WHERE PATHS DIVIDE.

THE great defects of our present educational and social systems are shown by the frequency with which people " miss their calling." By chance, necessity, or parental errors, we are pitchforked into certain positions, while our habits, inclinations, and capabilities lead us in an opposite direction. The artizan, mechanic, or farmer might often change places with the lawyer, doctor, or clergyman, to the mutual advantage of himself and his fellow men. The first duty in educating our children for this practical age is to discover, as soon as possible, the path in life to which they are best adapted, and then perfect them in this direction. The struggle for existence is becoming keener from year to year, and to be properly equipped for the battle we must have the kind of knowledge and wisdom which is applicable to the affairs of everyday life.

And yet, though Charles Langtry was not adapted for public speaking, it could scarcely be said that as a clergyman he was a failure. His athletic frame, chivalrous nature, and the dreamy indolence of his mind were not exactly the qualities required by a preacher of the gospel; but he was very popular, not only with his own congregation but with the public generally.

There was something attractive and kindly about him which drew people to him. His companionship caused no great mental strain; he had no air of superiority or self-righteousness, and people were not afraid to talk freely in his presence. There was no spirit of espionage in his pastoral visits. He was not continually looking for flaws in the orthodoxy of his hearers. He was one of them. He shared in their pastimes and interested himself in the affairs of everyday life. A game of cricket, a good dog, or a fast horse were legitimate subjects of discussion amongst the sterner sex, while with the ladies he could drink tea and talk knowingly of pies and puddings. When he appeared at the door his parishioners were not forced to make a mad rush for their Sunday clothes, nor their sanctimonious faces. Nor was it necessary to cook the "big potato" when he stayed for dinner. If the good wife happened to be boiling a pot of soup, he could sit by the stove and discuss it with her. They did not require to leave their work and sit down to entertain him. If they happened to be busy he amused himself with the children, or sat down at the organ and filled the place with melody. Very soon people learned to love him, and any insinuation as to his want of eloquence was, to many of his congregation, a declaration of war.

In this age of democracy the masses prefer a man who does not appear to look down upon them. For this very reason, the people's candidate, the man of the mud strata, will often defeat at the polls the gentleman of education and refinement.

Not, indeed, that Mr. Langtry lacked in either respect, nor that he was particularly democratic in his principles, but his lack of vanity and his natural benevolence created a feeling of fellowship in the hearts of those with whom he came in contact.

Mr. Sweetnam, his predecessor, had been a very eloquent man, but he was very aristocratic, and the congregation thought more of Mr. Langtry's kindness than of Mr. Sweetnam's eloquence.

We admire clever people, but we do not necessarily love them. We are fain to think that those in high positions are no better or purer than ourselves. Lincoln's memory is all the dearer to our hearts because we know that he was human. Not that Lincoln was ever popular in the ordinary sense. There is an isolation in greatness which prevents it. The tall, gigantic pine or oak will ever wave high and lonely above the scrubby beeches.

Another cause of Mr. Langtry's popularity was his wonderful power as a musician. While paying his pastoral visits, many a housewife stopped at her washtub to wipe away a tear. The eloquence of his soul seemed to flash from his finger-tips. The tones crept about the heart till the listener was wafted away from earthly cares into a land of bliss. He rarely played from copy, excepting in some new composition; he either memorized it or played whatever came uppermost in his mind. He needed no coaxing, for he loved to play, and he rarely left a house where there was an instrument without " feeling it," as he called it. Every piano or organ was a personal friend. To the meanest, wheeziest of them all, his touch was just as kind as when he sat before the grand organ in the church.

Musical critics from far and near came to hear him, and although they found fault with his technique, they never challenged his power of interpretation.

People rush to hear renowned professors, crowned with shaggy locks and glistening spectacles; to hear with hungry hearts the language of the soul; but, alas, too often do they ask for bread and receive a stone. In sumptuous halls where slavish fashion sits with lying plaudits in her hands; where heart and brain are fettered fast by Gotham's glitter, let tiresome technicality triumph; but at the humble hearth of human emotion, true genius in its simple garb receives its warmest welcome.

Charles Langtry had no Italian prefix to his name; he did not rush and dash with frenzied hands from bass to treble; he used no arts or tricks of touch and posture; but lounging lazily on his seat, with head thrown back, he searched for human souls.

Every key became a living, breathing thing which gave its voice and told its story. Sometimes they sang in chorus a glorious chant of praise, or through the shadows, deep and dark as death, they sobbed and sighed their tales of grief.

Every octave was a family and every ivory, white or black, was an individual.

Sometimes, in groups, they prophesied the coming of a nobler and a grander day, or, with a moan of anguish, told the martyrdom of man.

Had Charles Langtry followed music as a profession, not even his natural indolence would have prevented him from reaching the highest rung in the ladder of fame.

But, artist though he was, he had little conceit in his own attainments; in fact, he was his own severest critic.

He cared little for applause so that he satisfied himself, and no amount of appreciation pleased him, if either in conception or execution he fell short of his own ideal.

None of his hearers appreciated his musical genius more thoroughly than Mrs. Gordon, who, since little Davie's death, found great solace in her choir duties. His impromptus were a constant source of delight to her. They seemed to thaw the iciness about her heart.

Although she had been a constant visitor at the parsonage, she continually kept herself aloof from the young clergyman, and never allowed herself to be alone with him. He evidently understood and respected her motives. Latterly he had assisted her in this direction. Christina always convoyed her home from choir practice. Her big dog Nero was a constant companion and she did not fear to be alone.

Once, Charles had accompanied them, and had stolen an opportunity of getting her arm. This indiscretion cost her a night's sleep. She vowed that it would never happen again.

Now that her husband had gone, she would keep herself entirely apart. She would not only discontinue choir practice, but would absent herself from church, and cease her visits to Christina.

One day when her friend was coaxing her, she said, " No, Christina, you and your mother will have to do all the visiting till David comes home, and then I shall pay you back with interest. Why, think! I have a mill, a farm and two houses to manage. Then I have a young lady to chaperone, and you know lovers are hard to look after," she added with a laugh. " Indeed, I have so much to do that I have no time to fret. I am getting heavier every day. I haven't felt so cheerful and contented since I lost my little darling."

CHAPTER XLVI.

GOTHAM'S GRIEFS.

"CAN I go to the picnic, Marian?" said Nelly, holding up a pink envelope which she had just received.

"What picnic, dear?"

"The picnic at Snell's Lake, that the swells of Gowanstone are going to have. Maurice told me last night that he was appointed on one of the committees, and," she added with a blush, "he wants me to go with him."

Marian laid down the book which she was reading, and looked thoughtfully at her sister. "I wonder, Nelly, if I am not taking too much responsibility in allowing you and Mr. Fletcher to be so much together? Perhaps mother might not approve of it."

"Now, Mally dear, don't get cross with me," said Nelly, settling herself on her sister's lap.

"I'm not cross, dear, but you know I must not let this become serious before you have mother's approval. I approve of him myself. I think he is a gentleman. But you have only known him a few weeks, and it will never do, Nelly, to be head and ears in love with him before we know his history. It hasn't become serious already, has it?"

Poor Nelly turned rosy red. She hid her face on her sister's shoulder to cover her blushes. "I am afraid, Mally. Oh, you know. I don't like to say it, but I think I—love him already." Further confession was cut short by sobs.

"You needn't hide your face, Nelly. Look up and kiss me. I could see it myself. But do you think he loves you?"

Nelly fumbled at her apron and picked at the buttons on her sister's dress. "I—think—he—does."

"Did he ever tell you so?"

The fingers again toyed nervously with the buttons before the reply came. "He didn't just say that, but oh, you know, he has said little things that mean the same thing. Last night," and again she hid her face, " he kissed me."

"Oh!" exclaimed her sister, in mock surprise, " I suppose you got angry and sent him away."

" No, I didn't," came the smothered reply.

" What did you do, then ?"

" You won't be mad, Mally, will you ?"

" No, dear, I won't."

" Well," and her arms clung tighter, " I kissed him back. I couldn't help it."

Marian gave her sister a sympathetic squeeze, and with the moisture shining in her eyes, patted her on the head.

" Did I do wrong, Mally ?"

" It would be of little use to say that you did, when probably I would have done the same myself. Only, dear, you must be careful. You must make sure that he loves you before you give your heart away, holus bolus."

" Do you remember the tan boots I had when I went to Chicago that time ?"

" Yes, what about them ?"

" Well, I never told you because I thought Fred would. The very last day he drove you over to Gowanstone, Fred was in in Maurice's room at the hotel. Well, when Maurice lifted the lid of his trunk to take something out, there were my boots in a little corner by themselves. Fred teased me about it till I nearly cried, but I believe I was glad too."

Mrs. Gordon broke into a hearty laugh. " Well, dear, he must be badly smitten, though you really have a perfect foot. Well, well! I've heard of young ladies giving their lovers the mitten, but giving them the ' boots ' is generally the father's privilege. But where did you get the pair you have on ?"

" They came to the express office in Levisville. The box was prepaid and addressed to me. There was no letter or anything in the parcel to show where they came from."

" Oh, of course, he sent them to replace the others,

and you are both pleased with the exchange. I think he loves you, Nelly."

"Do you, Mally, you dear old thing; how can you tell?" and Nelly devoured her sister with kisses.

"Oh, just by the way he looks at you." For a time they sat in silence, each enjoying the pure sisterly sympathy of the other.

"If I had an invitation to the picnic, Nelly, and could go with you, it would be all correct. I promised mother I would chaperone you till she came home. You know people are very ready to talk about young girls. I don't care for picnics myself, dear, but if I get an invitation you shall go."

Snell's Lake was a small body of water covering about two hundred acres. It was situated on a range of hills to the northwards, about eight miles distant from Gowanstone.

The great stumbling-block in the way of its popularity as a pleasure resort, had, for many years, been its almost inaccessible position. Heretofore, the only means of access was a narrow causeway, which crept through ravines, clung to precipices, and was considered only fit for experienced horsemen or pedestrians.

During the present summer, however, a syndicate had purchased the lake and expended large sums of money in making a wide and properly graded road, protected at every dangerous point by a substantial railing.

Pavilions had been erected, and pleasure boats were furnished to picnic or excursion parties at reasonable rates. A spur-line of railway from Levisville was under construction, and the spot was expected to become famous.

The honor and prestige of opening this new summer resort, on the fifteenth of July, fell to the good people of Gowanstone.

Not the rag-tag and bob-tail, the rank and file, or the plodding plebeians who ignobly earned their daily bread by the sweat of their brow, but the patricians who either fed on political pap, or whose means of support were not outwardly visible.

The great difficulty of the whole affair fell upon the shoulders of the invitation committee. It was so hard to be *select*.

Mrs. A though eligible in herself, had a brother who had the pernicious habit of carrying his hod more gracefully than his whiskey.

Mrs. B was very nice, but her sister kept herself and bacchanalian husband by a boarding-house in the next town; and Mrs. C's cousin worked in the sewers. X's wife's mother had been a washerwoman. Y's paternal parent was a section foreman. Z kept up appearances, took his dinner (when he had one) at six o'clock, passed his days in idyllic idleness and had no visible means of support, but the trouble was, that owing to several little financial and legal documents he could not comfortably trot in the same class as the sheriff. This case was particularly touching. It was the *pièce de résistance*. To give a man, with such eminent qualifications for the upper class, the cold shoulder, for an officer whose father once kept a beer saloon on the Bowery was out of the question. The judge, himself, was not the clean potato, for he had a brother in Sing Sing and his father was in the asylum. The senator's reputation for poker-playing was somewhat shady, and Congressman Bates had anarchistic tendencies.

The committee were at their wit's end. There was no one to vouch for *them*. Several of them got offended at hints as to their own eligibility, and the whole affair would have been given up in disgust had it not been for the timely arrival of Sidney Dillon, the chairman. He reported that if they followed their original intention, there would not be left a corporal's guard.

The only ones he had found eligible under their original enactment were orphans, or those whose parentage and connections were unknown.

The only way out of the difficulty was to reduce the standard of qualifications, and include those who earned their living in a genteel sort of way, irrespective of family history altogether.

The first name in this class was Jamieson.

"Of course we must have *him*," said the chairman. "You simply can't run a picnic without him. As a rule, people don't know what to do when they get there. They either giggle to keep up their spirits, stand stupidly looking about them, or freeze up altogether. If we didn't invite Jamieson he would have a picnic on the following day that would put ours to shame. If he is there, he will take charge of everything and push it right along. Furthermore, we shall have his band; and last, but not least, there will be a big bill to pay."

The ominous silence which followed this announcement showed that Sydney's last argument had been very convincing.

"I move that Mr. Jamieson be chairman of the finance committee," said Senator Cox, clutching spasmodically at some small coins in his pocket.

"Second the motion," murmured Leslie Harper, the bank clerk, who up to this point had been quietly sucking his cane.

"Hadn't we better put Jamieson on the management committee too?"

"Not necessary," replied the chairman, "he will own the whole affair in two days."

"What about the pink and white Englishman?"

"Oh, you know, he's only a bookkeeper on a small salary."

"Yes, but he hasn't been at it long," said a young lady who evidently wished to condone his offence. "Put him on the working committee."

"I think he works more for love than money," remarked Mr. Dillon, with a smile. "I believe he has money of his own."

"Put him on the finance committee then," said the banker's wife. "Carried."

"What about Mr. Langtry and his sister?"

"We'll be only too glad to have him if he will come. He is a host in himself. They have a piano at the pavilion."

"Don't bother with his sister. She's a horrid old fright. She looks as if she had been packed away in a trunk for forty years and only brought out the day before yesterday."

"You forget that Mr. Langtry is no cad. She must be invited or he will not come, so that is settled," said the chairman.

After running over a long list of other names, some one suggested Mrs. Gordon.

This brought a perfect storm of opposition from the ladies, who made the most scathing remarks.

"She milks cows." "And hitches horses." "She does her own washing." Mrs. Carrol, whose perfumes were supposed to disinfect the plebeian proclivities of her connections, made the caustic comment that " Mrs. Gordon might have the odour of a teamster, and as for her sister, she is a perfect tomboy."

"A woman like Mrs. Gordon can do as she pleases," was Mr. Dillon's response. "Great beauty has privileges."

This was followed by the simultaneous exclamation that he was a wretch. "Great beauty, indeed! A regular sphinx."

"She is an heiress now, don't you know," exclaimed Mr. Harper, removing his cane for a moment.

"We won't believe it till we see it," said several others.

The chairman rapped on the table and called the meeting to order. Sydney's fearless candour was the strangest pillar of his social throne. People wondered why he dared to say things which no one else could. He never shirked the truth, though he generally clothed it in its least offensive garb.

Society followed him because he always led it. It was faithful to him because he did not court it. He seemed to know that the strange, fickle goddess spurns adulation and idolizes indifference.

Without deigning to take further notice of the spiteful comments, the chairman spoke in a quiet tone.

"At the last meeting you gave me the privilege of inviting two ladies. With your permission I shall send an invitation to Mrs. David Gordon."

And so another pink envelope found its way to Broadview.

CHAPTER XLVII.

PROPRIETY'S HOLIDAY.

THE place of rendezvous was truly a beautiful spot. The deep basin which surrounded the lake was densely wooded to the water's edge, and the dark green foliage of the trees formed an ideal outline to this little inland sea, which sparkled clear and cool in the summer sun.

This idyllic sheet of water had no visible inlet. It was supposed to be fed by subterranean springs from the surrounding hills, and its only outlet was a little stream which wound its way through wooded glens, rippled through ravines and plunged over precipices, till, supplemented by a score of its fellows, it became the "Speed."

Then, from a reckless rambler of hills and dales, a wanderer in the wilderness, it became a peaceful son of toil who gave prosaic power to whirling wheels, and, like a traitor, carried off the slaughtered giants who sometime gave it shelter from a sweltering sun.

Poor fallen heroes from the far off forest glade, who through the storms of ages smiled upon the streamlet's infant prattles, nor recked that e'er its rippling laugh or kindly kiss would turn to gross ingratitude.

It was along the margin of the forest stream that the new roadway ran, and as the picnickers with their procession of vehicles passed along, they made the dark green hills echo with their rejoicing.

The handsome uniforms and glistening brass instruments of the band stood out in bold relief against the foliage of the narrow pass, and when they came in sight of the lake the musicians fell into marching order, playing "Sherman's March to the Sea."

This little display had, of course, been arranged by Jamieson. It served the double purpose of inspiring the party with patriotic enthusiasm, and impressing upon the authorities of the lake the importance of their visitors.

But it was after their arrival that the genius of Jamieson shone forth.

Mounting the roof of his band-wagon, he shouted in stentorian voice his list of commands.

"The first part of the programme is boating and fishing, *ad libitum*, till one o'clock. Then the band will sound the reveille for lunch. Games will commence at three P. M., and dinner at seven. Last of all, every vehicle will be ready to start at nine-thirty."

He detailed his guests (for so he now considered them) into little parties, according to the size and capacity of the boats, shouting words of caution to one and all. He gave his orders with the skill of an experienced general, and somehow people had a habit of obeying him without knowing why. Others, perhaps more dignified, and clothed with more authority, might shout themselves hoarse and no one would pay the slightest attention, but let Jamieson give the word of command and everybody would fall into line. There was a soldierliness about his methods, a vigorousness about his arrangements, which made him a natural leader of men. Some might complain of or criticize his arrangements, but no one had the courage to show open disobedience. From the brewing of the lemonade to the wrappings of oil paper round the sandwiches, the minutest detail was arranged with clockwork precision. He watched with jealous eye for any lagging of the proceedings, and was always on the lookout for deserters.

Marian and Christina, accompanied by Nero (who had persisted in following them from Gowanstone) went off for a ramble in the woods. They preferred it to boating. Perhaps no two in the whole assembly were enjoying themselves more thoroughly than these.

Marian preferred strange trees to strange people. She fairly revelled in the trackless woods where the foot of man had never trod.

But Jamieson spied them, and their fate was sealed. Expostulation was useless. The idea of any one enjoying solitude was preposterous.

He locked Nero in the boat-house, threw him some food, and in a few moments two of his bandsmen were rowing them out on the lake, with the Stars and Stripes flying from the bow of the boat.

Poor Christina looked rather ancient in her new white muslin, which was cut with angular and painful precision. She sat facing the big drum-major, who (by the way) was an old bachelor, and at times she was very much embarrassed by his admiring glances.

Marian sat in the stern of the boat trailing her hand in the bright clear water, inwardly enjoying Christina's discomfort. About her apparel there was an unassuming plainness and artistic simplicity, which few could understand, and none could imitate. Every curve and line of her garments seemed to harmonize with and enchance the gracefulness of her figure. When you looked at her, you never seemed to notice her garments; they seemed to be a part of herself.

The grand old forest put her in a dreamy frame of mind. For a time the frivolities of life were forgotten. With her hat lying on her lap, her beautiful hair blowing carelessly about her neck and forehead, her lips half apart, she drank inspiration from the surroundings.

The gentlemen *would* look at her, they *would* comment upon her beauty as the boats passed and repassed each other. But the ladies had an entirely different impression. "I always knew she was a vulgar thing. The idea of taking up with those low, flashy bandsmen. It's enough to make one sick. She's like a country rustic who goes crazy over a uniform. She keeps that skinny Miss Langtry with her as a foil to show off her figure."

Fortunately, Marian could not hear these remarks. She would have been contented to pass the whole day in dreamy indolence, but unfortunately, Nero's howlings at the boat-house soon compelled her to return to his relief.

At the appointed time dinner came with its bustle and babble. It was to be as informal and as rustic as possible. The very atmosphere was full of reckless abandonment. And no wonder. When the judge took off his boots to run a race, his socks were seen to be full of holes; the sheriff broke a suspender and tore his trowsers, and Sydney Dillon actually went about all afternoon with his necktie all awry.

The senator told the same story over and over again. The banker's wife was a trifle hilarious. Mrs. Carrol went about with her hair hanging down her back; several ladies who had pretty feet had their dresses pinned up, and Leslie Harper went for several hours without a suck of his cane. They were actually going to eat with their knives, and hold chicken bones in their fingers. They were to laugh out loud if they were so inclined, and everybody was to go in for a good time. They were to have the glorious privilege of being natural. The Pecksniffs had failed to put in an appearance, and Mrs. Grundy was supposed to be at home.

Sydney Dillon playfully escorted Marian to a place near the head of the table. But her domestic instincts led her to lend a helping hand in the preparations.

While busy struggling with a can of salmon she broke the can-opener, and asked some gentleman to loan her a knife.

Charles Langtry, who had spent his whole day in fishing, was standing close by. Glad to be of any service, he produced his jack-knife. He almost begged her to let him open the can himself. But she refused.

"No, indeed, I won't be beaten like that." She attacked it more savagely than ever. But in a moment she gave a little cry. The knife had slipped off the hard smooth tin and sank deeply into her wrist.

Immediately Mr. Langtry was at her side, and as he withdrew the blade, the red blood spurted over his face.

The ladies screamed. Nelly fainted. Even the gentlemen turned pale. The intermittent jets of scarlet proved that some important vessel had been severed. Dr. Merrick, who was one of the party, pronounced it to be the interosseous artery.

"I must apply great pressure, for I have nothing with me to tie the vessel. Your hand will probably ache considerably. But you can bear it for an hour or two till you get home."

Soon she was going about with her hand in a sling, talking and laughing as cheerfully as ever. The accident had thrown a temporary gloom over the festivities. But she would make amends for her carelessness by being gayer than ever.

"Upon my word, Mrs. Gordon, blood-letting seems to agree with you," said the doctor.

"Indeed, I don't feel any the worse. Don't worry on my account but go on and enjoy yourselves." With a special effort she led the conversation, and did it so skillfully that she soon had the whole assembly in good humour, and the accident was apparently forgotten. Even Nelly was surprised at her sister's gaiety, while Nero, with his head to one side, made glances of inquiry at his mistress.

She was really over-doing herself. But the ordeal was soon over and with her dog at her heels she slipped away into the woods to quiet her nerves. With Nero as her companion she had nothing to fear. She followed a hunter's trail round the margin of the lake till she found herself on a little cleared mound which had evidently been a spot for some nomad's camp. She had gone quite a long distance round the arm of the lake, but she had a splendid view of the pavilion and boat-houses across the water.

The dusk was gathering, but the moon was coming up, and she loved to watch it shining peacefully on the placid waters of the lake. Placing her white woolen wrap on the little knoll, she threw herself down upon it, glad to be alone. She watched the boats moving to and fro on the shining water, and enjoyed the snatches of song that came floating up through the moonlight.

Soon the colored lights at the wharf were in full blaze, and the band opened the proceedings in true patriotic style by playing a medley overture of national airs including Yankee Doodle and the Star Spangled Banner. A lady soloist who came next and a speech which followed were too far away to be heard distinctly. Then came a cornet solo by the band master, followed by a quartette of male voices, which sounded very pleasing. After a short period of silence the piano gave its voice to the evening air, and even the first preliminary chords showed the touch of a master hand. It was Charles Langtry. No other hand could give the instrument the pulse and throb of life. It was evidently trying its voice like a bird preening its wings for flight. Then it let loose a perfect flood of melody, which came floating softly over the water and faintly echoed in the far-off hills. Not yet, however, did the sweet sounds crystallize into definiteness, but ran through the different shades of tone colour like the lights upon the balcony.

She knew that the player was looking at the lights, waiting for his theme to come to him, and until then would picture in sound anything that his eye chanced to fall upon.

Ha! There is a pause. The decision is made. There is a new tenderness of touch and tone. Gradually, through the echoing whispers of the accompaniment, woven like vines and leaves, the flower is budding into blossom.

Hark! Yes. It is the old familiar air: "Some Day I'll Wander Back Again," but surrounded with a perfect halo of beauty. Deep down, and scarcely discernible, is the counter-melody of "Annie Laurie," modestly telling its tale of love. Hush, there is a change in the movement.

The instrument is speaking now. Into the simple song theme there comes a flood of rosy light, and in its glow she sees the wooded hills and sloping fields of her girlhood's home. She sees the rosy sunset and hears the hum of insect life, broken only by the tinkle of the cow-bell and the whipoorwill's evensong. Then what? My God, yes! Her own voice singing to his harmonica. She can scarcely believe her ears. She unbuttons the band about her throat to ease her choking feeling. "I cannot, must not listen," she cries frantically as she stops her ears to shut out the low sobs of the bass solo which speaks as plainly as human tongue. It says that "for bonnie Annie Laurie he will lay him down and dee."

She listens again. He is in the middle of a passionate adagio which seems to numb her senses. It brings a peculiar feeling over her. But still, faintly through it all she hears her own voice in the original theme. The instrument fairly throbs with passion ; it seems to run the whole gamut of human emotions, till, with a reckless frenzy, comes a presto which rushes like a rocket to the sky, and bursting, falls in ashes to the earth.

All was still, so still that Marian could hear the beating of her heart. Her pent up emotions broke loose in a fit of sobbing. It seemed as if every fibre of her nature had been touched by the music. Memories of by gone days with all their freshness and their joy, their desires, passions and emotions came flooding upon her and she wept as if her heart would break.

Immediately after finishing his selection, Charles was requested by Christina to go in search of Mrs. Gordon, as she herself was timid about going into the woods.

"Very well, dear," he replied, "though perhaps she will not thank me."

"No matter, Charles, I don't like the idea of her being in the woods alone. She went in by that path."

Charles followed the trail on and on, till at last he spied her in a little clearing, half sitting and half reclining against a huge oak. Her wounded hand hung limply by her side, and with her face buried in her hands she was still sobbing.

A great wave of yearning and pity came over him. He felt a wild longing to take her in his arms. He threw himself down on his knees at her side.

"Heavens, Mrs. Gordon! Marian! You are sick and in pain. I will slacken the bandages for you."

He took the hand tenderly in his. When he removed the bandages he could not resist the impulse to kiss it. The hand was cold and numb with pressure. He kissed it again and again, while she only wept the more profusely. Removing all the pads but one he warmed her fingers between his own. He dare not trust himself to speak.

Her face was still buried in the handkerchief when the bandages were re-applied and his task completed. But he must say something.

"Marian," he whispers in low tremulous tones as he replaces her arm in the sling. "Don't weep or you will drive me frantic."

He stoops to look into her face, his arm slides over her shoulder, and, somehow, their lips meet in a long and clinging kiss.

That fatal kiss breaks down all reserve. With the fire of passion in her eyes, she throws herself upon his breast.

Time in his flight turns backwards. Locked in each other's arms, they are youthful lovers as of yore. All restraint is gone. The demon of passion takes possession of them. Honor and virtue are trembling in the balance.

But, suddenly, Nero comes bounding through the trees, and, with a savage growl, he springs at Langtry's throat.

CHAPTER XLVIII.

THE SKELETON OF THE FEAST.

Is there any awakening so rude; is there any disenchantment so terrible, as when we are suddenly revealed to ourselves in the light of lust. Can any tongue tell, or any pen picture the loathsome self-consciousness of having been the tool of passion?

To Marian the awakening was terrible. "Go, sir, go, and for the love of God, let us never meet again. Am I not low enough now?"

Charles Langtry stood hat in hand with his head bowed down "Marian, forgive me, I——"

"Don't dare to call me Marian!" she cried with a stamp of her foot. 'Thank God, I have the same loathing for you now that I have for myself. Away, away, and leave me alone to bear the shock of this stain upon my soul. I say I detest you. Go!"

She stood like a lioness at bay, her splendid figure drawn to its full height, her nostrils dilated and her eyes flashing. But he still stood as if rooted to the spot.

She placed her hands over her eyes and with a shudder, said: "Go, and let me thank God that Nero has saved me from worse than death. I may yet be fit to be the wife of an honest man."

"Oh, but the guilt was in my soul," she sobbed as she walked frantically to and fro. "I am a vile and loathsome creature."

Sinking on her knees beside the oak she clasped her hands in prayer.

"Oh God, I implore Thee by the sacredness of my marriage vows, and by the memory of the dear sweet face that looked up into mine and called me mother, to give me help and guidance. Thou hast saved my body from sin, but oh, merciful Father, teach me how to cleanse my soul from this foul stain; how once again to be worthy of the sacred name of wife. Guide me, oh God, in my duty from this hour, and, should suffering be my lot and my atonement, teach me to wear in humbleness Thy crown of thorns."

The young clergyman walked slowly and sadly along the path, but turned for a moment to look at the tear-stained face turned upwards to the stars. He knew that he was forgotten. The atmosphere around her seemed to change, and as she poured forth her prayer the light of a repentant soul shone in her eyes.

There, in the soft pale moonlight, surrounded by the weird shadows of the woods, with her faithful dog by her side, she seemed to shed a radiance on the scene around, and like a living statue plead for all who felt the yoke of human passion.

It seemed as if this warm, throbbing passionate woman had suddenly been transformed into an angel of light, who in the solemn stillness of the woods wept for the weakness of mankind, and held aloft the torch of charity and mercy.

As Mr. Langtry stole away the tears ran down his cheeks. "God will forgive me for loving such a noble creature. Every fibre of my being is drawn towards her. Nothing but death can break the tie that binds me to her. As well might I try to stop breathing, or by volition stay the beating of my heart, as try to cease loving that woman."

He walked on, scarcely knowing or noticing whither he was going till he came to a steep declivity, overlooking the rocks below. He stood for a moment looking down into the dark shadows. By one spring he might here end all his misery. The very possibilities of the spot had a fascination for him in his present mood. He threw himself down among the ferns and wild flowers.

Something light-coloured lying close by him on the bank caught his eye. He idly reached out to pick it up. It was a buff coloured glove, her glove; he knew it by its faint perfume. He kissed it greedily, and then lay toying with it in his hands.

"Why did God allow us to form a tie, which I, at least, can never break. Why did he allow human hands to separate those whom he created for each other? Surely, God can not be at variance with Nature. Is it wrong to eat and sleep and breathe? Do the little birds sin in choosing their mates? Do the flowers commit a sin in turning to the sunlight? No, by heaven, it is the law of man that errs."

He threw himself on his back and fairly groaned with anguish. "What have I to live for? Why should I live at all? My life has been one long disappointment. What need I fear in death? It can hold no suffering like life. Why not end it all here?"

For a time he gazed idly up at the stars, which in countless millions dotted the sky. Unconsciously he commenced humming a strain which the shining orbs suggested.

Soon the hollow vanities of life melted away like mist; his petty sorrows were forgotten and for a time he became an atom of the mother earth.

Gradually, however, his thoughts reverted to Marian. He pitied her for her suffering. It was surely greater than his. Should he not make life easier by helping her to forget him? Was it not his duty to go far away, beyond the reach of all temptation? And yet how could he throw up his position when his mother and Christina were dependent upon him for their daily bread? He must conquer himself, he must burn the selfishness from his soul and live for others as his sister did.

Poor Christina, whose simplicity and candour were almost childish, and whom he had been accustomed to regard as his inferior, must henceforth be his good angel. He must try to follow her footsteps.

At last he rose in a better frame of mind, thanking God for his preservation, and started toward the pavilion, whose lights he could occasionally see through the dense foliage.

He would, however, carefully avoid his sister and Nelly. He could not bear to be questioned.

The programme still went on, though it was now nearing a close, and the hour of departure would soon be at hand.

Nelly and her lover were enjoying the blissful elysium of love's young dream. This very evening he had poured forth his tale of love. On a shaded corner of the balcony they had exchanged vows and stolen kisses.

They wished that the music and moonlight might go on forever, and when the time for leaving arrived they were filled with disappointment. Everything then was hurry and bustle. Exactly at thirty minutes past nine the band waggon lead the procession for home.

Nobody wished to be left behind. The vehicles followed each other in rapid succession.

But where was Marian all this time? Nelly had not seen her, but Christina would know. "Christina," she shouted, "where are you?"

"Here, dear. Is Marian with you?"

"No. Is she not with you?" asked Nelly with an anxious quaver in her voice.

"I haven't seen her for hours. About an hour ago I sent Charles to hunt her up. Oh, here he comes now. Where is Mrs. Gordon, Charles?"

"I thought she was with you. Has she not returned yet?" inquired her brother in a tone of surprise. "She was at a little clearing away around the bay, and she wished to be alone. I understood, however, that she was coming shortly. Perhaps she has forgotten the hour."

"Poor Mally is so strange," said Nelly. "She was always so fond of the woods. She thinks the trees are company. But Nero is with her."

"May she not have missed her way back?" suggested Maurice, leading his vehicle forward in readiness.

"It is quite possible," replied Mr. Langtry. "We shall go in search of her at once. Here, bring that light; it will be a guide."

"Listen! I believe I heard Nero howling away in that direction," exclaimed Nelly. "Oh dear, I am sure there is something wrong. Listen! There it goes again."

A dismal, plaintive howl came floating over the water and faintly echoed through the hills.

Nelly grasped Christina's arm and broke into a fit of sobbing. "Oh, hurry, hurry! Let us go. Nero wouldn't howl like that for nothing. Oh, oh! It was so selfish of me not to think of her before. Oh, poor Mally!"

"Don't cry, Nelly. She may have merely missed her way in coming out," said Charles, with an assumed calmness in his voice though he was inwardly quaking with fear.

Perhaps she had expiated her uncommitted sin by *doing* what he had only *thought* of. Perhaps she had thrown herself into the lake in a fit of self-condemnation.

In a moment Maurice came with another lantern and the search party started out. The path was very narrow. At various points it was difficult to get through the thick foliage.

They made their way in single file to a point where the path divided. There they paused and shouted. But the echoes which followed were more confusing than the silence. Nero's answering howl seemed to come from a dozen different points.

"Here," cried Mr. Langtry excitedly, "you ladies stop here. We are going too slow. Maurice and I will run ahead. I can go to the very spot where she was. Don't be afraid. We will leave you a light;" and the two men went rushing and scrambling through the branches.

Nelly and Christina seated themselves on the edge of the bank, with the light between them, holding each other's hands. Under ordinary circumstances they would have started at the slightest sound. Every rustling leaf would have started a fresh fear. But their anxiety and suspense overcame all else. The men were gone only a few moments when they heard a crackling in the underbrush behind them. Before they had time to scream Nero came bounding upon them and covered them with caresses.

With joyful bark and coaxing whine the dog trotted along the path leading further into the woods, returning again and again with a dumb invitation to follow him.

"Shall we call them, Christina?" said Nelly, trembling with fear.

"Better not. The echoes would only confuse and mislead them. They might think we had strayed or fallen into the lake. We'll follow Nero. I'm not afraid now. I shall hold on by his tail. You take the lantern. Here. God of Heaven! look at my hands and dress. And you too, Nelly, are covered with blood. She is *bleeding* to death. Stop! Don't scream! Don't faint, Nelly, for the love of God! We may save her! As you love your sister catch my dress and follow me."

Nero in his eagerness drags them breathlessly along. Branches catch their clothes and scratch their faces, but they never slacken their speed. They stumble over logs, they trip over brushwood. They are panting with exertion and fear. Look! There's something white on the path ahead. Christina stumbles and falls. But Nero bounds onwards. He reaches the spot, stoops over the object, and gives a piteous whine. Nelly rushes forward.

In a moment piercing, agonizing shrieks are echoing through the hills, for there, face downwards in a pool of blood, lay the lifeless form of Marian Gordon.

CHAPTER XLIX.

VICARIOUS ATONEMENT.

Dr. Bennet was sitting in his office on the evening of the fifteenth, quietly enjoying a smoke and carelessly scanning the evening papers. He had been busy all day and felt quite tired, so much so that he proposed going to bed as soon as he had finished his cigar. Suddenly there came a violent ringing at his telephone. "Ah, I thought so," he growled to himself. "I felt certain that somebody was going to call me. Something urgent, too, by the ringing."

"Hello!—Yes, it's me—What?—Who did you say? Good God!" and he turned as pale as death. "Wait a minute——"

He ran frantically through the kitchen and out of the back door. "Dennis, Dennis! where are you?"

"'Ere," said the little man, running forward, "w'at is it?"

"The two mares and the light buggy, Dennis. Quick, now, quick! Here, Harriet, where are you? Take my cases out of the locker. All, mind you. And take them out to Dennis."

In a moment he was back at the telephone. "Hello!—At Springhill?—oh!—The doctor not home?—Fletcher, oh, yes—Still living when you left?—Thank God for that—Hello!—Is the doctor's wife there?—Well, tell her to give you some laudanum back with you—Ah, that's you, Mrs. Leopard—Yes, tincture opii—That's right—Say, Fletcher, hello there!—hurry back and pour a teaspoonful of that into her—Raise the foot of the bed—open the windows and let the air blow over her—Half a teaspoonful? No. Confound it, I said teaspoonful—Yes, yes—Sleep? No.—Poison, did you say?—Damn it! do what I tell you—Get out of there, and don't spare the horse!—Yes, head down and feet up—Stop—Langtry holding it? That's right.

Tell him not to stop the pressure for the fraction of a second. Get out now, or I'll be there before you."

In two minutes a pair of bays were gallopping madly up the street, the doctor in his usual position, and the stumpy little ostler clinging to a fragmentary portion of the seat.

The citizens sitting chatting on their doorsteps, enjoying the coolness of the evening, ran into the street as the flying vehicle passed.

"Why, that's Dr. Bennet. Was the team running away?"

"No, I don't think so."

"I wonder what's happened."

"Somebody is dying or very near to it."

"Let us go down and ask Harriet."

"Pshaw! she wouldn't know."

"Never mind, we'll hear soon enough in the morning. I'd hate to be a doctor."

"Me too," and the little group dispersed.

But, on, on, go the dashing bays. Up hills, down dales and along level stretches. With lips set and head drawn to one side the doctor sits holding his reins and urging his flying team. Ever and anon the buggy swings to one side or jumps through a ditch to pass some leisurely conveyance which is too slow to turn out.

Dennis gradually slides from his sitting posture into the bottom of the vehicle behind, but the driver takes no notice. They are nearing the mountain. In the distance a whole line of vehicles is approaching from the opposite direction. It is the picnickers from the lake, singing and shouting in merry chorus with the band in front.

Suddenly the long line stops, and Jamieson leaping to the roof of his band-waggon shouts in his loudest tones: "Vehicles ahoy! Look out for a runaway team. Close up behind and keep to the right."

Yes, there are two dark, leaping forms approaching in their mad career. Several men jump out and prepare to stop them, when suddenly they recognize the figure in the buggy.

"By Jove! it's the doctor. He's driving like mad. What's up, Doctor. What's wrong? Who's sick?"

But the bays never slackened their speed, and the rigid form in the vehicle never moved or spoke.

Flying beasts with dilated nostrils and foam-flecked sides, a silk hat shining in the bright moonlight, a pair of legs dangling behind, and a cloud of dust was all that the picnickers saw. The outside wheels tore up pieces of turf from the grassy rim of the roadway, bumped over rotten sticks as if they were portions of a pavement; and disappeared in the deep shadows of the wayside trees.

The songs and laughter ceased. All were awed into silence. They knew that some soul was trembling on the verge of eternity.

Now comes the climb up the mountain side, but still the bays rush on.

"You'll kill them, Doctor," comes from the back of the vehicle.

"Can't help it, Dennis."

"I'm afraid of Kate, Doctor."

"Yes, she's getting winded, but if she falls I'll mount Bess."

"I'll roll out behind and lighten you."

"All right, come behind, in case of accidents."

In a few seconds a dark object drops from the vehicle and rolls in the dust, but on, on, go the clattering hoofs and snorting nostrils.

They have reached the top. A great sigh of relief comes from the driver. Now they are tearing along the upland, when down goes one of the animals on its knees.

In a moment the driver is in front of his team. Pole, harness and whiffletrees are still sound. Good. Ha! There's the stream close by. Down the bank he runs and brings up his shining hat full of water. First Kate and then Bess greedily empties the strange vessel. But this causes a few moments' delay, and delay may be fatal.

"Now, my beauties," and away they go again faster than ever. Then they turn to the left and meet the fresh, cool westerly breeze which gives new life to the panting steeds. "Come, Kate, come! Radial artery likely. Hi, there, Bess. Gross carelessness some place. Ha, there's the lake lights. If I can only get reaction. No, it is somebody with a lantern. Go along there. Come, Kate."

The light moves hurriedly to the side of the road, and somebody shouts at him as he sweeps by, "Hurry, Doctor, she's still alive."

A swish of the whip was the only reply as the whirling vehicle spins round a curve and goes tearing through the canopy of trees towards the pavilion.

"Here he comes! Here he comes!" shouted a score of anxious voices.

Almost before he knew it the doctor was lifted from his buggy and pushed into the sick room.

"Oh, Doctor, will she live?" cried Nelly sinking on her knees at the bedside where, white as wax, lay her sister's prostrate form.

Without answering he pushed Nelly aside and laid his ear over Marian's heart. Charles Langtry, with large beads of perspiration on his brow, sat holding the wounded wrist. Maurice, with fear-stricken face, was pacing the floor, Nero lay trembling under the bed, and Christina stood by her brother's side quietly awaiting orders.

The hours of anguish through which they had passed since they found her lifeless form in the woods had told on every face. When they brought her to the pavilion the crowd had gone. Dr. Merrick had left an hour earlier.

At Springhill, a small village about three miles away, was a resident physician, and Maurice drove there in search of him. Not finding him at home he had telephoned to Gowanstone from there, and now, after two hours of agonizing anxiety, a helping hand had come.

But was it not too late? She had never spoken and only once opened her eyes. Her clothing and even the ground where she lay were found fairly soaked with blood. Every drop of the vitalizing fluid must have left her body.

All but Nelly and Mr. Langtry had given up hope.

They eagerly watched the physician's face as he listened for the faint throbs of his patient's heart.

But they could learn nothing from the closed eyes and compressed lips.

Within the shapely bald head a momentous struggle was going on which showed not on the face. He was standing at the bar of his own conscience, which told him that a human life was in his hands. Sometimes it urged caution, and sometimes courage, but in any case, it told him to be true.

At last he sprang up with an air of decision. Nelly caught him by the arm. "Oh, Doctor, will she live?"

"Can't say. She may be dead in an hour or well in a week. I'll tell you before I go. Now clear the room! Out, every one of you but Mr. Langtry and Christina. Did you give her what I told you, Fletcher?"

"No, we were afraid. They all said it would put her asleep and she would never wake up. We gave her half."

"Damn such work. Your cowardice may have cost her life. Clear out! Christina, bring hot water, salt, and baking soda. You have hot water ready? Good! It's a God's blessing *you* are here."

As soon as the room was cleared the old man put his hand on Langtry's shoulder. "Can you spare, or rather, are you willing, to spare some blood for this woman?"

Langtry's face turned a shade paler but he did not hesitate. "Certainly, with all my heart."

"I may want a good deal."

The clergyman gave a glance of inexpressible tenderness at the white face on the pillows. A curious light shone in his eyes as he met the doctor's gaze.

"You can have it all, and welcome. Don't spare it, if it will save her. But you had better put something here in place of my thumb. I might not be able to hold it when I get weak. I never fainted in my life and won't now if I can help it, but I might fall before you got through. I can lie on a lounge, and then you would not have to watch me."

Outside in the moonlight the anxious watchers

walked to and fro in agonies of suspense. Only a short time before the place echoed with mirth and music. Not three hours ago Nelly thought she was the happiest being on earth, and now—Oh, it was dreadful. She could not, dared not, think of losing Marian. An hour passed and no word came from the sick room.

"Maurice, please go and look in the window. Listen and see if you can hear anything. This suspense is awful. How shall I ever be able to face them all after this?" and she broke into another fit of sobbing.

For a long time not a sound came through the open window. All was still as death. At last there came a noise of footsteps and subdued voices, followed by an exclamation that threw them weeping in each other's arms. It was the doctor's voice. " By God, she'll live. We've saved her."

A moment later Christina appeared at the door to make an announcement. " The doctor tells me to say that Mrs. Gordon will recover." In her white garment, she seemed like an angel of light, a herald of joy. Nobody cheered or shouted. Some smiled and some wept, but many did both. They all greeted each other with warm human sympathy, and in their hearts offered up a prayer of thanks.

But in the general rejoicing there were two whose joy was not unmixed with grief. Christina, who saw her brother lying faint and pale upon the lounge, and Dennis, who, with dust stained clothes and scratched cheeks, stood by the stable door weeping over the carcass of his beloved Kate.

CHAPTER L.

A CROWN OF THORNS.

In two weeks from the day of the accident, Marian was taken home to the farm, and though she could not be said to have fully recovered, the colour was already returning to her cheeks. Her wonderful vitality and recuperative powers were a source of delight to her physician. No princess of the blood royal ever received more careful and efficient nursing and attendance. Trained nurses, spacious rooms and delicacies of every kind were placed at her disposal. Christina remained and acted as a companion till her friend was out of all danger, while Fred, Nelly and Maurice were daily visitors.

They wished to cable to England an account of the accident, but the doctor forbade them. They might write, if they wished, but they must caution Mr. and Mrs. Halford not to mention it to David. They waited from day to day, till he convinced them that it was better to say nothing about it, or only mention it incidentally. Any way she was nearly well and there could be little use in frightening them, now that it was all over.

Jamieson at first felt that he had a grievance. The picnic could not be called an unqualified success when it had such a semi-tragic ending. He had spared no pains or expense to make the affair successful, and a gorgeous success it would have been, only for the foolhardiness of a woman with a knife. His military instincts chided him for leaving such a possibility open. He should either have had the work all done by a competent person, or have taken with him proper tools for the purpose. However, he made up his mind that such an accident would never happen again where he had charge.

Some blamed Dr. Merrick for passing so lightly

over so serious a wound, but a great many claimed that it was Mrs. Gordon's own fault for not having gone home where it could have been properly attended to.

However that might be, every one was very kind and considerate. The news of the scene at the pavilion was not an hour in Gowanstone next day, when the iron-founder despatched a whole cargo of delicacies, flowers, fruit and wine.

The gossips of the town had, of course, considerable material for romancing. But there was a vague unsatisfactoriness about it all, which made it impossible to fasten a scandal upon any one in particular. The story had so many versions that nobody knew which to believe. One thing certain was, that since that very day Mr. Langtry had looked dreadfully unlike himself. His face was pale and haggard, his lips were almost white, and he carried his head to one side, as if his neck were stiff. When questioned as to his illness he gave evasive and unsatisfactory replies.

It was whispered around that the doctor took all the blood out of Mr. Langtry to supply Mrs. Gordon, actually pumped it from his arm into hers, but the improbability of this story branded it as a canard.

Like many other things, however, the picnic was a nine days' wonder. Now that Mrs. Gordon had returned to Broadview she was soon forgotten.

During her illness she had many opportunities of reflecting over the chain of events in which both her life and her honour had almost been lost. She was deeply conscious of the errors of her girlhood, but she had gathered the impression that time and education had purified her. Since then she had never been conscious of an impure thought, but the terrible scene in the woods convinced her that the demon of sensuality still lurked within her. She had not thought it possible that she could so far have forgotten herself, even for a moment. She must surely have been mad. Unlike many others, that day she had not tasted the champagne, but the music seemed to unhinge her in some way. It seemed to stir up her emotions till she lost control of them, and, unfortunately, temptation had come in a moment of weakness. She shuddered to think of the awful abyss over which she had almost precipitated herself. " Why am I so constituted as to feel an irresistible attraction for Charles Langtry? Is there something wrong in my physical make-up, or is it mental? Are my passions too strong, or do I lack control? Am I really a monster, or an ordinary human being?" She wondered if she were like other women, and whether, under similar circumstances, they might also stumble. Yet it mattered little, for even if others did sin it was no excuse for her guilt. She did not deceive herself. She felt that she had fallen, that it was Nero, poor, dear Nero, who had saved her from herself.

What should she do? In what direction did her duty lie? Would she ever have peace of mind again? How could she look her husband in the face, with such a secret in her soul? Must her life henceforth be a continuous lie? Supposing that she told him all, how would he receive it? Would he not be likely to cast her off and throw disgrace not only on herself but others?

Day after day she tortured herself for a solution of this problem. She did not object to suffering herself if it could be so arranged, but to bring disgrace on her parents or her innocent sister was an ordeal she could not face. Oh, dear! Why had they not left her a little while longer in the woods? Why had the doctor not been an hour later, or why had she not thrown herself into the lake? Was she like the condemned criminal, saved only to more thoroughly expiate her sin?

Her brain was a battle ground where contending forces fought for supremacy, but where each encounter only caused confusion and left victory still trembling in the balance.

She pitied Charles Langtry. She knew that his sufferings must almost equal her own. She was sorry that she had spoken so severely to him, when she knew that she was as much at fault as he was. She had not seen him since, nor did she know any of the particulars of her miraculous recovery. When she recovered consciousness that night she remembered only Christina and the doctor. She could recall a strange vision of Charles lying upon a couch in deathly paleness, but now she fancied that it was only the result of her disordered imagination.

"I have been afraid to trust myself alone with him. But the spell is broken now forever. I can only pity him, poor fellow."

On the sixth day, when she was strong enough to sit up in bed, Mrs. Stearns, whose husband was caretaker of the lake property, brought in her baby boy. The little fellow had eyes and hair like her dear wee Davie's. Marian took a great fancy to him. She spent hours in watching his prattles. Sometimes she smiled at the little tricks and gestures, and often she wept over something that reminded her of her lost darling. Toying and playing with the innocent babe she caught her first glimpse of a star of hope. It shone through all the gloom of moral darkness, through all the clouds of doubt and fear, and pointed out the pathway of eternal right. Come what might she must clear her soul before the memory of her little one. "I shall follow no guide but truth, and no path but duty," she said to herself.

From that time her strength came back with a bound. She was not long at the farm till she began to take a share of the work. Her manner had undergone a subtle change. Even Fred noticed and commented upon it. There was a deeper earnestness about her face, a graver tone to her speech. Seared into her soul with letters of fire was the motto, "Trust in God and do the right." Her daily round of labour helped her to crush the last germs of selfishness and deceit which lurked within her heart.

Oh, labour! Down-trodden, despised labour! Thou art the benefactor and preserver of our race. Thou bringest rest to frenzied brains and chasest morbid fancies from our sight. Thou art a beacon light amid the shifting sands of crime and madness, disease and death. Truly, truly, may we say, "*Labor omnia vincit!*"

CHAPTER LI.

A DOCUMENTARY DIAGNOSIS.

THE time of Gordon's probation had barely elapsed when Dr. Bennet received the following letter from his patient:

"DEAR DOCTOR:—I take the liberty of writing a few days ahead of time, but the seven weeks will have expired before this letter reaches you. You did not tell me the character or quality of the epistle I was to send, so I am at a loss to know just where to commence.

"In order, however, to give you a fair opportunity of judging the condition of my nervous system, I shall write whatever is uppermost in my mind, without any particular aim or effort. When I write again or when I return I shall give you a recital of my experiences in "the land of brown heath and shaggy wood," where, for three weeks I amused myself relic hunting and visiting the various spots of interest connected with the memory of Scotland's famous dead. But now I am in London.

"I have just returned from a stroll in Hyde Park, where I found an object-lesson which gave me food for thought. I have never seen such a collection of splendid-looking men and women as were driving and riding about the park this afternoon. The splendid physiques, robust health and refined looks of the women were simply astonishing, while the men were strong, active, clean and wholesome-looking. Just fancy meeting a score of women of the same type as my wife. It is enough to give one confidence in the future of our race. Not that any of them were (in my opinion) equal to her for that beauty of the human form divine which she possesses in an extraordinary degree. But, if you will allow me to use the phrase, they seemed to belong to exactly the same class of human animals.

"Now don't laugh, for I am bound to tell you everything. An odd little thing happened to me one evening last week. Come to think of it now, it must have been the fifteenth, for I reached London on the fourteenth, and it was the next evening. I had been spending the afternoon at the Zoological Gardens and was hurrying back to my lodgings on St. James Street, when I was certain I heard my wife call me. I stood stone still for a moment. My heart almost leapt into my mouth. The soft silvery ring of her voice was so distinct that I was perfectly stupefied, and for a moment I was foolish enough to imagine that it was her. I walked back half a block, looking right and left. Of course, it was a silly notion. The call I heard was probably the shout of a newsboy or hawker.

"Had this happened at night I might have become alarmed and cabled you to know if anything was wrong, but it was still daylight (somewhere between six and seven), so I went to a concert hall and laughed it off. Now, to-day, in the park I took a *sudden, intense longing to see her*, and I felt like taking the first boat home.

"I give you this experience for what it is worth, either as a symptom of a deranged nervous system, or as what some lunatics would call an occult manifestation. I fancy I see you smiling at this and charging it up to neurasthenia or some other outlandish name which you doctors give to diseases you don't understand.

"But to resume our original topic. I was going to suggest to you that the English nobility have done one good thing for the race if they have preserved such splendid specimens of the genus homo. You can't go down the Whitechapel district and then stand in the park, saying that one man is as good as another. Not even *your* democratic ideas could stand the shock. Perhaps I am oversensitive or I may be prejudiced, but the atmosphere of these 'aristocrats' had an exhilarating effect on me. If countenances are any index of character, they must be both refined and intelligent.

"Some literary fellow (I don't remember who it was), said that virtue was as rare in the upper classes as beauty was in the lower, but a statement of that kind carries with it its own contradiction. There may be exceptions, but as a rule well developed forms, open countenances, rosy cheeks and flashing eyes are not the product of dissipation and vice. It seems more likely that these results are due to centuries of good food, fresh air, cleanliness, vigourous exercise and suitable surroundings.

"I would a thousand times rather place the destiny of the world in such hands than distribute it in votes amongst such a mob as I saw at an open-air meeting the other night where a labour agitator was holding forth. Supposing we admit democracy to be the goal, we are surely rushing too fast. Moderate education and intelligence should precede the franchise. If I, as an individual, must be a slave, I prefer an intelligent master.

"I am convinced that the political atmosphere here is purer than ours.

"I have had two opportunities of visiting the House of Commons, and I feel assured that the majority of these representatives of the people are conscientiously doing what they conceive to be their duty. It is not alone the intellectual giants of the Gladstone and Beaconsfield type who are far beyond the reach of sordid selfishness, but the rank and file of these men (let their abilities be what they may) have unimpeachable motives. Too many of our fellows are 'out for the stuff;' simply, I believe, because as a rule the rabble prefers a man of its own stamp.

"I fancy I can see you growling at my rank toryism, but this dose will help to offset the many villainous potions you have given me. Ha, ha, ha!

"I left Mr. and Mrs. Halford at Boscastle, where the 'squire is visiting some of his boyhood acquaintances and arranging for my wife's legacy, which now amounts to about four thousand pounds.

"By the way, I must tell you that my respected father-in-law is a blue-blood of the best Cornish stock. This is another of those cases in which extravagance swallowed up the whole generation, stock, lock and barrel. This is the kind of thing we Americans laugh at, but, at the same time, we are willing, with our bags of dollars, to buy titled paupers for our sons-in-law. In spite of our boasted democracy the Baron de Bung-starter, with a dilapidated castle on the Rhine, the Duke of Debits, whose ancestral home is shingled with mortgages, and Count Pedro, whose quarters are carpeted with playing cards and unpaid bills, receive a thousand times more homage in New York than in London. They cut a larger figure. The Americans are democratic in theory, and the English in practice. Take that for dessert.

" But now, no more politics. I am both eating and sleeping well. I cannot say just when my insomnia left me, but it is gone, and I hope for good.

" I have so much to write about that I scarcely know when to quit. I remember, though, you always told me to stop writing or reading at the first sensation of weariness, so I think I will quit and go to bed.

" Before closing, however, I will admit that my principal object in writing is to hear from my wife. Just at this very moment I would give a good deal for one look at her.

" A promise is a promise, but to tell you the truth, I am on the point of rebelling, and if I don't hear from her soon I will write myself. They say a patient is out of danger when he rebels against his medicine, and by the time you receive this letter I shall be in open mutiny.

" Tell my wife to send a photo with her letter, and that I will count the days till I hear from her.
" Your disobedient patient,
" D. GORDON."

" N. B. By the way, Doctor, I had a little experience in Edinburgh which might, if not instructive, be amusing. At a music hall there I heard a Scottish vocalist sing ' Hail to the Chief ' in costume, and it fairly electrified me. He was a splendid singer, and he made me fancy I could see the kilted clans marching down the glen to the sound of the pibroch. I felt downright wicked, as if I wanted to kill ' twa at a blow '. For two pins I would have fought with my next neighbour.

" Now, was that a neurotic symptom, as you would call it, or was it an ebullition of Hielan' blood?

I love the land of the Stars and Stripes. It is the land of freedom and progress. It is the only country that I would care to live in, but deep down in my heart there must be a spot dedicated to 'Scotland yet.'"

The doctor fumbled the letter over and over. Although David's politics were not to his taste, he was pleased with the philosophical tone of the letter, and was fully convinced that Gordon was a well man again.

He enclosed it with a note to Mrs. Gordon at Broadview, and sent Maurice Fletcher with it that very evening.

"DEAR MADAM :—Enclosed find letter from Mr. Gordon. He seems quite well again. You may write him now, but tell him nothing of your accident nor of business.

"Yours,
"GEORGE BENNET."

What a delight the letter was to Marian, and how kind of the crusty old doctor to send it without waiting for the mail. She read it over and over again, till the portion referring to herself was learned by heart. Who shall say it was vanity that prompted her to kiss it? A new chamber in her heart seemed to open, and from it rushed forth a flood of benevolence. The world seemed brighter and better. In the stillness of the night she said to herself "Now I know what love is."

Next morning a cablegram flashed under the Atlantic with greetings to a husband from his loving wife.

CHAPTER LII.

THE WAGES OF SIN.

GORDON did not wait for the doctor's permission to write, for a few days after the arrival of his first communication there came a letter to Marian herself, which was brimming over with tenderness.

"Such a dear, sweet letter. I had no idea, that he loved me so fondly. He never told me so before. Why does he never talk to me like this? He's afraid I would think him silly. If he only knew how often I have hungered for a little tenderness."

Gordon was, indeed, a peculiar man in this respect. He seemed to consider any display of emotion or sentiment as *infra dig*. At concert hall or opera house, if anything were likely to move him to tears, he would scowl and look fierce, to hide what he thought was a weakness. Not even to his wife did he come out of his shell of reserve. He would just as soon have gone about naked, as to have had the public see the tender spots in his heart. He rather prided himself on being a rationalist, but in spite of all that his nature had more than its share of the emotional. In spite of kisses and caresses his wife felt that there were chambers in his heart to which she had never gained admission. Now, however, he had put upon paper a depth of feeling which he was probably too proud to express in person, and his wife got a glimpse of the hidden treasures of his inner nature.

Truly, we are strange mortals! Let us go to a lecture or entertainment where our expectations run high, and very frequently we come away thoroughly dissatisfied; while on another occasion, when our anticipations are not inflated, we will loudly applaud the same talent. Some one else may tell us of the good qualities of friend, companion, husband, or wife, and we pay little attention, but let us of our own accord accidentally discover some long-hidden, unsuspected virtue, and our hearts go out to them at once. Where we discover one treasure we expect to find another, and in our imagination see virtues which possibly do not exist.

The letter was a source of pleasure to Marian. For several days she stole occasionally into some quiet corner to read it over and over again, or to look at the photograph which it enclosed. One evening, when she thought all the others had retired, she was fondly kissing the letter when Nelly caught her in the act.

"Oh, shame, Mally! I caught you nicely, you crazy old spooney. Don't try to make fun of *me* again. Shame!" and pouncing upon her sister's knee she gave her a sympathetic hug. "I don't care, I just think David is a dry old stick. I never saw him kiss you or call you a pet name yet."

"Well, dear, David is not a man who wears his heart on his sleeve."

"I don't care. When I get married (if I ever do)," said Nellie with a blush, "he will have to be attentive and let people see that he loves me. He'll have to keep telling me about it, too."

"Oh, indeed, I suppose you and Maurice have it all arranged? David and I will have to come and see you, just to learn how to behave to each other."

They were about to retire for the night when they heard someone driving rapidly up the lane.

"It must be Maurice again, and me all topsy-turvey," said Nelly, running for shelter in headlong haste, while Marian prepared to go to the door.

What was their surprise when, with a short preliminary knock, Dr. Bennet entered the room without waiting for anyone to admit him, and marching up to Marian with his whip in his hand, said, "Charles Langtry is dying, and he, or rather his sister, wishes you to come at once."

"What!" exclaimed Marian, springing to her feet and seizing him by the arm, while her very lips turned white. "Great heavens, Doctor, it cannot be true!" she added in a hoarse whisper.

"It is only too true," replied the physician, tapping

the floor with his whip. " I don't think he will see daylight, and that is why I want you to come now."

" Was it an accident ?" she murmured, dropping into a chair.

The doctor did not immediately reply but addressed himself to Nelly. "Go and get Mrs. Gordon's wraps and your own. You shall go with her. We must start right away."

As soon as Nelly had left the room he answered Mrs. Gordon's question. "A neglected dog bite followed by blood poisoning."

Marian gave a low moan. She would have fallen to the floor had not the doctor assisted her to the door and given her a drink of water.

" He made me promise," continued the doctor in a low tone, " not to tell the cause of the trouble to anyone, but of course you know already."

Marian's only reply was a groan of anguish, as she sat with her face buried in her hands.

" Hush! here's your sister! Be careful of your questions before her. Hurry now, for it is a long drive."

As Mrs. Gordon stepped into the doctor's vehicle she felt like a criminal going up for trial. The very leaves of the wayside trees, as they drove along, seemed to be whispering " murderess." Her thoughts came in rapid succession. " Oh, God! what a monster I am. I must have been mad. Poor fellow! he never told me he was hurt and I was inhuman enough not to ask him. Nero must be killed, the wicked brute ; and yet the poor dog was only doing his duty. But now this man must die. All his manly prime and beauty will soon be rotting in the grave, and those hands whose magic touch could turn ivory keys into heart strings will be food for worms. Poor Christina and Mrs. Langtry. He was their joy and their pride. Yes, and their only support too. Oh, it is terrible to think of it."

Had she been alone that minute, with the means at hand, she would probably have ended her life. She would have carried out the sentence of her own conscience, which said that for this man's life her own must be given.

The doctor had lit a cigar and was smoking as complacently as if he were driving his steeds for pleasure, instead of hurrying to a deathbed. There was little cause for haste as far as he was concerned, for Charles Langtry was beyond all earthly power. The patient in his ravings had revealed not only the story of his wounds, but of his boyhood as well.

The doctor was not surprised. Here was the disturbing element which had deflected Mrs. Gordon's electrical affinity. He took everything as a matter of course. For thirty years he had been analysing his fellow-creatures, and in the green-room of life had seen the sham of outward show. Accustomed to seeing society in its shirt sleeves, he knew men as they were, not as they seemed to be. He conceived that the man who had once been the lover of such a woman would remain her lover as long as life lasted. On the other hand, he was sure that he who first aroused the great magnetic possibilities of Mrs. Gordon, would always have a powerful influence over her. It was the old story of the loadstone and the magnet. It rather pleased him to know that this very power had been strong enough to overcome the scruples of those whom he knew to be morally and mentally far above the average. It was a verification of his theory, a proof that every human being was an electrical entity. Nor did it lower Mrs. Gordon one whit in his estimation, or change his high opinion of the young clergyman. He could form an idea of the wonderful force of the temptation which they had to resist. Even in the purest hearts he had detected spots where lurked the germs of evil, and in the brightest minds had marked the serpent's trail.

He smoked on in silence, occasionally taking his cigar from his lips to urge his team, but never offering to open a conversation. His own conscience was smiting him hip and thigh.

If Mr. Langtry's veins had been filled with rich pure blood, if he had been in his usual condition, the dog bite (bad as it was), would not have been fatal. But he had been "bled white," to give life to Mrs. Gordon; his natural power of resistance had been sadly weakened, and neglect had done the rest.

In doing his duty to Mrs. Gordon, had the doctor forgotten what was due to Mr. Langtry? Had he borrowed too freely from the generous giver? Had he allowed his peculiar devotion for this woman to swerve him from the strict path of duty? The only balm to his conscience was that, at the time, he was not aware of the clergyman's wound.

At last Marian spoke. "How long has he been ill?"

"He has not been well for some time, but they only called me in the night before last."

"Is he delirious?"

"He was last night, but he is quite clear now, at least, as clear as a dying man can be."

"Who stayed with him last night?"

"I did."

"Any one else?"

"No, I sent Christina and the mother to bed."

Marian gave a great sight of relief. "Thank God for that," she said to herself, and relapsed into silence.

She sat holding Nelly's hand in hers. She was thankful for the darkness which hid her from prying eyes. She would have given her life to have her soul as stainless as her sister's. She wondered how Nelly, so innocent, should have such a monster for a sister.

When she met Christina's gaze and saw her face pale with suffering, she sank weeping on her knees in front of her.

"Don't cry, dear," said the sorrow stricken sister, putting her hand on Marian's head. "Take off your wraps. It is terrible, but we must try and bear it. When you get warmed go into the room. He wishes to see you alone. Something about his music, I think."

Mrs. Langtry came from the sick room, weeping as if her heart would break. "Oh, Marian, my boy, my boy! Why couldn't I die first? Why should I have lived to see this day? He heard your voice. He wants you to go in now."

With faltering step, and bated breath, Marian went softly into the room and Christina closed the door behind her. One look at his pallid face told her his hour had come. She fell on her knees at the bedside, and buried her face in the bed clothes.

"Oh God, Charles, I have murdered you."

"Don't," he replied faintly. "You *shall* not talk like that."

"It was my fault, Charles. Oh, it is terrible, to think of you suffering, and me in health. I wish I could change places with you."

"No, Marian, it was my fault. I stirred up your emotions by the love tale I played. I knew it would unnerve you, but some inward demon lured me on. God forgive me, but it was the first time I ever put sensuality and voluptuousness into a theme or accompaniment. I never even tried it before."

He paused for breath. "I think it was—because I felt—so sorry about your hand."

For a moment a faint smile of triumph flashed over his face, then he drew a long breath and rubbed his eyes in a dazed sort of way. "May God forgive my sin. I tempted a pure, virtuous woman—and now I am—suffering the consequences. I, who should be—a leader and a teacher of men."

"Then why can't I die, too? My sin was even greater than yours. I was unfaithful (in spirit) to my marriage vows. Some terrible thing will happen me, and I don't care how soon. I am a monster, I tell you. I was not human enough to ask if you were hurt. There is no death or suffering too bad for me."

He put his hand on her shining hair and looked at her pityingly.

"Marian, I suppose you have your faults like other mortals, but to me you are the most honest, purest, most human, noblest woman in the world. I pity you for the torture you will give yourself."

She still kept her face buried to shut out the sight of her victim. She could not bear to see the sunken, ghastly face which, but for her, would beam with manly health and beauty. After resting a few moments with his eyes closed he spoke again.

"If your mother had not separated us our lives would have been one grand, sweet song. You would have inspired me to great and noble things."

He feebly reached out and took one of her hands in his. He lay for a few moments fondling it.

"I would, with you at my side, have given—the world a song of love and praise that would have echoed through all the ages. Quick! I feel the inspiration now—quick, a pencil and—some paper—or it will pass."

He tried to raise himself on his elbow, but fell back on his pillow exhausted.

"No—my music days—are over. And yet—ah, well—what matter—let it pass."

He was panting from exertion. She gave him a few spoonfuls of water to moisten his lips. Then she seated herself by the side of the bed and buried her face in her hands.

"Show me—the arm that was hurt. It's a good thing—there isn't—much scar. It is—a beautiful hand. This is the finger—I put the ring on—the night—I carried you—through the stream. Don't you remember?—how it got fast—and I had—to cut it off—and spoiled the ring—your finger—got scratched—with the knife—and it bled—but I—kissed it—till it stopped. Didn't I?" and he raised her hand to his lips.

"Oh, God! I cannot bear it any longer," she groaned, as she rocked herself to and fro. "I must call Christina and your mother."

"Forgive me," pleaded the dying man. "You know —my mind—is weak. Let me have—your hand. It cannot matter now. It makes—me strong. You are —rich now, I hear. You will see—to Christina—and mother?"

"Charles, before God I promise that they shall never want. I shall put them beyond the reach of want. It is the only atonement I can make to them and you for the great wrong I have done."

The invalid's eye flashed as he looked at her. "I say you—have done me—no wrong. It wasn't Nero —killed me. It was—neglect. The doctor can—tell you so too. Don't cry. It is better—for me to go. I couldn't live—in peace—without you."

She rose to her feet and stood leaning against the bed-post, with her face hidden in her handkerchief, while he caressed her hand.

"Won't you—kiss me—and let me feel—your face—against mine for a minute? It is no harm—is it?" She stooped down and laid her cheek upon his. He kissed her repeatedly and feebly put his arms about her neck.

"There, you can—call the rest. My sight is—getting dim. God—will forgive—you—and me."

They sat for an hour watching him grow feebler, while from time to time the doctor took his watch and measured the ebbing tide of life.

The dying man kissed his mother and sister and tried to whisper words of comfort in their ears.

They knelt on either side of the bed, bowed down with their great sorrow. For nearly an hour not a word was spoken, and they thought that he had become unconscious, but he opened his eyes and seemed to be looking for someone. Christina motioned Marian to come forward, and she stooped to catch the feeble sounds that came from his lips. His breath was coming thick and fast. She could scarcely understand him.

"Don't—shoot—the—dog—he—"

But the sentence was never finished, for with one wild final throb his heart stood still.

CHAPTER LIII.

GILDING A GRIEF.

IF anything is needed to convince us of our insignificance, or give us to understand that the world can get along without us, it is the rapidity with which we are forgotten when we are gone. There is always someone willing and ready to take our place. " The King is dead, long live the King," still echoes along the line.

In a small community like Gowanstone, however, the suddenness of Mr. Langtry's death was quite a shock. The deceased had persistently refused to see any other physician than Dr. Bennet. But people looked askance at the doctor, and thought there must be something wrong when so robust a man as Mr. Langtry went off so suddenly.

He, perhaps, more than any other citizen, was loved by all with whom he came in contact. He was widely known throughout the district as a rare musician and a liberal patron of manly sports. Eminent divines, marksmen, anglers and athletes, all mourned his loss. Together with the citizens, they attended the funeral and looked solemn, while the usual number of lachrymose females wept over the coffin. The local papers wrote up lengthy obituaries eulogising his social qualities and musical abilities, his successor preached a funeral sermon, and everything went on as before.

Dr. Bennet and Mrs. Gordon were executors to an estate which consisted only of the small balance of an unpaid salary, and a huge pile of music in manuscript. The doctor ruefully wondered what was to be done. But he did not remain long in suspense, for on the following day his co-executor called at his office to discuss the situation.

" You know, Doctor, I shall have plenty of money when David comes home, but here is five hundred dollars anyway. Could we not arrange it so that they would think it came out of the estate?"

"He has no estate," replied the doctor, with a sad smile.

"There is his music."

Her companion shook his head and snapped his fingers, but Marian was persistent.

"I think you are wrong, Doctor. I believe those manuscripts are worth thousands of dollars. Charles Langtry never wrote meaningless music."

"He was certainly more than a pianist. He was an artist; but it does not follow that he was an eminent composer."

"Well, you give them the money," she said, depositing a roll of bills on the table. "You know they will want mournings."

"Really, Mrs. Gordon, I can't see the sense of spending money so foolishly when it may be needed in many other ways."

She turned her beautiful eyes full upon him for a moment. "Don't you see it will employ their minds getting it ready. It will give them a temporary motive and help them to live through their grief? They are not philosophers like yourself, Doctor; they are only weak women."

The doctor wiped his spectacles thoughtfully but did not reply.

"You could employ a man to decorate the grave and they could go to see it every day. Don't you think it would help to soften their grief?" she asked, with a sob in her throat and the moisture in her eyes.

"I suppose it would," replied her companion, blowing his nose. "You would require some plans for the workmen. They would need something to guide them."

"Well, you see, Christina and I could do that. It would always be doing something for his memory. It is all the comfort they have, poor souls." Here the speaker broke down and moved away to the window to hide her tears, while the doctor fumbled and fussed with some papers on his desk.

In a few moments she came back and stood facing

him. " He asked me not to shoot the dog, but I will have to send him away for awhile. Poor Nero, he is such a faithful brute, too, although he is getting too cross lately."

"I suppose they will soon have to move out of the parsonage," remarked the doctor, who wished to change the subject.

" Yes, but they have two weeks yet, or more if necessary. I am staying with them now altogether, just to keep them company. It may keep them from noticing their loss so much."

" Do you think it would be of any use to have a sale, not of the furniture, of course, but of his horses vehicles, and sundries, and, perhaps, the piano?"

" It would not matter much about those other things, but I would not think of selling the piano. It was his companion. They would not care to part with it."

" Very well, I will attend to the matter," replied the doctor. "In the meantime, there is no hurry about the music."

" Not at present. By the way, I have secured them a house. It is a cheerful spot and has a flower garden. If you think of anything more you can let me know. Good-bye."

"Gordon was right," said the doctor to himself as the door closed behind his visitor. " There is some hope for the race as long as such women exist. There was neither false modesty nor brazenness in her face when she spoke of the dog; nothing but pure, honest candour."

He lit a cigar and puffed away thoughtfully. " I could have loved such a woman. Humph!" and he took a pinch of snuff. "Poor Langtry. Well, well, Burns was right.

"What's done we partly may compute,
But know not what's resisted."

Marian seemed to forget her own troubles in her sympathy for the Langtrys. Her new duties in providing and arranging for her bereaved friends were a positive comfort to her during these dark days. What with moving, resettling, sewing and decorating the grave she was continually in the company of Christina and her mother.

Then poor Nelly had *her* troubles. Mr. Tracy of Denver was going to tour Australia with his ball team during the winter, and had offered Maurice the financial management of his opera house for six months at a good salary.

Fletcher's duties as bookkeeper would cease as soon as Mr. Gordon came home. Having nothing else in view, Maurice had accepted the offer. He wished to take Nelly with him as his wife, and the poor girl was in a quandary.

She was sure that her mother would not consent to so hasty a marriage. Indeed, she was afraid that her parents might not consent at all to the union. Hope, however, was strong within her, and she went on preparing in the expectation of soon having a home of her own.

As the time for David's return approached Marian applied herself to the task of studying her duty to her husband. During his absence his business interests had been well guarded by Maurice. He would have no reason to complain on that account. She had decided to tell him the whole truth, but, as the time drew nigh, she became more timid. " Oh, it is hard to do right. He will never forgive me. I love him and I could not bear to lose him. He is so good and pure. Ah, me! it is only those who stumble that pity those who fall." And yet she felt that, though the day of the picnic was the darkest one in her life, she was *since then* a better woman. It was as if she had been groping along in the dark, close to the edge of a precipice, and a flash of light had shown her where she stood.

CHAPER LIV.

THE ROSE AND ITS THORN.

"JUST landed. Will reach home to-morrow evening. All's well."

This was the telegram which set Mrs. Gordon's heart all of a flutter, and turned her pale and red by turns. "Here, Nelly, read this," she cried excitedly. "How would it be, if we got everything ready this afternoon, and ran down to Dearborn Junction to-morrow to meet them?"

"Good. That's splendid," replied her sister, with delight. "Now I know why somebody got such a nice travelling dress. Oh, but you are a cunning one. A person would think it was your lover coming to see you."

"So it is my lover. Why not? By the way, Nelly, did you ever hear him say lately how he liked my hair done up," she inquired with a little flush.

"Yes. You remember the time he came to see you over home, just after Davie died? Well, you had it done up in fluffy, loose plaits, and I could see that he noticed it. He didn't say anything, but I knew he liked it, for I saw him admiring you when your back was turned."

"Well, come, dear, and let us try it now."

They spent nearly the whole afternoon in toilet experiments. Nelly acted as maid and critic. The new dress had to be tried on. "Really it is very plain," was Nelly's comment, "but you look just as if you had been poured into it. I am beginning to find you out, Mally. It is not the dress that looks so nice, it is yourself. In this case, it is a woman with a dress on, and not a dress with a woman in it."

The gown was really an artistic triumph, and when the finishing touches were put on her sister's toilet, Nelly exclaimed, "Well, if David Gordon's heart don't jump when he sees you, it will be because he hasn't got one. But how did you come to think of going to Dearborn?"

"Why, Nelly," said Marian, colouring slightly, "if I wish to give my lover a kiss, I don't want all Gowanstone staring at me. If we met at the station here, he would be ashamed to kiss me, so I would have to do it all myself."

"You spooney old thing, you are worse than me. You will just be in the same fix, though, in the train, as you would at the station."

"No, indeed. The spectators will be all strangers, and I won't need to care so much. But what are those tears for, dear? You must be getting hysterical."

"Your lover is coming home, but mine is going away. I don't care. Mother will just have to let me go. I'll just die, if he goes away."

"Never mind, dear," said Mrs. Gordon, sympathetically, taking her in her arms. "I will help you all I can. But you don't know how nice it is to get a love letter every other day. It is nearly as good as seeing him. It will come all right, Nelly. Now, dry your eyes, and we will get everything ready for to-morrow."

Next day, at two o'clock in the afternoon, two ladies were promenading the station platform at Dearborn Junction, waiting impatiently for the express from New York. A cold, raw November wind was blowing from the north, but they were clad in fur-trimmed garments and seemed perfectly indifferent to the weather. If anything, the sharp wind only served to deepen the colour in their cheeks and to enhance their beauty.

Every few moments they stopped and gazed along the level stretch of track where the glistening rails seemed to fade into the sky. It was thirty minutes past the time, and the train was not yet in sight. The manner of the taller lady was full of excitement. She walked to and fro with a short, nervous step, stopping every few seconds to look to the eastward, and occasionally heaving a deep sigh.

"Look, Nelly, yonder is a speck of smoke. It is coming now. Oh, dear! I am all unstrung. Let us sit down for a moment. My heart is all of a flutter."

"Don't be a goose, Mally. Look at me. I am not excited."

"Am I looking all right, Nelly? How is my hair? Push that hairpin in a little tighter. There."

"You are simply lovely. Really and truly, Marian, you are. You look like a duchess. That grey fur is so becoming. My! how we will surprise them all," continued Nelly, gleefully. "You'll make for David, I suppose, but I'll rush for father, the dear old soul. Look, it's almost here! Don't stand so close. It frightens me," she added, as the locomotive came rushing in with slackening speed and hissing jets of steam.

The motion of the train had barely ceased when they mounted the steps of the first coach.

The stop was only a momentary one. Before they had crushed their way through the first car the train was again going at full speed. Coach after coach was gone through in like manner without discovering the looked-for faces. They began to fear that the travellers had missed their train.

"Ah, here is the conductor; we will ask him."

"Have you any other passengers for Gowanstone?" asked Marian with beating heart, as she handed him her tickets.

"Yes. I think there are two or three in the last sleeper."

"Can we get through? It seems so crowded."

The official, with a polite bow and an admiring glance, volunteered to escort them himself.

In a few moments they caught a glimpse of their mother's massive figure sitting with her back towards them.

"There they are!" They swooped down on the old couple unawares, fairly smothering them with kisses. "But where is David?" said Marian, with a tremor in her voice as she looked excitedly along the rows of seats. "Quick, where is he?"

Mrs. Halford laughed with exasperating coolness. "Well, now, Marian, it were like this here. We had a compartment or stateroom to ourselves last night, but David didn't sleep very well, so, after dinner him went to lay down and told us not to disturb him till us were near home."

"Which compartment?" she asked, glancing from one end of the coach to the other.

"Mother is only teazing you," said her father. "He's right in there."

Whether it was the swaying of the train or her own excitement which made her stagger, Marian could not tell, but she could scarcely walk straight to the door, which faced toward the rear of the car. She gently pushed it open, and the first thing which caught her sight was her husband asleep on the sofa. How quickly she noticed every feature, and every change in his countenance or apparel.

There was a faint streak of grey on his temples, but his face was more plump than it had been for years, and he seemed ever so much handsomer.

She stole in on tiptoe and stood over him for a moment as if afraid to disturb his slumbers. She closed the door gently. She had him all to herself, while she feasted her eyes upon him.

She rolled back her fur collar, pushed her hat further back on her head and knelt gently beside him till a pair of rosy lips were pushed under his mustache, and a cool pink cheek rested against his.

What a vision met the sleeper's gaze when he awoke and found himself in his wife's arms. "There's a pair of gloves for me, and another, and another," she said, kissing him greedily.

"Why, darling, it is you. Are we there already?"

"No, but I am here. I could not wait any longer, so I came to meet you," was her laughing reply.

"Here sit on my knee and let me look at you."

"I am pretty heavy," she said coquettishly, as she accepted the invitation. "I weigh about a hundred and sixty-five. Shocking, isn't it? But you are a good deal stouter, too."

He did not speak for a time, but sat gazing fondly at her while she arranged his tie, the blue-spotted silk specially donned for the occasion.

"Marian, I do believe you are the most beautiful woman in the world."

"Is that so?" she replied archly. "I was beginning to feel jealous of the beautiful ladies you met in the park."

He shook his head and smiled. "I was just thinking that it was a great *privilege* to have the love of such a lovely woman."

"I do love you, David," she responded, as she kissed him again and again, "and never so much as now. I have fallen in love with you in earnest this time. Now I will fix you up. We must not let them see we have been spooning. Where is your hairbrush? A comb will do. I see you are shaved differently, but I think you look nicer. The grey hairs become you wonderfully, but I don't want too many of them. You are only a boy yet, you know."

David sat very demurely submitting to the combing process. He was content to admire the pink ears and cheeks, the shapely neck, the deep blue eyes and silken hair of the woman on his knee.

How long this billing and cooing would have continued it was impossible to say, though Gordon wished it might last forever, but a knock at the door interrupted them.

"Are you two not done spooning yet?" asked Nelly. "May I come in?"

"Yes, come in, Nelly."

David felt abashed, and was about to push his wife from his knee.

"No, sir," protested Marian, clinging tighter. "You always pretend before people that you don't care much about me, but now you've got to kiss me right before Nelly, and not let on to be such a bluebeard.

"You've got to tell me that you love me, and right before her too. I am going to break you off your bad habits. There now, that's a good boy," she continued with a triumphant glance at Nelly. "You can kiss her too. Come, Nelly, you needn't be so shy. He is just as nice as your fellow."

"Oh, she has got a fellow then," said David, saluting her. "Aha! and who is the lucky man?"

"You shut up, Marian Gordon, or I'll tell on you," retorted the young girl saucily. "Why, David, she got up before daylight this morning to catch the nine o'clock train."

"Oh, that's nothing, *she* has actually threatened to run away with Maurice."

"It wouldn't be any more than my big sister did," replied Nelly gingerly, whereat they all laughed. "I suppose now, if you are through hugging and kissing, I may bring father and mother in. Then we will all be together like Brown's cows."

That night the little brick cottage at Gowanstone was the scene of a happy family reunion, but the thorn peeped through the rose when David asked: "Where's Nero?"

CHAPTER LV.

A THUNDERBOLT FROM A BLUE SKY.

WHEN Mrs. Halford arrived in Gowanstone she resolved to remain there a week or so before returning to Broadview. She did not feel like taking off her holiday garments all at once, and going into the work at home. She would make a short stay at her daughter's, and thus gradually accommodate herself to everyday life.

But she had reasons of far greater importance. Nelly's affairs had to be discussed and settled, and although she had made up her mind to give her consent to the match, yet she must hold them in suspense for a time, in order to give them all a sense of her importance. Indeed, since the first, Mrs. Halford had been kind and confidential with the young Englishman. He held the key to a secret which she did not wish to have opened. It would never do to let Marian discover her illegitimacy, or that she herself, instead of being the child of poor but honest parents, was the fruit of an illicit love. It was not, however, through fear of exposure that she finally gave her consent, for she had a high opinion of the young Englishman, and she saw that Nelly loved him. She had interfered once in love affairs and had only made matters worse for herself and her daughter. She wouldn't repeat the experiment.

Maurice had discharged his duties with credit to himself and satisfaction to his employer. He was very loath to leave for the South. Nelly coaxed him to give up the situation altogether, but his word was given and he remained firm. However, Mrs. Halford agreed to his returning in three months to claim his bride.

The mistress of Broadview was very much pleased with the homage she received in Gowanstone. Besides being wealthy herself, her daughter was now an heiress, and her husband was a relic of a defunct line of aristocrats. The *élite* of the town stumbled over each other in paying their respects to Mrs. Gordon and her mother. From the dry goods clerk behind his counter to the banker in his office, there was a distinct change of manner towards them.

This servility was as distasteful to Mrs. Gordon as it was pleasing to her mother. Dame Fortune's smiles had no visible effect either on Marian's face or her apparel. She was glad to be rich to be able to help her husband, or the Langtrys. It would give her an increased power of doing good to others.

Mrs. Halford, however, had another motive for remaining in the neighbourhood a few days longer than she otherwise would have done. She had of course heard, months ago, of Mr. Langtry's death, and it had been quite a shock to her. Fate this time had played into her hands, had removed him far more effectively than Mr. Slade could have done. She would be reasonably entitled to a portion of her money back.

Since coming home, odd and contradictory rumours had reached her ears, and to gratify her curiosity, if for no other reason, she must probe the matter to the bottom. First was the story of Charles Langtry's movements at the picnic, and the hint that her daughter's life had been saved by blood taken from his veins. This was disturbing enough, but matters looked even worse, when she learned that the wound which caused

Langtry's death, was received on the fateful day at Snell's Lake. The deceased had at one time called his wound a boil, and, another time, said that his neck had been hurt by the branch of a tree. He had gone to the picnic well and hearty, and next day was pale and bloodless. To cap the climax, the clergyman had sent for Marian when on his death-bed.

Mrs. Halford divined by her daughter's evasive replies to her questions, that there was some reason for keeping secret the details of Charles Langtry's illness and death. As a matter of duty, she paid a visit of condolence to the bereaved mother and sister. From Christina she pumped all that she could of her brother's sudden decease.

"Your brother sent for Marian that night, Christina?"

"Yes. It was about his music. You see, it was all he had."

"Oh! and what are her going to do about it?"

"I don't really know, Aunt Jane, but Marian thinks there is a fortune in it. One of the publishers has already advanced five hundred on it. Charles seemed to think that Mrs. Gordon was the only one who understood his compositions."

"Poor fellow. His neck got hurt, did it not, the day of the picnic?"

"I don't know what started it, but it turned to blood poisoning at last."

In spite of all inquiries, Mrs. Halford could learn nothing satisfactory from Christina.

Before leaving, however, she produced a parcel, from which she took some presents for the bereaved ones, and she asked permission to contribute something towards the erection of a head-stone. She did not know what her daughter's intentions, as executor, were, but she inwardly vowed that many a roll of butter or box of poultry would find its way from Broadview. She also decided to present them with a cow, as soon as they were fairly settled in their new premises.

As a last resource Mrs. Halford resolved to apply to Dr. Bennet for the information she required. Surely he would know all about it. She would learn the truth from him.

She would not confess it to herself, but sometimes a suspicion came over her that Mr. Slade had some indirect hand in the matter. The idea was ridiculous in a way, and yet it seemed odd that Langtry should have been mysteriously removed at the very time when the lawyer was laying his plans.

At any rate, she decided to have done with the legal gentleman and to withdraw her deposits from his bank.

She tried to satisfy herself and ease her conscience by the knowledge that she was in no way contributory to the clergyman's death. She was haunted by horrible dreams and nightmares, and in every case the corpse of the dead man and the figure of the great lawyer seemed mysteriously connected.

Her intended donation towards the tombstone would furnish her with an excuse for visiting the doctor. She would extract from him enough to satisfy her own mind.

"That were a sad thing, Doctor, about Mr. Langtry, were it not?" she said, in her slow, deliberate way, after some remarks about her trip and the weather.

"Yes. Mr. Langtry was a fine young man. A gentleman and a musician."

"It were blood poisoning, were it not?" she asked, looking him straight in the eyes.

The doctor nodded, without speaking. He saw at once what her errand was, and was amused at the egotism of this woman, who thought to turn him inside out.

"What are the cause of blood poisoning?"

"Absorption of pus into the circulation," he replied, taking refuge in technicalities and looking wise.

"It seems odd how a boil on his neck would take him off so sudden," she remarked, trying a fresh tack.

"It does, indeed," was the assuring reply.

"I knew a young man over at Levisville that had blood poisoning from a boil, but they poulticed it and gave him whiskey. It brought him around, but him were weak for a long time."

The tone of Mrs. Halford's voice seemed to insinuate that with proper treatment Mr. Langtry would have recovered. It was an attempt to put him on the defensive, to force him into details.

"It was a good thing the young man got better," responded the physician in a sympathetic tone. "It must have been a relief to his parents. It is hard to see people cut down in their prime."

Something about the corners of the doctor's mouth told his visitor that she was being laughed at.

Her eyes gleamed and her colour deepened, but her words were as deliberate as ever.

"Well," she said, with a sigh, "I shall not keep you from some poor creature who may be dying *without* your help. Here am fifty dollars towards a headstone. You are executor, I hear."

"Yes, along with your daughter. Everything is to be divided equally between Christina and her mother."

"Oh, yes, you made the will yourself. You must find it very handy to be able for it. You have a great *experience* in it, no doubt. I were going to see the tombstone agent, but you have, no doubt, *particular* acquaintance with him. I shall leave the design to your *practiced taste*—and—*ripe experience*."

With this parting shot she bowed her way out of the door, with a glow in her eye, and walked rapidly homewards.

She was just passing the office of the *Gowanstone Herald* when something on a bulletin board caught her eye.

SLADE OF LEVISVILLE ABSCONDS!

THE SLICK SOLICITOR SLIDES!

Twenty-Five Thousand of the City's Money Gone,
Besides Ten Times that Amount
In Private Funds!

NO CLUE TO HIS WHEREABOUTS!

The sight left her eyes and she fell unconscious on the sidewalk. Retribution had come had last.

CHAPTER LVI.

THE EVILS OF PROCRASTINATION.

The defalcation of so prominent a financial pillar as Daniel Slade was a great shock to the people of Levisville. To hundreds it meant poverty and ruin. The widows' and orphans' mite went as well as private fortunes. For a time there was a panic in the local money market. People lost confidence in each other. Everybody wanted their own, and a number of other failures came as a natural consequence. The defaulter had taken everything he could, and had given himself a good week's start.

From a capitalist Mrs. Halford fell to the level of a common farmer, with nothing left but the homestead. Very few gave her any sympathy except her own. Her husband tried to console her by reminding her that they were still as well off as they were in the old log house of Gore Farm. He recalled the stringent circumstances through which they had fought their way before, and pointed out that they still had a home left.

Marian also gave her mother the closest, deepest sympathy, and endeavoured in many ways to lighten the blow. She assured her mother that she had plenty for all.

But nothing seemed to give any consolation to the broken-spirited woman. Mrs. Halford was like Samson when shorn of his locks. She seemed to lose health, strength and all interest in everything. For weeks she ate little and slept less, and when she arose from her bed of sickness she seemed to be twenty years older.

In the meantime, Marian forgot her own troubles in giving consolation to others. Her resolution to confess all to her husband had never been put in force. She was afraid to bring more trouble upon her mother at present, and was patiently awaiting some favourable time and opportunity. But fate took the matter in its own hands.

David had been home about four weeks, when one afternoon, he had occasion to run over to the house for some papers he had forgotten. He entered through the side door, and went to his private desk, without making his presence known.

His wife and Christina Langtry were talking together in the dining-room. Through the half open door he could hear every word that was said. He paid little attention to their conversation, for his mind was busy with other matters, and Christina was a constant visitor, until a peculiar tremor in his wife's voice caught his ear. "Poor fellow, he said you were to give me this. It is the very one I gave him years and years ago."

"Yes," replied Christina, with a sob. "He always kept it locked away. That evening before you came, he told me it was for you. I had seen him kissing it time and again, but I did not know why he prized it so. I forgot it till I found it to-day."

"Hush, dear, we will not speak of it. I shall keep it for his sake."

David, having finished his errand, went out again unnoticed. He was annoyed by what he had just heard. He recalled Langtry's sudden indisposition in the church at Boston, and remembered that words dropped here and there had a strange significance when looked at in certain lights. Versions of the picnic accident, and rumours that the clergyman had sent for Marian to his death-bed, all came to him from outside sources.

Gordon was not naturally prone to suspicion, but he felt that he had reasonable grounds for it. The fact that his wife had never taken him into her confidence, or referred to any link in this chain of occurrences was not very reassuring. If there was nothing to hide, then why hide it.

An hour afterwards, he saw her going down the street with Christina, and the benevolence of her countenance, together with her quiet womanly dignity and grace, made him feel ashamed of his suspicions.

"Tush! a man would be a villain, who could suspect her for a moment. She is honesty and candour itself."

Before evening he had forgotten all about it. He came home to his supper in as good spirits as usual. Some friends dropped in soon afterwards, and the evening was spent very pleasantly at whist and chess. After escorting one of his lady visitors home, he proceeded to lock up the house as usual. While passing through the dining-room, he noticed a book in a very unusual position, behind some dishes on the sideboard. He took it up to see what it was.

It was an Anglican prayer-book, with a peculiarly antiquated style of binding. He opened it up, to look through it, when his eye fell upon some verses on the fly leaf, indited:

"With undying love to Charles from Marian."

While he was reading the verses there fell to the floor, first, a piece of pale blue ribbon, such as his wife always used to tie her hair, and then, oh horror, a glove which he recognized as one worn by her just previous to his departure for England.

"By Heavens, I will end this mystery at once," and crushing the tokens in his hand, he bounded up the stair, two steps at a time.

His wife was standing before her mirror undoing her luxurious hair, looking as beautiful and as innocent as ever.

In a moment he was holding the open book before her, and in a tone which she had never heard him use before said, "Is that your writing?"

Now Marian had not only neglected to hide the prayer book, but she had forgotten that ever the verses had been written till they met her gaze. It seemed like a ghost from the past. She turned white to the lips and, trembling with fear, seated herself on the edge of the bed. When she saw his face hardened with suspicion she almost lost courage to face the ordeal.

"Can't you speak?" he repeated. "Is that your writing?"

"Yes," she faltered, "but that was years before I ever saw you."

"What about this, then?" he demanded, holding out the ribbon.

"My God," she said to herself, "where has he found that? Why did I not look into the prayer-book or put it away?"

"Have you lost your tongue?" he asked in sarcastic tones.

"It is a piece of hair ribbon I used to wear."

"How did *he* come by it? Do you know?"

"Yes," she answered, with trembling lips, as she sank on her knees at his feet and burst into tears.

He was sitting on the edge of the bed with the tell-tale book in his hands, looking at her with a fierceness which was dreadful to behold.

"Oh, David! Please let me speak! As God is my judge, I intended to tell you all, when you were in a forgiving mood."

"Go ahead, then, I will listen patiently—if I can."

With her face buried in her hands and resting against his knees, she sobbed out the story of her girlhood. With her usual conscientious candour, she told the whole truth, without sparing herself or setting forth any extenuating circumstances.

He listened to the story without comment, but his lips were set and his hands clenched as if he were about to strike some one.

"So, then," he sneered, "that ribbon was given and taken as a badge of lost purity."

He laughed, a hard, bitter, cynical laugh, and attempted to rise, but she held him fast.

He looked down at her beautiful neck and shoulders, half covered with her silky, flowing hair, and wondered how such a beautiful exterior could cover anything but virtue. For himself, he could conscientiously say that his life had been pure. He had never been guilty of an unchaste thought. There had been only one woman in the world for him and that was his wife.

But his own innocence only made him more severe on the frailties of others. Another hard, bitter laugh.

"And did the affair end there?"

Poor, foolish, frightened Marian. Why did she

answer, yes? She wished to tell him all, but surely it would be better to wait till his bitterness had subsided.

"You lie, you traitress! Look at this!" he cried fiercely, holding up her glove. "By God! my impulse is to trample the life out of you!" he shouted, as he threw her on the floor and held his heel above her. "Oh, I shall go mad!" and holding his hands to his throbbing temples he paced the room like a caged lion.

Marian rose to her feet and stood confronting him. All fear was gone now.

"Shame on you for a coward, David Gordon!" she exclaimed, with deep luminousness in her eyes. "Like a ruffian you have bullied me and tried to frighten me. I did not know that Charles Langtry had that glove, nor do I know now how he came by it, but I do know that he loved me to the hour of his death. All your violence shall not prevent me from telling the truth. You shall not frighten me into being a liar and a coward again as you did a moment ago. The very wound that caused his death saved your wife's honour. Whether you cast me off to-night, scatter my brains on these walls, or strangle me where I stand, I will tell the truth as a duty I owe to you, to my dead child and the God above us. It is a duty I owe to the conscience which, in a moment of passion, I did stain.

"In the flood tide of emotion I did for a moment forget my wifely vows. Nay, do not start. Nero saved me from myself, although, God forgive me, I did return Mr. Langtry's kisses. It would be of little use to tell you how his music stirred up my emotions and unchained my passions. You could not understand.

"From that moment I have loathed myself and despised the woman who would sin, even in thought. I have wept and prayed for wisdom and strength to conquer my base self and to make this confession. Charles Langtry, on his deathbed, was pleased that my honour had been saved, even at the cost of his life. He was glad to die, that both he and I might be out of temptation's way. He begged me to kiss him that night, when his cheek was growing cold, and not for all the pain and torture of a dozen lives, or all the shame and sorrow you could heap upon me, would I have refused. It was a pure and holy kiss, which helped to cleanse his soul and mine.

"Oh, David," she cried, sinking on her knees before him. "I did not seek temptation. It came upon me like an avalanche, and all my health and strength became my weakenss. I did not know my passions were so strong, and I so weak. Help me, oh, help me to purify myself in the sight of my little darling that is dead and gone."

Gordon was still pacing the floor, torn asunder by various impulses. Sometimes he felt like taking her in his arms and mingling his tears with hers, and sometimes he was awed by the eloquence of her face and tongue.

"David," she went on beseechingly, as she held out her arms to him, "I was afraid to lose your love. Since I have seen my own unworthiness I have loved you more and more. I have only just learned to know what love is. There is not, and never can be, words or tears to atone for an error like mine, and yet I feel that the great Creator of the Universe has shown me the path of peace. Do not, in pity's name, inflict disgrace upon those who love me, or blight the life of purity and innocence. If you must publish my misdeeds, or place the brand of shame upon my brow, take me some place far away and do not bring grey hairs in sorrow to the grave.

"Take me in your arms again, and my soul shall be an open chamber shining with the light of love. Come and help me to whiten it with purity. Don't turn away, David. Remember, we are all human. There are none perfect, nay, not one. You should forgive me when God has."

She paused to see if he would speak, but he still paced the floor in silence.

"Whether you trample me under your feet, and bury me beneath a mountain of shame and suffering, or whether you take me to your heart again, my tortured conscience has already told me to seek for peace in the pathway of eternal right, and that, if I gain not your forgiveness, I shall earn the blessings of the eternal God."

Marian's plea might have succeeded, but David's eye fell upon the accursed tokens, now scattered on the floor, and the demon of jealousy conquered. Pushing her from him, he rushed from the room. She heard him rapidly descending the stairs. Slamming the front door behind him, he walked hurriedly down the street

---

CHAPTER LVII.

OIL ON TROUBLED WATERS.

"HELLO, Gordon! Where are you off to in such a hurry?"

The speaker was Dr. Bennet, with whom David collided as he turned a corner of the street, and the familiar voice brought him to his senses just as if he had suddenly awakened from some terrible dream.

"I just came out to cool my head, Doctor. I wasn't feeling extra well."

"Is that so?" queried his companion with sudden interest. "You weren't in bed, were you?"

"No," replied Gordon, "but I thought if I took a walk before going to bed I would sleep all the better."

The doctor stole a glance at him as they passed a lamp on the street. "Quite right. Come along to my office and have a chat. It isn't midnight yet."

Once inside of his sanctum, the lynx-eyed physician discovered that there was something amiss.

"You've been speculating again, Gordon?"

"No, honour bright, I have not. Fact is, I don't need to, now."

"Why, man, your pupil is contracted to a pin point!" exclaimed the doctor, putting his hand on Gordon's head and looking into his eyes. "Too much excitement going on here," he continued, tapping his patient on the head with his forefinger. "You are not David Gordon now. You are the other fellow, and not an extra good fellow at that. Wait, I'll fix you a dose to take right away."

"The storm has broken, then," said the old man to himself. "Just like her to tell everything and to take all the blame upon herself. Tush, she is worth a dozen of him or any other man that I know of. I must caution him, though, or he might do something rash."

"Here, drink this, Gordon, and don't allow yourself to get excited. Extreme passion, in you, might be destructive. Keep down the pressure. Your father before you was a passionate man. Sometimes it was hard for him to keep himself in hand."

David drank the medicine and sat for a time looking into the fire in sullen silence. The doctor pretended to take no notice of his mood and went on speaking of things in the abstract after their usual style of conversation.

"I often think, Gordon, we are strange mortals. We all look upon passion as an enormity, excepting in the form in which we happen to possess it ourselves. For instance, I might call you a fool, or sneer at you for allowing your *temper* to control you. You in turn would despise the insane infatuation of the *gambler*. He, in his turn would sneer at the stupid folly of the *drunkard*, who would feel thankful, when sober, that he was not a *libertine* like his neighbour. The *licentious man* will scoff at the idiot who loses his head with temper or liquor, and the *pious swindler*, whose vices are all well varnished, will pat himself on the back because he is regular in his habits, and will thank God that he is not as other men are. And so it goes all the way around; each of us having sympathy with our fellows only in proportion as their faults resemble our own. Of the defaulter who runs away with a million of money, the *greedy* man will say : 'By Jove, he must be a clever fellow.' Of the individual who knocks his man down for an insulting word, the *passionate* man will say : ' He's the stuff.' To the outraged husband who shoots the destroyer of his happiness, the *jealous* will give sympathy, and for the intemperate man who disgraces himself the *wine-bibbers* will have a score of excuses. Of the voluptuary who levants with some beautiful woman the *sensual* man will say, with a wink: 'Well, you can't blame him;' and to the daring plunges of the speculator, the *gambler* will give applause. But the greedy man has the same contempt for the others that they have for him. In fact, we are all saints if you keep us away from our peccadilloes."

The doctor's incisive logic seemed to soothe Gordon even though it bore heavily on him at times. But he spoke only in monosyllables. "Yes." "That's so." "Quite true," and sat looking into the fire with a peculiar expression on his face. He rose several times to go, but the doctor detained him.

"Sit down, man, sit down. You couldn't sleep if you were home, and I don't feel like sleeping myself. You never told me yet of your pedestrian trip through the Highlands."

But, do what he could, the doctor could not get his patient to take any interest in the conversation.

"I'll try some tobacco on him," said the old man to himself, "and then I'll appeal to his generosity. Here, Gordon, try a cigar, they're extra quality. Here's a match. Now, be sociable. You know I have little company outside of yourself. I felt lonesome till I met you to-night."

They gradually opened up a discussion of politics, which the host kept up till the hard, sullen look had left Gordon's face, and when his visitor finally stepped out into the night the doctor congratulated himself on having thrown oil on the troubled waters.

Meanwhile Marian sat on her bed in a condition of semi-stupor. She could think of nothing. She could do nothing but wait and wait, without knowing what she was waiting for. She sat aimlessly picking at the coverlet and tracing its patterns with her fingers. At last the clock in the hall struck twelve and she roused herself. She became anxious. Where could David have gone? What could have happened him?

She raised a window and looked toward the mill, half expecting to see a light in his office. But all was dark. For a long time she sat in the chilly night wind, watching and listening for footsteps. The swish of the water at the sluiceway made her think of the mill-pond.

She shivered and shuddered. "Surely he would not be so foolish. No, no, I will not think of it."

She put down the window and sat shivering by the heater. She was alone in the house, but that did not give her any alarm. Indeed, she was thankful that there had been none to see or hear the terrible scene through which she had just passed.

But would he never come? The suspense was terrible. "O God, surely there cannot be another life lost through a wretch like me. If he will only come home. If he is only spared I can bear all else. O God, pity him, and help him to bear his burden!"

The clock strikes two, and she commences to pace the floor frantically.

"I will bear it no longer. I will go and search for him. I will go to Dr. Bennet. He will befriend me.

"Hark! there's the front door, and his dear, familiar step in the hall. Oh, the music of it. Thank God, I can bear it all, now that my darling is safe," and she dropped on her knees at the bedside laughing and crying in the same breath.

After what seemed a long time she heard him moving about down stairs. The clock struck three. Then she heard him coming up the stairs, and as he passed her door he tossed a letter into the room.

"MADAM:—I shall not trust myself to further discuss the painful disclosures of to-night, because I am afraid I shall lose control of my temper and do or say something which I would afterwards have cause to regret. As it is, the fact that I did in a sense lay violent hands on you, is an indelible stain on my honour as a gentleman. I can neither forgive myself nor her who caused me to appear like a brawling ruffian in my own eyes."

Marian wiped away her tears and shook her head. "Oh, that terrible pride of his. I can pity the shame he feels, poor fellow. He has seen himself just as I saw myself on that terrible night in the woods. Poor dear, he is only human. But I must read on."

"I feel that I am no longer a gentleman, that the

stain on my conscience is one which I shall carry to my grave."—" So is mine, David, so is mine," she murmured.—" I have settled on a definite course of action, and your rejection or approval of the same shall decide whether we continue to live under the same roof. I have decided that we shall *never again* live as husband and wife. I shall occupy my own apartments and you yours. Of these apartments you shall have your choice. There shall be no communication between us, except in the presence of strangers, when we shall address each other with courtesy and civility in order to keep up appearances. I shall engage a housekeeper as soon as possible, and, as it is better that we should meet as little as possible, you can arrange the meals at different hours.

"In the matter of household and personal expenses, you are at liberty to do as you have always done. You may come and go as you like "—here a sentence was crossed out but she managed to decipher it—" but I shall always expect you to have due consideration for the name you bear——"

She paused to wipe her eyes. She was pleased that the cruel words had been crossed out. It seemed like a faint spark of hope. But she eagerly read on.

" You are at liberty to entertain your friends and relatives whenever you see fit, and I shall always endeavor to treat them with courtesy and respect. It will not be necessary for you to reply to this letter unless you intend to leave the premises, for I wish, *now*, to cut off all communication. If you should at any time wish to take action for divorce, I shall not defend any suit you may bring against me.
" DAVID GORDON."

"Divorce! Oh, David, David, why need you have mentioned that hateful word? I would rather be your slave, or your servant, than wear a coronet."

She rose to her feet with clasped hands and streaming eyes, and turned her face upward in prayer.

" Thank heaven, I know the worst now. I shall try

to bear with patience the penalty of my sin. I shall carry my cross with resignation, but, please God, I shall win him back yet."

CHAPTER LVIII.

ADVERSITY'S JEWEL.

A YEAR, a long, dreary year, had passed away since the estrangement of Gordon and his wife, and yet apparently they were as far from a reconciliation as ever. They lived under the same roof, but to Marian her husband seemed further away than when he was on the other side of the Alantic.

Yet she had the comfort of seeing him every day. For this, alone, she was thankful. It was like a ray of sunshine upon her lonely path. Sometimes she lost all hope and wished herself in her grave, but this was only at rare intervals; for generally she was firm in the faith that she would win him back again.

She had the satisfaction of knowing that no other woman was filling her place in his heart, and that she could depend upon him living a pure life.

Gordon was a man of very regular habits and this fact gave her several daily opportunities of stealing a look at him. Protected by the curtains of her window, she could see him coming to and from his meals. But soon there came a time when this did not satisfy her, and she concocted various schemes for enlarging her opportunities. The mirrored side-board in the dining-room was so arranged that she could see him at his meals without being seen, and, all unknown to him, she had the pleasure of cooking his favourite dishes.

Then she always attended to his rooms. She found it a great comfort to be able to do little acts of kindness for him. She could read the books that he read, and think the same thoughts. She could add little adornments and comforts to his chamber; watch for ravelled threads and missing buttons.

One day she was nearly caught in the act of tidying his room when he came back about the middle of the forenoon for a missing bunch of keys. Too late to escape through the door, she darted into the closet, with her heart pounding like a sledge hammer. What if he should discover her? What would she do? She would risk all and take him bodily in her arms. But in a few moments he was gone again. Her excitement was all in vain.

It taught her a lesson, however. She made up her mind that if the time ever did come, when he should discover her in her stealthy acts of kindness, she would risk all rebuffs, and try to overwhelm him with tenderness.

She was fortunate in having an excellent housekeeper at her service. When Gordon employed this domestic, he gave her to understand that she was to look upon Mrs. Gordon as her mistress. She was a middle-aged spinster, with a kindly heart and a still tongue, and she had the sovereign virtue of attending faithfully to her duties.

Soon she came under the spell of Marian's magnetic influence. There arose between the two women a mutual understanding and affection, which, on Martha Temple's part, almost amounted to devotion.

For what reason the young couple were separated Martha did not know, but how any living creature could help loving her mistress she was at a loss to understand.

She did not attempt to pry into what did not concern her, but she was convinced that the fault lay with Mr. Gordon. She soon discovered that her mistress dearly loved her husband, and she gradually learned to know just what Mrs. Gordon wished her to do. She became an astute and faithful ally of her mistress, readily becoming a party to any little plan which would give her increased opportunities of seeing and coming in contact with her husband. But this must be done without making her motive apparent, for Martha could see that Mrs. Gordon was very sensitive, and did not wish any one to notice the estrangement between her and her husband. Whenever

David praised a dish of food Martha was sure to tell her mistress of it, and one day, when he said that his study was the coziest little spot in America, Mrs. Gordon actually opened her piano.

Occasionally, little obstacles arose which taxed Marian's ingenuity to the utmost. The window of David's office, through which she could see him at almost any hour of the day, would occasionally become so opaque with dust that she was cheated out of this pleasure. It took a long time to get Martha to understand, from hints and inuendos, that the office windows occasionally needed cleaning. The dust, Marian said, not only looked untidy, but it shut out a certain amount of light, and the office was already too dark for the good of Mr. Gordon's eyesight.

Ah, me! what strange creatures women are. Their love will grow and thrive upon the most meagre sustenance, and starve from feeding. Difficulties do not destroy, nor obstacles overcome, ther devotion. In fact, adversity only adds to their adoration. Infinitesimal crumbs will serve to keep alive the glow within their hearts, while in luxury's lap it dies from satiety.

The only breaks in the monotony of her life were her occasional visits to Broadview. But she never remained long. Martha was not a particularly good cook, and David's creature comforts could not be neglected. After a day's absence she seemed to be on pins and needles till she got home again. She grew hungry for a look at his face.

Besides, Broadview was lonely without Nelly, who, with her husband, was now settled in Denver and who, judging from her letters, was as happy as the day was long.

Sometimes there were visitors. The doctor, Mr. Jamieson, the banker, and occasionally her father and mother.

On these occasions her manner was a triumph. No one could have discerned anything in her demeanour towards her husband which would lead any one to suspect that there was any estrangement between them. "God knows it is no trouble for me to act the loving wife to David Gordon. It 's a rôle I can play without prompting," she said to herself.

But *he* could not cover his embarrassment so well. Not only the doctor, but their other acquaintances, soon discovered that all was not well between husband and wife.

On one occasion her father spoke of it with moisture in his eyes, but she kissed away his tears.

"You dear, imaginative old daddy, you think I ought to be fondled and kissed all the time. David is not unkind. It is only his manner. He is so taken up with his books that he is absent-minded. So don't you be talking like that, or I'll pull your ears," and she finished by giving him a kiss.

But the estrangement was really no secret. *She* attended church and *he* did not, consequently, that was supposed to be the cause of their alienation. David knew this and preferred that the public should look upon him as a bigot rather than upon his wife with suspicion.

Once the pastor preached a sermon on the text, "Be ye not unequally yoked with unbelievers," and she took him to task severely for misrepresenting agnostics. She gave the speaker to understand that a repetition of the offence would mean her withdrawal from the church. There was no quicker way of rousing her to arms than by making the slightest hint at her husband's shortcomings.

She took advantage of every opportunity to soften him. By intuition she seemed to know just how he wished her to act in the presence of strangers, and she was generally conscious of his approval. Little acts of kindness and tenderness were done under the pretence of formality. Many a little march she stole upon him in this way. Nor was there at these times any servility in her attitude towards him; if anything, rather the contrary.

The doctor noticed her tactics one cold evening when Gordon was going out with him.

They had almost reached the gate when she called him back with a tone of authority. "Here, David, you must not go out without a muffler of some kind."

Snatching a plaid, she followed him out and adjusted it round his neck and shoulders. The doctor noticed, even in the dark, that while she was muffling him up she kept her face very close to his, and took a little longer time than was necessary.

"Pooh," he thought, "there's little need for me to worry about her. She'll conquer him yet. She fairly worships that man and he doesn't deserve it."

Christina was a great help to her during these trying times. Together they went about assisting the poor and needy in that quiet, unostentatious way which does good by stealth. Her life expanded with her sympathies. Though she had no offspring of her own to love, the sick and unfortunate were all her children.

"Do you know, Christina, it has taken me all my life to learn what you always knew by intuition."

"Don't flatter me, Marian. I never learned very much. I was always a dunce at school."

"You have taught me more, dear, than all my books and teachers. You have shown me by example how to find happiness in its highest form, by putting away all consideration for self, and living for others. I do believe that every crime, every sin, and every vice, is but a modification, in one way or another, of that greatest curse to mankind, selfishness."

CHAPTER LIX.

BILL NIGER'S "KETCH."

SOMETIMES the best qualities of our natures can be brought to light only by adversity Suffering and sorrow are the great crucibles which separate the dross from the gold, but like the various ores our natures require different times for the completion of the process.

The death of Gordon's mother and his child each in turn softened the sharp outlines of his character, but the peculiar trial he had undergone since his estrangement from his wife had a greater effect than either.

At first he dropped into a deep vein of cynicism in which he lost all faith in his fellow creatures. He reasoned that if the woman who had been his model of human perfection could deceive him there was surely no one in the wide world whom he could trust. His ultimatum was, "Nobody really cares for anybody else. Life is nothing but a sham from the cradle to the grave."

The only thing which prevented him from becoming a miserable misanthrope was the memory of his mother, whose kindly, honest face beamed at him from a picture in his room. It shone through his cynicism like the sun breaking through a mist.

The companionship of the doctor was also of great assistance. Many a pleasant hour they spent together.

Gordon was slow to discover that his estimate of his fellow creatures had been too heroic; his opinion of himself too much coloured by prejudice. Both egoism and egotism prevented him from discovering his own deficiencies.

On the evening of the quarrel with his wife, however, he caught a glimpse of his baser self. The doctor's incisive logic gradually awakened his inward consciousness, and he made the astonishing discovery that, if weighed in the balance, there was a possibility of *his* being found wanting. The vision he got of himself and his fellow creatures through the lens of the doctor's logic gave him the shock of his life. It changed the colour of his mental horizon. His friend's philosophy convinced him that mankind, instead of consisting of angel and demons, heroes and villains, was simply a mixture of good and bad in every possible variety and proportion. He had always *known* that, but somehow he had never thoroughly realized it till the lesson was brought home to him in his own person. Then he learned with surprise and chagrin that one of those spotted creatures was David Gordon.

Many a man will repeat a truism all his life and loudly shout "hear, hear!" whenever it is proclaimed, without ever having become embued with the spirit of it. Thousands of rogues have lived and died with the firm conviction that they were honest men, simply because they did not burglarize their neighbour's house or refuse to pay a debt which they could not legally repudiate.

Moral truths are only valuable in proportion as we apply them to our everyday lives. Let some one say, "To err is human," and we will all shout "Amen;" but let any one try to show us *where we have erred*, and vanity will immediately clap its hands over our ears and eyes.

Gordon had looked for perfection in his wife, and immediately she confessed her human frailties he had put her from him as unfit for his companionship. He confessed to himself that if he had it all to do over again, he would act in a different manner. But the die was cast. He had chosen his own path and must follow it. He really, in his heart, forgave his wife *her own* sins, but not the one that she had caused *him* to commit. It was hard to forgive any one who had lowered him in his own estimation.

He could not, in the face of all he had said, offer the olive-branch to his wife. Besides, he felt that his actions must have destroyed her affection for him, and a wife without love would be insufferable. He must "dree his weird."

But an event entirely unforeseen was about to mark the turning point of his life.

It was a beautiful afternoon in March, when old Sol was giving his first promise of spring, and David was sitting at his office window ruminating on the absence of his wife, who had gone on a visit to her sister at Denver.

She had been absent only a few days when he made a discovery which furnished him with material for his present thoughtful mood. Both at the table and in his rooms there was a great falling off in attention. The cooking was not so much to his taste; his slippers were never in their usual corner; the water in his bath was not tempered, and a dozen little things were out of their usual place.

He was not a man of luxurious habits, and never once thought of complaining. He could live contentedly on the simplest food, so long as it was clean; and all the other trifles were easily overcome by a little extra precaution on his own part. But it suddenly dawned upon him that his wife, for the past eighteen months, had been studying his every comfort without hope of reward or recognition. "She must love me still or she could not, would not, do it."

In spite of all his efforts to concentrate his energies on his ledger, his mind would wander back to the discovery he had made. A feeling of tenderness seemed to creep around his heart.

The warmth of the sun heralded a change of season; it promised to supplant snow banks by green fields. Little rivulets from the melting snow were running in every direction, glistening in the bright sunlight, and the Speed was swollen to many times its natural size. At noon Gordon had completely opened his sluiceway to make room for the great volume of dark, muddy water which had worn a wide gap in the ice by its mad rush for the final plunge at the weir. He did nothing all afternoon but gaze at the rushing water in his millpond and think of his absent wife.

It was now after four o'clock, for the children were coming from school, and he was about to make another attack on his ledgers, when he noticed two boys in a very precarious position. They were out on the pond, at the edge of the ice, breaking off pieces with a stick, and watching them glide away with the current.

He rose to warn them of their danger. But before he reached the corner of the mill, one of the lads had fallen through the ice, and the other was running towards the shore shouting for help. The rotten ice had given way. The poor lad, wedged in between several loose blocks, was keeping his head above water as best he could, and giving vent to the most heartrending cries.

Gordon seized several boards from a pile of lumber, and ran to the rescue. Cautiously placing them in front of him, he approached step by step. He was almost within reach of the lad, when the whole foundation gave way. In a second he, too, was floundering in the icy water.

The excitement on the bank was now intense. The town bell was sounding the alarm.

Gordon still held to his plank. Pushing it over upon a sound portion of ice, he managed to scramble to his feet again, amid cheers from the spectators.

He was comparatively safe now. But unfortunately, his floundering had only served to loosen the block to which the boy clung, and it was now gradually being sucked out into the current.

"Hang on, sonny, for dear life. Don't be afraid, I'll catch you." Waiting only to throw off his coat and cap, David sprang into the seething water.

There was a hoarse shout from the shore, and a wail of despair. "They're lost, they're lost. The weir, the weir," was the general cry. Through it all, Jamieson's voice was heard, calling for pikes and ropes.

But Gordon did not despair of accomplishing his object. He knew the conformation of the dam, and had confidence in himself. Soon he was alongside the boy. While they were drifting down the raging torrent, he was pushing his charge further upon the ice block. He feared that it might break, and all would be lost. His plan was to cross the current to the opposite side, and be carried into a little bay, at the far side of the weir, directly in line with the other edge of the stream. His arms and legs were numb with cold, but he bent himself to his task, and swam with all his might. Down they came with the torrent. For a few moments, the suspense was terrible. Would the swimmer succeed in crossing the current, or would they both be swept over the weir?

"He's gaining! He's gaining! Look! Hurrah, they are saved!" as David with a final push sent the ice, with its cargo, into the little bay. He heard a cheer as the little fellow went within the reach of safety.

But his final push must have been too much for him. He suddenly seemed to lose all power of himself. In a moment his head was underneath the water. He felt, at last, that his hour had came. The memories of a life-time were crowded into a few seconds.

"Great God, he has sunk! No! there's his head again. But the current has got him. He's lost! he's lost!"

The struggle for breath as he went down somewhat rallied him from his numbness. But it was too late. A terrible roaring was in his ear. As he caught a final glimpse of the pale faces on the bridge overhead, he was dimly conscious that he would soon be in eternity.

A vision of his wife on her knees before him was his last spark of consciousness. Something seemed to strike him on the head, and all was blank.

Hark! there is a hoarse shout. Something has caught him. A dozen strong hands are ready to pull him up.

"Why, it's Bill Niger that has caught him. Look out, Bill. Don't send the pike through him."

"Keep quiet, there. It is the other end of the pike I have, with a wire on it."

"By heavens! the old man's wire is round his arm."

"Order!" shouted Jamieson. "Easy, Bill. Don't try to pull him up. You might drop him. Catch my feet, you fellows," and in a moment the iron-founder was dangling beneath the bridge, clutching at the garments of the drowning man.

There was a moment of suspense as the limp body was pulled up.

"Is he dead? Is he dead?" was the whispered question on every lip, and every heart stood still.

"Make way for the doctor! Is he dead, Doctor?"

"Dead, no! Don't you see he is bleeding. He'll soon be all right." A ringing, rousing cheer went up from the crowd.

What though they laughed and joked as he was being hurried home to warm blankets? What though they chaffed Bill Niger about his wire-pulling, and threatened to have him fined for fishing out of season? Many a one secretly wiped the moisture from his eyes, and slipped a piece of silver into the old man's pocket.

To laugh and joke in the midst of calamity, and to extract humour from even the most tragic situations, is the privilege of Americans.

But their appreciation of the heroic deed was none the less genuine. Before sunset the news was flashed over the wires to the press of a continent.

CHAPTER LX.

A WELCOME VISITOR.

WHEN Gordon recovered consciousness he was lying snugly in bed, surrounded by a dozen smiling faces.

"Is the boy safe?" was his first question.

"Safe and sound, thanks to you."

"Something hit me on the head?" he said, feeling for the wound on his forehead.

"No, you hit the weir post, and Bill Niger here snared you by the arm."

"Yes, just like a sucker," growled the old fisherman, "and many a one I've snared in my time. I hain't been fishing twenty years for nothing."

Gordon almost joined in the hearty laugh that went round, but poor old Bill couldn't see where the joke was.

"You'll have to reform now, Bill, since you've tackled bigger game, and become a fisher of men," remarked the doctor facetiously.

"It is really wrong to allow this merriment," he continued, "only I don't think you'll be much the worse for your cold bath, Gordon."

"I believe if I had not been accustomed to a cold bath, I never would have had the courage to jump in."

"No, nor you wouldn't have stood it. But now we'll away and let you rest for a while. Come, come. Out every one of you. The fun is all over now. He'll be at work to-morrow."

Sure enough, when the boy's parents called next day to pour out their thanks, Gordon was over at the mill as usual, the only trace of his great struggle being a patch on his forehead.

Though David made light of it himself the community did not. The next two days were spent in receiving the congratulations of everybody for miles around. He felt heartily sick of the whole affair. He casually wondered whether old Bill had really done him a good turn. He had, at least so far as his own consciousness was concerned, crossed the big divide, and since there was no pleasure in life, he thought there was little in his rescue to cause rejoicing.

"A person has only to die once; I might as well have made a job of it. Life is not worth living anyway," was his sentiment.

"Allow me to congratulate you," said a voice at his shoulder. Wheeling round, David found himself face to face with the long-lost Senger.

"Why, how do you do, Professor? I am really glad to see you. How is the world using you?"

His visitor's garb itself was almost sufficient reply. He wore the same venerable coat and his trousers were patched at the knees. His jewelry had vanished, his neck-tie was only a pretence, and his stockingless feet were peeping through his shoes. But his smile was cheerful and reassuring.

"Though poor in worldly goods I am rich in experience. I have been chasing that fleeting shadow, happiness, like most of my fellows, and perhaps, have come as near to it as any of them. There are none so poor as those who have lost the power of enjoying life."

"I don't exactly catch your meaning, Professor."

"The poorest men in the world are, first, those who are the victims of ennui, those who have been satiated with the pleasures of life; and second, those who have lost faith, confidence and interest in their fellow-creatures. Now, poor as I am," he continued, looking at his dilapidated garment, "I have still confidence in humanity, and can still admire the deed of heroism you performed but two days gone."

"Stop, Professor, please. I have heard enough of that. When did you arrive?"

"Just this morning. I think I shall stay over till Monday. I am billing the town for a lecture to-morrow night."

"Oh. On what subject?"

"On phrenology. You know one must live," he added, with a gesture of apology. "Besides, I give them good value. There *are* truths, you know, in phrenology."

David smiled. "Oh, certainly; and that reminds me that I wish to get some more of your pamphlets. But do you know, I have a fancy to hear you give a lecture on theology. If you are going to stay over Sunday, why not? Jamieson will give you Science Hall. He built it because the town council once refused to let an agnostic lecture in the town hall. It is open to every civil, respectable man on any question or topic, be he Hindoo or Hottentot. I am certain you would have a good audience."

The professor looked grave. "I would prefer giving a sermon, though I have never tried it. But," he added, thoughtfully, "I must follow my own convictions, and not speak to please any individual or set of individuals. In matters of conscience one must be true to oneself."

"Certainly, certainly! The truth as you see it. I have been at church only once since I was a boy, and then the services were postponed. But no matter whether you are orthodox or heterodox, you shall have a good hearing."

"I would not care to discuss theology. The subject is too speculative. But I could preach a sermon on practical Christianity."

"Good!" exclaimed David. "Let it be practical, by all means. That's the spirit of the age. But here comes the doctor. Let us hear what he says."

Dr. Bennet's eyes fairly sparkled with delight when he beheld his long-lost specimen. In his enthusiasm he almost took Mr. Senger in his arms.

After a number of explanations had been given as to the professor's long silence, the doctor asked:

"How long are you going to stay, Professor?"

"Only till Monday."

The physician gave David a knowing look, as much as to say, "we will see about that."

"We were just discussing, before you came in, the

advisability of the professor's giving us a sermon on Sunday," explained David. "Or, shall we call it a lecture? It's all the same thing."

"I beg your pardon, Mr. Gordon," exclaimed the professor, "there is a vast difference," and he held up two fingers to emphasize his words.

"Indeed," said David, with an amused smile, "let us hear the difference. But first, take a chair."

Mr. Senger seated himself in a big arm chair, and with his fingers extended before him, commenced his explanation.

"A lecture is directed to our mental, and a sermon to our moral natures. The one is an appeal to reason, and the other to sentiment."

Gordon broke into a hearty laugh. "You are very hard on the preachers. You remind me of Burns' couplet:

"'To mix faith and sense
On any pretense
Is heretic, damnable error.'"

"Ah, the bard was in a cynical mood when he said that. Sentiment and reason are as inseparably connected as the mental and physical in ourselves."

The doctor sat on a pile of empty sacks, fairly beaming with interest, but taking no part in the discussion.

"A lecture," continued the professor, "is presumably for the purpose of elucidating truths, while a sermon is devoted to the application of them to human life. There is the same difference between a lecture and a sermon as there is between the tweed or the broadcloth which hangs in the dealer's window and a suit of clothes on a customer's back. The lecture may supply the cloth, but the sermon is the scissors and sewing machine which make a garment of it."

"You are a hard man to stick, Professor," rejoined David with a laugh. "Your explanation is true, inasmuch as the average sermon does cut and carve truth most unmercifully." This sally brought forth another laugh all round, but the professor was quite undaunted.

"Your millstones are terrible mutilators of wheat, and yet you keep them whirling to prepare the food for our stomachs. Very well. Every church should be a tailor shop where truth is fitted to the peculiar needs or conditions of the community."

"One would infer from your discourse, Professor, that there is no morality outside of religion. Do you mean to say that one cannot be morally perfect without being a Christian?"

"Any one who is morally perfect is unconsciously a Christian, in the sense that he is a follower of Christ's precepts."

"There are very few Christians, then, I take it. But supposing a Mahommedan were morally perfect, would he be a Christian?" asked Gordon with a smile.

The doctor gleefully rubbed his left arm but did not speak. Here was a poser, he thought.

"If you were familiar with the teachings of Maho, met," replied Mr. Senger, "you would see that one could not be morally perfect while he adhered to that faith. But a man may attend services in a mosque or temple, and if he is morally perfect, even though he never heard of Christ, he is still a Christian in the *highest sense*. Supposing I ask three boys to solve a problem for me. One does it by arithmetic, another by algebra, and still another by mensuration or Euclid, but what matter so long as they all get the correct answer and all reach the same conclusion? If a man reaches moral perfection by Mohammedanism, Hindooism, or any other ism, he is practically a Christian. All he lacks is the label. We use the word Christian to represent moral perfection, because, so far as we are concerned, Christ was the only *living example*. It appears to me you have a wrong impression, Gordon. You think that Christ wanted adulation and flattery. No such thing. His motives were not governed by selfishness and vanity. He little cared for praise and lip-service, so long as his teachings, his truths, were *accepted* and *practiced*."

"Look here, Professor. Suppose that a man is honest, sober, industrious and honorable; that he does his duty to his wife and children, and obeys the laws of the land. Would you place him as first class in your moral category?"

Mr. Senger smiled and shook his head.

"Well, by heavens," retorted David, "there are very few who fill the bill. If you were dealing with the public, you would find it out."

"Those are only the foundation stones of morality," replied the professor. "If *that were all*, there would be no kindness, charity, mercy, or love. Morality, without the higher qualities as taught by Christ, would be just as incomplete as mathematics would be with only arithmetic. What could we do in solving the great engineering problems of the world, without the higher mathematics? Well, we are just as helpless in solving the problem of a perfect life, without the higher and nobler qualities which form the great superstructure of morality. Remember it is not sufficient to say, 'Well, I never did any one any *harm*. That is only negative morality. We must do *good*, and leave the world better than we found it. There are errors of *omission*, as well as errors of *commission*."

Gordon felt that he was losing ground.

"Pshaw! It does not seem to matter much, whether you steal, cheat or lie. The worst villain unhung, who believes in Christ (or says he does) is far better in the eyes of the church than the honest man who does not. Common morality is good enough for me."

The professor again shook his head.

"Christ shows us that the man who professes to believe in him and does not endeavour to follow his precepts is a liar, a thief, and the truth is not in him. A man may believe the story of the crucifixion; he may believe that such a being as Christ really did exist, but that amounts to nothing. Credulity is not a virtue. Faith without works is only a mockery," continued the speaker, snapping his fingers. "Furthermore, I contend that ordinary morality (as you call it), is not sufficient for a man who performs a deed of heroism. No ordinary ethics prompted you to jump to almost certain death to save that boy. You have the works without the faith, the goods without the label, ha, ha, ha!"

Gordon was completely cornered, and he knew it

"Am I never to hear the last of that? Is it fair to drag that out against me in an argument of this kind?"

"He was only tailoring truth a little for you," said the doctor, "but you can finish your argument on Sunday, Professor."

"Indeed, Doctor, I am afraid I have a heavy task before me. No ordinary discourse will do for two such keen critics. I must go even now and prepare myself."

"Wait a moment, Professor, you must come and dine with me," exclaimed the doctor.

"Thank you very much, but I shall deny myself the pleasure, until I can present myself in more suitable guise."

"Pooh, man! I am a bachelor. We shall dine by ourselves, though I must tell you the fare will be very plain," and, with a knowing wink at Gordon, the doctor bore away his prize in triumph.

CHAPTER LXI.

SAPPING AND MINING.

"OH, my hero! Oh, my darling! I told you, Nelly, that something had happened when that vision of him came before me at the matinée yesterday. To think he should be so near death and me thousands of miles away. I must go, dear. I cannot stay a moment longer."

"Yes, but Mally, the papers say that he is not seriously hurt. Look! It says only a slight scalp wound."

"I don't care, I *must* go. Don't keep me, dear, but come and help me pack up. Is this the latest time-table?"

"Yes, I think so."

"Well, I can catch the Limited in forty minutes. Let us hurry. I can make it."

"Won't you have something to eat, dear?"

SAPPING AND MINING.

"No, Nelly, not a bite. It would choke me. Hurry, hurry."

While they were getting ready a telegram was handed in, addressed to "Mrs. Maurice Fletcher, Denver."

"Gordon is all right. He is working as usual.
GEO. BENNET."

"There now, dear, it is no use getting excited," said Nelly, as Marian snatched the telegram and kissed it. "The poor old doctor knew you would be worrying your heart out about him, and even sent the message to *me* so as not to frighten you. Now you can wait till to-morrow."

"Don't coax me, Nelly dear. I shall come back soon. But I shall not rest till I see his dear face again."

Before Maurice was aware of her intentions, Marian was flying homewards as fast as steam could carry her.

All night long she lay awake in her berth, thinking of her wickedness in not having long ago broken down the barriers of reserve and taken him by sheer force. What if the wire had missed his arm, and he had gone to his death, without a word of forgiveness between them? It was terrible to think of it.

At first she could not eat. But when it occurred to her that want of food and sleep would make her look haggard she changed her tactics. On the second day of her journey she secured a stateroom, and remained in bed the greater part of the time.

"I shall not go to him, looking pale and faded. I will lay siege to his heart with all the power and strategy at my command. I shall spare no art or wile to bring him to my arms again. I have remained passive long enough. I shall be aggressive now. He has taught me a lesson in courage. He has set me a noble example. I shall be wise as the serpent, and innocent as the dove. I shall win. I know and feel the inspiration of Victory."

But she must gird on her armour. She must preserve her complexion by taking plenty of sleep. When the train stopped at Chicago she secured a bath which revived her wonderfully.

On Saturday morning again, before reaching home, she took advantage of the seclusion of her state-room, to give herself a vigourous sponging, and when she left the train at Gowanstone, there was not a trace of fatigue in her face.

When David, from his office window, saw the omnibus from the station drive up to his gate, his heart beat more quickly. He instinctively guessed that his wife's unexpected return was due to his little escapade. In fact, he had hoped that she would come. It would be an evidence that she still cared for him.

At the house a different scene was being enacted. The moment that Marian was inside her own door she burst into tears.

"Is he all right, Martha?"

"Yes, ma'm. He's at the mill, he is."

"Did he eat his dinner all right?"

"Not quite so well as he generally does, ma'm."

"What underclothes has he on?"

"I couldn't say, ma'm. Miss Langtry hunted up the things. She gave him some extra, she did."

"Christina is an angel. But was it all true that I read in the papers?"

"Yes, and more, ma'm, because I seed it myself. It was awful, it was. They bringed him in and put him in your bed, they did, because it was handy. And the doctor sewed up his head."

Marian sprang up and caught her by the arm. "Don't deceive me, Martha. You said he was quite well."

"So he is, ma'm, and only for the stickin' plasters on his head, you would never know the difference."

"Run, then, please, and tell Christina to come right away. Tell her I am home and wish to see her very particularly."

As soon as she was alone she stole into the room, *her room*, where *he* had passed one night. Looking around to make sure that no one would see her, she kissed the pillows where his head had been. There was a roll of sticking-plaster on the little table and a distinct smell of iodoform about the room, while in the pin-cushion was a strangely shaped, curved needle. There was also a watersoaked collar and tie in the wash-stand drawer. She pounced upon these, and after covering them with kisses, slipped them into her pocket.

"Christina, would you like to see through the mill this afternoon," said Marian, with a pleading look at her friend, after they had finished their sisterly greetings.

"Yes," replied Christina, trying to look unconscious; "I have often wondered what it looked like inside. Shall we go now?"

"Yes, yes. Just as soon as I have had a wash and changed my dress. I will lend you my gossamer to keep the dust off."

"And what will you do?"

"Oh, I shall wear some old thing that the dust won't hurt. Anything will do."

As Marian ran to her room she bit her tongue at the fib. If it took all the dresses in her wardrobe, she would have something suitable for the rôle she was about to play. Tush, what was a dress in a warfare of this kind?"

She had already studied many hours over this question, and when she had finished her toilet there was a distinct air of coyness about her from her hat to her boots. There was a dash of carelessness here and a trace of coquettishness there which could be seen but not understood. She would approach him with a mixture of ingenuousness and simplicity, totally ignoring the past. She had a new rôle to play. The stake she was playing for was dearer than life.

Her heart was beating wildly as she ran up the steps leading to his office with Christina at her heels. She timidly knocked, and in reply to his gruff "Come in," she opened the door and stood face to face with the man for whom she would have died.

Gordon bade them the time of day, and offered them chairs, while he stood leaning against his desk waiting for them to speak. His heart was thumping like a sledge hammer. But, though his face was pale, he preserved his outward calmness.

When Marian saw the patch on his forehead she felt like taking her hero bodily in her arms. It cost her quite an effort to keep the look of tenderness from her face. "This is the man I called a coward. But I will make amends now."

"Mr. Gordon," she said, politely, addressing him as though he were a perfect stranger, "we have come to congratulate you and express the admiration which every woman feels for a deed of heroism. Courage is the quality of all others which we women admire. I feel it both a pleasure and a duty to offer you my hand."

Poor David! His face turned scarlet. Speech failed him. But he held out his hand and she shook it as respectfully as if she did not long to kiss it.

"It was a noble deed, Mr. Gordon," said Christina, offering her hand in turn.

David Gordon disliked flattery in its ordinary, fulsome, palpable form, but below the outward crust of his nature there lay a deep vein of vanity. His wife's words and her respectful, serene tone touched a tender spot. His embarrassed attitude and heightened colour told Marian that her aim had been true and her judgment sound. She smiled inwardly at this loophole in his armour, and yet she felt that she could love him all the more for being able to laugh at him a little.

"Really, it makes me feel ridiculous to have it mentioned," he protested when he finally recovered himself. "It was done on the spur of the moment. Any one would have done the same."

"But there was only one who did," replied Marian, archly, as she prepared to land another broadside. "Heroes are not so plentiful," and she turned her face away with the same instinct that once caused her to shut her eyes when she fired off a gun.

She was very uncertain as to how her last shot would tell. She moved over to the window which overlooked the pond. "What a sinner I am to hit this poor fellow on a weak spot," she said to herself, with a sob in her throat. "I don't care. *He is a hero* and I *love* him. I'm fond of flattery myself. *Who isn't*, if it is skilfully given? But it is cowardly, and I won't do it again."

"Would you ladies like to see through the mill?" he asked in a kindly tone.

"We would be delighted. That is, if it is not too much trouble."

"No trouble at all. We will go right now. Just follow me." Donning his white cap, he led them out among the whirling wheels, where the noise of the machinery, and the rushing sound of grain, made conversation impossible.

Up and down he led them amongst bins, hoppers and elevators, shouting in their ears, from time to time, a minute explanation of the course taken by the wheat on its way to make the white, sweet-smelling flour. Everything which seemed so intricate to them was so simple to him, and though he seemed to go about quite carelessly among the wheels, he was very careful of the safety of his visitors. In spite of this, however, Marian was continually getting into dangerous positions.

He was kept busy looking after her. She had a thousand questions to ask, and of course, had to put her lips close to his ear in order to be heard. Even Christina smiled at the childish perversity with which her friend insisted on looking into every bin and hopper which required his assistance to reach, and though she could generally romp like a tomboy, she could not now dismount from a box without Mr. Gordon's assistance. She was weaving an invisible web about him, like the spider with the fly. She felt that she was gaining ground, and her spirits rose in proportion. All embarrasment on her part was gone. Her face beamed with pleasure.

Once, as if by accident, her lips touched his ear, and several times her hair grazed his cheek. But the climax came when the frilling of her dress got caught in a gearing.

A careless swish of her skirt threw it among some cogged wheels. With a relentless grasp they commenced to drag her in.

Gordon immediately caught her in his arms. With a herculean wrench, he tore her loose.

At first she seemed a little frightened, but when her husband released her from his arms she was a rosy red. It was all over in a trice. But short as the time was, her cheek lay for a full second against his.

The gearings were not speeded very high, and the danger was not very great, but she was now under an obligation to him. She had something to apologize for. She had displayed her inferiority.

In thanking him for his presence of mind, she managed to keep the lovelight from her eye. She preserved with difficulty her original manner. In apologizing for the fright she had given him, she begged him to overlook her silly recklessness, and added, that she never dreamt of any danger, on account of *his* being at hand.

But she had still another opportunity, when they reached the office. "Christina, will you please run over to the house for some pins? I have only two here. I can't go out on the street this way."

The wheels had taken a large bite out of her gown, leaving it in tatters. With her head bent over her shoulder she made several futile attempts to secure some loose pieces.

"Mr. Gordon, will you please fasten that for me? Dear me, what a silly thing I was not to think of what I was doing. I'm sure you won't care to have such troublesome visitors very often. I feel that I have been a nuisance. A child would have known better."

Davit knelt down and commenced his task, while she, peeping over her shoulder, gave orders. From the dainty frills and laces underneath there came a faint perfume. Poor David scarcely knew what he was doing. But she artfully kept him struggling with the fragment till Christina arrived.

"It is too bad, Christina. I needn't have troubled you. Mr. Gordon has done bravely. Now, if you will loan me your gossamer we will go."

Gordon was by this time almost mesmerized by her arts, and all the more so that she seemed quite unconscious of them.

As they were about to pass through the door a notice posted nearby caught Marian's eye. She read aloud:

"A SERMON IN SCIENCE HALL,

Sunday, March 21st.

Professor Senger will give an address on Practical Christianity. Come one *and all*.

F. Senger."

"Would you like to go, Christina?" she continued, turning suddenly to her friend with a coaxing look on her face. "It's to-morrow, you know."

"I think I would. I have heard that the strange old man is very clever."

"I shall be glad to escort you both," said David. "It was at my suggestion that the lecture was announced. Come for dinner to-morrow, Miss Langtry, and we shall all go together."

Marian bowed an acknowledgment. "Thanks, a thousand thanks for your kind invitation, Mr. Gordon. Also for your kindness, patience and—" here she paused with a gentle smile—" your presence of mind. Good afternoon."

Marian could scarcely walk home with decorum. She felt as if she could hop, skip, and jump, like a school-girl. When they reached the house she caught Christina in her arms and swung her round with a velocity that threatened destruction to the furniture. She kissed Martha, "cut up" like a youngster, and wound up at the piano with " Home, sweet home."

Christina on her way home wondered if the episode of the dress were really an accident, or whether it was done on a sudden impulse. Had her friend reached a point where she would risk life, limb, everything, to to bring her husband back to her? Was the toss of her flounces into the wheels the last throw of the dice, where everything is won or lost?

Ah, Christina! Deeper thinkers and greater philosophers could only, like yourself, have guessed. Who can measure the hidden impulses and motives of the human heart? The warp and woof of love and life are woven in mystery.

Mrs. Gordon was a woman.

CHAPTER LXII.

A LAY SERMON.

On Sunday afternoon, at least half an hour before the appointed time, every seat in Science Hall was taken up. It had been commonly reported that the professor was going to preach to the agnostics, but whether *pro* or *con*, nobody could tell.

It would have been hard, however, to find a more intelligent, liberal and friendly audience than that which had gathered to hear what the eccentric old man had to say. A few of the ultra-orthodox felt uneasy and out of place. The hall seemed to them to have an atmosphere of ungodliness.

The drop curtain which ornamented the front of the stage, represented a Mayday scene, where lads and lasses danced around the Maypole, and a very fair steel engraving of the Bard of Avon decorated the archway at the top. Through the half-open stage door, they could catch glimpses of wigs, swords, bright costumes, bloodthirsty bowie-knives, and superannuated blunderbusses. Indeed, to some, it was a terrible place for the word of God to be spoken, and they occasionally knelt for a prayer of disinfection. But the bulk of the audience having often been to the hall to hear dramatic entertainments, took everything as a matter of course.

At last the speaker appeared, Bible in hand, wearing the same threadbare coat, but his hat was now of a more reputable shape, and his nether garments were quite new. With spotless collar and cuffs, and a shirt fresh from the laundry, he had a decidedly respectable appearance.

When the curtain went up, the professor was discovered in the foreground of a rocky cañon, through which ran a turbulent stream with its rushing rapids and tumbling waterfalls. The scenery was good. The towering cliffs and mountain peaks with which the old man was surrounded, gave him a weird and somewhat prophetic appearance.

Another surprise, however, was in store for the audience. Just at this moment the members of Jamieson's orchestra came creeping up through the little door under the stage and took their places with their music in front of them.

It still wanted a quarter of an hour of the appointed time, and the professor, drawing his chair to the front of the stage, entertained his audience by speaking in a quiet, conversational style.

"No doubt it may seem odd to many of you to hear the gospel of Christ from a scenery-decked stage. In fact, it is a surprise to myself. And yet I confess I feel the inspiration of the grand old mountains there. True, they are only paintings, but yet they suggest the eternal. They give us a hint of the magnificence of the universe.

"Perhaps I may be mistaken, but it seems to me that it could not be wrong for a preacher of the gospel to be surrounded by scenery in keeping with his text. The impressiveness of Christ's sermon on the mount was, no doubt, augmented by the surroundings.

"Many advanced churches have orchestras, just as we have here to-day, and if the ear helps us to form higher conceptions and nobler ideas, why not the eye?

"I never thought of it before, and perhaps I should not speak of it now, but I have a fancy that grand scenery would make us more devout and reverential, would help us to forget our narrow little selves.

"It may be that we are all slaves to custom. We all have prejudices against innovations; but it is just possible that the church may change its opinion. There is no inspiration in bare walls, and if we take away the prejudice against the scenery, I don't see what harm there could be. It has certainly lent great force to the educative power of the stage.

"I don't see why truth should not be made attractive; clad in up-to-date clothing. Take the music, for instance, of our hymns and anthems. There cannot be any doubt that it has done much to neutralize the cruelty of creeds and beautify thought. Yet there was a time when a violin, trombone, or even an organ, was considered too ungodly for a place of worship.

"But now I see the time is up.

"The orchestra will kindly open with the doxology."

Immediately that grand old song of praise, that anthem of love which will live as long as water runs and grass grows, was echoing through the hall. Some stood up and some sat still, but all sang from their hearts.

"The white light of the violins" called for purity of thought; the clarionet and cornet declared their faith in the future of mankind; the flute warbled of the joys of righteousness; the bass with its deep, soft hum told of the peace which passeth all understanding; the grave old trombone spoke of the stern duties of life; and all joined in greeting the great Creator of the universe. Neither time nor usage can wither the beauty of that grand old air, whose mellowing tones of peace and love are universal and eternal.

It is a fitting theme to tune our hearts for grave and sacred thought. When the professor commenced his prayer the audience listened with bated breath.

"O God, Thou symbol of love and truth, let us here express a wish that our understanding may be enlarged sufficiently to comprehend in spirit and letter the subject before us to-day. Let prejudice, hate and superstition be expelled from our souls, and let us come together as fellow-creatures. Let us meet, not in the arrogance of knowledge, but in the humbleness of that ignorance we must all feel in the presence of the eternal. Let us sympathize with each other in the darkness which surrounds the question of whence and whither; the darkness which is only penetrated by the star of hope. Let us take each other lovingly by the hand and search earnestly for truth. He who truly seeks shall truly find. Amen!"

The ring of sincerity in the speaker's tones had a powerful effect on his hearers. There was not a soul in the hall who did not feel that the professor's heart was in his words. Next he gave out a hymn. Here a hitch in the proceedings occurred

He gave out the wrong hymn, and the musicians not being prepared for this did not attempt to play, but the professor started to sing in a loud sonorous voice, not only the wrong hymn but the wrong time and tune, if indeed, it could be called a tune at all. For nearly a whole verse he struggled on alone in a way that put many in a cold sweat. Some giggled, and some frowned, but all felt uneasy.

A pang of pity for the poor old man shot through David's heart. Would he never quit, or would somebody never put him right till he became a laughing stock? He felt like getting up in his seat, and asking him to omit the singing, when as if in answer to his wish, Marian's clear sweet voice went ringing through the hall, and in a moment the audience joined her.

"How kind; how brave of her," thought David. "She has saved the whole proceedings from becoming ridiculous." Reaching under her cape, he gave her hand a squeeze. The rich colour mounted to her cheek and brow, but she kept on singing. She sang as she had never sung before. She felt that in that clasp their souls had touched once more.

When the hymn was ended, the professor was so exhausted by his vocal efforts that he required a short breathing spell, and he asked that the collection be taken up. In the absence of the regulation plate, he handed over his hat. There was a touch of humour in the situation. But those who smiled did so good naturedly, and the contributions were fairly liberal. While this was going on he spoke a few words on the efficacy of prayer.

"As far as I can judge, a prayer is not intended so much to invoke the personal assistance of an Almighty Being, as to arouse the proper feeling in our own hearts. A prayer is simply a wish, a high and earnest thought; and by expressing it aloud, we hope to arouse the best and noblest elements of each other's nature. If we have such thoughts and desires it must be right to express them, in order that others may be influenced thereby. A prayer like a hymn is a tuning of our minds to the subject in hand, a tilling of the soil on which to sow the seeds of truth. For the same reason that a conscientious violinist will always be careful to delicately tune his instrument before attempting some great selection, so I think, will prayer always hold a place with earnest, conscientious seekers for truth.

The collection having been completed and the hat deposited on the table, the speaker took a drink of water, and commenced:

"KIND FRIENDS:—First let me apologize beforehand for the rambling nature of my remarks, partly due to my inexperience and partly to the irregular way in which ideas come upon me. Besides, I shall probably never have an opportunity of meeting you again, and wishing to go over as much ground as possible I shall take no particular verse or chapter, but speak broadly on the question before us. In this intelligent audience, there are no doubt many classes of thinkers, and, instead of emphasizing your differences, I shall try to show you a common ground where we can all give each other our sympathies.

"I think I am safe in saying that he who tries to accentuate your differences, to erect barriers of prejudice between you, is an evil disposed person, no matter what position he occupies, or what the colour of his coat may be. I would like to show you that we are not nearly so far apart as we imagine, that a great many of our prejudices are founded on misapprehension.

"We shall proceed cautiously, in order to avoid any misunderstanding, and if any one wishes to ask a question, I shall consider it a privilege to answer it, if I can.

"I am not going to claim, at the outset, that truth originated with Christ. We can all readily understand that truth must have been co-existent with space and matter, co-eternal with God. Perhaps I had better pause and make myself clear on this point, for the word God may convey a different idea to each and every one of you. I ask you, however, to let me use the word to-day as a symbol of truth, wisdom, righteousness, charity and love, in fact, *all good*, and then we shall understand each other.

"*You* may be a materialist and hold there is nothing but the unchanging laws of force and matter. *You* may be an agnostic and say that you don't know; or *you* may be a deist, in whose mind there is an imprint of an omnipotent and all-wise Being. Now, as this is not a discourse on theology, we will agree to differ on this point, but we can all join hands on a more important, a more practical one, viz., *that we all have due reverence and love for God*, no matter what ideas of the eternal may exist in your minds.

"No materialist will claim that there is anything wrong in loving *good;* no agnostic can smile at you for worshipping *truth*, and no rationalist will try to reason away your adoration for *charity* and *mercy*. In omnipotence and omniscience there is enough for every man to worship, call it by what name ye may.

"Now, if we all understand each other, we shall return to the teachings of Him, whom we, as Christian people, regard as the representative of God. Other ages and other nations have had their Saviours, who shot out of the darkness of ignorance, and, in shedding the light of truth, sacrificed themselves for suffering humanity. But though I might wish to say a word or pay a tribute of respect to those great spirits, it will be more than sufficient for us to consider the life and teachings of Christ.

"Unfortunately, creeds and clericalisms have distorted and misapplied his teachings, have surrounded them with an atmosphere of mystery and supernaturalism, which makes it appear as if they are only applicable to a future life and not to this one.

"Just last Sunday I went to hear a sermon in one of our neighbouring cities. I have not the slightest doubt that the pastor was a sincere and conscientious man, for he had an honest face, but he actually gave his hearers to understand that Christ's object was to use the earth as a stamping-ground where everything (excepting the church in general and *his* in particular) might be allowed to go to rack and ruin, and our only duty was a great scramble to secure, by hook or crook, a clear title to mansions in the sky. Think of it. If Christ had been on earth, if he could have heard the words of that man, he would have shed tears of pity. He would have said, 'Father, forgive him, he knows not what he does.' In the midst of human ignorance even the gods stand appalled.

"The very technicality, intricate phraseology, and cant of the pulpit has been, I am sorry to say, the proverbial bushel under which the light has been hidden. The complexity of the average sermon surrounds the whole question with a haze that is almost impenetrable to the human intellect.

"But we must not allow Christianity to suffer in our estimation, because of the faulty methods of expounding it, now in use. We can well afford to throw away all sanctimonious phrases, all pretense, all mystery, and speak in the language of the present time, using the same every-day English with which we might discuss any other grave topic.

"We do not need to be afraid of the great truths of Christianity. All the hammering and pounding will only make the true metal shine the brighter. Daylight reveals greater beauty. Christ's teachings, read in the light of common sense, in the light of reason, not taken by one single text but read as a whole, are intended for to-day and to-morrow; for Sunday and Saturday.

"He wished us to be better husbands and wives, better fathers and mothers, better mechanics, better citizens and better men. He wished us to have more just laws, purer government, higher education, healthier homes, cleaner bodies and purer souls. He knew that in teaching us how to *live*, he was teaching us how to *die*; that to live properly in this world, was the best preparation for another. He found the world groaning under the yoke of superstition and priestcraft. The rich and the powerful, the cunning and the unscrupulous, made slaves of the masses. They used their superstition to bandage their eyes and their ignorance to forge their own chains.

"He appealed to the people in every possible way, and used every means at his command to impress upon them the light of truth.

"Away through all the vistas of the future, through all the tangled webs of cause and effect, he saw the rocks upon which civilization was apt to split. He foresaw the struggles of might and right, labour and capital, hunger and luxury. He taught moral, social, and political reform to the masses, and to the individual he gave lessons in honesty, industry, economy, cleanliness, mercy, charity and love.

Oh, the love, the exquisite, universal love of Christ ! Oh, the sympathy and tenderness of that mighty heart ! Let us stop for a moment and try to grasp the meaning of it.

"You love your wife and your child. You could suffer the tortures of death to save them from pain. But what about your neighbour of whom you are jealous or with whom you have had a quarrel? Perhaps he goes to a different church, or possibly does not go at all. Can you say to yourself, " Well, poor Jones ain't a bad fellow. He has to work hard from daylight till dark. He has said some hard things about me, but so have I about him. He has a hard time to get along. I see a chance to give him a lift, poor fellow, and I'll do it. I won't let him know about it, because it would make him feel embarrassed. I'll stop abusing him, too, whether he does me or not." You go out of your way to help him. You contradict any slanderous stories about him and you feel better. Somehow, the sun seems to shine brighter, the birds sing more sweetly, and the air is more exhilarating. Your step is more joyful, your eye is brighter. You have an impression that there is a man in your clothes.

" But you have only just got nicely started to be a Christian. When you extend that loving sympathy to *all mankind*, from the drunkard in the ditch to the tyrant in purple robes ; from the prisoner in the cell to the savage in the wilderness ; then you have the *spirit of Christ* in your heart, no matter whether you call yourself agnostic, atheist or materialist.

"On the other hand, remember that no matter how often you go to church, no matter how many psalms you sing, or how long a grace you may say before dinner; no matter whether you are an elder or a deacon, or how ably you can discuss doctrinal points, unless you have the love of Christ in your heart you are no Christian. Remember that going to church will no more make you a Christian than carrying a violin under your arm will make you a musician. Christianity is a *life;* not a *creed.*

"It is no disgrace to be a freethinker. Christ himself was a freethinker. He was unbeliever in the religions of his time. He threw aside all creeds and dogmas, and looked only to the eternal God for inspiration.

"But he was preaching heresy. The priests were in danger of losing their high positions. The tyrants, land-grabbers, and usurers would be shorn of their power. They saw nothing but decreased revenue and loss of prestige in the new conditions of which Christ preached.

"The doctrine of the brotherhood of man was not acceptable where class legislation made slaves of some and tyrants of others. The rich and the powerful said that he must die, and in order to impress upon the people that he was an impostor he must suffer death in the company of thieves. Don't I beg of you, get the impression that the primary object of Christ's sufferings was to appease divine wrath. Do not for pity's sake slander the name of the great Creator of the universe by such a doctrine. Do not poison your minds with such infamy. Remember always that *God is Love*.

"Don't let theologians divide you up into classes and groups by doctrinal fences. Don't let them feed any prejudice in your mind against your neighbour, because he happens to have a different conception of the eternal. Leave quibbling over doctrinal points to professional religionists. Cling to the love of Christ as your Rock of Ages. Remember that *true religion* is broad enough for every man whose motto is 'love truth and do the right.'

"Remember that Christ asserted the right of private judgment. The men who to-day ostracize the agnostic are the lineal descendants of those who spat upon His garments as He was led to the cross. Remember that there is no conflict between science and religion. If science quarrels with creeds, doctrines and dogmas, so much the worse for the dogmas. Science is *truth* itself and is a *part* of religion, but only a part. Science may show inaccuracies of Biblical history, or that the writers of the gospel had a limited knowledge of the natural sciences, but that does not shake the foundation of religion.

"Some conscientious thinkers may argue that cause and effect, force and matter, are the beginning and end of all; that science (as we know it) is the only guiding star of life. What about emotion and sentiment? What prompts our noblest deeds? Is it science which causes the starving mother to give her last crust to her child? Was it science that opened the father's arms to the prodigal son, or prompted Christ to give his life for us? How much science is there in a mother's holy kiss to her first-born? Does science bid us weep over our dead? Can you figure on a slate the love of a husband for his wife, or a patriot for his country? Can you measure off with a tape the deeds of heroism in every country and every clime? Deeds which give their inspiration to poesy and song, which warm with the throb of life the great master-pieces of canvas and marble. Are we merely machines, living automatons, aggregations of atoms?

"No, a thousand times no. Love must be the handmaiden of truth. The star of hope must shine over the open grave, and the religion which stands the test of time or fills the wants of man *must* needs be adorned with flowers of love, and clustered with buds of hope and charity."

CHAPTER LXIII.

TURNING TOWARDS THE SUN.

How much longer the sermon would have continued no one knew, but suddenly the speaker passed his hand over his forehead and sank into his chair. At first he turned very pale. Then a deep flush came over his cheek and forehead. Everyone saw that something was wrong. The doctor, fearing that the professor would suddenly develop his *alter ego*, ran forward and bathed his head with cold water. He ordered the windows to be opened, as the room was very close, and he unbuttoned his patient's coat which was too tight to allow of free breathing. But in a moment he was sorry he had done so, for it opened to full view the wretched poverty of the professor.

He had no waistcoat, and nothing but a fragment of a shirt was left, fastened here and there by threads and strings. His shining shirt was only a "dickie." One could see at a glance that there had been great difficulty in getting anything to fasten it to. For suspenders he had pieces of twine, knotted and tied in the most inexplicable manner.

What a tale of poverty and want was there. Nobody laughed or smiled. They all felt sad. The doctor hurriedly re-buttoned the coat, but the tale had been told.

Marian swallowed a lump in her throat, shook the contents of her purse into her husband's hand, and motioned him to go forward. A murmur of applause went round the assembly when Jamieson followed suit with a ten-dollar bill. Again the hat was passed around, and many a piece of silver went to swell the original contribution.

The professor fortunately soon recovered from his temporary indisposition. He addressed a few parting words to his audience.

With tears glistening in his eyes he said, "Your generosity, good people, has overwhelmed me. Your kind attention to my rambling discourse, has made this the day of my life. You have loaded me down with wealth, and lifted a weight off my mind. In coming here I spent my last half dollar for a railway ticket, and I was at a loss to know how I was going to pay for my lodgings. I have been in sore straits, but thank God I have cheated no man. Let me say as a last greeting that your kind sympathy with me and with each other gives ample evidence that the spirit of Christ has been with us. Good-by and God bless you."

At this, the orchestra broke into an unknown anthem of praise and peace, which held the audience spell-bound with its deep religious fervour, while through it all like an undercurrent were the familiar strains of "America."

Many did not agree with the letter of Mr. Senger's

discourse, but all subscribed to the spirit of love and charity with which it was embued.

And then the music was soul inspiring. They all wondered where the closing anthem had come from. Surely some master hand had been at work in its instrumental adaptation and arrangement.

There was one who knew it was the work of a hand that now lay cold in death, of a heart that was truly religious. The manuscript had been loaned to Mr. Jamieson by Mrs. Gordon.

If one could judge by the comments and criticisms which came from the various groups on their way home, the professor's earnestness had reached the hearts of some, and given many others food for thought.

For the first time in a year and a half Gordon offered his arm to his wife. She pulled her veil over her face to hide its joy. Her hand trembled as she placed it on his arm.

Christina took a sudden notion to walk beside an old lady whom she was accustomed to visit, and left the pair to themselves. Neither of them spoke. *Her* heart was too full for utterance, and *he* was lost in contemplation of the discourse to which he had just listened.

It seemed to her as if the distance home was all too short. By a slight pressure of his arm as they neared their gate, she led him past, and they went for a long walk through the town. She was proud of the privilege of walking with her husband, as proud as any maiden of her first lover, or a bride of her bridegroom.

He was absent-minded and distraught. His brain was in a whirl with new thoughts, new ideas, and he walked along, scarcely knowing whither he was going. He left it to his wife to greet or salute the friends and acquaintances they met from time to time.

Not till they reached home did their eyes meet. She noticed a strange, puzzled look upon his face. But they parted without a word, she going to her room, and he climbing the stairs to his. She felt that the time had not yet arrived to unbosom herself.

It was a relief for Marian to be alone, to have a "good cry." She threw herself down on her bed and wept like a child. But they were tears of joy. The clouds were lifting; the sunshine was coming. He would soon be her own again.

"Hark! he is walking the floor above. Poor fellow! I know his head is aching. If I could only bathe it for him. But this crying will never do. He must not see my eyes red with weeping. Hark! he is coming down the stairs. Perhaps he is coming to me now."

She jumped up with beating heart and hurriedly removed the tear-stains from her face. But his footsteps passed her door.

"Martha, will you please tell Mrs. Gordon that I shall bring Professor Senger here to tea to-night," she heard him say, and in a moment he went out through the front door.

She ran to the window and watched him cross the street. "Perhaps he is going to the doctor's to get something for his head. No, he is going the other way. Well, I shall go myself and then dress. Poor fellow, I must wait till he gets over the shock which the sermon has given him. The doctor will know what to give me for his headache."

"Now, I shall dress for *him*," she said when she returned. "We shall have dinner instead of tea. I shall wear the amber satin he got for me in Boston. It is out of fashion now, but he will not know that, and there will be nobody here to laugh at me. Then the locket and chain he gave me on the road that Sunday. Yes, and the tie I spoiled for him the morning he tried to milk."

"Dear me, I'm afraid I'm getting more vain as I grow older," she continued, as she posed and turned in front of the mirror. "But it cannot be wrong to dress for the man I love when he is my husband. I cannot wait any longer. If he does not take me in his arms to-night I shall take him in mine. Poor fellow, I know the sermon stirred up his very soul I know the storm going on in his brain. I can see by his face that he thinks his whole life has been a mistake. If he only had a good cry it would do him good. I will take pity on him and give in first. I will sink my pride and go on my knees to him if necessary."

Marian went on talking to herself as she prepared to come forth in all the wealth of her womanly beauty. To-night she would make her final effort.

CHAPTER LXIV.

RECONCILIATION.

DAVID had not gone far, when he met the professor walking up and down the sidewalk, looking the very picture of despair.

"Well, Professor, are you not feeling well?" inquired David, as he approached.

"No," replied the old man, feebly. "I ordered dinner half an hour ago, but the cook told me, very saucily, that there would be no dinner till seven o'clock. I can't even get a biscuit; the shops, of course, are all closed. Just think! Now I am flooded with wealth and can't get a bite to eat. I was to go to tea with the doctor, but he was called away."

"I have just come for the special purpose of inviting you to tea with me, but that won't be for an hour yet. You are staying at the Union? Well, come, and we'll get something right away."

Taking the professor by the arm, David escorted him into the hotel and asked for the landlord. "Ah, goodday, Mr. Grady. Would you kindly get Mr. Senger a little lunch? He tells me he is just starving."

"It is his own fault, Mr. Gordon. He does not come at meal time. The clerk says he has not been at the table since yesterday morning. He is more trouble than he is all worth. He has an extra room full of trunks and rubbish of all kinds. The chambermaids complain that he throws all the bedding on the floor, and sleeps between two ticks of his own. He has spilt ink all over the carpet, and every morning his room is like a box-stall with confusion." During this arraignment Mr. Senger sat staring at the landlord in a dazed sort of way, but never ventured to reply.

"Why, sir," continued mine host with an injured air, "the gentleman in the next room complained that he sang psalms half the night and sang damned badly at that."

The professor here broke in with an explanation. "I was only practising the hymns for to-day's service. My voice was out of training."

This was too much for Gordon's gravity. He laughed till the tears ran down his cheeks. The amazed looks of both the professor and the landlord only added fuel to the fire. They must have thought that Gordon had taken leave of his senses, for in spite of all his efforts he could not contain himself.

Meantime Mr. Senger was expostulating with the landlord, but David did not catch what they were saying.

"Tell the waiter, Mr. Grady, to bring some biscuits, cheese and some milk," said Gordon, wiping his eyes. "Mr. Senger, please go into the dining-room. I shall join you in a moment. I wish to speak to Mr. Grady."

"I just wanted to say," continued David as soon as they were alone, "that I will make good any damage done."

"Oh, that's all right, Mr. Gordon. Dr. Bennet has already guaranteed him, or I would not have kept him. He told me it would be no harm to starve him a little for his health's sake. But he has starved himself, for he never came to the table."

"I think the poor old fellow had no money, and he was afraid he would not be able to pay up."

"Well, but the doctor guaranteed him, Mr. Gordon."

"Quite true, but the professor did not know it. And perhaps if he had it would have made no difference, because he will not be dependent on anybody."

The landlord nodded and scratched his head. "I promised the doctor to keep him here till he gets a place ready at his own house. I guess he must be going to experiment on the old fellow. The doctor is a queer fish. He's got some game on foot, but he can make a sausage of him for all I care. I'll be glad to get rid of him."

As soon as David entered the dining-room, the professor invited him to sit in, and grandiloquently ordered the waiter to attend to his friend's wants.

Just to humour him Gordon pretended to munch a biscuit, while listening to his companion's flow of conversation. Mr. Senger was all sunshine now.

"I was just trying to think of the name of that—Major of Sir Walter Scott's, who wore a wide belt, and pulled it up a notch for every meal that he missed. Oh, yes. Dugald Dalgetty it was. Rather a good idea, I think. The want of normal pressure on the gastric walls is one of the causes of that horrible sensation known as hunger. I have read up the best authorities on the question. An occasional sip of castor-oil is a splendid thing to relieve it. Seems to act by causing a certain amount of nausea. I dined very sparingly at the doctor's yesterday, and I have felt quite gaunt since then. I took my last sip of oil before going to the hall."

David sat bolt upright in his chair. "Do you mean to say you have fasted since then?"

"I could not help myself. I had some change from the sale of my pamphlets, but I required some stationery to prepare my sermon, and clean linen to deliver it in. I have sometimes gone in debt for lodgings, but never for meals."

"Why didn't you tell me last night?"

"What! cry poverty? Never! Now that I am rich I can afford to confess. The rich man likes to tell of his past poverty, just as the newly fledged penitent likes to rehearse his past sins," and jingling some coins in his pocket the professor laughed merrily.

"You don't believe much in sudden conversion, then?" inquired David.

The old man elevated his eyebrows. "That depends altogether on the individual. In some cases the whole truth may come with a bound, but as a rule it takes years and often a lifetime. The average sudden conversion, with its wailings and lamentations, is entirely emotional, a sort of moral hysteria."

"But great truths may dawn upon a person suddenly without the emotional element," remarked David. "Don't you think so?"

"Oh, yes. A question has often baffled me for years and then flashed upon me in a moment."

"Now, Professor, if you have finished we will go," said Gordon, taking a parcel from under his coat. "You'll kindly do me a favour if you will accept this as a loan. Or if you like you can buy them. It is a shirt and a pair of suspenders. Take them up-stairs and don't be long in getting ready, for the time is nearly up. You can pay me to-morrow."

Gordon of course expected that his wife would preside at the table as was her custom on all such occasions, but he was prepared for no such vision as met his eyes when Marian came into the room.

He was so completely carried away with admiration that he had barely presence of mind enough to say, "Professor Senger, allowed me to introduce you to Mrs. Gordon."

"Ah yes," responded the professor with a courtly bow. "The lady who came to my assistance in the singing. I am proud of the opportunity of thanking you for your kindness, and of complimenting you on your voice."

Never in his life had David seen his wife looking so beautiful. The neatly fitting amber satin gown displayed the curves of her figure to the greatest advantage. Her face was full of animation, and her cheek had the bloom of a peach. He was reminded of an expression of his mother's, "I gar myself believe, lassie, that I can see yere bonnie shape, richt through yer claes." Through a filmy gauzy substance, he could trace the outlines of her beautiful arms, while the cut of her corsage showed her creamy neck and a tiny speck of snowy bosom. Then the chain and locket and the milk-stained tie brought a score of tender memories over him, till he almost forgot his guest. He had only just rallied from the effects of the sermon, when his brain was again set in a whirl by his wife's surpassing beauty.

The events of the day had been too much for him. He seemed to be at a loss what to say or do.

Marian explained to her guest that her husband was subject to headaches. " I went over to the doctor's, David—(it was usually Mr. Gordon)—and got a powder for you. Better take it before you sit in to dinner," she continued, dissolving it in a wine glass and giving it to him to drink. "Come now, Professor, if you please, dinner is waiting."

" That medicine looks like antipyrin, phenacetin, or some of those tar preparations," said the professor, as they took their seat at the table. " Very good thing, I believe, if not taken too frequently, but very depressing I have found in my own case."

" You have some knowledge of medicine then," said Mrs. Gordon with surprise.

" Yes, madam. In studying the brain from a phrenological stand-point, I found it necessary to acquaint myself with generalities."

Mr. Senger was eating with great gusto, notwithstanding his recent lunch. Gordon began to think that Dr. Bennet's theory was correct. Marian, womanlike, was particularly pleased to see her guest enjoying his meal, and assisted him very diligently.

" Can I help you to a little more salmon, Mr. Senger ?"

"Thank you, yes. I am very fond of fish. People don't eat enough fish."

" We generally have it every Friday, but it came late this week."

The professor gave an inquiring glance at his hostess and then at David. Marian, understanding his implied question, answered with a smile. " Oh no, we are not Catholics, but the dealers generally supply them for Friday."

" Well now, Mrs. Gordon, just think of the Protestant who laughs at Catholics for eating fish on Friday, just as if Friday was not as good a day for eating fish as any other. In a climate like this we could with advantage abstain from eating meat at least two days per week, instead of one."

" You believe in Lent, then ?" queried David.

"Most assuredly I do," replied the professor, helping himself to another piece of salmon. "Lent is one of the wisest and best institutions the Church has ever given us.

"Just think of people, in even a much warmer climate than this, eating meat all the year round. Why, it would have brought on diseases of all kinds."

He paused for a moment to drink some tea. "In olden times you know, Mrs. Gordon, the priests combined within themselves the three professions of *medicine*, *law*, and *divinity*. It was their duty to look after the health of the people, and they found it necessary to cut off animal food before the heat of summer set in. It was necessary, not only for the physical but the moral health of the people. If you wish to make a man or a dog savage, feed him on meat. People have laughed and sneered at the idea of different articles of food having an effect upon our moral natures, but it is now an established fact."

"Yes, but why make Lent a religious ordinance?" inquired David.

"Why? For the best of all reasons. To have it strictly adhered to. The Catholic Church is a paternal, or rather, I might say a maternal one, and the priests knew perfectly well that if they told the people it was for the good of their health, nobody would have paid much attention to it, for then, as now, people were very careless about their bodies."

"The masses must surely have been very ignorant and superstitious," remarked Gordon.

"All the more reason for making it a religious observance and giving it an air of mystery. Pshaw! The same thing goes on to-day. Doctors still play the same old tricks upon their patients. If they order a man to go home and take a dose of salts, he will conclude that his case has been slighted, but if he gets magnesium sulphate and aqua written on a prescription, he is quite satisfied so long as the taste is concealed; but more especially if the bottle is covered with blue paper, and the directions caution him not to expose it to the light."

"I wish Dr. Bennet was here," said Marian, laughing heartily.

"He will tell you that I am quite correct. If you yourself, Mrs. Gordon, had a bottle of medicine which you were at liberty to take at any time, you would soon lose faith in it. But if you were told to take a certain number of drops so many minutes after eating, and cautioned strictly to keep it in a cool place, your faith would be firm as a rock."

"You believe in humbug, then, Professor," laughed the host.

"Humbug is not the proper term. We must take people as we find them. Reason is a faculty which the average man does not exercise to any serious extent. We must appeal to his credulity, or, if you like, to his faith. In fact we all have a weakness for believing things we don't comprehend, something that appeals to our imagination."

Gordon laughed and shook his head.

"Oh, but it is positively true," repeated the professor with great emphasis. "I am quite sure your physician would be able to point out many instances in your own case. Let me tell you a little story. It is a perfectly true one. Dr. Abernethy, the famous Scotch physician, of whom most people have heard, once had a very wealthy but refractory patient, whom we will call Mr. B. His real ailment, it seems, was want of exercise, lack of activity, and while the doctor invariably gave him a big bottle of medicine, he tried to impress upon him the absolute necessity of exercise, but all to no purpose. Finally, the doctor told his patient that he could do nothing for him, but that a certain herb physician away in the Highlands at Glen Parridge (or some such name) would be able to cure him. The patient decided to go. But on inquiry he found that the only way to reach the outlandish place was to make a journey on foot. So he packed his knapsack and set forth. About two months afterwards the patient met the doctor on the street and threatened to cane him for sending him on a fool's errand, for there was no such herb-doctor in existence as the one to whom he had been recommended, and his trip was all for nothing. But Mr. B was a well man again."

Before the professor had quite finished his story the

hostess broke into a hearty laugh. "What about your trip to the old country, David?"

Gordon coloured a little, and then joined in the merriment, till the peals of laughter startled Martha in the kitchen.

"Now that you have explained Lent," said David, "perhaps you can tell us if the ceremony of anointing with oil has a like foundation."

The professor paused a moment to stow away a piece of cold fowl.

"Certainly. Some clever priest, no doubt, discovered that anointing with oil saved many a life. It was a remedy which succeeded where all else failed, and probably came to be looked upon as a last resort. Only last Friday Dr. Bennet told me that he had saved a child's life by inunctions of oil."

They had now finished dinner, and they adjourned to the parlor, where David threw himself on a lounge, leaving his wife to conduct the conversation.

"I suppose the counting of beads has some reasonable explanation as well?"

"Quite so. People in those days could not read. Every bead represents a high and holy thought. It is simply a silent prayer. Often the poor servant girl who tells her beads is more devout than her mistress who mechanically mumbles her prayers. Protestants accuse Catholics of idolatry because they wear a cross. But it is only an emblem, and to people who lack imagination such emblems are useful."

Marian was delighted with the old man's conversation. He seemed to make everything so clear and simple. "How is it, Mr. Senger, that all other denominations hate the Catholic Church? Don't you think they ought to respect it as being the first Christian Church?"

"They should indeed, Mrs. Gordon. It always reminds me of precocious children, railing at their mother for her old-fashioned ways. We should remember that Catholicism nursed us in our infancy, guarded our health, clothed the naked and fed the hungry. It looked after the moral, physical, and spiritual welfare of the people. It carried us over gerat chasms of chaos. It preserved the fine arts. Not even the cruelties of the inquisition, nor the fires of Smithfield, should make us forget what is due to the Mother Church."

"That is how it has appeared to me. The churches have different vestments, different methods, differently constructed places of worship, and they vary a good deal in the formality of their rites; but they are all supposed to teach the precepts of Christ. Why should there be any contention or jealousy between them?"

The old man laughed. "Your question reminds me of that little poem of Southey's,

> "'Now tell us all about the war,
> And what they killed each other for.'

"I am afraid, Mrs. Gordon, that my reply will be as unsatisfactory as old Caspar's was.

"I might as well," he continued, "go out on the street and knock down the first man I meet, because he does not wear my kind of a hat; pick a quarrel with my neighbour because the roof of his house has a different pitch; or boycot the man across the way for not eating his meals at the same time as I do."

"It does seem silly, doesn't it? If people would only stop to think of it, there would be less strife in the world."

"And yet eminent divines and learned doctors will spend the best of their days learning dead languages, reading history, and stuffing their brains with the lore of ages, to quibble, whittle, or cheese-pare over some insignificant doctrinal point. A lifetime is spent fitting up a craft to weather the storms of a teapot."

Marian noticed that her guest's face was becoming flushed. He excused himself several times for yawning. His manner was changing as well. He became uneasy. He fidgeted in his chair. Of course she pretended not to notice it. She endeavoured to keep up the conversation. But the yawning became more persistent, and he finally rose to take his leave.

"I have a great deal of writing to do to-morrow.

My pamphlet on Light must be got ready for the publisher. The people shall not say that Senger left them in darkness."

David escorted his guest to the door and apologized for his dullness, but the professor paid no attention, and with a curt " good-night " was gone.

When Gordon returned to the parlor his wife had left the room, ostensibly to get a drink of water, but really to calm her beating heart and renew her courage, for *now* was the appointed time.

He threw himself down on the lounge wondering whether she would come back. He had not long to wait. She came in and seated herself beside the table where he could not see her without turning around.

" Does your head ache, David ?" she asked, timidly. Her heart almost stood still, waiting for his reply.

" Yes. But it is a good deal better than it was."

"Will you let me bathe it with cologne?" she asked, growing bolder.

" If it will not be too much trouble."

Eagerly she hurried to her room for her cologne bottle and a towel. Kneeling beside him she spread the towel for his head to rest upon, and soothingly laid her hand on his brow.

But she could not bear the yearning look in his eyes.

With a sudden impulse she snatched him in her arms, pressed his head to her panting bosom, and covered his face with tears and kisses. With a great sob he threw his arms around her neck and wept like a child.

She bent over him, cooing like a mother to her babe, and kissing away his tears, while he sobbed out, " Oh, Marian, I am not worthy of you. I can see it all now. You are mine till death."

CHAPTER LXV.

CHRISTMAS CHIMES.

It is the 24th of December, but the weather is more like that of October, for the air is balmy and the sunshine is warm. It is like a last remnant of summer, and all who can avail themselves of the opportunity are airing themselves or their children.

A stranger would scarcely recognize Gowanstone after six years, it had become so enlarged and improved. The streets are now paved, and most of the vacant lots are covered with fine buildings. Old structures have disappeared and new ones have taken their places, but the lawn beside the mill cottage still flourishes fresh and green like an oasis in the desert of brick and mortar. The cottage itself is no longer a cottage. It is now a mansion, with bay windows and decorated gables, while, in stained glass over the door, is the word " Metapedia."

Even the old mill, the most venerable landmark of the place, has passed away. On the corner is a huge stone structure with dust-stained windows and towering chimney, while away at the top in letters of wire are the names, Gordon & Fletcher.

But it is not only on the main streets where changes can be observed, for up on the hill where formerly there were nothing but pasture fields, there are now a score of handsome residences; indeed, Hope Hill (as it is now called), has become the residential part of the town.

Down the street leading from this quarter, a woman is trundling a baby carriage with one hand, and leading a little boy with the other.

The little fellow trotting along at her side is dressed in full Highland costume, plaid, philabeg, sash and cairngoram brooch, and he marches along with a pride in his step and a significance in his manner which shows he is keenly conscious of his gay habiliments.

People who meet this little group turn to look after

them, to smile at the fantastic costume of the little fellow, and admire the woman he is calling Mamma, a splendid, handsome, robust woman, with a smile of contentment on her face.

"Run, Davie," she said to the little boy, "there's papa coming," and off went the kilted warrior, running and shouting.

A man in a suit of grey tweed had just turned the corner, and was walking rapidly towards them. His head was bent as if in deep thought and his face was not visible, but the slight greyness of his hair and whiskers seemed to blend with the colour of his garments, and only for his firm, elastic step and erect form, he might have been mistaken for a man of fifty.

"Hello, papa!" shouted the little warrior. "Don't you like me now?" He stood upright with arms outstretched, in order to display his grandeur to greater advantage.

The father held up his hands in admiration. "Well, well. It is you, Davie. This is one of mamma's surprises, I guess. And she has picked the right tartan, too."

"Mamma says I am a Scoshman; am I, papa?"

"Oh, I suppose so, but you are an American too you must remember, and may be President some day. You mustn't forget that, Davie," and he lifted the little fellow in his arms.

"What do you think of your clansman?" said his wife, laughing pleasantly as they met.

"He looks like a thoroughbred Hielandman now," he replied. "Here, Davie, kiss mamma." As he reached the son over to kiss his mother, he deftly snatched a kiss for himself.

"Oh, David, for shame, and right here on the street. If any of the Herchemers see us they will be scandalized," she exclaimed, looking rapidly around. But the love-light in her eye showed that she was not displeased, and she slyly pressed his hand in token of appreciation.

"I have the greatest news for you, mamma," said David with enthusiasm, "and the greatest surprise. You couldn't imagine what a Christmas-box I got to-day. You couldn't guess if you tried a thousand times."

"I thought there was something buoyant and joyful in your step," replied his wife with a fond look of ownership, as she brushed some dust off his sleeve. "I can read your very walk. But you haven't kissed little Elsie yet."

He stooped over the carriage and kissed the rosy infant who was fast asleep. "I'll wheel it for you," and he took the handle of the vehicle from his wife, for the up-grade was getting steeper.

"We can't go to Broadview, to-morrow, dear," he continued, watching his wife's face.

"What! Not go to Fred's wedding! Surely David, you are joking. Why, I have promised," she added in a firmer tone, "and am all ready to catch the six o'clock train. You promised too, dear," she continued in a tone of reproach. "You know I love Fred."

Gordon laughed at the look of concern in his wife's face.

"We'll have to remain at home to receive callers. They've elected me Mayor of Gowanstone by acclamation, and according to the time-honoured custom of the town, we must have a reception to-morrow."

A flush of fond pride and surprise came over her face. "What! Mayor of Gowanstone! Well, well," and stepping closely to his side she gave his hand a squeeze.

"Just wait, Your Worship, till I get you home and see if you don't get a touzling. I actually feel like an anarchist and shall take pleasure in pulling the ears of the town's first magistrate. We are all rebels at heart, as far as authority is concerned. I shall get even with it now. Just wait, my boy, till I get you home," she added with a merry laugh and a look of mischievous tenderness.

"I am sorry to disappoint Fred, but really it can't be helped," said David, returning the squeeze of her hand. "But there will be plenty there without us. Grandma, Grandpa, Uncle Maurice, Aunt Nelly and little Willie, are all going over this evening. I told them to call for Davie. Was that right?"

The mother looked fondly at the little form marching away in front of them. "Yes, I'm glad you did. I promised Davie a ride in the 'toot,' and I wouldn't like the little dear to be disappointed. He'll go any place with his grandpa. The bride and groom will be here in a few days anyway. Besides, Nelly can take over my presents. I don't like to break a promise, but it can't be helped. I had a letter from Fred to-day, and he tells me that Grazely has given the bride the old Gore hundred, excepting the old log house and six acres, which he offers as a Christmas' box to father and mother to use as a camping place for summer. He says that Clara expects her Uncle Innes, Mr. Fetterly, and Mr. Tracy over to her wedding, all the way from Denver."

"Is that so? There will be lots of fun where Fetterly is. Jake used to live next door to the old shoe shop when father was living.

"And so the old folks again own the spot where they started life. It will be like old times. But now, dear, you must put on your thinking cap. We must not be behindhand in our entertainment. The whole town will be here in some form or other. Brass bands, societies, athletic clubs, and all the prominent citizens from Congressman Darrow down to the clerk of the court, or sergeant of police."

Gordon was as full of enthusiasm as a ten year old boy. He seemed completely carried away by the exuberance of his spirits.

"It was such a surprise," he went on. "I never dreamt of such a thing. I was invoicing some cars of flour when in came Browning, Geoffry, Switzer, Mills, Davis, and Maurice.

"'How do you do, your Worship?' said Maurice, catching my hand.

"I looked at them in astonishment.

"'Damn it, man,' said Browning, 'You are Mayor of the town by acclamation,' and they all laughed and pulled me around. Of course I had to go over and make a speech. I don't know whether I spoke well or ill, but I got plenty of applause. Do you know though, I was afraid of breaking down."

"Not a bit of fear of you breaking down," said his wife, with a smile of confidence. "You'll always go through with what you undertake."

"Yes, but I was so taken by surprise. I would rather have faced a regiment of soldiers than that audience to-day."

"Grandma Gordon used to sometimes call you 'a fechtin' Hielandman.' There is another," she added, pointing to the kilted clansman strutting along in front. "He'll fight all day for a straw, and then give away a whole sheaf."

As soon as they were inside their own door his wife caught him in her arms and kissed him till little Davie became jealous. She swung him around, touzled his hair, and finally led him to the kitchen by the ear, introducing him to Martha as "His Worship, the Mayor."

"Now, Marian, please quit teasing me, and let us get down to business. You and Martha will have to look well to your commissariat department. Maurice told me to leave it all to you, so now remember. I'll do anything I can, but you will have to take charge of the arrangements yourself. For to-morrow, at least, Gowanstone will be under petticoat government."

They had, indeed, a very busy afternoon and evening. Several of the neighbours kindly called to assist in the preparations. Sidney Dillon, who engineered the decorations, was to be master of ceremonies.

But it was Christmas' eve, and Santa Claus must not be forgotten. Not only had they to attend to the stockings of a number of poor children, but there was a list of indigents and invalids, whom Marian kept under her care. It was nearly midnight when they sat down to wait for the Christmas' chimes. She sat on his knee with her arm around him, gazing thoughtfully into the blazing hearth.

"This is the proudest day of our lives, Marian. Don't you feel it so?"

For a few moments she did not speak, but sat running her fingers through his hair.

"Do you remember the evening after the professor's first sermon, when I went to bathe your head and you took me in your arms? Every kiss you gave me was a jewel, every tear that dropped from your face to mine seemed to cleanse my soul. That night, as you slept in my arms, I lay awake watching you for hours. Not for all the gold, or pomp, or power that this poor world contains, would I have surrendered that privilege of having your head upon my bosom. Your kisses had put a wreath upon my forehead; they had crowned me queen of your heart and home. There, in my own room, where for many sleepless nights I mourned and wept for the honours I had lost, where in the loneliness of my isolation I expiated my sin, where visions of suicide and madness harassed my soul, you did call me by the dear and sacred name of wife, and there I had you for my own again. What, sir Mayor," she asked, smiling through her tears, " is your victory, or your crown compared to mine?"

A silent embrace was his only reply.

Wiping her eyes, she went on in low, tender tones.

" David, we who are so rich in love, so rich in worldly goods, must not forget our poor, suffering, joyless fellow-creatures. We must not be *selfish*."

"Why, darling, I don't think you need to chide yourself on that account. Didn't you, this very night, send parcels to half the houses in the town? Perhaps if we asked the doctor, he might say that your sweetmeats are ill-directed benevolence, after all."

Marian smiled. " Poor old doctor, he pretends to ignore little acts of kindness and charity, but I have often caught him at it on the sly. He pretends to keep the professor for what he can learn from him, and that he is helping to write some scientific work, but I feel positive that he loves Mr. Senger for his own sake. I was thinking that besides the children there are some old people to remember. Peter McQueen may be out of tobacco. The poor-warden will not buy it for him, so I have to keep him supplied myself."

"Do you actually buy tobacco?" laughed David. "What will the grocer think? He knows I don't smoke now. You should have told him who it was for."

"I never thought of it. Please don't interrupt me.

Mrs. Reeves needs a new pair of spectacles. She can't read now with those she has. I must find out what grade or number she wears, and take them to her to-morrow. Last week I got Mr. Sutherland to take me to see those poor fellows who are in for robbery and ——"

"Really, Marian," interrupted her husband, "I like to see you giving charity, but to go to the jail is carrying the thing too far. What could you say to those ruffians?"

"Oh, I just sympathized with them. I told them *I* often had wicked, vicious impulses, and that all along it was a fight to keep oneself from doing wrong."

Gordon broke into a hearty laugh. "Oh, yes, I suppose you told them that you came within an ace of being a burglar yourself."

She placed her hand over his lips to check interruption, and went on.

"The younger one was sulky at first, poor fellow. He seemed to think I came to look at him, like a wild beast, but I gave him some flowers, and I took down the address of his sister. The other has a wife and two children. He does not want them to know he is in jail. The poor fellow told me he could not get work and was driven to steal. His wife lives at Otterville. Christina went over to see her and took her some sewing, for which she paid in advance."

Gordon half closed his eyes to look at this woman, this wife of his, who, without fear, would follow her good intentions even to the mouth of hell. There was a reckless daring about her charity which defied Mrs. Grundy and put ridicule to rout. No wonder that Sydney Dillon always said that Mrs. Gordon was privileged to do as she pleased. Fancy this beautiful woman sitting in friendly conclave with burglars.

"I imagine I can see Sutherland," said David, with a smile. "Were you not afraid?"

"No. One does not think of that. You feel so sorry for them."

"Well, but they might strangle you, the villains."

"Don't call them names, David. We don't know

what their temptations and surroundings may have been.

"Now that I think of it, don't forget to send the buggy round to-morrow for Christina and her mother. It will make them feel sure that we did not invite them merely out of courtesy."

"Very well. Oh, by the way," he continued, slapping his knee, "that reminds me of something else. I forget to tell you about the music publishers. I got a letter from Boston to-day. They offer to take the rest of the manuscript on the same terms. They sent a cheque by mail and the pictures by express, so that they would be in time for to-morrow."

"What pictures do you mean?"

"Well, it was an idea of my own. One is an oil painting (life size) of Charles, and the other is an illuminated parchment, containing some of the high tributes which the Boston critics are paying to his genius. They were not very expensive, and I thought they would make a suitable Christmas gift for Christina and her mother."

Marian turned pale and the moisture came into her eyes.

"David," she said, placing her hands on his shoulders, "the picture is for *them*, but the message is for *me;* a message from your soul to mine of complete forgiveness.

"But hark! There are the Christmas chimes."

Their voices were suddenly hushed as the clear, sweet tones rang out on the midnight air. They rose to their feet, and standing side by side in the holy temple of home, their memories flew back through the ages, and their hearts filled with reverence for ONE *who loved his fellow-men.*

THE END.

www.ingramcontent.com/pod-product-compliance
Lightning Source LLC
Chambersburg PA
CBHW051248300426
44114CB00011B/937